DATE DUE

DEMCO 38-296

A Ming Society

A Ming Society

T'ai-ho County, Kiangsi,
Fourteenth to Seventeenth
Centuries

John W. Dardess

UNIVERSITY OF CALIFORNIA PRESS

Berkeley · Los Angeles · London

University of California Press
Berkeley and Los Angeles, California

University of California Press, Ltd.
London, England

© 1996 by
The Regents of the University of California

Library of Congress Cataloging-in-Publication Data

Dardess, John W., 1937–
    A Ming society : T'ai-ho County, Kiangsi,
fourteenth to seventeenth centuries / John W.
Dardess.
        p.   cm.
    Includes bibliographical references and index.
    ISBN 0-520-20425-5 (alk. paper)
    1. T'ai-ho hsien (Kiangsi Province, China)—
Social conditions.   2. China—History—Ming
dynasty, 1368-1644.   I. Title.
    HN740.T55D37   1996
    306'.0951'222—dc20   96-3631

Printed in the United States of America
9   8   7   6   5   4   3   2   1

In memory of my grandfather
John C. Dardess
1871–1955

Contents

Illustrations

MAPS

TABLES

Acknowledgments

Writers are personally responsible for whatever they write, but no one finishes a work like this one without help from other people. Jerry Stannard (who has, alas, since departed this life) helped me with problems of botanical identification. Lee Williams and Bob McColl helped me acquire and interpret Landsat images of T'ai-ho County. Gene Carvalho and Vicki Fu Doll helped me get microfilms of rare works. Marsha Weidner and Chou Yeong-chau helped me identify and locate paintings. Jay Alexander, Wallace Johnson, Betsy Kuznesof, Don McCoy, Keith McMahon, and Carolyn and Lynn Nelson either critiqued draft chapters or discussed some of the general issues I take up. I must thank the *Harvard Journal of Asiatic Studies* for publishing an early version of the first two chapters. The University of Kansas granted me sabbatical leave in the fall of 1991, during which time I drafted several of the later chapters. The original manuscript was a bit ungainly, and I am deeply indebted to Sheila Levine of the University of California Press for steering it over its several hurdles, and to the press's readers, whose comments and suggestions were crucial in helping me to decide how to slim it down and improve it.

August 1995

Introduction

This book is about T'ai-ho County, Kiangsi Province, in Ming dynasty China (1368–1644). It is a social history of a locality in its national context. The point of the book is to show how the people of T'ai-ho County adapted and readapted themselves, in their individual and collective behavior, to the exigencies of life in the great entity that was Ming China, in which they considered themselves active participants.

Ming China's territory was the size of France eight times over. Kiangsi Province was (and is) roughly the size of the state of Wisconsin. Chi-an Prefecture (of which T'ai-ho was one of nine component counties) was slightly larger than the state of Vermont. But these three large units are too unwieldy to serve as canvases for social history of any but the most generalized kind. T'ai-ho County was (and is) about 80 percent the size of the state of Rhode Island. It has appreciable size and yet is small enough that one can get to know nearly all of the families that lived there and get good glimpses of the thoughts and behavior of the family members and their friends and neighbors at various moments through the nearly three centuries of Ming rule.

Another reason for keying on T'ai-ho as a vehicle for exploring Ming social history is the existence of good sources for it. It happens that some twenty collected works by authors who were native sons have been preserved. All these are of Ming date, ranging from the fourteenth to the seventeenth century. There is probably only a handful of other counties in Ming China with anything comparable in quantity and temporal range.

To focus on one county, out of more than a thousand of them, in a big realm like Ming China is, of course, to raise the question how typical or representative it is of the rest. I cannot adequately answer that question. It is safe to say that T'ai-ho bears little resemblance to T'an-ch'eng, the deprived and stricken county of seventeenth-century Shan-tung described by Jonathan Spence in his *The Death of Woman Wang*. T'ai-ho may or may not be a typical member of a class of counties in Kiangsi Province, or south China generally, of middling productivity, dense population, and high rates of socioacademic success in the Ming era. Certainly in the fifteenth century, its leading native sons considered it a very special place. The sixteenth century residents seem not to have cared about it one way or the other.

What did it mean to be part of the Ming realm, part of China's civi-lization? In the first half of the fifteenth century, the relationship of T'ai-ho to China was a bit like that of Virginia and its luminaries to the emerging national order of late-eighteenth-century America, although Kiangsi elites were not among the "professionalizing" architects of the new Ming order. (Men from Chekiang were). In the early fifteenth cen-tury, following the prince of Yen's seizure of power in 1402, an unusu-ally large number of T'ai-ho men began to enter Ming service as offi-cials, and a handful of them reached the very highest positions in the Ming state. By that time, a collective identity as T'ai-ho men (rather than as Chi-an or Kiangsi men) had been defined and reinforced, espe-cially in aesthetic perceptions of local life and landscape. Genealogical research and the composing of obituaries helped to pin down individual identity and place in social hierarchy. Friendships and marriage connec-tions were carefully noted and celebrated as well.

But, rather as the election of Andrew Jackson in 1829 effectively ended the dominance of Virginia and Massachusetts elites in the af-fairs of the American republic, the reenthronement of the T'ien-shun emperor in the Peking palace coup of 1457 ended for good the extraor-dinary dominance of great T'ai-ho men (Yang Shih-ch'i, Wang Chih, Ch'en Hsun, Hsiao Tzu) in the highest reaches of Ming government.

The repercussions of that dramatic turnover at the top were far-reaching. For many in T'ai-ho, it dissipated a robust sense of worldly optimism. The rate of recruitment of county men into Ming bureauc-racy declined by half—while, ironically, the size of the local body of *sheng-yuan* (county students) expanded. Appreciation for the local landscape dimmed. People cease to flaunt their pride in being T'ai-ho natives. The growth rate of the county's upper class decreased, and emi-gration was encouraged. Powerful lineage organizations emerged in the countryside, replacing the looser family associations of the past. It was necessary to redefine one's place in China's civilization. The great men of sixteenth-century T'ai-ho (Lo Ch'in-shun, Ou-yang Te, Hu Chih) were not statesmen primarily but Confucian philosophers of national renown and influence, for whom the important spheres of social and intellectual interaction were personal, familial, collegial, and national. T'ai-ho County as such held no special place in their affections. Lo Ch'in-shun and Ou-yang Te were so much opposed to each other as thinkers that nothing like a T'ai-ho "school" had any chance of emerging.

But where did a local patriotism centered upon T'ai-ho County come from in the first place? Little is known of the county in the Sung (960–1279). In the Sung, it was Chi-an Prefecture that served, in the social consciousness of the elite, as a principal center of civilized life and as a forum for the most intense feelings of local pride and national patriotism and for native literary tradition. People boasted of "our Chi" or "our Lu-ling," whatever their actual county of residence within the prefecture. (A history of Chi-an Prefecture in the Sung has yet to be written, but Robert P. Hymes's *Statesmen and Gentlemen*, which is a social history of the elite of the neighboring prefecture of Fu-chou in the Sung, shows what could be done.) Somehow, between the end of the Sung and the forming of the Ming in 1368, Chi-an Prefecture broke apart in all respects save for its administrative function in the apparatus of the imperial state. Thus, whereas in the Sung, the literati of T'ai-ho County were, as far as one can tell, culturally and socially indistinguishable from the literati of the prefecture as a whole, around the middle of the fourteenth century there emerged a wholly independent literature whose authors considered themselves natives of "our T'ai-ho" and took little interest in either Chi-an Prefecture or Kiangsi Province. It is not clear what brought about this change. It was only after the dust had cleared that the T'ai-ho literati began to write in quantity, and so it is from that point that the story must begin.

·   ·   ·

There are three parts to this book. The first part is a physical and aesthetic reconstruction of the county as landscape. The second part takes up resource management, family formation, lineage organization, and civil service recruitment, and points up how living conditions and social opportunities changed in T'ai-ho as the Ming centuries wore on. The third part considers changing aspects of life in the greater world of Ming China, as reflected by the personal writings and experiences of some major figures who happened to be natives of the county. The strongest general impression conveyed by these chapters is that Ming literati culture was plastic and polycephalous and always susceptible to new waves of ideas that demanded a rethinking of accepted attitudes toward self and society.

But why would anyone want to read about one county? The short-coming of selecting literati from just one county, whatever the method shows of Ming cultural change generally, is that the results are by no means tantamount to general cultural history itself. T'ai-ho County is not Ming China writ small. What is true of Kiangsi Province is not nec-essarily true of the richer and more highly developed Kiangnan region. But the whole of Ming China is too huge and diffuse to manage dia-chronically in any detail. The advantage of confining one's attention to T'ai-ho people is that doing so makes it possible to look at a portion of Ming history through time and in detail; to show how differently the world presented itself to Wang Chih in the fifteenth century as com-pared to, say, Ou-yang Te in the sixteenth, or to Hsiao Shih-wei in the seventeenth.

Even more, the political and social organization of late imperial China was such that counties mattered greatly to it: as the critical points in political hierarchy where central government met society at large; as the (mainly rural) seedbeds and sources of identity for national elites; and as places to which those elites returned on leave or upon re-tirement, places which demanded from them no small part of their pa-tronage, influence, and writing skills. Most of what is known of T'ai-ho comes by way of information furnished by the local literati who suc-ceeded at the national level. As the generations passed, the thinking of the literati changed, and their ways of expressing local patronage and influence changed as well. T'ai-ho is worth reading about because its history is not simply local history; its history gives evidence for the re-ciprocality of the relationship between local conditions and national de-velopments in later imperial China.

The third part shows the impact of a series of waves, in part intellec-tual, in part sociopsychological, that surged through T'ai-ho County and caught up so many of the local elite—students, teachers, writers, wealthy benefactors, officials—in their swirls. A wave typically lasted a generation or two before it receded, and another wave, coming from some different direction, and with a different profile, replaced it. These waves usually came from somewhere outside T'ai-ho. It was the func-tion of the great local literati to perceive these waves as they came, to modify and interpret them, and, in a few cases, to try to resist them.

It looks as though five waves rolled through T'ai-ho over the course of the period from the fourteenth to the seventeenth century. Wave one crested in the middle and late Yuan dynasty and featured a strong belief in the efficacy of an arrogant and naive individualism. Wave two, whose early signs Liu Sung perceived, was soon after creatively interpreted by Yang Shih-ch'i to feature the development of local patriotism and an ethic of cooperation as an answer to the problem of how best to adjust to the emperor-driven autocratic order of Ming China in the early fifteenth century. Wave three is harder to define, but a major political and psychological break occurred in 1449, with the Mongols' capture of the Cheng-t'ung emperor, after which Ming autocracy was never again the same. From that point on, the emperors could never quite recapture policy initiative or the national moral high ground. In these circumstances, Yin Chih repudiated T'ai-ho patriotism and the cooperative ethic. To a degree, wave three resembled wave one. Yin Chih saw the fourth wave coming, and he did what he could to stop it.

The fourth wave featured the sixteenth-century Ming intelligentsia's seizure of the nation's moral high ground, through its break with the official orthodoxy and its rethinking and redevelopment of the Confucian heritage in the light of a desire to elaborate a new, self-centered idealism (Wang Yang-ming's was, of course, the greatest name involved in this movement). The elite of T'ai-ho County were swamped by this wave. Most swam enthusiastically with it. Lo Ch'in-shun, for all his apparent resistance, in effect joined in by creatively rethinking the received Ch'eng-Chu orthodoxy rather than just stubbornly defending it. Figures like Ou-yang Te and Liu K'uei swam buoyantly in the new tide. Others, like Wang Ssu and Hu Chih, thrashed about in it with difficulty, but they joined in nonetheless.

Chang Chü-cheng's suppression of philosophical discussion in the late sixteenth century broke the back of the Wang Yang-ming schools, at least in their sloganized forms (the "extending the innate knowledge" of Ou-yang Te, the "search for benevolence" of Hu Chih, etc.). The cultural world of seventeenth-century China was diverse, and not all of its currents reached T'ai-ho. One current that certainly did was the lay Buddhist revival, whose impact can be seen in the life of the garden builder and aesthete Hsiao Shih-wei. The lay Buddhist revival was the fifth and final wave.

I have not tried to write balanced and comprehensive biographies of the T'ai-ho literati. Their lives each raise certain problems of interpreting and adapting to the world, and I have tried to identify and pursue those problems instead. (The *Dictionary of Ming Biography* contains standard short sketches of the lives of Yang Shih-ch'i, Wang Chih, Lo Ch'in-shun, Ou-yang Te, and Hu Chih.)

All translations from Chinese sources are my own. Many local place names defy convenient translation, but I have given English-language versions whenever those can easily be done.

PART ONE

The Setting

CHAPTER I

The Land: Its Settlement, Use, and Appreciation

PATTERNS OF SETTLEMENT

T'ai-ho County was not a tiny place. In size it measured 1,028 square miles,[1] which is about 85 percent the size of the state of Rhode Island (1,214 square miles). Located on the Kan River, some 150 miles south of the Kiangsi provincial capital of Nanchang, T'ai-ho stretched seventy-five miles east to west and was about thirty miles deep at its thickest point north to south.

The county contained six large subdivisions called *hsiang*, or "cantons" (see map 1).[2] These had no administrative use in the Ming period. They simply served to identify physiographically coherent regions. Five of the six cantons took in a main Kan River tributary and its feeders, each tributary forming a natural conduit for settlement and communication. The "metropolitan" canton, Ch'ien-ch'iu (Thousand Autumns), with the county seat at its center, straddled the Kan and the lower reaches of several of its tributaries.

The six cantons were in turn divided into seventy lower-echelon units called *tu*, or townships, which did have an administrative function. They were numbered consecutively. Beginning with the canton of Jen-shan (Benevolent and Good) in the northeast, officials placed township number 1 in the first cropland below the watershed of the Jen-shan River. Then they kept plotting, down that stream and up the next one and so on through the county, insofar as topography allowed. The townships served as quota assignment areas for taxes and services.

9

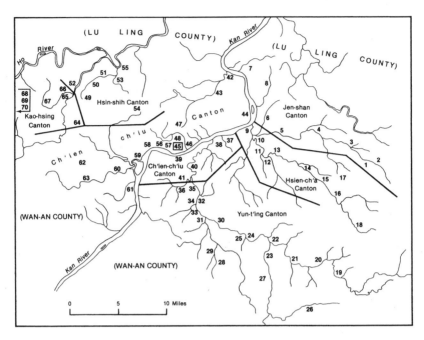

Map 1. T'ai-ho County in the Ming: Cantons and Townships. Maps 1 and
2 are reprinted from John W. Dardess, "A Ming Landscape: Settlement, Land
Use, Labor, and Estheticism in T'ai-ho County, Kiangsi," *Harvard Journal of
Asiatic Studies* 49, no. 2 (December 1989): 295–364.

Though their exact boundaries can no longer be determined, some seem to
have encompassed several square miles of crop- and residential land.

At the bottom of the fiscal-administrative hierarchy lay some 250
rural wards, in T'ai-ho called *li*. Although county, cantons, townships,
and wards together made up what is technically known as a "nested"
hierarchy of units, the wards were clearly creatures of compromise between imperial administration and local society. Localism is evident in
the way in which the wards were named. Many were named after local
features—for example, Shan-t'ien (Mountain Field), Lo-chiang (Snail
River), and the like. Several wards were concurrently known by more
than one name: T'ao-yuan (Peach Spring), Ssu-hsia (Under the Temple),
and Shih-t'ai (Stone Terrace) were all names for the same ward in township 12. Other wards had script variants: Shen-ch'i (in township 4) was
written both as Deep Creek and as Sash Creek. And there were dupli-
cated names, as well as one triplicate (three different wards all named
Nan-ch'i, or South Creek). Ward names commonly served as choronyms

for dominant local lineages—for example, the Shan-t'ien Yin, the T'ao-yuan Hsiao, etc.

Upon this unsystematic local toponymy, the early Ming state tried to impose order and control, not by redesigning the microgeography but by treating each ward as though it were also a uniform population unit, each consisting of 110 taxpaying households as its core.[3] It then grouped these theoretically uniform wards into the serially numbered townships. Each township contained anywhere from one to twelve wards. In the Ming, the total number of wards wavered between 250 and 260.

Although modern detailed maps show many of these old wards as discrete dots, suggesting punctiform villages, it is clear that in the Ming they were in fact microregions and not settlements as such. They *included* the actual, physical settlements that were points of departure for local land-use systems.

Of these actual settlements, the largest was the little walled city that served as the county seat. Like the county, it too was called T'ai-ho. It sat on prime alluvial land on the north shore of the Kan, not directly on the water, but slightly inland, so as to escape flooding and erosion. The area within the walls (about a third of a square mile), together with an outer extension of suburban and farming space, was designated for fiscal purposes as township 45. There was no further subdivision into wards, however.

In the Ming and Ch'ing, the city proper had an oblong shape, with an interior network of streets and lanes that featured many odd bends and irregularities (see map 2). Public buildings (like the magistrate's yamen and the K'uai-ko, or Happy Tower, a local landmark) were placed erratically. Certainly the forces of traditional urban planning had been weak here.

The streets were narrow, at best wide enough to admit the horsecarts that, in the Ming period, daily hauled produce in from the countryside. The residential lanes were very narrow. The whole effect was one of crowding. John Nieuhoff, accompanying a Dutch embassy up the Kan in 1655, described T'ai-ho as a small city, set in a "charming" landscape, with well-paved but very narrow streets.[4] Congestion had already been evident centuries before: a twelfth-century observer wrote that a multistory house owned by one Ch'en Ch'eng, though near the Kan River, gave him no prospect on it because "hundreds of houses belonging to people in the market block out the view."[5]

People lived in the city for reasons of livelihood. Some lines of trade

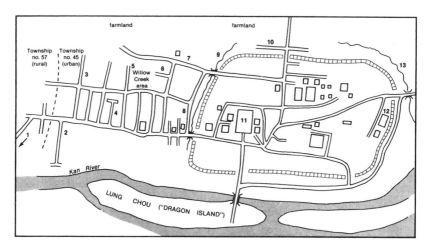

Map 2.   T'ai-ho City and Its Suburb in Ming Times: (1) To township 56 and
P'o-t'ang k'ou (2) Hollow Street (Ao-chieh) (3) Kao-ying Lane (4) Moat Head
Lane (Hao-t'ou hsiang) (5) Old Well Lane (Ku-ching hsiang) (6) Fishpond
Lane (Yü-ch'ih hsiang) (7) Grass Garden Lane (Mao-yuan hsiang) (8) Back
Street (Hou-chieh) (9) Refined Creek (Hsiu-ch'i) (10) Lane of Successful
Officials (Ch'iu-tzu hsiang) (11) County magistrate's office (12) Happy Tower
(K'uai-ko) (13) Clear Creek (Ch'ing-ch'i).

required a certain density of customers, which is why in the fifteenth
century the family of Ch'en Hsun—whose fortune was based on land
speculation and grain dealing—lived in the east part of the city, "inter-
mixed with the other classes of people," their buildings "packed like
fish scales" against those of their neighbors. But willow and sophora
trees shaded the front, and a studio was placed in back, far enough from
the horsecart traffic and marketplace clamor that none of the noise
could be heard.[6]

Others did less well. Liu O (1295–1352) moved from his kinsmen's
rural home to a house near the east wall, which "one entered through
a mean alley, reaching a mean dwelling where his family lived frugally,"
and where he eked out a living as a professional tutor.[7] Medical practitioners were also drawn to the city. So was a more transient assortment of indigents, child-monks, litigants, government students, yamen
underlings, and the like. In the late sixteenth century, a writer remarked
that there were "several myriad" city families, including "a thousand"
government clerks and lictors in T'ai-ho city, but that was surely guess-
work. No official enumeration of the city population of Ming or Ch'ing
date seems to have survived.[8]

While the city attracted the needy and ambitious, it also clearly re-pelled many of the affluent, whose fortunes had already been made. Through the Ming, there took place a steady exodus of wealthy people from the inner city (or the crowded parts of the western suburb) for the rest and quiet of rural places.[9]

Suburban spread beyond the city walls of T'ai-ho was not uniform in every direction. South of the city, the Kan River shore lay vacant. East of the city, suburbs failed to grow, probably because of flooding. To the north, the suburb hugged the city wall, along a street called Ch'iu-tzu hsiang (Lane of Successful Officials), where families such as the Hsiao and the Tseng supervised the labor of their bondsmen in soils of "top fertility."[10]

The west side was different. From the two west gates of the city, par-allel roads led out for a half mile, laced together by a network of inte-rior lanes. This western suburb straddled a soil frontier between fine alluvial sand along the Kan River to the south and a more mixed and productive alluvium to the north.[11] Intensive farming estates lined the suburb's north edge. Dense settlement continued westward for an-other mile, where urban township met rural townships 56 and 57. A citylike community developed in P'o-t'ang-k'ou (Broken Reservoir Mouth Ward, township 56).[12]

Out in the broad countryside of T'ai-ho County, rural settlements were not uniform in size or appearance. They ranged from isolated resi-dences, to peasant hamlets, to elite residences whose buildings were scattered about, to densely clustered, citylike communities, like that of the Cheng family in township 35. The family numbered "a thousand and several hundreds," and their "tile roofs look like fish scales, rising up in a dense mass, just like city residences, wherever you look."[13]

By taking actual centers of settlement, whatever their size or form, as starting points, it is possible to use the literary evidence to show that the human use of landscape in T'ai-ho in Ming times was organized into a system of distinct rings or zones. Taken together, these land-use zones demonstrate that several very different kinds of land all had a crucial part to play in sustaining over a considerable period of time a sizable population at a respectable level of affluence, sophistication, and social organization. Yet T'ai-ho's was a subsistence landscape, not a heavily commercialized one.

Starting from any center of settlement and proceeding outward, one entered first an innermost area of intensively worked garden space (*yuan, p'u*), often with room in it somewhere for dogs, pigs, and chick-

ens. Gardens were minuscule in total acreage, but they were heavily
worked and very productive. Next, beyond the gardens, one came upon
the fields (*t'ien*), larger in area than gardens but commonly lower in per-
acre productivity and not as heavily worked. Finally, somewhere beyond both gardens and fields there stretched an enormous outer enve-
lope of uncultivated space that was an absolutely essential component
of T'ai-ho's subsistence landscape, though on average its per-acre yields
were lowest of all. (There is an ancient word for that space—*tse*—but
the T'ai-ho writers never used it.)[14]

A few technical words of ancient Mediterranean origin will help in
the understanding of these landscapes. If what goes on in the garden
(*hortus*) is "horticulture," then what goes on in the field (*ager*) is "agriculture," and those words will be used with these restricted applica-
tions in mind. The exploitation of uncultivated space, essential in many
premodern subsistence economies, has all but vanished in modern
times, as has the old vocabulary that once named and described it. But
the old noun "march" means just the right thing: a mosaic of hacked-
up forest, groves of lopped shrubs or trees interspersed with grassy or
weedy glades. The rarely used adjective "nemoral" derives from the
analogous *nemus*, or "wooded pasture," of ancient Italy. And so one
may refer to the three principal subsistence zones as horticultural, agricultural, and nemoral.

HORTICULTURE IN T'AI-HO

What sort of horticulture was T'ai-ho's? J. G. Hawkes has constructed a
general typology, indeed a continuum, of gardening modes, which may
be of help in answering the question. At one extreme of this continuum
there is the *jíbaro*, an apparently planless jumble of subsistence plants
of every possible sort, each species being represented by only a few individuals. At the other extreme lies commercialized monoculture, with
large areas planted to a single species.[15] T'ai-ho's gardens seem to have
filled much of the continuum without reaching the extremes.

Some commercial horticulture has been noted in passing already.
There are further examples. The late-fourteenth-century gardens of Lo
Hui-ch'ing (of Hsia-mu Ward, township 39) featured single species
growing in such quantity as to suggest a commercial operation: "in the
west part of the garden, green leeks stand thick-planted in a thousand beds, and behind his house, a myriad red fagara bushes grow
widely spaced."[16] In the early fifteenth century, on Lung-chou, the big

river island just south of T'ai-ho city, lived a certain Elder Yao, whose home was surrounded by woods and several tens of *mou* of fertile land. He grew, perhaps as outfield crops, hemp, millet, and soybeans, which yielded him several hundred *hu* yearly; but out of gratitude for the founding of the Ming and the return of peaceful conditions, he sent as a gift to the Yung-lo emperor "several tens of boxes of sugar cane, melons, and yams," which fact suggests, again, commercial gardening on some scale.[17]

In 1370, Buddhist monks funded the rebuilding of their temple on the south bank of the Kan from the proceeds of what surely was commercial gardening:

> The gardens attached to the temple amount to something over ten *mou,* and these are presently planted to several hundred fagara bushes, several hundred yams, a thousand or more leeks and cabbages, and several tens of [privet or ash] trees for [insect white-] wax. The pathways are broad and even, and the drainage channels ordered and regular. Hired laborers are assigned the task of cultivating with plows drawn by two-steer teams, and so rapidly do they go, that it is almost as though night, or a storm, were fast approaching.[18]

Most T'ai-ho gardens, however, seem to have been of the kitchen or subsistence type, located very close to the homesite, owing to the range and frequency of the labor demands they imposed. Besides planting, fertilizing, thinning, weeding, and hoeing, there was a need for daily watering, picking, and hand squashing of bugs, tasks that family members or domestic servants performed. While outfield crops, wet or dry, grew in unitary fields, gardens were usually subdivided into small rectangular plots or beds (*ch'i*), with each bed sporting a single species. There is no indication that the *jibaro* technique was much practiced. Fruit-bearing trees, however, were often scattered about a garden. A bamboo clump would serve as a windbreak, while brushwood fencing or a hedge would enclose the entire complex.

The following examples of garden descriptions seem to show that the T'ai-ho kitchen gardens held a certain diversity of plant species and that the mixtures differed from one garden to another, in response either to local conditions or to the food preferences of the family or to some small market opportunity. These examples also show that some of the literati contributed their own labor to subsistence gardens, and that they occasionally reflected upon the anxieties and satisfactions connected with that labor. The garden descriptions are vignettes, mostly poetic and always select, never complete.

Of some estate in T'ai-ho, fourteenth-century poet Liu Sung (1321–

81) writes: "light frost descends on the soybeans on the hilltop; sunset clouds rain their glow on the beds of amaranth."[19] The poet here contrasts soybeans in an outfield with the amaranth (cooked and eaten as a vegetable) in the garden bed. In another vignette, Liu Sung and some companions, passing along a road in winter, stopped to look into a well-hidden garden: "Where the streams from the back of the mountain converge, and a high stone path leads through the woods, we spotted the top of a tile roof outlined against the hill beyond, with thick hedging all around the place. So we spread apart the foliage and saw leeks in beds; we pulled aside the vines and there came to view a peach tree by a creek."[20]

T'ai-ho philosopher Lo Ch'in-shun (1465–1547) wrote of a garden, probably somewhere in the south part of T'ai-ho, "where the melon vines spread about after the rain, while in the grove, the oranges bend the boughs in midautumn."[21] Some garden description was off-season: "Melon vines in the garden, long bedraggled in the cold; the yam vines, too, have collapsed since the coming of fall. A light rain has wet the dark path below the flowers; a passing cloud has shaded over the bamboo-fringed pond."[22] A ruined garden, just west of the county seat, prompted this description sometime during the wars of the fourteenth century: "The bamboo clump was long ago cut down, and the once flourishing apricot trees are knocked flat. The fragrant fagara is drooped and wilting; the fine oranges, insect-ridden too."[23] In the sixteenth century, T'ai-ho philosopher Hu Chih (1517–85) noted his own garden in its seasonal decline: "The idled garden has everywhere grown to weeds, and the wattle gate is open now to the dogs and pigs. The last bitter oranges (*Citrus aurantium*) were picked after the frost, but a few vegetables still linger in the rain."[24]

The luffa was a useful member of the melon family—its dried fibers made scouring pads. It also climbed and thus used little space, as Liu Sung noted in Ho-ch'i (Grain Creek Ward, township 65): "Several peasant homes lie hidden in the yellow bamboo; the road by here twists up and down the hills and ridges. The dogs bark at the wattle gate below the sweetgum tree, and, on this cold day, the luffa twines all along the hedge-fence."[25]

A fiber crop like hemp might be posted to the outfields, but it might also be brought in and gardened. Ramie (*Boehmeria nivea*, a nettle), on the other hand, had to be gardened and did not produce well if handled as an outfield crop. A perennial grown from rootstock, ramie requires intensive care—watering, heavy fertilizing, plus winter bedding, and periodic replanting. After laborious hand processing, the stripped stems of this plant yield an excellent fabric called summer cloth or grasscloth. Liu Sung carefully described it:

> Many families south of the Kan raise ramie;
> They first burn the soil, then next year they mound it, and fence it off.
> When the old stems are harvested, new stems come up,
> And you can get three harvests a year.
> The girl of the family to the east, with her fine features,
> Weaves white ramie and makes spring clothing.
> Early in the morning she goes to the garden to defoliate the stalks;
> She peels away the green skins, and comes away with an armful.
> Next she goes and rinses the fibers in the pond,
> Then, deftly using a round knife, she scrapes them:
> It's like snakes shedding their skins, or scales and bristles flying off;
> You touch the clouds of fiber now, and their smoothness surprises you.
> It's taken her a month to ready everything for the loom.[26]

The garden was, of course, principally a source of household food. Thanks to the mild climate, T'ai-ho gardens could provide some fresh produce all year. When he was an official in Peking, Wang Chih (1379–1462) reminisced that around his home in the western suburb there were "about ten *mou* of garden, all planted to vegetables, mostly radish [not the European or American radish but a plant closer to the Japanese daikon]. That we'd pick in winter, cut it up together with yam, add leek, salt, and bean paste, and boil for soup. Not even the rarest and richest of foods could surpass that, and everyone in the family loved to eat it."[27]

Some literati performed garden labor in person. Liang Lan (1343–1410), a local writer, ended a day's work in his Willow Creek garden physically exhausted but spiritually euphoric. But as Liu Sung grubbed about his garden one spring day, his thoughts ran off in several different directions. He thought of the coming harvest from his peach trees, now in bloom, and of the melons that, months later, would ripen from the seeds he now held in his hand. He could dream ahead to "soft, sweet, golden yellow vegetables" and to "pickled, jade-green relish." He had some firm ideas about gardening technique: hemp should be widely spaced; peasants often sowed it too thickly and got puny plants as a result. Similarly, melon had to be planted with a lot of room for the vines to spread. The south side of the Kan River, where he lived (in Chu-lin Ward, township 38), featured a sandy alluvium, which was no good for water spinach (*Ipomoea aquatica*) or for "crystal onion," a famous local specialty. Lettuce you ate raw, but rape-turnip you could pickle. He half thought of compiling handbooks on farming and vegetables. He must have already planted his seeds because nothing had germinated. If the weeds had flowered (he sighed as he hoed them up), then why had the melons not set fruit? The wheat on the high ridge was stunted and sere because it got no rain after it was planted the previous fall. Weeding was toilsome and unending. The millet had sprouted on the high ground to the east, but the weeds had gotten ahead of it; and they had to be taken out, else if it did rain, it would do the crop no good. He had planted (edible) chrysanthemums too close to a tree, which had since leafed out and was now shading the plants, so that they looked sickly. He wished someone would come relieve him of the watering pot so that he could go eat. On top of it all, the tax assessor had come by to register his mulberry and fruit trees.[28]

AGRICULTURE IN FIELD AND PADDY

One could garden any crop one pleased, but traditional field agriculture in T'ai-ho, dry or wet, was limited to a narrow range of plants (rice, wheat, millet, taro, etc.) that can be seen to have certain features in common, foremost among these being an amenability to "mass production" techniques, including an ability to give satisfactory results despite relative neglect. If whatever was grown in gardens was worked at intensively (one plant at a time), then whatever was grown in fields was something that could be handled extensively (many plants at a time).

The greater the number of individual plants needed to produce a given amount of food, the greater is the likelihood of that species being made an outfield crop in a subsistence landscape. And plant for plant, even rice yields little. Thus as long as enough space is available in the landscape, rice along with the other grains will be exiled some distance from the homesite, where the plants and their fruits (kernels) will be handled in the greatest possible quantities on the fewest possible occasions. For the T'ai-ho literati, the location and nature of the staple crops clearly reduced their aesthetic interest. The literati also looked distantly upon the episodic, massed labor that was commonly expended upon such crops.

Dry, that is, nonirrigated, field crops known to have been raised in T'ai-ho in Ming times included spring-ripening wheat, buckwheat, and millet and fall-ripening soybeans. These were planted in any arable land that could not be turned into paddy, or, as occasionally in the case of soybeans, in harvested and drained paddy. In T'ai-ho, these crops provided common local foods (millet gruel, buckwheat cakes, bean paste, bean curd, etc.), and they probably also served to reduce dependency on the main staple, which was rice. Taro is also mentioned as having been grown in fields, and it must have been an important source of starch for some families.

A few fleeting glimpses of dry field crops are available. A peasant hamlet, nestled against the march, is described in enough detail by Liu Sung that field crops can be distinguished from garden fairly sharply: "In the pass between the hills they grow wheat, and at the head of the pass, hemp. The door of the earthen hut is dark, no stir within. The neighbor's yard is fenced against tigers, and in it, children feed a pet crow. Fine mountains, like green jade, rise on either side; flowing streams lace the garden plots, spilling white foam. Late in the day the adults come home with their hoes in the light rain; poppies have dropped their petals all over the courtyard."[29] In Nan-ch'üan (South Drain Ward, township 56) there is broad level upland and "fruiting millet, thick in the fields."[30] Along a twisting path that approaches a mountain hamlet, wheat has been planted in ridges of soil; by fall, these ridges will be weed covered, and peasants may snare rabbits there. At Liu Sung's home in Chu-lin Ward, some of his wheat seems to be gardened, i.e., planted in "continuous beds," near mulberry, while the rest of it is planted out on "high ridges" beyond the reach of irrigation water, where, later perhaps, after the wheat is harvested, soybeans will be sown. A bondsman delivers Liu the report that "sunshine in the irrigated fields has made the rice dark green; rain on the hill-ridges has made the soybeans flower profusely."[31]

Because of severe population and livestock losses in the wars of the mid–fourteenth century, much agricultural land in T'ai-ho was temporarily abandoned. In these circumstances a truly extensive mode of field management was here and there adopted as the wars ended, creating for a time a sharp contrast between outfield agriculture and intensive, homebound horticulture. Ancient words for fallow fields appeared in the poetry; weeds and scrub were burned to provide an initial fertilizer of ash when the fallow was brought back into production. In a "three-or-four family hamlet" somewhere in northwest T'ai-ho, "the young children are looking for mandarin oranges; the peasant wives have been planting melon since daybreak. At midday they eat their fill of rice, then away they go to burn off the fallow fields."[32] In T'ao-yüan (Peach Spring Ward, township 12), "eight or nine families live by the green mountain; they set fires and then cultivate, and so are accustomed to using the weeding spade (hao-ch'an)."[33] Such fields might lie far from the homestead: "the peasants are taking lunch in the newly-opened fallow, so their wattle-gated yards are quiet; a dog sleeps in the fallen flowers at the base of the fence."[34] The burning of weeds and brush, accomplished during the fall or winter, made a notable spectacle. "The wind tosses the bright hot fire all about, and the mountains front and rear reflect the conflagration. When spring comes, the rains will break up the black ashes, and the wheat fields below the mountain will be loose and fertile."[35] How long into the Ming the technique of fallowing and burning was continued is not known.

It was surely rice, however, that was the primary field crop in the landscape and economy of T'ai-ho in Ming times. This, the most productive of the earth's staple grains, could be treated more and more as a horticultural item whenever population pressure on the land grew intense enough, as it did in some parts of China. In Ming T'ai-ho, such pressures apparently were seldom felt. Rice plants in T'ai-ho appear to have been germinated in thick seed beds prior to their transplantation into the paddy, so there was something of an early horticultural phase in the life cycle of rice. But, by and large, rice belonged to the realm of extensive grain cropping, although it stood in its own rather peculiar domain, quite apart from the dry crops.

Essential to paddy rice in T'ai-ho were the diversion and manipulation of small streams running down from hills and mountains and the modification of valley floors into a gently cascading series of small, level water fields through the building of appropriately placed balks. Seasonal irregularities in water availability made it necessary to construct gravity-flow reservoirs along the upper and middle courses of small streams (big streams, like the Kan, were useless for irrigating rice). The reservoirs were commonly constructed by means of permanent lateral diking (*pei*), which pushed a stream from one side and used natural formations on the other side to guide the flow into one or more holding pools, from which water could be released as needed. Along the lower courses of streams, it was often necessary to lift the water to field level, and this was sometimes done by meeting the stream head-on with permanent or temporary dams.

The laying out of the basic infrastructure, the continued need for upkeep and repair, and the perennial problems of water supply and distribution ensured that rice agriculture could not normally be accomplished by one family, or one hamlet. In Ming T'ai-ho, rice production was handled either through a landlord-tenant system or, alternatively, by bondsmen working under the close supervision of their master.

Among the T'ai-ho literati, only Liu Sung ever reflected aesthetically upon paddy as it lay in the larger landscape, and then but once, where he also inserted a slight down-note: "It's the third month of the year, and the sun and wind have just followed the rain; below the mountain, rice field after rice field is deep in rolling water. The sprouts make a single sheet, like green fabric; but when the wild spotted ducks come, they'll have no place to alight."[36]

What accounts for the curious disproportion between the prominence of rice in the landscape and the paucity of references to it in the poetry and descriptive prose of the local literati? To the Western eye, the rice paddies of interior south China have a picturesque quality suggestive, at certain times of year, of lush green lawns, but in China they must nowhere have been considered particularly attractive, as witnessed by the rarity of their depiction in traditional Chinese landscape art.

Nor was rice-field labor at all discussed by the T'ai-ho literati; even though Wang Chih said that he once guided a plow through a paddy and Liu Sung, that he once helped carry sheaves. Why the omission, given that the literati did discuss garden labor in detail? The answer does not, apparently, lie in an aversion to physical labor as such. The omission may have had something to do with the cooperative, massed character of the labor conducted in rice fields, often under supervision, and to group singing or the beat of a gong.[37] A literatus as gardener worked alone, or nearly so, and could see and think about the results of his own work. The paddy laborer was but part of a team, a worker whose individual effort was lost somewhere in the team's final product. It is probably for that reason that the literati regarded rice-field labor as socially beneath them.

THE MANY USES OF THE MARCH

Beyond the fields lay the vast marches of T'ai-ho. If gardened spaces were small, heavily worked, and tended constantly and fields, larger, worked spasmodically, and visited often, then the march lands were spaces that were vast, untended, and visited only occasionally. Their relative neglect surely did not mean that the marches were inconsequential to livelihood. In fact, of the three zones, it may have been the agricultural zone that ranked last. At least one gathers as much from Wang Chen's *Nung shu* of 1313, a monument in China's technical literature on farming. According to Wang Chen (who was once a magistrate in northern Kiangsi), the pioneer homesteader should locate himself below a mountain and near water; use grass, brush, and other materials close at hand for building; and lay out vegetable beds first of all. Then, if the opportunity arises later, he may extend his farming space to include the fruits, fibers, and grains.[38]

As may be ascertained from fiscal data from the year 1610 (and closely confirmed by a U.S. Army map of 1954), T'ai-ho contained some 144 to 147 square miles of rice paddy, about 14 percent of its total area.[39] Thus something approaching 85 percent of all available space in the county would have been given over to nemoral pursuits of many different kinds: grazing, hunting, gathering, mining, industry, and the like.

Land-use zones that shaped themselves around settlements in the flatter parts of medieval Europe, starting from a settlement and proceeding outwards from it, had first gardens, then plowed fields, and then a degraded "boundary forest" (home of herbs, wild fruit, game, small timber for fuel and carpentry, foliage for fodder, glades or "lawns" for grazing, and perhaps some mining or industry). Outermost lay wilderness, with big virgin timber.[40]

T'ai-ho County diverged slightly from this pattern because its rough, unglaciated topography meant that flat, farmed land met slope not gradually but at sharp, abrupt angles. In T'ai-ho it was elevation as well as distance that dictated the location of nemoral space. As noted earlier, homesites often backed directly into the base of some steep incline so as to afford the inhabitants a convenient avenue of access into the semi-wild and its resources. Thus a fairly distant ring in a flat landscape of old Europe might have begun as a very close one in T'ai-ho.

Among the many essential uses for T'ai-ho's vast march country was the grazing of livestock. In the absence of fodder rotations in field cropping, or of specially maintained and fenced meadow, grazing was conducted at some distance from homesites, in grassy glades and patches.

The grazing animals were goats (*yang*) and "yellow cows," or zebu cattle (*niu, huang-niu*). In Kiangsi, the massive water buffalo predominated in the great lake plains of the north. The zebu is a smaller animal whose lighter build and lesser strength are counterbalanced by its lower forage requirements and especially by its superior ability to negotiate steep inclines and craggy rocks in search of scarce grass.[41] It and not the water buffalo appears to have been the predominant bovine in T'ai-ho.

A zebu cow was a costly investment—for T'ai-ho's resident Confucian philosopher Lo Ch'in-shun, as well as for the lowliest peasant.[42] In a mid-fourteenth-century poem, Liu Sung told of a peasant family that tended its cow as carefully as it would a child. "They went lightly with the whip, so as not to hurt it; and when one winter snow and frost killed all the green grass, they fed it salted soup and rice chaff. They grieved to see it thin, as their lives depended on it. They kept it warm and dry in its wooden-doored earthen stall, and day and night they guarded it against theft." Despite the care, the cow came to a sad end, seized by a marauding army and driven off to be slaughtered for its meat.[43]

The main purpose of the cow was to plow rice fields in the spring, but sometimes other uses were devised. In the late fourteenth century, a peasant from a hamlet "by the bamboo grove, where three or four families live, and the path down to the river makes a bend," saved enough to buy a young cow, which he then hitched to a cart to haul water.[44]

One can follow these animals as they move, under constant human supervision, from their shelters near the homestead out to the marches to graze, and back again. Chou Shih-hsiu's late-fourteenth-century poem follows a herder with his long flute as he takes his yellow cows further and further off. The cows have already chewed away the grass on the sandspits and creek margins, so the herder takes them first to a "good place to the west, where rich grass grows on the open slope and flat hilltop." When they have grazed that, he moves them even further to "a remote valley where no one goes, where the crows caw and the wild goats [takins?] run by," where they must chew on clumps of ear-high grass growing among sharp, flesh-tearing rocks.[45] Animals homeward bound from grazing are pictured in a different part of T'ai-ho in the fourteenth century, when sometimes the older members of the Hsiao people of Shih-kang (Stone Hill Ward, township 10), having "strolled with their canes out along the field balks, would come home in the evening in the company of a servant or two, singing songs as they followed behind the returning herd of cows and goats."[46]

A basic characteristic of march country is the alternation of open glades with wooded groves, and because of this characteristic, the T'ai-ho herders (*mu-t'ung*) regularly crossed paths with wood gatherers (*ch'iao*) as they made their way, inbound or outbound, from centers of settlement. Wood collectors were not lumbermen felling whole trees or clear-cutting forest patches. They were, rather, harvesters of woody suckers and branches, dry or green, that they bundled and portered for sale or their own use as fuel, material for fences, fodder, or compost.

The technical name for this activity is coppicing, and a coppice (or copse) is a grove of trees that periodically undergoes heavy pruning.

Coppicing keeps trees in the rapid growth phase of their life cycles and permits high rates of annual per-acre output, ten or more times as much as in unmanaged or clear-cut forest.[47] Many of the common trees to be found in T'ai-ho's marches (willows, ailanthus, osmanthus, evergreen oaks, etc.) would have responded well to such treatment.

In the march landscape of Peach Spring Ward in township 12, one might have encountered, as Liu Sung did, "a mountain girl, carrying off firewood on her back, her hair hanging down in two braids."[48] Perhaps her home was nearby, tucked into the foot of a coppiced slope. Peasant families found it convenient to have their homes in such sites, with both "fields and brush near at hand," where at sundown the menfolk might be found, just after they had returned with their loads of fuel, laughing and sharing out cups of rice-beer and lying down placidly drunk in their rude doorways.[49]

City residents had to buy their fuel in the city markets. To service their needs, whole families of full-time wood collectors made their homes right in the mountainous country to the north and west. At Ma-shan (Horse Mountain, township 47), near some of the tombs of the Ch'ing-ch'i Yang lineage and the Taoist Temple of the Great Mystery (*T'ai-hsuan kuan*), lived some dozen families in the sixteenth century, all of the same surname, and all of them woodsmen. From Teng-k'o ling (Mount Success-in-the-Examinations), about two miles north of the city, wood collectors and herdsmen of the early fifteenth century followed a well-worn path along a ravine that led from highland brush and forage down to city markets. Commercial gathering, aimed at regular sales in the city, also afforded a living for several other families who lived contentedly enough "in thatched huts deep in the woods." Chou Shih-hsiu described them one morning in the fourteenth century honing their hatchets on whetstones and then setting off with their vine-ropes "right up the green mountain." They had already taken enough deadwood and ailanthus, and now they were after green branches and osmanthus. These they planned to bundle and take directly to the city for sale. With the proceeds, they figured to buy rice and other foodstuffs for their parents and dependents back home. Their occupation let them legally escape the tax and service responsibilities that burdened most people.[50]

The wood collector also escaped the farmer's worries over flood and drought. But while the people of medieval Europe tended to regard the woodcutters and other denizens of the wilderness margins with suspicion, the literati of T'ai-ho saw them as harmless. Indeed, behind every real wood gatherer stood symbolically some local literatus, envious of his fiscal and spiritual freedoms and attracted to the aesthetic setting of his laboring routines. Thus Wang Huan (d. 1423) of Mei-kang (Apricot Hill Ward, township 8) styled himself "wood gatherer" and named the small building housing his private study the Studio of the Wood Gatherer in the Snow (*Ch'iao-hsueh chai*).[51]

And what may have been mere idle conceit for Wang Huan was a matter of romantic, hands-on engagement for Hu Yun-chung, a failed but proud examination taker of the late fourteenth century. "He is," wrote his friend Chou Shih-hsiu,

> attracted to the mountains and thick greenery south of his home, and whenever he can take the time from managing his fields and gardens, he puts on a headband of kudzu cloth, fetches a feather parasol, and, accompanied by a young servant, proceeds hatchet in hand to a place he likes, where a stream splashes over rocks under a dark canopy of pine and bamboo, and there he amuses himself gathering brush. His explanation is this:
>
> "Men are born into this world with different inclinations. Some you see are like flies and birds, thronging and swarming in noisy markets, competing for goods and profits, and delighting in maximizing their take. Such men have gone irretrievably astray, and cannot know the true happiness possessed by us wood gatherers.
>
> "As for me, I set out in the morning as the sun rises, the fog lifts, and lone clouds float by. I wade across a clear stream, sit enraptured under a dense tree, and let out a long yell as the wind starts to pick up. Not even the immortals beyond this world have a greater contentment. Mind you, I'm not like Chu Mai-ch'en of the Han dynasty, who grubbed bent-backed for firewood, just working until the day he could achieve office at last. When I finish cutting branches late in the day, the setting sun is on the mountains, the smoky landscape darkens, the calls of the wildlife echo back and forth, and deer pass by in file. Then I grope my way back through the vines and out of the valley, parting the thickets and traversing the wild moor, with hardly enough of a bundle to cook a pot of bean soup with. As I reach my gate, my children welcome me—unlike Chu Mai-ch'en, ambitious but stooped with toil, whose foolish wife deserted him.
>
> "Home now from collecting, the moon rises over the upper story where I have zither and books and the mats spread out. I lean out and view all creation, then I order up rice-beer and drink as I like. I don't know whether Heaven and Earth can provide any greater contentment than this. After all, luxurious villas and pleasure gardens eventually fall to ruin, and the status and perquisites of office are vulnerable to sudden loss. I see no pleasure in those, and I guess that's why I find it in wood collecting."[52]

In addition to such amateurish wood gathering, the literati of early Ming T'ai-ho also entered march country for wild and medicinal plants,

which engaged their practical, scholarly, and aesthetic interests. Some
built mountain houses right in the march. Behind one such house, early
in the Ming, "a green mountain loses itself in clouds," and "along the
cliffs to the west, one can sometimes see deer herds pass by." The owner
had put medicinal plants out to dry by an unfrequented, pine-shaded
window. In Shen-ch'i Ward, a special house was built in the march for
an ill parent, close to the sources of curative herbs, which were bundled
and placed in the courtyard.[53] Inside Hsiao Tzu's home in Nan-ch'i
Ward (township 59), medicinal plants hung along a special rafter, and
on a rainy day in spring, the camphorlike odor of the dried birthwort
(*Asarum* sp.) was particularly fragrant.[54]

Amateur botanizing was in vogue in T'ai-ho among the literati early
in the Ming. Liu Sung recounted seeing on a mountain path near
Shuang-chiang-k'ou (near township 66) an odd plant that for lack of
flowers he could not identify, and so he picked it in the hope that some
local resident might be able to tell him what it was.[55] Liang Ch'ien
(1366–1418) and his friends liked to read and discuss the classic medical texts and take plant-hunting field trips along the upper reaches of
the creeks in the back country. Accompanied by a servant carrying a
box, they would stop to taste the herbs they found, make drawings
of them, and deposit the specimens in the box, talking all the while.
Finally, as darkness fell, they would grope their way home through
the vines.[56]

The occasional wild species was sometimes simply noted, without
reference to its possible uses, medicinal or otherwise. Liu Sung passed
by a *chü-yu* tree as it spread its aroma along a road in Ho-ch'i (township
65). Its notable fragrance probably identifies this one as the *Wu chü-yu*,
or *Evodia rutaecarpa*, with its medicinal fruits, not noted by Liu.[57] It
was presumably a wild climbing evergreen fig (*Ficus pumila*) that Liu,
on another occasion, saw twining up among the bamboo at the water's
edge in Ho-ch'i.[58] Along the southeastern edge of the county, a glimpse
could be had from a library window of "the wild green woods on the
mountains, with the wind rising, and the dew not yet dry on the green
and yellow mountain orange," that is, the *Fortunella hindsii*, a relative of the kumquat.[59] No indication was given whether, or how, these
plants were used, but some sense of the variety and, here and there,
the density of the understory flora of the march country of early Ming
T'ai-ho was well conveyed.

Early in the Ming, then, the literati and common people of T'ai-
ho regularly combed the marches in search of brush and herbs, vari-

ously for consumption, sale, or recreation. Both classes hunted as well. Among the fauna known to have inhabited the marches were rabbit, several species of deer, fox, boar, "mountain ox" (perhaps takin), tiger, and one or more species of primate.

One could hear the chatter of monkeys of some sort in the highest, isolated mountains of the southern perimeter of the county in the mid-fourteenth century, and they are known to have lived in the higher parts of Mount Wu (about ten miles west of the county seat) as late as the early eighteenth. They were hunted and sold for their fur, or as pets.[60]

Early in the Ming, elite sportsmen, alone or in parties, penetrated the wild in pursuit of game. Liu Sung's nephew Liu Chung-ch'i (of T'ai-yuan Ward, township 33) was "as a youth unusually spirited and fond of hunting from horseback with bow and arrow. Once accompanying a hunting party deep in the mountains, he came upon a fierce tiger, and rising ahead alone, he killed it. The experience strengthened his mind."[61]

While such "baronial" standards of behavior were still accepted (as early in the Ming they were), gentlemen also hunted with trained dogs, "long accustomed to their master's habits, responding eagerly to his looks and gestures" as they plunged through thorn thickets and sharp rocks after fleeing quarry.[62] Rugged terrain provided the setting for excitement and sudden drama; a remote ravine in the mountains along the southeastern perimeter of the county set the stage for an incident involving Hu Ju-lin (stalwart and gregarious member of a "big house," student of the Confucian classics, and sporting huntsman). A tiger jumped him before he could cock the trigger of his crossbow. Eventually wood collectors, hearing a din, came to investigate. They found Hu unconscious on the ground, but the tiger could not reach him to kill him because Hu's favorite hunting dog, though overmatched, managed to keep harassing it. The woodsmen chased off the tiger, but when Hu revived and offered them rewards, they declined, arguing that it was the dog and not they that had really saved his life. When the dog died of its wounds a few days later, Hu gave it an elaborate, human-style burial.[63] If the display seems jocular, the sentiment was surely sincere.

Peasants, settled on the edges of the tiger-infested wilds of the southeastern part of T'ai-ho, were also vulnerable to alarming feline intrusions. In the still of a moonlit night one might be jolted awake by the clamor of squawking chickens, bellowing cattle, barking dogs, and yelling men with bamboo sticks chasing off a prowling tiger.[64] The big cats were also known to attack in broad daylight, crouching, as one did, in thick grass, then springing upon the back of a grazing yellow cow, tearing its flesh and bloodying it, until finally the menfolk drove it away.[65]

The value of wild game was such that when it was depleted, as it was in the canton of Hsien-ch'a by at least the mid-Ming, a community compact (*hsiang-yueh*) that imposed hunting and fishing restrictions was organized.[66] Yet game still abounded in the mountains of the county's southeastern border as late as the mid–seventeenth century, as evidenced by the fact that specialized, non-elite "hunting households" (*she-hu*) lived there in sufficient number to merit their incorporation into a county defense militia.[67] Still, it appears that as game was pushed ever further away, hunting declined in social esteem. Literati sport hunting died out later in the Ming, and the seventeenth-century revival of Buddhist thought, along with Buddhism's animal-releasing rituals and its revulsion against all meat and slaughter, may have played a part in that.

Fishing on the natural watercourses, large and small, also took place. Fish were bred or farmed in T'ai-ho's many man-made ponds and reservoirs. But just as hunters and gatherers penetrated march country for subsistence or sport, so too fishermen took to the wild waters to plunder nature's own supply of fish.

One might find fishing folk living two families, ten mouths, to a small, broad-beamed boat.[68] An oldest son might work the net, a second son the oar, while the youngest did the cooking.[69] In the late fourteenth century, somewhere near township 66, a fishing family fished through the four seasons of the year; the father sang as he rowed out on the broad Ho shui (Grain River), and though some of his family used fishing cormorants, he preferred using nets. Toward nightfall, they would dock on the riverbank and collect their cooking fuel right there. They neither plowed nor planted; yet they all had food and clothes enough.[70]

In the early fifteenth century, Yen Tsung-tan was locally known as an eccentric sporting fisherman, taking his boat back and forth along the big Kan River between T'ai-ho and Kan-chou city some seventy-five miles south and insisting upon using a fishing-pole, not nets, so as to show that he did not have to make a living at this pursuit. Though he lacked learning, "he was polite to the students and scholars he met, and did not act boorishly with them."[71] There were also land-bound sport fishermen, like the arrogant but convivial Liu Ang (1372–1429). His estate in Tung-ch'ang (township 41) bordered upon some islands and flats toward the mouth of a small Kan tributary. His parties featured zither playing, singing, and board games. When he and his guests grew

tired of those amusements, they would all take rice-beer and go down
to the river and fish.[72]

•   •   •

It is also into the nemoral reaches that one must look for examples of
what little industry and mining T'ai-ho County had in Ming times. T'ai-
ho's few industries could be found in remote sites, surrounded by near
wilderness, where water power, fuel, and raw materials were available.
In the extreme southeast, about twenty-five straight-line miles from the
county seat, modern detailed maps show a small but conspicuous ex-
panse of irrigated paddy hedged about by rugged mountains. That was
the site of Lang-ch'uan Ward (township 26) in Yun-t'ing Canton. Access
to it was by way of a long, narrow ravine some ten miles in length. "The
cliffs on either side embrace hundreds of mountain peaks," wrote Liu
Sung in a poem. "Creeks cross and recross the road, skirting and pierc-
ing the grass; daylight lights but half the forest, the rest [the opposite
side] is secluded pine. Here a water-driven trip hammer is at work in the
autumn rain; there a kiln burning stone pours thick smoke into the evening air."[73]

In the twelfth century, China's paper industry began to move into
remote mountain country in search of bamboo, then a new raw material for making paper. In this connection, the industrial valley of Lang-
ch'uan came to produce a high-grade bamboo paper good enough that
the Yuan dynasty after 1279 used it as stock for its paper currency. The
county has also produced modest quantities of a fine-quality "furry-
edged" paper from the Ming period on into modern times.[74]

Mining, like industry, is an activity of uncultivated space, or of space
rendered uncultivable. As it happened, T'ai-ho's two gypsum mines
were each located within a few miles of the county seat, where ugly
evidence of occasional attempts at large-scale digging were easily visible. Mining was widely believed to hurt the great veins along which, in
geomantic theory, vital forces coursed through the county landscape. In
the view of the literati, small-scale peasant digging was tolerable, but
ambitious tunneling and shafting by greedy entrepreneurs was not. In
Chung-pu Ward (township 6), "pile after pile of mine tailings" signaled
to Liu Sung what was afoot in the latter part of the fourteenth century.
Pinkish gypsum, in deposits several inches thick, "white dragon bones
hidden deep in the yellow earth," attracted the operators, despite official bans. Miners with basket-encased lamps bored deep into the gyp-
sum-laden hills, and so strong was the lure of profit that even when the

tunnels collapsed ahead, those behind dug on all the same. Liu had no objection to people taking a little gypsum to steam or dissolve for medicinal purposes, but the huge output at Chung-pu was instead mixed with salt from Kwangtung, heated to achieve a uniform color, and finally distributed to retail salt merchants, who would rush off with their boats and carts full, never bothering to check the illegally adulterated stuff for taste. The noxious business threatened "irreparable damage to the earth's veins." Liu could only wish for a god to come and trample the whole place flat.[75]

The other deposit, whiter gypsum in thinner veins, lay in one or more hills in the vicinity of Mount Wu. Local peasants used a little of this gypsum to make bean curd for sale, and physicians used it to make "medicinal cakes." That was legitimate. But several times during the Ming, big operators opened the works, recruiting laborers from among vagrants and undesirables (who were accused of conducting robberies at night, after work), until tunnel collapses and a great public outcry shut the business down. Early in the seventeenth century, a local entrepreneur opened the Mount Wu works yet again, this time as an imperial monopoly under eunuch patronage. In 1602 and 1603, official memorials of protest against this outrage stressed the geomantic harm, the low per-load price of gypsum, the damage to people's homes, graves, and fields, and the likelihood of riot.[76] (The Wan-li emperor ignored these protests, and their actual effect is uncertain.)

The literati's dislike for gouging the earth extended to deep wells, but curiously it did not extend to the ravages of soil erosion. In fact, the only early discussion of soil erosion focused upon its visually positive effects. In 1367, Liu Sung and his brother discovered a place, perhaps somewhere in township 41, where a stream had cut so low a canyon through an agricultural plain that the farmers could not reach it for irrigation. Long before, a big dam had been built to remedy the problem, and over time, the water falling into the spillway below the dam had eaten away an enormous hole full of fantastic erosional formations. Liu Sung gave the scene a long, detailed, aesthetic description.[77]

Most of T'ai-ho's march country seems to have been neither owned nor taxed but picked over at will within whatever loose restrictions local custom or agreement imposed. Tomb sites, which were preferably and typically located on uncultivable, semiwild, sloping land, were major exceptions. In T'ai-ho these sites were selected with the advice of professional geomancers, and the tombs carefully constructed so that the ancestors, comfortably interred in their shallow hillside niches, might forever radiate good influences upon their living descendants. Subtle and exacting criteria for good tomb location guaranteed intense competition for choice sites, and that competition in turn forced the growth of legal protection for assertions of ownership. (A late-fifteenth-century magistrate complained that the bulk of the litigation he handled centered upon disputes over tomb sites.)[78]

The tombs of the great common-descent groups and lineages were not concentrated in one place but scattered far and wide, and thus upkeep and seasonal visits became major efforts in management and logistics. In 1439, it took the Grand Secretary Yang Shih-ch'i more than a month to tour by sedan chair thirty-two scattered ancestral tombs in T'ai-ho County alone (there were yet other tombs in neighboring counties). He found one tomb site encroached upon by home builders, and he directed that the offenders be prosecuted at once. He mentioned by name eighteen tomb watchers (none of them Yangs) who were authorized to receive payments of cloth or cash whenever the Yang kinsmen appeared on their seasonal visits.

The Yang tombs also had a place in the subsistence economy. Yang Shih-ch'i instructed his junior kinsmen that each of their families should take turns cutting grass and brush off the tumuli, in order that each might get an equal share of the fuel. He also had them issue permits to the tomb watchers empowering them to harvest the brush along the outskirts of the tombs. No one was to cut trees off the grave sites, however, unless they grew thick enough to harbor tigers or snakes, in which case the culled trees were to be evenly divided among the Yang families.[79]

The tombs in T'ai-ho's nemoral hillsides were sacred; yet nemoral space never quite acquired the transcendent aura that it once had in the paganisms of the West. No Diana coursed in T'ai-ho's groves and glades; no druids conducted rites under holy clumps of trees. The Podocarpus trees, male and female, that grew by a Buddhist hermitage in Ku-kang (Old Hill Ward, township 22) elicited appreciation of their strange dioecious botany, but they suggested nothing holy.[80] Sacred space in T'ai-ho lay at the highest elevations, on the mountaintops, as will be noted in a moment.

In sum, then, three principal regimes of land use have been singled out: the horticultural, the agricultural, and the nemoral. It has been argued that because the working energies of the people were perforce concentrated nearest their homes, scattering and fading with increasing distance, a basic pattern of land use emerged, with each land-use zone

contributing its specific range of essential goods to the subsistence economy. Early in the Ming, the literati took a certain role in this economy—describing it, rhapsodizing upon it, and personally contributing
labor to those activities (like gardening, wood collecting, or hunting)
whose marginal productivity was high.

There are, to be sure, some ambiguities in this simple trizonal system. Where in it, for example, does one place afforestation? Here and
there in T'ai-ho, members of affluent common-descent groups removed
cutover scrub from certain hillsides and planted patches of single-spe-
cies forest in its place. Examples include the Yang of Shang-yuan-t'ang
(Upper Spring Pond, township 43) and the Tseng of Tang-yuan (township 29), who reportedly pioneered the local planting of the China fir
(*shan*, probably *Cunninghamia sinensis*) around the mid–fifteenth century.[81] The Kuo lineage, already domiciled for centuries at Kao-p'ing
(township 61) when Liu Sung wrote about them, had long-established
plantings of pine, camphor, and three species of oak: "the taller trees
reach to the clouds, while the shorter blanket the mountains; their yield
provides fuel and building materials."[82] In the sixteenth century, Yin
Ch'u-yung of Kuan-ch'i (Irrigation Creek Ward, township 14) planted
"several *li* of pine (i.e., rows of pine totaling about a mile in length),
which successfully grew into a forest. He offered the advice that pine
would not flourish just anywhere and required an appropriate topography: "The pine tree is dark in color and grows very tall. If it is not well-
rooted, it will grow twisted and skewed and won't mature properly.
That is why it must be planted on level hilltops and broad elevations. It
is useless to plant such places to crops, because weeds will shade them
out and the scrub will defeat them, which is another reason why pine is
best there."[83]

Another ambiguity was the survival in T'ai-ho of watery or marshy
places where useful lines of what probably were endogenous species
managed to hold their own against the encroachments of garden
and field. Water plants such as sweet flag (*Calamus* sp.), water shield
(*Brasenia*), water caltrop (*Trapa*), perennial wild rice (*Zizania*), cattail
(*Typha*), arrowhead (*Sagittaria*), and fringed water lily (*Limnanthe-
mum*) grew in such places. All of them were consumable as famine
foods, or as delicacies, and seem to have been remnants of a primordial
southern diet of "water shield, eels, wild rice, taro soup, [and] baked
turtle," constituents in what Hui-lin Li has called a "distinct system"
of aquaculture.[84] All the plants can, of course, be deliberately cultivated,
but in T'ai-ho their description often suggests a wild or semiwild state.

Local description also includes, alongside the water plants listed above, weedy terrestrial plants that were confined only with the greatest difficulty to narrow marginal locations, always threatening to spread forth at the slightest opportunity. Some of those weeds too were used as famine foods.

Wild rice grew in thick clumps where fishermen in their boats might encounter it.[85] Somewhere near Liu Sung's home, "in the spring wind, mulberry trees fringe the continuous plots of wheat; and in the autumn rain, wild rice and cattail front the pine-covered slope."[86] Here the poet has contrasted the thin filament of one stand against the broad patch of the other. During the wars of the mid–fourteenth century, starving children took baskets out to the idled fields, and though it was already early spring, nothing was green, owing to an exceptionally cold winter: "The cattail and the fringed water lily haven't yet sprouted at the water's edge, but the sweet shepherd's purse [Capsella bursa-pastoris] has emerged from the mud and flowered," and so they picked that to eat.[87] In township 56, "a deep wood encloses an empty guesthouse . . . , the flowering water shield grows broad-leaved in the creek."[88]

When garden vegetables failed for lack of water, Liu Sung and Wang Tzu-ch'i contented themselves with a pauper's soup of lamb's-quarter (Chenopodium sp.).[89] Wild amaranth (probably Amaranthus viridis) spread as a "traveler" in fall gardens, and if the melon vines were bug ridden, and the eggplant weed choked, one might be pleased enough to pick it to boil for soup or chop for pickling.[90] At the homestead of the Wen family near Mount Wu, shepherd's purse grew apace with the wheat in the spring snow.[91] The weedy cereal called pai (Echinochloa crus-galli) could grow either in abandoned dry fields or, as a rice-mimic, in wet places; "starvelings, thin as storks" went into deserted fields to harvest it in famine times. On an "old mountain estate, inhabited by a few families with their dogs and chickens, the hamlet is desolate after the wars, and plowmen are few, and so the cattail and the pai stand tall in fields flooded by fall rains."[92]

SCENIC LANDSCAPES

The literati of early Ming T'ai-ho also reflected upon the landscape of their native county in its wider, more inclusive, and more specifically scenic dimensions. Scenic appreciation was a social activity in which the younger cohorts of literati, many with good prospects for official careers, developed a sense of identity and comradeship. Scenic outings, literary descriptions, and artistic representations enhanced emotional identification with native place, which was useful psychic capital to have in the distant and uncertain world of imperial bureaucracy.

Wang Chih lived to become minister of personnel, one of the highest imperial offices of his time. Home on leave in 1422, his star already on the rise, he described at great length an outing he took with some sixteen promising local literati up to the summits of Mount Wu, west of the county seat. Struck by the grandeur of the view from one of these summits, he remarked:

> the rest of us climbed the Wu-po Hill, then pushed ourselves to the top of a crag. Here there were no more big trees, just yellow grass and dwarf bamboo. The view was bright and clear in all directions. Right beneath our feet, and extending for several hundred li, as far as our eyes could see, there lay a scenic expanse of villages, bamboo groves and tree clumps, and smoke and clouds. The big mountains in the south part of the county loomed about like jade tablets. There was the Kan River, flowing in from the west, making its bend in front of the county seat, and then continuing on east, until the smaller mountains hid it and you couldn't see it any more. Inside and outside the city walls you could make out the different government offices, people's homes, and Buddhist and Taoist temples, even though they were packed as tight as the teeth of a comb, or the scales of a fish. I sighed and said to the others: "This truly is a magnificent county. If we hadn't taken this trip, we would never have fully grasped its scenic scale."[93]

There existed local landscape artists in T'ai-ho in the early Ming. Their work is now lost, but comments upon it remain. Nowhere did the commentators say that this art had any value as art. Rather, they took it as a literal but necessarily secondhand likeness of its subject. Looking at a landscape painting was a flimsier experience than viewing the actual landscape that it tried to portray. As Wang Chih put it in a poem he placed on a painting of Hsiao Tzu's home in Nan-ch'i (township 59): "The artist Li has executed this painting with rare skill; yet how can looking at a painting be as good as observing the real thing?"[94] Thus landscape art was here a technique whereby a scene was made portable so as to provide those far from the native soil with something to stimulate sentimental attachments and nostalgic reverie. Hsiao Tzu served in the Han-lin Academy in Peking, and the painting of his Nan-ch'i home would simply have helped him reconstruct a fond and familiar scene in his mind.

But there were other and more important uses for T'ai-ho's landscape art. For example, Wang Chih's mother's family, also surnamed

Hsiao, lived in Lu-kang (Fortune Hill, township 55), some ten miles northwest of the county seat. Their estate was "surrounded by a land-scape [*ching-wu*] of clear creeks and scenic mountains." Wang's maternal uncle Hsiao K'o (1358–1411) selected the best views, which he called "The Eight Scenes at Fortune Hill," and he devised these labels for them:

Wood Gatherer's Cottage at Fortune Hill
Gathering of Gulls at Snail Cove
Fishing in a Snowfall at Cheng Island
Farming beneath Clouds in Tung Ward
Morning Colors on Gap Mountain
Autumn Sounds on Mount Wu-lao
Moonlight after Rain on Apricot Creek
Clear Wind in Bamboo Pass

He used to sit and sing in those places. He always wanted to have a good lyricist write descriptive poems about them, but he died without having done it. Fortunately, his son, Hsiao Fu-te, has been able to fulfill his wish. This year he brought his own paintings of the eight scenes to Peking, and Lung Shih-yü [Lung Wen, 1409–59], of the Central Drafting Office, helped him in arranging to have various officials here write poems about them. I was asked to provide the preface. . . .

These eight scenes have always been there in Lu-kang, but until the right people were found, they just languished unappreciated in their remoteness and obscurity. Now thanks to Hsiao Fu-te and his father, the beauty of these places has been shown, and that is surely Lu-kang's good fortune, because, as the saying goes, it is people that make a place scenic, just as a man's talent becomes apparent only when it is put to use.[95]

Here a rural T'ai-ho estate has become something more than a holding that affords a livelihood. Art and poetry have commuted it into the recognizable coin of the national aesthetic tradition. The tiny, obscure locality of Lu-kang has won at least a momentary place on the national scenic map, and the Hsiao family has itself gained by its determined promotion of these scenes. Social recognition among Peking officialdom will have injured neither their standing in local society nor their hopes for official careers for themselves. In this way, T'ai-ho's local landscapes could be made to serve as social currency in the wider world beyond.

And T'ai-ho's scenic excellences could also be directed inward, offering psychic benefits to the local landlord and contributing to peaceful relations among the laborers on his detached estate. Wang Chih described how:

> Twenty *li* [about 7 miles] south of T'ai-ho there is a place called Nan-yuan [South Garden], with luxuriant forests and broad fields. A range of mountains coming from Feng-ling in Lang-ch'uan [township 26] divides and encloses Nan-yuan to the east and west, about seven or eight *li* away. A small river, with its source in Hsing-kuo County, flows northwest to join the Kan, and as it comes through here, the water becomes clear and attractive. Given so scenic a landscape, the inhabitants of this place are honest and simple, showing little sign of crime or strife. This is one reason why my friend, Hsiao Chung-ling, has his detached estate here.
>
> As far as the eye can see, all the fine fields and deep ponds are owned by him, and he himself directs his slaves [*t'ung-nu*] in the plowing and planting. There is an abundance of everything: rice, soybeans, wheat, vegetables, fish, turtles. Recently his son was appointed magistrate in T'eng County [in Kwangsi], so now there is also a salary income. Hsiao Chung-ling can relax, drink with his guests, and share the enjoyment of this place.
>
> This enjoyment consists of everything that strikes the ear and eye. You look off to the mountains, shaded by dense growths of pine and cypress, and your eye follows the deer as they file up and down. You look out on the river, and there you watch the boats sail by, and the birds and fish as they swim. Your hear the singing of the wood collectors and fishermen; you observe the traffic of plowmen and herdsmen. Once I was going to Shan-t'ien [township 31] and passed through here en route. A slave pointed out the Hsiao detached estate and identified it for me. I would have paid Hsiao Chung-ling a visit, but he wasn't at home at the time. But I did linger and look around awhile.
>
> There was a time when I was home on leave when I thought about setting up a farming estate for my retirement, but I never did it. There was good field and garden land available, but either it lacked a scenic river, without which the wise cannot be content; or else it lacked forested mountain, without which the benevolent are dissatisfied. There are very few places that, like Nan-yuan, have all of it. It is therefore appropriate that Hsiao should seek to preserve his enjoyment by asking me to write this account.
>
> Yet the scenic dimensions of Nan-yuan do not stop here. If you look even further off, then to the south you notice the high peaks of the San-ku [Three Gazers] side by side, rearing a thousand feet up into the clouds. The local teacher Hsiao Tzu-ching [Hsiao Ch'u, 1064–1130] once had a studio out there. Off to the east is Mount Wang, immense and overpowering, like a racing dragon or recumbent tiger. That is where in the Chin era [265–419 A.D.] Wang Tzu-yao, the immortal, ascended into the sky. But just as the pure and lofty unworldliness of these places transcends the life and death of individuals, so too Hsiao Chung-ling, as he contemplates these distant reaches, must surely achieve a transcendental joy that lies beyond landscape and cannot be communicated to others.[96]

Unlike the series of disconnected scenes at Lu-kang, the Nan-yuan landscape was holistic and complete. The land-use zones succeeded each other with distance; wild water and nemoral slopes enclosed a secure subsistence base that delighted the senses as much as it filled the larder. It was a "Confucian" landscape in that its aesthetics reinforced moral values and social harmony. But beyond the march, on a spiritual-geographical frontier in the far distance, there lay a higher region, this one a Taoist landscape of awesome peaks and world-transcending promise. Below it stretched the humanized landscape of subsistence routine and social obligation, while above flashed a wild, formless skyscape of transcendence, freedom, and joy, the Taoist paradise of the upper atmosphere which the adepts of old had supposedly attained.

The elevated site of the Lung-ch'eng ssu, a rebuilt Buddhist temple in township 8, conveyed a strong sense of otherworldliness to Liang Ch'ien early in the fifteenth century:

Here the hills approach from several hundred *li* to the southwest, undulating like an uninterrupted chain of dragons. They make a forested ring around the temple, hence its name [Dragon Wall]. You can see the Kan River far off in one direction, and the San-ku peaks in another. You find yourself among steep cliffs with endless green and idle rustling sounds. Atop the heights, you are among the mist-clad pines and cypress, so far from the everyday world that it is like being up among the sacred mountains T'ien-t'ai and Lu-shan.[97]

From the lowland home of a physician in Kuan-ch'ao (township 31), the view of the distant mountains at certain moments also conveyed a hint of paradise: "Whenever the rain stops and the mist evaporates, the play of light and shadow creates rich patterns so unworldly that one is reminded of P'eng-hu and Yuan-ch'ao [mythical island abodes of the immortals]."[98]

The relationship between these two realms, one earthly and the other ethereal, was pointed up by Wang Chih while he was living in Peking. He had had forty pictures made and mounted into a long scroll. Thirty-eight of the pictures made up a detailed panorama of all the "mountain and river" scenery of his native T'ai-ho County. "When off duty I look at this," he wrote, "and it is like having the views I knew from long ago right before my eyes. My spirits rise and my heart relaxes. What is it but this painting that lets me enjoy these mountains and forests right here in Peking?"

But two of the pictures were not about scenic landscape. They featured immortals, "floating in the void" and "journeying beyond the everyday world." Their being there was not an incongruity. If landscape somehow lost its charm, then their purpose became clear. Wang Chih explained:

> On second thought, it occurred to me that the landscape of my county was enjoyable when I saw it long ago, but I have long been away and am unsure what changes may have taken place in it. It all depends on the quality of our magistrates. If they have all been good magistrates, who have gained the co-operation of the people and have brought on Heaven's bounty, then the flora and fauna will have flourished even more; the mountains will have become even finer and the waters clearer, and the pleasure of it all will have increased. But this is not what I hear. I fear that what I used to enjoy now looks lamentable, and that the local people must be envying the immortals on their transcendental journey.[99]

Whether in fact the landscape of T'ai-ho began notably to deteriorate in the mid–fifteenth century, owing to official maladministration or to other causes, is uncertain. What soon did occur, however, was a definite end to earlier literati preoccupations with the beauty or grandeur of local landscape in the round. By the sixteenth century, there were signs that some major shifts in attitudes toward nature and landscape were taking place. The clues are several, and they trace an interesting trajectory.

The first clue centers about Kuo Hsu (1456–1532), the only T'ai-ho native ever to achieve anything close to national recognition as an artist. As an artist and literatus, he would be expected to have devoted some of the same loving attention to his native scenery as had the literati before him, who wrote but did not paint. Yet that was not the case. Kuo Hsu developed his artistic ideas on his travels, and though he did live at home for periods of time, none of his work ever explicitly featured T'ai-ho scenes.[100] That is surely strange. All intellectual and emotional contact with the earlier T'ai-ho tradition seems to have broken off. The county landscapes that, just two generations earlier, had inspired so much description and comment, somehow failed to make an impression upon Kuo Hsu.

This curious deflation of T'ai-ho's scenic inheritance is nowhere directly explained, but it does help build a context for understanding the acceptance of certain new aesthetic fashions from outside. An early example of this is the Tzu-i yuan (Garden of Self-Satisfaction) laid out by Liu Che (1541–1611), a member of a wealthy family of K'an-ch'i in township 63. Liu Che is said to have planned the garden in imitation of a style developed in the city of Soochow, in the Yangtze delta region.

This showpiece surrounded a library and a museum and boasted plantings of "a myriad bamboo, a thousand rows of cypress, ancient *Prunus mume* [Japanese apricot], gnarled pines, red-flowered peach, an osmanthus grove, tubsful of lotus, potsful of orchids, and noted flowers scattered about the courtyard."[101] Again, it is an interesting question why, given the already celebrated picturesqueness of the natural and man-made landscapes of T'ai-ho, it was now felt appropriate to indulge in an expensive, contrived, and inward-turned creation of this sort. (Rural insecurity may have been a factor.)

Excursions changed, too. In earlier times, Liu Sung and Wang Chih and their friends had reached the mountains of T'ai-ho on horseback and scaled them on foot. In the 1660s, however, the literati hiked no more; instead they were taken as tourists by sedan-chair across the rice paddies and up Mount Yü-hua, where rest pavilions awaited them, and where, after a lunch of boiled mallow and rice-beer, they would not explore or botanize but unpack and examine books and paintings by a clear, cold stream.[102] The large and small worlds of nature have been pushed here from the center to the edges of consciousness.

Atop Mount Wang stood an altar, erected in the early fourteenth century by Hsiao Te-t'ung of Peach Spring Ward (township 12), of bricks manufactured at the base of the mountain by hired laborers, then painfully hauled to the top. There, sacrifices to Wang Tzu-yao and other ancient Taoist adepts proved effective against flood, drought, disease, and childlessness.[103] In 1671, more than three centuries after its construction, that altar still stood, and the common people still visited it on foot. The literati, however, now enjoyed some wholly new facilities. Chang Chen-sheng, a retired official from neighboring Lu-ling County (and also a noted Confucian writer) put a battalion of bondsmen (*t'ung-p'u*) to work hacking out of the rock and forest a scenic route to the top of Mount Wang that chair bearers could negotiate. The stone-paved path bridged streams and skirted rocky deeps, and all along it were built pavilions, rest houses, and storied structures, each with its own name, easily some twenty in all.[104] This development provided comfort and amusement for literati tourism. Once again, nature found itself modified and outdone by artifice.

No literatus of the early Ming had ever written of the landscape as Hsiao Shih-wei did in his diary. His entry for November 4, 1635, reads: "Yang Chai-yun [Yang Chia-tso] and I waited for K'ang Lin-ting [K'ang Ch'eng-tsu] at Pointed Star Hill [to the west of the county seat]. This is a bald mountain, but it is higher than the surrounding hills and so affords something of a view. There is a stone cliff behind with a big split in it, the best scenic attraction here, but unfortunately it is spoiled by a detestable ramshackle house built right in the middle of it."[105] If this house had been noticed at all in the early Ming, it would probably have been considered an appropriate component of the landscape not a cause for offense as here.

An outstanding achievement among the new landscape fashions in T'ai-ho was the nationally celebrated Ch'un-fou yuan (Spring Floating Garden), planned and built by the same Hsiao Shih-wei in the 1620s, and located in the Willow Creek area of the western suburb.

The Spring Floating Garden was a completely man-made scenic landscape. Hsiao had channels dug to make creeks, soil and rock piled up to make mountains, winding paths laid out, bridges and pavilions erected, and plantings put in. "In every instance," we are told, "he exhausted all possibilities and exercised every cleverness to make this garden different from anyone else's."[106] Hsiao Shih-wei himself wrote a descriptive guide to the park. An excerpt from the middle of it may suffice to give its flavor:

> At the end of the Path of Allurement, there is an island, from which the distant trees viewed by moonlight look like so much shepherd's purse. On this island sits Bowl Mountain, half of which looks like it were about to topple into the lake. The mountain looks like a bowl if you view it from the lake; but if you stand on it, and look out on the lake, it is quite like being on a snail that is plowing its way through a dish of water. Looking down from there, you see fish swimming in the tips of the reflected branches of the trees, people walking as if in a mirror, and all the shadows of the trees following you along in midcurrent.[107]

Some complex illusions have been effected here. Mountains, islands, lakes, usually the remote components of a scenic landscape, reachable only with difficulty, have been miniaturized and placed close in. Moreover, this walk-through wilderness is intended to be appreciated less for itself than for its capacity to spring perceptual surprises on the viewer, to suggest imaginative permutations of one thing into something else. Distant trees look like weeds, a toy mountain becomes now a bowl, now a snail's shell; fish seem to swim in trees. Although Hsiao Shih-wei had close personal connections to people whom Frederic Wakeman has styled the "Romantic" literati of seventeenth-century China, with their "esthetic sensuality," "sybaritic laxity," and egocentrism,[108] the Spring Floating Garden seems rather to have tried to express a certain intellectuality. Perhaps it embodied in some way the combination of Buddhist epistemology and intellectual Taoism that Hsiao Shih-wei is said to have adopted in his now lost commentary on the Buddhist text known as the *Awakening of Faith*.[109]

The new-style gardens of T'ai-ho, affordable by only a few very wealthy men, take us far indeed from the land uses of the workaday world that the early Ming literati celebrated. The identity of some of the plantings that graced these garden underscores the point. Beside such traditional local stocks as camphor trees, bamboo, osmanthus, and magnolia, new and exotic species appear for the first time, most likely as special purchases. Both the Garden of Self-Satisfaction and the Spring Floating Garden boasted specimens of the red-petaled, double-flowered peach (*fei-t'ao*), a plant with ornamental rather than economic value, and almost assuredly an import.

Hsiao Shih-wei noted in his diary on November 13, 1635: "the crab-apple is all abloom, and there are a few blossoms open on the peaches and plums. The narcissus has put out some luxuriant and lovely bunches of flowers. Later I went over to the Pan-jo Temple to check on the chrysanthemums. The best variety is the 'frost-defying yellow,' but the variety called 'gold sparrow tongue' grown by my younger brother is almost as good." On December 2, he observed that the hydrangea (or viburnum), the "human-faced peach," and the quince had all flowered and that the crabapple was still blooming despite the frost.[110]

The crabapple in question is specified by Hsiao as the *hsi-fu hai-t'ang,* a spectacular small tree, profusely adorned in season with rose-colored blossoms. H. L. Li identifies it as the *Malus floribunda,* perhaps a hybrid, and in any case a native of north China.[111] The so-called human-faced peach is not a peach but the *Dracontomelum dao,* a tropical member of the cashew family, and is, in T'ai-ho, far to the north of its native range. The quince is specifically the *t'ieh-keng hai-t'ang* (*Chaenomeles lagenaria*), or "Japanese quince," also cultivated for its floral display.

There is a certain consistency between the cultivation of these new and exotic ornamental plants and the shift of aesthetic interest from the natural or subsistence landscape to the manufactured miniature. Both gardens seem like deliberate attempts to ignore anything local or commonplace. The Garden of Self-Satisfaction and the Spring Floating Garden combined national fashion and personal idiosyncrasy, but they had no particular connection to T'ai-ho. They could have been put almost anywhere in south China.

As in the mid–fourteenth, so again in the mid–seventeenth century, T'ai-ho County suffered the depredations and upheavals of prolonged

civil war (albeit with very different consequences for landscape appreciation). In 1662, a visitor, Shih Jun-chang, found the county "aswarm
with bandits, and thorny scrub growing in what once had been people's
homes." He further noted that "wherever you look, you see signs of
abandonment . . . and you realize that before the upheavals, there must
have been a dense and thriving population of mountain people here."[112]
In 1677, a local writer, Liang Kung, described T'ai-ho as still lying in
ruins—its schools wrecked, its markets and shops closed, and its fields
unworked.[113]

The Spring Floating Garden was an early casualty. By 1662, "wood
gatherers and herders had taken everything away," and all that remained
were weeds and ruined walls and pavilions, such that "the onlooker
would hardly guess that all this was once the garden."[114] No matter.
The old garden had fronted on an artificial lake called Lake T'ao, made
up of several excavated and interconnected ponds. During the troubled
1660s and 1670s, Hsiao Shih-wei's nephew and heir, Hsiao Po-sheng
(1619–ca. 1678), created a new Buddhist temple complex and resort on
a different side of this lake. The old garden had been in its day a resort
where elite guests (including members of the Restoration Society) had
been welcome to stay, and Hsiao Po-sheng continued to offer such hospitality. One famous guest of his, Fang I-chih, commented that since
Lake T'ao was not wide and wild like a real lake but calm and sheltered,
it should be renamed Winding Shore.[115]

This new resort included a Buddhist temple (called the Sandalwood
Incense Region of Wisdom), a Garden of the Buddhist Householder,
and a structure called the Tower of Great Compassion, which contained apartments for guests, as did a nearby hermitage (called the I-an,
or Shou-shan an). Hsiao Po-sheng's personal showpiece garden, the Tun-
p'u (Garden of Escape) with its lotus pond, seems to have been laid out
in part of what had been the old Spring Floating Garden. The Garden
of Escape featured a grove of fine sophora trees plus tea bushes and medicinal herbs; its gardeners were skilled in the making of tiny boats of
orchids and toy sedan-chairs of bamboo, as well as in brewing tea and
in the distilling of a fiery vodka, a Hsiao family specialty. The extraordinary wealth of the Hsiao family, only slightly depleted by the wars,
made possible all this construction; there in Willow Creek lay a small
paradise of repose in a county where "all around lay ruined places and
bald-topped hills."[116]

In June and July of 1670, Fang I-chih and the Buddhist abbot Chung-
ch'ien had a bamboo raft built and got together a small boating party

on Lake T'ao. One of the participants was a local writer, Wang Yü-k'uo. His account of the party evidences a Buddhist reading of landscape, with a deliberate search for its ambiguities and double meanings:

> We waited at Plum Mound, east of the tower, for the moon to rise. A breeze blew in the fragrant lotus, and mist clung in the reflected elms. Soon there was light in the night clouds behind the trees, and the bright moon, round as a basket, rose above the west pagoda. We boarded the raft and rowed among the reflections of the bamboo and cypress. The moon appeared and disappeared as the raft turned this way and that. The two slaves [*t'ung*] at the oars had never been on the lake before, and had to ask directions. We gave them directions and got extraordinary views at every turn. The mountains beyond seemed to follow us in an aimless way; the most darkly foliaged one was Mount Yü-hua.
>
> Presently we heard a slight noise like a brook, coming from the tall trees. It turned out to be an old peasant, working a well-sweep with his foot. He must have been very tired, and we laughed at our enjoying our relaxation while he enjoyed his labor. We were all simply following our inclinations.
>
> We then caught glimpses of lamps burning in the Garden of the Buddhist Householder. The garden people had seen our raft coming, and had lit and placed lamps on shore. We rowed to the temple and landed there. . . . The abbot P'ing-yuan served us tea and snacks, and we discussed the recent history of this place, and while we were regretting not having toured here in the earlier days, the water clock in the tower sounded three times.
>
> So we left the temple and anchored in the broadest and brightest part of the lake. The moon was directly overhead, the water reflected the sky perfectly, and we agreed that it was probably a mistake to consider the lake a miniature, and not a big and wide one after all. Then a breeze ruffled the trees, the night air turned chilly, and the abbot Chung-ch'ien pulled his robe around his head. We ordered the two slaves to row back at once, but they got lost among the islets and couldn't find the way.
>
> The lake used to serve as a place for the Buddhist ceremony of releasing living things, so the fish here were tame. But the birds on shore rose in alarm and twittered among the trees when they heard us talking. That surprised us, and it showed we hadn't yet completely tired of the excursion.
>
> The lake is only about one *li* from the city wall, so close that we could hear very sharply the sound of something being split. We sighed that although we often want to take some rice-beer and boat about on a body of water under the full moon, armed troops on shore will investigate anything unusual and yell at you if you try. That did not happen to us this time, because the lake is hidden among trees, so we enjoyed ourselves just as we pleased.[117]

Thus, while menials rowed them over the moonlit artificial lake, the literati read the landscape as though it were all a demonstration lesson in the phenomenology of the *Awakening of Faith*. Opposites blurred and erased each other. Each new sensation posed a momentary contradiction, then resolved itself in some higher synthesis. Work merged with leisure, and the small blended with the big. The past entangled itself in the moving time of the present, the tame intergraded with the wild, and even military repression enveloped freedom.

Another famous visitor, the Ming loyalist Wei Hsi, described a boating excursion on Ch'ing-ch'i (Clear Creek), just east of the city, in June 1677. He liked the daytime view there but regretted the absence of any pavilion to sit in. Hsiao Po-sheng arranged a nighttime boating excursion under the moon and on the crest of a chance flood. As the members of the party contemplated their reflections in the calm, moonlit floodwater, their real-life anxieties dissolved. The experience created a joyous frame of mind that, everyone insisted, merited permanent remembrance after the party was over. "It is the inclinations we have in everyday life that create joy," remarked Hsiao Po-sheng. "If we can achieve this joy in ourselves, then no matter where we are, we will be in a waterscape [like this one]."[118]

And so ends the late Ming trajectory leading to increasingly attenuated forms of landscape appreciation. From the early Ming discovery of beauty and value in the real world of nature and life on the land, one ends in the late Ming and early Ch'ing's determination to ignore or avoid that world, with the creation of toy fantasies in artificial lakes and landscaped gardens, and a preference for moonlit surrealisms to the daylight world of settlement, work, and subsistence. As one ponders this cycle of landscape interpretation by the T'ai-ho literati, and all the things it might mean, it is hard to dismiss the suspicion that in T'ai-ho these changing perceptions were to some degree driven by changing social opportunity and social consciousness—that starting in the sixteenth century an optimistic world of local security and favorable opportunity for the literati gradually soured; that a more limited, more problematical, and more distasteful world replaced it; and that the changing perceptions of landscape perhaps served as a sort of barometer for the changing pressures of society. The chapters in the next section attempt to explore what some of those pressures may have been.

PART TWO

The Pressures of Change

CHAPTER 2

Managing the Local Wealth

It is next to impossible to talk about the "economy" of T'ai-ho; seldom does anything resembling conventional economic data emerge from the sources. Western-derived categories of thinking about production, consumption, and exchange soon shrivel for want of the right kinds of facts to flesh them out. And yet the Ming literati often discussed what one might call resource management—although never with some dehumanized goal of efficiency in mind. Instead, at least early on, resource management was viewed within a framework of aesthetic description and was structured by a deep concern for visible manifestations of ethical *social* behavior. Significantly, in the sixteenth century, the framework for discussing resources shifted toward statecraft and equity.

While the local "economy" is a topic impossible to pursue very far, it would not be out of place here to try to locate T'ai-ho County in the broader context of the rural socioeconomic order of later imperial China, as that issue is currently understood. The debate about how best to typify that order has moved away from characterizing it as "feudal" or "manorial" and seems to focus on a formula balancing "landlordism" with "gentry society." Landlordism, as an exploitive form of rural control, occurs with a free market in land and a partible inheritance system; whereas gentry society results from education and local engagements with the imperial examination system and entails a moral and social obligation to provide local services.[1] However, China's "landlords" came in many sizes and shapes, and the labor they deployed

ranged from free tenants to land-bound serfs, from hired labor to inden-
tured labor to slave labor, in a slithery and unstable variety of admix-
tures and combinations. It appears that interior Kiangsi generally was
hospitable to large estates (of both the compact and scattered variety)
in the Sung and, to a lesser extent, later and that the labor force consisted of a wide assortment of tenants, tenant serfs, and bondspeople.
Some bondspeople worked in the household, others in the fields. Ming
law explicitly recognized a status distinction between free people (*liang-
jen*) and bondspeople.[2] All that can be said of T'ai-ho in the Ming is that
it surely contained some large estates—privately controlled early on and
many of them lineage-controlled later—and that there were tenants and
bondspeople at work on estates of various sizes throughout the Ming.
In the absence of appropriate documentation (deeds and contracts, account books, intensive literati discussions of the issue as such), it is impossible to analyze rural socioeconomic relations in detail.

Another way to approach the problem of rural order in late imperial China is simply to label the locally dominant people as "elites" with
a wide and flexible repertoire of strategies at their disposal, in which
landowning, education, and degree holding were usual but not necessarily indispensable elements. Elites could also engage in such things as
philanthropy, commerce, moneylending, managing, brokering, and militia leadership, as local conditions and broad historical change might
dictate.[3] In the case of T'ai-ho, this chapter will show that, indeed, local
elites changed their strategies in the sixteenth century—from an earlier
"baronial" style of landowning toward the duller, grayer, less picturable
tasks of managing corporate lineage estates and moneylending, the latter often outside the province altogether. Ownership and management
appear to have parted ways more and more.

As far as the "economic history" of T'ai-ho goes, suffice it to say that
T'ai-ho seems to follow in broad outline the phases in the long growth
curve that Robert Hartwell traced out for the whole peripheral zone of
the middle Yangtze macroregion, in which zone T'ai-ho is to be found.[4]
Thus the peripheral zone underwent "frontier settlement" in the years
2–742 (the county dates back to the third century and was renamed
T'ai-ho in the year 591). Then in the years 742–1170, it entered a boom
phase of "rapid development" (T'ai-ho's largest irrigation work was
built during the years 926–929. Native literati authored new works on
agricultural plants and tools in 1094 and 1201, but no works appeared
after that. The last big irrigation project was completed around 1348.)

After "rapid development," it entered an "equilibrium" phase that in theory lasted from 1170 to 1948–and, indeed, there is no evidence for any significant new growth spurts in the T'ai-ho economy from Ming times down to the founding of the People's Republic of China in 1949.[5] But there were a series of reconstructions following civil wars (e.g., in the 1380s and 1390s, 1680s, 1870s, 1950s) and incremental changes here and there (in population and in the increasing use of silver in the late Ming). These developments elicited local adaptations, and this chapter will show some of the responses occasioned by changing conditions in the early and mid-Ming.

Beyond question, the mainstay of the T'ai-ho economy in the Ming was rice production. Some 14 percent of the county's 1,028 square miles was devoted to that crop. Soils were on the whole poor, and total annual yields in good or excellent years were in the range of 600–700,000 piculs (1 picul equals 103 liters, or 2.84 bushels). A pauper's dole in the Ming was pretty much standardized at 3.5 piculs a year, so the county could, after taxes, feed a maximum of some 170–200,000 people on rice alone. Reasonably reliable population returns are few and scattered: 212,834 (1391); 583,759 (1851); 413,213 (1982).[6] Evidently there was not always a great surplus of rice, and T'ai-ho people in the Ming indeed ate other starchy things grown locally, like wheat, millet gruel, buckwheat cakes, and taro.[7] There are no data to show when, or how often, T'ai-ho was a net exporter of rice to other parts of China in Ming times.

Occasionally, local literati made sweeping comments about what might be styled the moral-political economy of their native county. Some time in the late fourteenth century, for instance, when the county was still suffering the effects of the late Yuan civil wars, Liu Sung (1321–81) remarked that despite its location on the great Kan River artery, T'ai-ho was an unattractive place. "The housing is crude, the fields idle or sterile, and the common people are poor and frugal," he stated. "There are no special products or food surpluses, and thus no way to amass commercial wealth. Officials and outsiders of high status consider us as beneath contempt; traveling merchants and envoys put up for the night here and then proceed immediately on." But the meagerness of the economy was, he asserted, compensated for by the sincerity, solid simplicity, and righteousness of the county's *shih* (Confucian literati), who judged people by moral standards, not by their wealth.[8]

By the early fifteenth century, some decades later, things had improved. Wang Chih asserted that the county was flourishing, that there were no more abandoned fields or idle people.[9] He described his county glowingly to a Peking colleague (who had just learned he had been appointed magistrate in T'ai-ho), boasting how the gentlemen observed decorum and obeyed the laws, how the students diligently applied themselves to preparing for examinations, and how "the ordinary people work in the fields, ship goods upriver to the Yangtze, trade in the local markets for a 10 percent profit wherewith to support their parents, wives, and children, and enjoy the pleasure of having 'gotten it for themselves.' " T'ai-ho was scenic and not as unruly as the administrative guidebooks said, and it was self-sufficient in ("produced its own") horses, oxen, sheep, swine, tea, bamboo shoots, fish, turtles, fruit, vegetables, and kudzu and ramie cloth.[10] The land easily supported the population, he remarked on a later occasion, and no one in T'ai-ho starved or froze except in a very bad year.[11] Ch'en Hsun once compared his native T'ai-ho to all the other counties of Ming China: its population and tax yield were half or less of those of the "rich and busy" counties of the realm, but it had ten times the people and tax yield of "thinly populated and poor counties"; so, he wrote, "you can say that it isn't a small place at all."[12]

But generalizations such as these are few, and the above statements (which I have not quoted in full) are mostly briefs on behalf of the local people's innate respect for law and fiscal obligations and their amenability to sound moral guidance. In order to proceed further with the topic of local resources and their exploitation, embedded as always in an ethical and social (or, later, administrative) matrix, it is necessary to descend to detail at ground level and look for descriptions of how different people in this and that part of the county managed their wealth. It turns out that there took place in sixteenth-century T'ai-ho something of a sea change in wealth managing, a phenomenon that coincides roughly in time with changes in aesthetic appreciation, as well as in demography, in modes of lineage formation, and in rates of bureaucratic recruitment, topics to be taken up in subsequent chapters.

WEALTH MANAGEMENT IN AN ERA
OF RECONSTRUCTION (CA. 1360–1460)

I would like to turn first to rural livelihood and introduce some of the local descriptions of family-based farming operations. Some of these operations appear to have been varied and complex. From a focal point of residence, some managerial families extended a wide span of control over several different types of landscape; and the mix of products from those landscapes was said to afford them self-sufficiency, perhaps even affluence.

The Kuo family of Kao-p'ing (High Flat Ward, township 61) are a case in point. Basic to their well-being was water control. Out of the Tiao-ch'i (Dock Creek) Hills and their scenic heights came a twisting, fast-flowing stream, splashing along a low diversion dike for about two-thirds of a mile until it poured into rock-edged T'ai-hsin (Great New) Reservoir, which also collected other streams and was several hundred *mou* in size. Edible bamboo grew nearby. "Their ponds and reservoirs are variously large and small, deep and shallow," wrote Liu Sung. "All of them are either rock-edged or bamboo-wattled to prevent leakage, so that the water level remains high even in drought years. They are also good for bream, tench, and other fish and [indecipherable] water birds, that hatch in spring and are plump by fall, when they are taken to the kitchen and prepared as food for guests." Next in the discussion come the Kuo fields. "Their fields wind about between two mountains, and so are narrow here and wide there. Some are high, and some low-lying. They are good for early and late rice, fragrant rice, glutinous millet, and wheat. From these they ferment beers and make cakes for the fall and winter sacrifices." From fields, the description jumps abruptly to the wild. "There are fine rabbit, fox, musk-deer, and wild [indecipherable] for hunting." Finally, the discussion turns to the settlement: "Where they live there are many field men and wood gatherers, but there are no merchants with their slick practices, nor do the customs feature fighting and aggression."[13] These descriptive fragments, jumbled as they are, do portray an achieved ideal of self-sufficiency, apparently free of any significant engagement with the market economy.[14]

Some years later, probably in the early 1420s, P'eng Ts'un-wen came to Peking on some business, perhaps a tax transport mission, and persuaded native son Wang Chih to write a description of the family estate in Ta-kuan Ward (township 25), about twenty miles southeast of the county seat, where the P'engs had been living some ten generations. As with the Kuo holdings in township 61, so here too water control was emphasized by Wang as essential to farm operations. P'eng Ts'un-wen was fortunate to have plenty of water. "Beside the creeks lie fine fields and fertile soil, suitable for glutinous and nonglutinous rice. Springs pour out [from the hills] on all sides, and those fields that lie at the same elevation [as the creeks] never lack for irrigation water. Where the fields are high relative to the creeks, temporary earthen dams are built to make the creeks flow laterally, so that the rest of the fields get enough water, after which [the dams] are cut. So there is no worry about drought, and all the fields produce regularly." The rest of Wang's essay underlines the delights of life on this estate, the rites to the soil god, the harvest celebration (in which the bondspeople participate alongside the family members), and the abundance of fruits and vegetables and livestock and fish.[15]

Water access, high-grade fields, and diversified production also created a base for self-sufficiency for some of the Liang people. Liang Lin (a contemporary of P'eng Ts'un-wen) managed a holding in Ch'ang-ch'i (Long Creek Ward, township 60), several miles west of the county seat. Streams from the hills fed White Rock Reservoir, and Long Creek was its effluent, which, before it emptied into the Kan River, irrigated "several thousand *mou* of fields." Liang Lin's fields lay along the upper part of Long Creek, where he supervised bondsmen (*t'ung-nu*) in the cultivation of soybeans, wheat, millet, and rice. In the creek grew cattail, wild rice, and other esculent waterweeds. He also raised horses, asses, oxen, goats, fish, turtles, geese, and ducks.[16]

The semitechnical term here used for Liang Lin's holding is *pieh-yeh*, literally "separate property," or "detached estate." In some current economic writing, the term is rather mechanically taken to mean an absentee estate, but it is clear in the T'ai-ho examples that it means only that the family's main base or original home lay somewhere else, no more.[17] (Liang Lin was a grandnephew of Liang Lan, so the family's main base would have been Moat Head Lane in the western suburb of T'ai-ho.) Similarly, some members of the Yen family of T'ai-ho city had a *pieh-yeh* a few miles to the northwest in Lung-men (Dragon Gate Ward, township 57). There were "rich fields, rich soil, and gardens with waterways meandering all about. All this yields enough in grain, hemp, mulberry, fish, fruits, and vegetables to make for self-sufficiency in food and clothing."[18] Neither of these was an absentee estate; both were founded and managed by heads of family branches.

Some of the above estates may have been compact in their layout, but certainly other holdings were scattered. Thus Liang Lan (1343–1410) built a detached house with five *mou* of garden plots in the Willow Creek neighborhood of T'ai-ho's western suburb, where he grew hemp and vegetables and hoed the weeds himself; but he also owned large grain fields elsewhere, worked by bondsmen, and from time to time he took a horsecart out to those fields to supervise.[19]

Liu Sung and Chou Shih-hsiu (1354–1402) were both landlords as well as scholar-officials with literary skills and pretensions, and their poems touch upon estate layout, wealth management, and rural class relations. Before becoming a Ming official in 1370 and after his retirement a few years later, Liu Sung was a minor landlord in Chu-lin Ward (township 38), near the south bank of the Kan. He lived in a flatland hamlet (ts'un) with no access to semiwild space and thus had to have a peasant or tenant deliver firewood to his gate. He reportedly owned and managed fifty mou of fields, a holding that was small by the standards of the time.[20] We know that Liu did grub about in his garden, but much of his land was out of his sight and immediate reach and was rented to rice-farming tenants.

Two mou of these fields, which he said he could not work himself, he "registered" (i.e., rented?) to a certain "farm father" (nung-fu) in return for a "pint or peck" of grain payment. This fellow cheated him in good years. One year a bad drought struck; because Liu's granary was empty, he could not meet his tax payment, and so reluctantly he pressed the obstreperous tenant. Yet, he told himself, he should not hate the poor fellow; the tax collector was a better target for his anger.[21]

Early one morning, Liu visited another peasant. The fellow swept out his yard, offered rice soup, and called out his sons to bow to the guest. It was a bad year, and the vegetables looked poorly; yet this family still managed a fine decorum that put Liu's mind at ease. Why, wondered Liu, did the "noble" despise such people and maintain a stern and distant attitude toward them, such as policemen had for thieves and bandits?[22]

In the spring of some better year, Liu slept over at a tenant's house. He awoke early, when the fellow opened the door to go out and feed his cow. Through the open door, rice came into view, and Liu had a glimpse of "a field full of green sprouts, waving in white water." Then early one morning of a sixth month, Liu set out from his own home and proceeded some distance over the broad fields to the foot of some hills, where he spent the day watching and helping with the rice harvest. The peasants (presumably tenants) reaped the paddy and brought the sheaves to their yard. It was a good harvest; and rice-beer was brought out in happy celebration, and plans were made to make a report at the soil god's altar the next day.[23]

Later a tenant came to visit, bearing a pot of the rice-beer he had just brewed from *no*, the so-called glutinous rice harvested in the fall. Disarmed by this courtesy and mindful of the "twenty years of civil war" just past, during which field agriculture had ceased and people had been glad enough just to eat chaff, Liu found he did not have the heart to ask about "pints and pecks," i.e., his rent payment.[24]

Liu stated that these rice-farming tenants had suffered grievously in the civil wars of the 1350s and 1360s; he had seen starving mothers throw infants they could not feed into the river, and much else. It was odd for him, therefore, to hear now at rice-transplanting time the newest generation of young peasants singing as though there had been no war at all: "North and south of the hamlet, there is plenty of spring rain; as the cuckoo with his thousand notes ignores the work of men, so too the youngsters, ignorant of the bitterness of war, sing songs redolent of peaceful times as they push in the rice seedlings."[25]

Liu Sung never described his own home. Chou Shih-hsiu did. Chou's home was in Chü-kang (Hill of the Provincial Graduate, in township 55). It was a new construction, set up in what had been a remote and desolate place. His wife, Hu Shu-hsien (1358–1439), directed the building of the home and the purchase of nearby fields. She supervised the labor and budgeted the annual yield "to provide food, clothing, sacrificial supplies, and requirements for guests."[26] Chou penned an elaborate description of the home base, with its studio, pool, bridge, ancestral temple, and pavilion for viewing the "rippling green" of all the surrounding scenery. These facilities were dispersed among creeks, springs, and hummocks, taking advantage of a natural topography that apparently needed little alteration, thus preserving an uncrowded and distinctly rural ambience.[27]

What must have been some of the distant tenant hamlets attached to this estate were described by Chou in several poems. Chou's poems deliver an idyllic picture; yet Chou, like Liu Sung, placed peasant society at a social as well as spatial distance from himself. Both literati regarded peasantry as almost a separate social type.

"The field families," wrote Liu, "live in a nook by the mountains; they've built thatched huts there, two by two. Chickens and piglets wander about, but the hemp and mulberry prevent their escape. The people there talk and laugh with an even temper, they work and rest with utter reason. Surely they reflect the trueness of Heaven itself, and that's why they claim no personal ownership of things."[28]

"Humble doorways loom by the dark path," wrote Chou,

and a crooked lane goes down to the inlet. Here ten families, two or three surnames, have been living side by side for generations. The smoke from their fires intermingles wherever you look; so too, in their routines, the people cooperate. One man's son heads the house on the west, while another's daughter is his neighbor's wife. A cold fall wind blows at the soil god's shrine, while piglets and rice-beer are sacrificed to the Ancestor of the Fields, to whom the old shaman burns paper money, while boys pound on a bronze drum. Mist drapes the sugarcane garden in silence, and drizzling rain falls on the taro field as the people come home after the rites, spread mats, and chat, half drunk.[29]

In another hamlet of "three or four families by a bamboo grove," there were "bed after bed of long peppers [*Piper longum,* for market?] and trees all yellow with loquats." Uneducated, yet decorous in their behavior, the inhabitants "for untold generations have lived their entire lives here."[30]

There is no ready explanation why the peasants and their homes and hamlets and their social behavior, described so vividly by Liu Sung and Chou Shih-hsiu, were never again described by the T'ai-ho literati. By the sixteenth century, however, the literati were beginning to lose interest in the natural world and the humanized landscape; perhaps the peasantry was an early victim of this changing outlook.

·   ·   ·

It is clear that Liu Sung and probably also Chou Shih-hsiu were but minor landlords. Far above them stood a class of very rich men and their families. Their great wealth was derived from their control over critical aspects of rice production (water, land, labor, storage, etc.).

That a small minority of big growers predominated here (as most elsewhere in south China) is obvious first of all in the very fiscal geography of the county. T'ai-ho's seventy townships (sixty-nine of them rural) each embraced from one to twelve wards. Each ward was understood by imperial government to comprise 110 taxpaying households (*hu*) — that is, fiscal families or family-like units that owned, or (to use a more appropriate, looser word) controlled, rice fields and grew, or rather managed the production of, rice. Early in the Ming, the heads of the ten wealthiest households in each ward were singled out to form a special pool among whose members rotated annually the duty of supervising rice-tax collections as *li-chang,* or "ward leaders." And above the ward leaders presided an even richer set of private citizens, the *liang-chang,* or "tax captains," who in the early Ming were collectively the linchpin of the county tax-gathering apparatus. It was their job to gather the rice tax collected by the ward leaders, to store it, and eventually to direct its shipment to whatever depot the government specified.

Little is known of any of T'ai-ho's ward leaders. More is known of its tax captains. Yang Shih-ch'i gave details of the tax captaincy system as it operated in T'ai-ho in the early Ming:

> For the managing of taxes, the central government has set up tax districts [*ch'ü*], with a regular [tax captain] and two assistants in charge of each. Rich producers have been selected to fill these positions. For some twenty years, the captaincies changed every year, until in 1424, the Ministry of Revenue restored the older system of permanent captaincies, with the richest producers in charge. This was because [many of the small taxpayers] were taking advantage of the yearly changes to escape making their payments. But the result now is that the captains, taking advantage of their permanency, have willfully harmed the lesser people and have made them suffer.
>
> Our T'ai-ho has twelve tax districts and thirty-six regular and assistant tax captains; and among them, scarcely one in ten does not harm the people.[31]

Yang Shih-ch'i wrote this in an epitaph for Hsiao Ying (1379–1428), who had been one of the exceptions, a well-liked tax captain. Hsiao Ying had been a leading member of a common-descent group that utterly dominated T'ao-yuan (Peach Spring Ward), which was the only ward in township 12. The Peach Spring Hsiao are a prime example of what the literati of early Ming T'ai-ho meant when they said that great wealth derived principally from rice production. Their remarks about these Hsiao afford as good a look as can be had into the disposition and management of such an enterprise.

The founder was one Hsiao Po-yuan, originally from further north in Kiangsi, who was appointed vice magistrate of T'ai-ho in 1126. On leaving office, he decided to make his home in scenic Peach Spring Ward. Nothing is known about how he and his descendants managed to acquire so much land, but the civil wars of the mid–fourteenth century may have provided some opportunities. The brothers Hsiao Ssu-ho and Ssu-hsien led a militia and defended township 12 so well that not once was the place molested. Teachers and writers from elsewhere in T'ai-ho, fleeing war, found refuge in Peach Spring, and they left behind poems of appreciation that Yang Shih-ch'i later commented on in great detail.

The early Ming government appointed Hsiao Ssu-hsien a tax captain. His sons and nephews and their descendants continued to perform in that office, either in annual rotation or on a permanent basis, until the system withered away, at some point now unknown, in the course of the sixteenth century.

Early in the Ming, the Hsiao maintained a primary school, called the Nan-hsun Academy, exclusively for the tutoring of their children. Several of T'ai-ho's promising junior literati taught there for short periods. Yang Shih-ch'i was one; he was a tutor from 1399 to 1400. He thoroughly enjoyed his stint. He later recalled his employer, Hsiao Lien (1340–1419), as well read, and a quipster as well: "at big gatherings of guests, whenever heated arguments arose, he would interrupt with a few words that convincingly settled the issue. But sometimes he would interrupt with a few words in jest: then everyone would fall over laughing, while Hsiao would just keep sitting there with a straight face." His son Hsiao Ying (who was a tax captain) used to put on a short coat and sun hat and take books, basket, and spade out to the rice fields; and when he got tired of weeding, he would sit on a balk and chant and sing until darkness fell. He named the house where he lived Plow and Study. He enjoyed consorting with literati, and he prided himself on his ability to make poems. "That was the sort of fellow he was," wrote Yang Shih-ch'i.

The Peach Spring Hsiao were at times managed as one big joint family, sharing a common kitchen and budget. Their seasonal ceremonies were impressive to onlookers. And Yang Shih-ch'i remembered sitting in the guest seat in their main hall while his employer, Hsiao Lien, sat in the east seat, and a hundred or more juniors lined up in two files, all well dressed and well behaved.[32]

Indeed, the Hsiao common-descent group was undergoing a population explosion early in the Ming. Ch'en Hsun noted, in a detailed preface to their genealogy, an expansion of one segment, counting males only, from one to ten to thirty-one (the generation of Hsiao Ssu-ho and Ssu-hsien) to "nearly fifty" in Hsiao Lien's generation. Ch'en also described the Hsiao holdings in rice fields, but he placed his description in what was for him its appropriate sociomoral context:

> There are quite a few common-descent groups of the Hsiao surname in T'ai-ho. It is only the Peach Spring Hsiao that are famous all over the county's six cantons for being able simultaneously to study the classics, to produce admired leaders, and to sustain ritual observances, as well as possess great wealth in gardens and fields. There are assuredly others with great wealth in gardens and fields, but they don't observe the rituals. There are many whose members study the classics, but they are not so rich. Some excel

in some areas and not in others; some in three of them, but not in the fourth. Only the Peach Spring Hsiao excel in all four . . .

These Hsiao live in houses packed right next to each other, a hundred this way and a thousand that, with the junior and senior branches all neighbors to each other. Recitations from the schoolroom can be heard from dawn to dark, with the senior males teaching, and the juniors learning . . .

South of the Kan River, half the landscape is taken up by mountains and rivers. Only 30 or 40 percent of the land is arable. Common people who can buy as much as several tens of *ch'ing* [several thousand *mou*] of gardens and fields are doing very well indeed . . . There are usually one or two individuals among these Hsiao who have several tens of *ch'ing* of land, enough to put them in the top rank [of landowners] in our county. That is why these Hsiao [as a group] are ranked first in our county.

To some extent, rich Hsiao may have exploited poor ones. Some of the Hsiao fields were worked by bondspeople, who may or may not have been kin. Thus one finds Tax Captain Hsiao Tzu (1375–1432) assigning bondspeople their jobs at plowing and weeding.[33]

One can find a dozen or more other men, from a dozen other common-descent groups of T'ai-ho, who served as tax captains in the early Ming years. For example, there were the unrelated Hsiao of South Creek Ward (township 59), where Hsiao Pao (1400–60) and his brothers for thirty years took turns serving as tax captains, so effectively that they incurred neither the hatred of the locals nor reproof from government.[34] There was K'ang Wei-chin (1393–1460, of Hsiu-ch'i, on the west side of T'ai-ho city), whose duty as tax captain was onerous because there he had to collect from a large number of small taxpayers; but he got the local officials to petition the court to allow him to "consolidate" the payments in some way, thus easing the burdens for everyone.[35] Tax Captain Lo Chi (1387–1459), from Hsia-ching (Summer Path), somewhere in Yun-t'ing Canton, dug into his own pockets to pay the taxes of people who were having difficulties.[36] (Whether Lo Chi secured rights over their rice fields in return is not stated.)

Some of T'ai-ho's big rice growers who were appointed tax captains suffered grievously for failed performance. One of the Chang men of Sha-li Ward (township 66), late in making a delivery, was exiled to a military garrison and had his property confiscated as punishment.[37] Hsiao Yen-ming of Chang-ch'i (Camphor Creek Ward, township 41) had trouble making collections, and his family's holdings too were confiscated.[38] Wang T'ien-ti (1303–84, of Nan-fu Ward, township 61) was accused by neighbors of falsely reporting his holdings at the time fields were first surveyed for tax purposes in the 1370s, and his lands were confiscated; but like the Chang and Hsiao, he soon either got back his lands or acquired new ones. As an overseer of some sort, he was put in charge of forwarding that part of the county rice tax that had to be deposited in Chi-an Prefecture, which task he acquitted well for a number of years.[39]

It appears as though Tax Captain Hsiao Chi (1352–1422, of Wangshan Ward, township 17) nominally avoided confiscation by donating his rice fields together with the tenants on them (*tien*) as a gift to the Ming state. Why? These Hsiao (who were not related to any of the Hsiao mentioned above) had led a local defense militia in the 1350s and 1360s; and with the founding of the Ming, some of the family members not only were made tax captains but were made subject to permanent military service as well. Hsiao Chi and his two brothers thought the tax captaincy too heavy a burden. They agreed that they had no need of their huge income—that it was enough just to live in an era free of war—"so they offered all their ancestral fields to the government and gave up their shop in the market, so as to devote themselves to a life of rural leisure." Then one brother left to take a military post on the Chekiang coast, and the other for some unknown reason landed in prison. Hsiao Chi, the sole remaining brother, then worked hard to rebuild the old livelihood for the sake of his old mother and his many dependent kin. "He increased his animal herds, planted rice, and developed new fields on the north side of Mount Wang and also in Stone Inkslab Flat. He built a reservoir at Lung-t'an that was several tens of *chang* deep and irrigated several thousand *mou*. So as his fields expanded, his family prospered."[40] If that meant he had to serve again as tax captain, his epitaph does not so indicate.

·   ·   ·

If one were to hazard a general profile of the big rice growers of T'ai-ho County in the early Ming, one might point out a few prominent features. The growers belonged to large common-descent groups that dominated one or another rural ward. Specifically, they were members of exceptionally rich families within those larger kinship groups. It was not the entire kinship group that was rich. It appears that T'ai-ho's rice plutocracy was a hereditary, small-family affair—in the cases at least of the Peach Spring Hsiao and the unrelated South Creek Hsiao, where the tax captaincies passed from father to sons and then rotated among the sons.

But wealth managing did not just involve unpaid local tax-administration. It also involved making large "charitable" donations of unhusked

rice to special granaries to alleviate scarcities and making loans available
at low interest to prevent famine. Tax captains were among the donors
because by giving they could relieve themselves and their families of
the captaincies. The local gazetteers preserve what looks like a complete
listing of major rice donors, and the local literati wrote about some of
the donors in detail.

Public donations of rice began in earnest in the 1440s, in response
to Grand Secretary Yang Shih-ch'i's nationwide famine insurance plan.
Yang's plan may have been inspired in part by earlier voluntary action
undertaken by his former employers, the Peach Spring Hsiao. In 1434,
T'ai-ho had a bad drought, which was followed in 1435 by a rice shortage, and the fear was that yet another bad year might be disastrous. So
Hsiao Hsiang built a "charitable granary" (i-lin) in Peach Spring Ward
and filled it with three thousand piculs of (unhusked) rice for the benefit
of the "little people" (hsi-min). Rather than bribe the local clerks, Hsiao
managed the granary himself for a year, until 1437, when Yü Yao, assistant prefect of Chi-an and acting magistrate of T'ai-ho (and a protégé
and personal appointee of Yang's), ascertained that the granary then
held twelve hundred piculs, and took it under state management. In
1438, in reward for his efforts, Hsiao Hsiang was given official honors
as a "philanthropic commoner" (i-min), and his family was excused of
services.[41]

When Yang Shih-ch'i's plan for a national system of famine insurance granaries (yü-pei ts'ang) was promulgated in July 1440, ten more
T'ai-ho rice growers volunteered to build granaries and fill them with
unhusked rice. Each man put two thousand piculs (after milling, about
eight hundred) in a granary of his own making and agreed to let county
government supervise the disbursements. In return, the donor's family
was relieved of services, and the donor was officially designated a philanthropic commoner in a document issued by the court in Peking and
sealed by the emperor himself. Several T'ai-ho donors went to Peking to
thank the emperor in person, and in turn, they were given a banquet by
the Court of Imperial Entertainments.[42]

Droughts bad enough to occasion mention in the Veritable Records
of the court continued through the summer of 1442. From 1447 to
1450 came a series of ruinous floods, which were followed again by
droughts from 1452 to 1457. A prolonged subsistence crisis was the
result. Civil disorder threatened. The rebellions of Yeh Tsung-mao and
Teng Mao-ch'i, raging in Fukien and Chekiang Provinces to the east,
spilled over into Kiangsi. The Veritable Records noted in March 1449

that some men in T'ai-ho, imitating the Fukien bandits, were organizing gangs to conduct looting.[43] Ch'en Hsun noted in alarm how poor and shiftless people in the prefecture were beginning to raid the rice stores of the "big houses."[44]

It was time to intervene. Grand Secretary Ch'en Hsun arranged for the appointment of a prefect capable of suppressing the looters. He also pushed the appointment of Han Yung (1422–78) as governor (hsun-fu) of Kiangsi Province. Governor Han Yung came to Kiangsi and found the earlier rice reserves depleted; and, on his urging, the court authorized in 1452 more generous awards for smaller contributions: for twelve hundred piculs (unhusked) rice, each donor would be made an honorary official (i-kuan), with the right to wear the cap and belt of an office holder.[45] Eight T'ai-ho rice growers responded to that offer; the names of six of them are listed in a long national honor roll of donors copied into the Veritable Records. They also received service relief and imperial thank-you notes.[46]

In 1455, the rice granaries were empty again. Poor harvests had left borrowers unable to repay. It was hard to encourage new contributions. Han Yung therefore increased the rewards: higher official emblems, in return for larger donations. The response in T'ai-ho was good: seventeen donors each set aside two thousand piculs.[47]

Rice donations by big T'ai-ho growers continued until around the turn of the sixteenth century. Fifty donors are listed for the Ch'eng-hua era (1465–87), and twenty-eight for the Hung-chih period (1488–1505). However, these later donations are no longer listed by amount. The contributors got official caps and belts for buying rice rather than for providing stipulated quantities in kind, as earlier. This change must reflect a growing prevalence of silver in the south China economy. It coincides with the emerging occupation of moneylending and the increasing use of silver to finance such things as the building of lineage temples.

Altogether, 106 T'ai-ho contributors are listed by name. Most are identified by local address (township or ward), which makes it possible to identify them further as members of no less than sixty-four different common-descent groups spread geographically over almost all of the county's rice-producing territory. Eleven common-descent groups had members who made three or more contributions (the Peach Spring Hsiao made the most—nine). Twelve groups contributed twice, and forty-two once. If these reserves were never enough to reach everyone in T'ai-ho, they seem at least to have deterred price gouging and dispelled anxieties about food availability. Their wide geographical dispersion inside the county sufficed to dampen the social upheavals that had disturbed Kiangsi's neighbors to the east. In Peking, Grand Secretaries Yang Shih-ch'i and Ch'en Hsun (who were native sons of T'ai-ho) knew that food shortages created social chaos, and they devised plans and appointed officials to see that rice was made available. Still, it bears noting that the persistent subsistence crises that T'ai-ho underwent in the latter half of the fifteenth century coincide precisely in time with a significant decline in the growth rate of the upper class and with strong signs that increasing numbers of both upper and lower classes were beginning to emigrate from T'ai-ho altogether (see chapter 3).

•   •   •

It seems curious that the large quantities of rice indicated by the size of the donations of the fifteenth century could have been amassed by single individuals. (The contributions were never made in the name of common-descent groups acting collectively. They were always made in the name of rich individuals, who reaped the honors, and whose immediate families received the service exemptions; the individuals happened also to be members of larger common-descent groups.)

China's was a partible inheritance system, which in the light of the typically large families of T'ai-ho's upper class, should have quickly made the large-scale control (or ownership) of rice fields by any single person a rarity. Yet, evidently, that was not the case. The sources give certain hints as to why, within the families and common-descent groups of T'ai-ho, inequality in control of land occurred as often as it did.

First of all, a style of ruthless self-aggrandizement was at work in central Kiangsi, at least in the early Ming. Liu Ch'iu (1392–1443, of An-fu County) noted, with deep disgust, the existence of the young man of acquisitive instinct and managerial aptitude, who, even while his parents were still alive, created a personal fortune, never caring that his own living standards far exceeded theirs or that, while he prospered, the orphans of his brothers were fast descending into poverty and hunger. Some people admired such men: "As [the acquisitive man's] fortune grows and his lands expand," wrote Liu, "his power increases to the point that his neighbors are awed into according him admiration and respect."[48]

In T'ai-ho, by means fair or foul, Grand Secretary Yang Shih-ch'i's entrepreneurial son Yang Chi acquired some substantial tracts of land; but in 1443, locals accused him of murder and other crimes, and he was arrested and imprisoned. Yang Shih-ch'i, distraught, instructed his family to return all his son's acquisitions to their former owners and to divest themselves of all distant and low-yield fields. He insisted that the Yang estate be compact and small in size. "Confucian families like ours," he wrote, "should not be thinking about enrichment. The household should not have registered under it any more than 120 or 130 piculs [worth of] fields and thirty or forty piculs of [tax?] rice, which is just enough for a year's subsistence. Don't by any means acquire more, or you'll overburden your descendants. You as parents have to think ahead, so remember that if you have too many fields and too much rice [registered] to the household, your heirs will have an impossible time bearing the taxes and services." He repeated the point in another letter. "If you have too many fields you'll have a heavy burden of taxes and services, and you'll make your heirs go bankrupt trying to render them."[49]

An ethos of selfish acquisitiveness surely helps explain the rise of a rice plutocracy in T'ai-ho, but rather than complain about that ethos, the T'ai-ho literati preferred to talk about such acts of generosity and altruism as their own rich men engaged in. For example, Kuo Yen-hui (1386–1458) contributed property that he had acquired personally to the estate of his deceased father so that enlarged and equalized shares might then be inherited by himself and all his brothers.[50] That arrangement was presented as a praiseworthy act of personal unselfishness for the sake of family.

Second, the ideal of equal partition could not prevent free transfers or forcible seizures of property. For example, late in the fourteenth century, in Yung-chiang Ward (township 49), the brothers of Wang Ku-p'ing reportedly ganged together and took away his property. Wang Ku-p'ing did not protest; he had enough to live adequately and to educate his two sons, both of whom eventually became minor officials. "Working the fields is just an occupation for common people," Wang declared. "Working at education is for gentlemen."[51]

In Yen-chuang Ward (township 64), Chiang Hsuan (1350–1404) gained esteem when he overcame the reluctance of his two older brothers and persuaded them to take his share of their father's estate. Of course, the brothers had to bear the tax and service burdens. Chiang Hsuan kept just enough to live on, but he went on to build a large estate of his own and to endow ritual and charitable institutions for all the Chiang kin, rich and poor. Yang Shih-ch'i thought well of him for that and married one of his daughters to one of Chiang's ten grandsons.[52]

Civil war destruction created space for individual estate-building early in the Ming. A contemporary of Chiang Hsuan's was Lo An-tao (1346–1426). Because he was orphaned young, Lo's uncles seized his original inheritance in Tu-yuan Ward (township 57). Lo moved in with his father-in-law, in Hsiu-ch'i in T'ai-ho city, and went on to build a wholly new estate of his own in Hou-t'ang Ward (also in township 57). So big a landowner did he become that he was made a tax captain, reportedly a kind one who paid shortfalls out of his own pocket. (He also abetted T'ai-ho's early Ming population boom, with five sons, one daughter, fifteen grandsons, six granddaughters, thirty great-grandsons, and sixteen great-granddaughters.)[53]

Prominent on the official lists of large grain donors were the Lung of Kan-chu Ward (township 54). (Five of them purchased famine insurance rice in return for the caps and belts of official status in the period 1465–1505.) The Lung had been rich and prominent in T'ai-ho for centuries, but the estate in question was one that had passed through the hands of Lung Chü (1366–1424), a one-time *sheng-yuan* (county student) who left school to take care of his parents. Wang Chih, a friend and frequent visitor, noted that Lung Chü "supervised the labor of the bondsmen" in the "fine and irrigated fields" at Kan-chu.[54] The size of the estate is unknown, but the heirs cooperated to keep it intact. Lung Chü had five sons. The oldest and youngest were imperial officials, and they yielded their property shares. Of the remaining three brothers, Lung Shu-chao (1390–1445) doled charity and built a library and school; another, Lung Shu-hsuan (1393–1447), "managed the fields and gardens and supervised the farmwork and thus created a prosperous livelihood [for all]."[55]

The next generation of Lungs consisted of fourteen males or more. Five of them were officials or government teachers; three others won caps and belts as large grain donors. The custom of fraternal property-sharing continued. Lung Wen (1408–59), an official, let his older brother Lung Kuang, who stayed home to manage the fields, take all his inherited property.[56]

A good question is to what degree did the desire for education and elite social standing reduce competition among the Lung heirs for inheritance shares and so allow a large holding in rice fields to remain intact over several generations. At all events, these Lung were wealthy still at the time of Lung Tsung-wu (1542–1609), when they built and endowed a large lineage temple. (It may also be noted that the Peach

Spring Hsiao invested in education and also organized themselves into a lineage in the fifteenth and sixteenth centuries.) Official salaries, plus a certain Confucian disdain for crude acts of self-aggrandizement, may have softened property claims in a few cases, and so helped a few large holdings to persist beyond the point where the population growth of descendants would otherwise have reduced them to small bits.

But there is no reason to suppose that the Lung and Hsiao cases were typical. It was not just seizures and disclaimers but also the equal inheritance system itself that tended to work in favor of inequalities and thus in favor of a pattern of larger and smaller estates.

Liu Sung insisted that it was always essential to equalize inheritance shares to avoid strife among brothers. If one brother should die prematurely and without a male heir of his own, a nephew should be appointed to conduct the sacrifices in his memory, but that nephew should not inherit his dead uncle's property. That property must be divided among his surviving brothers. The nephew should be simply a ritual heir, without property claim.[57]

However, Kuo Pien (1470–1542, of North Gate, T'ai-ho city) did not follow this rule. When his younger brother died without heir, the question was how to apportion shares among the three nephews of Kuo Pien (sons of his two older brothers) and his own five sons. Kuo Pien appointed his own youngest son his younger brother's heir, but he did not think it right for that son to get the whole share (tantamount to Kuo Pien's getting half his own father's property). So, Kuo Pien cut that share into four parts, with his youngest son receiving one, and his nephews the other three.

This was given as an equitable arrangement, but the arithmetic of it shows a strong skewing in favor of the oldest brother's son (.3125 of Kuo Pien's father's estate), followed by the two sons of the second brother (each .1875), and last of all Kuo Pien's own five sons (each with .0625).[58]

Similarly, Liang Lan divided his estate evenly between his sons Liang Ch'ien (1366–1418) and Liang Hun (1370–1434). But Liang Ch'ien himself had four sons, and Liang Hun only one; so what was an equal partition for the first set of heirs was definitely not so for the second. (Liang Hun offered to redivide the estate to remedy that imbalance, but Liang Ch'ien modestly refused to agree to that.)[59]

For reasons seldom made clear, T'ai-ho parents sometimes knowingly divided their estate into unequal shares, in effect ignoring the equal-partition rule altogether. That practice, unquestionably, contributed to landowning inequalities. Favoritism of this kind seems often to have been practiced in families consisting of sets of stepchildren (brothers by different mothers).

For example, Ch'en Chu-i owned "less than a hundred *mou* of rice paddy" near the T'ai-ho city wall. He and his wife willed one-third to the older son, Ch'en Mo (ca. 1305–ca. 1389), and two-thirds to the younger, Ch'en Yung (1320–97). Ch'en Mo had three sons; Ch'en Yung had but two. The parents' motive is hard to fathom. It may be that Ch'en Chu-i's wife favored the younger son because he was hers. Ch'en Mo may have been her stepson. A Confucian tutor by trade, Ch'en Mo argued that because the estate was small, Ch'en Yung should get all of it; but his mother (or stepmother) refused to go as far as that, and Ch'en Mo was made to keep his third.[60]

When Wang Lin-chao of Nan-fu Ward partitioned his estate, he gave the greater share to his younger son by his then current wife and slighted his older son, Wang Yen-jui (1378–1445), whose own mother had died. Dutifully, Wang Yen-jui accepted the smaller share and even shouldered his father's tax and service liabilities; but perhaps some resentment can be seen in his pointed insistence that his own four sons and their heirs share equally in his own estate.[61]

Hsiao Chen (1432–1501, of Lung-p'o Ward, either in township 6 or in 32) found himself the unwilling beneficiary of an unequal partition. When his father died, his mother slighted his two older half-brothers and gave him "too many" fields. So when at length his mother died, Hsiao Chen destroyed the deed and returned to his half-brothers their fair share of the inheritance. Hsiao Chen achieved a *chin-shih* degree and ended his career as Nanking minister of works (civil service grade 2A); and instead of amassing personal property, he built a lineage temple and made an endowment, under the collective management of his kinsmen, of the rice fields that he had bought or inherited.[62] Lands placed under lineage temple control could not be privatized or sold. This was a sign of changing patterns of rice field control in T'ai-ho.

A contemporary of Hsiao Chen's was Teng Ting (d. 1504). Teng was the son of his father's second wife, but his father favored his sons by his first and left him but a few "distant and unproductive *mou*" as his share. More spurred than soured by that treatment, Teng won his *chin-shih* degree in 1484, rose to the grade 5A position of director in the Ministry of Justice in Nanking, and later devoted much money and effort to lineage organization and to an unavailing attempt to create a communal lineage economy (*ho tsu-jen kung-tsuan*).

The Ou-yang were a very large common-descent group of Shu-chiang Ward (township 61). In the early fifteenth century, they were a joint lineage of "several thousand fingers" (several hundred people) sharing a common budget. Later, one branch came under the leadership of Ou-yang Mien (1418–84), a full-time family manager, local leader, and benefactor (though never a major grain donor). He had five sons. Two or three survived him. The youngest survivor was Ou-yang Yung (1460–1539). In Ou-yang Mien's old age, "the older son managed the family, while [Ou-yang Yung] taught pupils and surrendered to [his older brother] all the several hundred *hu* he earned as tuition. When [Mien died and] the time came to divide the estate, the older brother got the best fields. [Ou-yang Yung] did not protest, and [in return for not protesting], whenever he found himself in need, [his brother] gave him relief."

Ou-yang Yung spent some years as a stipend student in Ch'ien-an County, on the frontier east of Peking, where kinsmen had been sent in military exile since early Ming; but after repeatedly failing examinations he gave up and returned to T'ai-ho, only to leave again and live the rest of his life in this or that official yamen with his famous son, Ou-yang Te.[63]

Thus the rice fields that Ou-yang Mien had controlled passed largely intact to one of his older sons, and Ou-yang Yung was, in effect, disinherited, though he retained at least a moral right to occasional relief from the yield of the land he had declined to lay claim to. The unnamed older brother's four sons seem to have inherited all shares in the estate. Neither of Ou-yang Yung's two sons, Ou-yang Te (1496–1554) or Ou-yang Yü, got anything. Nonetheless, Ou-yang Te intimately involved himself in the difficulties his cousins had with the management of their properties. From 1532 to 1537, when he was an official in Nanking, he sent home some twenty-five dated family letters, in which he counseled his cousins and their heirs in such matters as handling disputes, managing the bondsmen, and monitoring finances. In the first letter, he remarked that the income from field rents (*t'ien-tsu*) was enough to feed some thirty people altogether. Even though he corresponded with his family, later, when he came home on mourning leave, he boarded with his K'ang in-laws. He had no "home" of his own, and he scarcely visited his own kin.[64]

CHANGES IN THE SIXTEENTH CENTURY

Population regrowth in T'ai-ho in the century of peace following the founding of the Ming, accompanied by various indications that transactions in kind were being replaced by transactions in silver, lends an air of abstractness and grayness to the problems of local organization and management that the literati wrote about in the sixteenth century. Descriptions of the humanized landscape and personal character, common earlier, become rarer; personal authority and personal local relationships, though important, seem more limited or more diffused in their effect.

Take water control, for example. The early Ming literati loved to describe water, or talk about it in the context of the farming operations of some successful local magnate, often a grain donor or tax captain. But the writings of native son Ch'en Ch'ang-chi (ca. 1501–ca. 1570) look at local water control in the generalized context of imperial statecraft. Sometime during or after two successive drought years (1552–53), Ch'en prefaced a set of directives issued by the Kiangsi governor. In his preface, Ch'en remarked at length that most of Kiangsi's rice fields lay high above the rivers, so that farmers could seldom irrigate using river water directly. An elaborate infrastructure of dikes, channels, and reservoirs was, therefore, necessary to get water to high lying paddy. He noted that China's historical records, informative about irrigation elsewhere in the realm, were all but silent on Kiangsi, where, owing to the corrupt concealments of the landowners and the failure of local officials personally to investigate them, government records and gazetteers seriously undercounted irrigation works for tax purposes.

In Chi-an Prefecture, he pointed out, the paddies were very high, and they dried out very easily; but because the dikes and reservoirs were not recorded (and therefore not taxed), greedy estate builders eagerly acquired them in order to get rich. Sometimes the way to get even richer was not to release the water for irrigation at all but rather to impound it for powering mills and raising fish. Some water owners charged water-use fees to rice growers. Yet often, in the fifth and sixth lunar months, when rice sprouts reached a critical stage, the growers could only watch their crops shrivel and die because the landowners refused to release water. (It was thanks to the governor's orders that landowners were forced to release water in the severe drought of 1552–53.)

Ch'en also remarked favorably on efforts by the Chi-an prefect to register all irrigation works and to order water releases. Drought-wracked rice growers in T'ai-ho County were at last empowered to take water for their fields without fear of landowner retaliation.[65] In these instances, it is evident that Ch'en Ch'ang-chi's interest lay in devising effective procedures for state intervention in local water management, in the name of proportional equity as well as the local rice crop.

Take also the matter of handling famines, which Ch'en Ch'ang-chi also wrote about in detail. In the mid–sixteenth century, there was no more talk of large contributions in kind or in cash so as to ensure food supplies ahead of time. Instead, famines began striking the county with full severity, whereupon officials and local benefactors set up feeding stations and gave outright doles to the starving.

A case in point is a bad famine that dates to about the year 1545. Ch'en Ch'ang-chi wrote a long letter to the Kiangsi regional inspector about it:

> In the hills and valleys, all you see is red earth, where many of the people have died of starvation. In fields near the mountains and ravines, the yields have been very thin, and many of the people there have died of disease.
>
> In one of our townships, there lived little people of the Liu surname, only about two *li* [less than a mile] from my own house, where the husband and wife died of hunger, and their children not long after. I hadn't realized that. When I heard of it, I rushed over to help bury them, but their corpses were gone. And they lived so close by! If there can be casualties like that, and I didn't know about them, then I can guess there are many more casualties in places further away that I don't know about either.

The rest of Ch'en's long letter is a technical discussion of food relief. This time, unhusked grain to be distributed in T'ai-ho and elsewhere was going to come from provincial and other government sources. The hard part was actually putting food into the mouths of the truly needy. There were two matters to consider. One was dishonesty. Clerks, *li-chia* (ward service) personnel, and others in positions of access to relief grain were going to use various means to skim it. Some elite rural lineages would surely order their tenants (*tien-hu*) to pose as famine victims or would even send their own villainous juniors out to steal grain. The other difficulty was logistic. How did you get grain out into the vast rural areas, where most of the famine victims lived? Ch'en told T'ai-ho Magistrate Liao Hsuan that he should be able to reach 80–90 percent of the starving people by boat. The neediest were to get ten *tou* (one picul) unhusked grain each, the "middle poor" six *tou*, and the rest three or four (these amounts fed an adult male for two weeks to a month). People who lived beyond the reach of boats were to be given

.33 taels silver to buy their own grain (.33 taels was the approximate price for one picul of milled rice).[66]

The growing complexities of social and economic life in the sixteenth century prompted a range of responses in organization as well as in local statecraft. The formation of endowed lineage estates removed many of the best rice fields from the free market in land. Estates and individuals performed more and more of their transactions in silver rather than in kind. The tax captaincy system, based as it was on easily visible forms of personally owned wealth, faded out and was replaced by an organization of "county scribes" (*hsien-tsung*) and "ward scribes" (*li-shu*) and other appointees who were not necessarily owners of landed properties (some seem to have been agents acting on behalf of endowed lineages).

It is impossible to discuss wealth or resources in sixteenth-century T'ai-ho without mentioning silver, which was spreading long tentacles into the local rice-based economy.[67] Rice sales earned silver, or silver earned by other means was invested in rice fields, or both. Rather than rice being lent at interest, as earlier, silver was lent at interest, often far away from T'ai-ho County itself. T'ai-ho moneylenders occasionally found themselves "elected" by their relatives and neighbors to take part in land surveys and tax assessments.

All the signs indicate that these were new developments. Earlier on, commerce and agriculture had been more distinct. T'ai-ho merchants of the fourteenth century exported goods in kind, generally northward. Liu Sung, for example, wrote of men of the Yuan surname of Heng-kang (township 33) who were "big merchants traveling north and south with money and goods."[68] Members of the Wang people of Mei-kang (township 8), based in the nearby commercial town of Yung-ho in Lu-ling County, made regular trips to Shantung in north China to buy fish, salt, lacquer, and silk.[69] Lo T'ien-yü (1305–62, of Chiang-nan Ward, township 60) was inspired by the biographies of entrepreneurs he'd read about as a youth in Ssu-ma Ch'ien's *Shih chi,* and he resolved that he, too, would pursue a commercial career. "He became an expert speculator in wholesale goods . . . First he amassed agricultural products, then he shipped them downriver [toward the Yangtze] for sale."[70]

But Ming-era sources make scarcely any reference at all to bulk commerce of that sort. The lending of silver, much of it apparently small-scale, becomes suddenly noticeable in the sixteenth century. The lenders focused their business not northward but southward, sojourning for long periods in southern Kiangsi and in Kwangtung.

For instance, there was Hsiao Ch'ao-shang (1510–77) of Huang-kang (Phoenix Hill Ward, township 25), who tutored and lent silver in Kan-chou Prefecture, in southern Kiangsi, and earned enough to retrieve his large family back home from imminent impoverishment. Though "simple-minded and humble-looking" at first glance, Hsiao was put in charge of the community compact of Yun-t'ing Canton by the T'ai-ho magistrates in the 1560s and 1570s after he had returned home from sojourning.[71] Hu Hsi (1498–1580, of I-ho Ward, township 51), a former moneylender who had done business in Kwangtung, played a leading role in surveying local fields for tax purposes.[72] There are further examples of such moneylenders.

But what business was Cosunhoa in? Cosunhoa (or Cuotomhoa or Cotonhoa) was a T'ai-ho merchant sojourning in Nan-hsiung in northern Kwangtung who, around 1591, came to the Jesuit mission in Shao-chou to receive the faith from Matteo Ricci. Whatever his business was, he was a man of wealth, with forty people in his employ. He was baptized Giuseppe, and he put Ricci up in his home in 1592 and helped the mission by publishing Christian tracts. (Co or Cuo looks like a rendering of Kuo, but it is impossible to determine which of several T'ai-ho Kuo lineages Cosunhoa belonged to.)[73]

Reportedly the biggest entrepreneur of late Ming T'ai-ho was Wu Hsiang-shan of Heng-t'ang (a place about thirteen miles east of T'ai-ho city, probably in Jen-shan Canton). For his seventieth birthday celebration, an in-law wrote of him as follows:

> Chi-an Prefecture has thin soil and a dense population. Many of its people sojourn in other provinces, but most of them are small-time merchants who lack the intelligence and honesty necessary to get rich.
>
> Not so Wu Hsiang-shan of Hsia-ch'i [or Heng-t'ang] in T'ai-ho, who is a Chi Jan [a great merchant of the fifth century B.C.]. In his youth Wu was a student, but illness forced him to quit study, and he went to Kwangtung to collect debts for his father. The debtors were making annual interest payments but were still obligated for the principal, even after ten or more years. When Wu arrived he studied the debt contracts, and decided to collect only on the recent loans and cancel the old ones. He said: "Once the paid interest more or less matches the amount of the original loan, it is enough. It is too much to demand [full] repayment in such cases." The Kwangtung people were happy about that, and in a few years, Wu was earning more interest than ever, as people were coming from all over Kwangtung to borrow from him.
>
> [One day] Wu heard that prolonged rains had made the roads so slippery that rice peddlers from Shao-chou were wailing by the roadsides after falling and spilling their loads. He donated one hundred silver [taels] for food, so

that no one on the roads was ruined by the rains. The Kwangtung people then regarded Wu as they would a parent, and Wu's money loans spread everywhere in Kwangtung.

At home [in T'ai-ho], Wu dealt with his kinsmen and with the people of his canton in the same way, and earned the same gratitude. Wu would loan to everyone, and repeatedly, even when doing so exhausted his reserves. His idea was to lower the interest repayment rate and extend the life of the obligation. He made loans as though he were casting [seeds], and he took in the interest like one gathers a harvest. After a few decades, his family grew enormously rich.[74]

Wu Hsiang-shan's strategy for local dominance thus included education and moneylending. It also included marriage arrangements with scholar-official families of the region and local philanthropy (free burials, famine and winter relief, and the upkeep of bridges and a ferry).[75]

It is not known how, or whether, local government co-opted Wu Hsiang-shan into the sixteenth-century tax-collecting apparatus of county, township, and ward scribes. Generally, however, it was local elite strategy not to avoid but to preserve their fiscal registry as taxpaying households (*hu*) and to perform willingly and in person (not necessarily honestly and in person) those unpaid service roles that involved supervision and management.[76] The identity and nature of the local elites involved in tax supervision becomes clear in several sixteenth-century cases, some of them involving fraud.

An enormous shortfall in 1512 prompted the magistrate to encourage informers and to revise the registers to eliminate land ownership concealments. Native son Ou-yang To was on hand at the time, having just won his *chin-shih* degree, and he noted that such fraud could never have been perpetrated without the connivance of the county scribes.[77]

But surely neither Chang Ssu nor Kuo Lan participated in fraud. Chang Ssu (1465–1542, of Hou-tung Ward, township 5), a local benefactor and major purchaser of famine rice, was on duty as a "township scribe" (*tu-tsung*) in 1512. As such, his epitaph asserts, "he devoted his whole mind to the public good and rectified all cases of concealed ownership."[78] Kuo Lan (1468–1515) was from T'ai-ho city, where some members of his family were moneylenders and prominent purchasers of famine rice. His father-in-law purchased the post of vice magistrate in Chien-yang County in Fukien, and Kuo Lan, then a very young man, accompanied him there. Perhaps that is where he learned Taoist alchemy and the mathematics of areal measurement (*fang-t'ien ch'ü-hung chih shu*). Years later, in 1512, the magistrate appointed him a supervisor of county registers in T'ai-ho, in which task he showed both competence and honesty.[79]

In 1533, Magistrate Ch'en K'uei discovered a tax shortfall of nearly five thousand piculs, and so he consulted the ward scribes and checked their information against that in the county scribes' registers. Then he called in all the county scribes, showed them the discrepancies, gave them deadlines for revising their registers, and threatened penal sanctions if they failed to comply. They complied. Not trusting the county scribes any further, Magistrate Ch'en assigned the job of writing up the final revised master register to Kuo Yuan-ch'ang, a philanthropic commoner exempted from services and so not a member of the suspect upper-level tax-collecting corps.[80] It is interesting that while biographies or epitaphs of lower-level township and ward scribes and of local elites at the highest level are available, no county scribe seems to have been so honored.

Later lower-level servitors (local elites) include Wang Hsiao-yuan (1478–1545) of T'ai-ho's western suburb, where members of his family were moneylenders and traveling merchants. Wang served three times as city ward leader and was said to have been well regarded by the common people. A magistrate had him rectify tax registers. Wang exposed all the frauds. "All the frauds tried to bribe Wang, in hope of avoiding [exposure], but Wang haughtily refused them, and none was able to get away with it."[81] There was also Ou-yang Chieh (1493–1540) of Shu-chiang Ward. He was a family manager of sorts, not especially literate but "so very good at computation [suan-fa] that specialists deferred to his skill." He also arbitrated local disputes. He was twice made a scribe and put in charge of the ward registers.[82]

Also much involved in local tax matters was Yueh K'uei (1488–1568), once a promising sheng-yuan. After his ninth failed attempt at the provincial exams, he retired home to manage his family's rural estate in Ho-ch'i (Grain Creek Ward, township 65). The county magistrate appointed him "general overseer" of the people of the township and its wards (tu-li-jen tsung-ling) so that a field survey might be made. Yueh drew up a ten-point plan (no details given), of which the aim was to ensure equity and deter fraud. Even after he died, it is said that the local people used his plan in making their own tax assessments.[83] Chang Feng (1501–80+), who was Chang Ssu's son, retired from office in 1556 and lived at home in township 5, where he got the prefectural and censorial officials to accept his ten-point plan for use in making field surveys (again, no details given). Because he was a former official, his plan got wider endorsement and circulation than Yueh K'uei's did.[84]

In Lu-kang (Fortune Hill Ward, township 55), family manager and township scribe Hsiao Hsi (1502–1574) had charge of the field survey, and he was said to have acted justly, though he was not a man whom all his neighbors liked.[85] Wang Hsu-yü (d. 1578), a moneylender and former *sheng-yuan* from Wang-chia-yuan (Wang Family Garden Ward, township 31), was "elected" (*t'ui*) township scribe in response to the magistrate's request for nominations. Wang spent many days personally taking areal measurements of the fields, and the magistrate was well pleased with the quality of the register he turned in.[86]

Thus those drawn into the tax-collecting service apparatus of sixteenth-century T'ai-ho County included personally wealthy men (Chang Ssu, Kuo Yuan-ch'ang), educated men (Yueh K'uei), former officials (Chang Feng), moneylenders (Hu Hsi, Wang Hsu-yü), computational experts (Kuo Lan, Ou-yang Chieh), and others whose personal circumstances are not clear. All of them, however, can be traced to some well-established local lineage and address. And the state services those men performed were "elite" in their nature, because it can be demonstrated that there existed in T'ai-ho (and certainly elsewhere in China) a system of upper- and lower-level service categories which reflected socioeconomic class structure.

To show this split, it is first necessary to provide the essential units of account for collecting taxes and assigning services. These were, in descending order, the township (*tu*), the ward (*li*), the fiscal household (*hu*), and the serviceable male (*ting*).

Through the Ming, the townships numbered a constant seventy. The wards were variously reported as numbering 250 or 260. The number of households, however, fell by more than 25 percent—from 44,772 in 1391 to 32,713 in 1585. The number of serviceable males fell by more than 60 percent—from some 150,000 in 1391 to 49,921 in 1585. Meanwhile, actual population surely rose. What was going on here?

The decline in households must have been real. At least, indirect evidence points in that direction. Wang Shih-hsing (1547–98), an official and something of a cultural geographer, noted of Kiangsi Province generally:

> Kiangsi custom places great value on household status [*men-ti*]. The tax registers are based on the Yellow Registers of the early Ming, and the names of the township and ward chiefs are still the names of the ancestors as written in the old registers. The descendants perform the services without chang-

ing the names. A family may be poor and owe back taxes; yet as long as any serviceable males survive, they will do everything to remedy the situation, because they fear the humiliation and shame that will follow if some other family, even a newly rich one, is assigned the service of ward chief.[87]

If this pattern held true for T'ai-ho (and it may have, despite lack of direct testimony), then official registry as a fiscal household was a *social* honor for families to cling to as long as they could, not, as often with other assessments, a burden to escape or avoid. The decline in T'ai-ho's registered households would then have come about through real social processes of impoverishment and attrition. It is possible, too, that "the formal constituency [of the *hu*] remained frozen after the early Ming, though its real membership increased as population rose . . . [A] nuclear household in early Ming could grow to be an entire village segment by the end of the dynasty," as happened in parts of Kwangtung Province.[88]

It may, then, be hypothesized that a *hu* in T'ai-ho coincided with a localized lineage segment; indeed, that it *was* a lineage segment, in the fiscal domain.[89]

Further, it is known that T'ai-ho's lineage leaders used *ting* as units of account when levying contributions upon their members—e.g., the Willow Creek Ch'en in the 1540s.[90] These were, presumably, the same *ting* that the lineage leaders, when acting as household leaders, might assign state service responsibilities to.

That lineage leaders could impose, or excuse, state service responsibilities with some freedom of choice is shown in the case of the Yin of Hung-fu Ward (township 24), where Yin Chih (1427–1511) made such a decision about service responsibility. The case had to do with the widow of Yin Ch'ao-chi, a grandnephew of Yin Chih's and a former county clerk, who left one surviving son:

> The family of the widow [née Hsiao] lacked for serviceable males [*ting-nan*]. The bondsmen [*t'ung-p'u*] had all run away, the fields were weedy and unworked, and her neighbors thought she had become too poor to survive. [When she proved determined to carry on], Yin Chih directed that she was not to be burdened with household service responsibilities [*men-hu chü-i*]).[91]

Thus here it was a lineage leader and former official, Yin Chih, who determined whether or not widow Hsiao's young son, who was all she had for support, was or was not liable as a *ting* for local government services.

This bit of data is virtually all there is about the actual assigning of *ting* in T'ai-ho in Ming times. The statement makes sense if (1) the *ting* was not a real person in an actual census but an abstract unit of account in a township or ward quota and (2) it was lineage leaders generally that had the power to decide exactly who among their male memberships were personally liable for service in a given year, under the given *ting* quota.

The first assumption is supported by the extraordinary statement the T'ai-ho gazetteer of 1579 makes about "households and services" (*hu-i*):

> From [the period 1465–1505] to the present, the households never exceed forty thousand, and the *ting-k'ou* [serviceable males plus females subject to the salt tax] only amount to one hundred thousand or so. The present registers show no more than fifty thousand *ting*, which, even when measured against households and females, represent a decline from early Ming.
>
> The county has seventy townships, and in each township live the lineages [that comprise as many as] a thousand *ting*. At a general ratio of seven males for every three females, there must actually exist several hundred thousand *ting* altogether. But the custom is to prize landowning and to despise people of dependent status [*p'u*], so the numbers on the registers show few people of worth and many people of dependent status. Yet, even while taxes and services constantly increase, families of respected status study the classics generation after generation [and so win service exemptions], while those of dependent status refrain from protesting.
>
> This is so because each lineage has a lineage head, each household has a household head, each township has an old quota of service assignments [*ting-ch'ai*], and each [canton] has a compact and regulations for public security [*pao-chia*]. As long as local officials follow custom in managing all this, and make only such periodic adjustments in the registers as are consistent with equity, then the people will not be overburdened with fiscal demands and will be able to preserve their wealth, while the state will have the people in reality, even if not in name. This is how to find equity in inequity, to the benefit of both the public and private spheres. It is definitely unnecessary to count and register every single item.[92]

So there we have it. Officialdom openly acquiesced in what was conceded to be a serious undercount in the real population of serviceable males. This inequity was perpetrated at the expense of people of low status (presumably tenants and bondsmen), and the whole unfair arrangement was held in line through the authority of lineage and household leaders and the public security organs.

The T'ai-ho gazetteer notes that service exemptions (which were given to officials, *sheng-yuan*, and the like) did *not* include regular household services, that is, service as household, ward, or township leaders and scribes.[93]

The specific service assignments mentioned in the quotation above, for which the *ting* was the abstract unit of account, refer not to regular household services but to local variants of the standard four service categories of *li-chia, chün-yao* (equalized corvée), *i-chuan* (postal service), and *min-chuang* (militia service).[94] Those were lower-class services performed by menials. Upper-class services were essentially managerial in nature. Local epitaphs show that, indeed, those services were performed by noted lineage representatives. Those who performed those services had some control over those who performed menial services, probably by way of designating which men should, as *ting,* actually serve as militiamen, postal workers, guards, messengers, and the like. Whoever the men were who did the jobs demanded of the low-ranking "four service categories" (*ssu-ch'ai*), they never appear in the local epitaphs.

．　　．　　．

In compliance with a national trend, T'ai-ho County adopted the "Single Whip" tax-and-service system at some point in the Lung-ch'ing era (1567–72). The per-*ting* tax assessment was eliminated and replaced by an assessment on each picul of tax rice (in T'ai-ho, each picul of tax rice had .19094003 taels service silver added on).

Few local epitaphs are available for the late Ming, so the effect of the new system is difficult to gauge. There is some discussion for Kiangsi Province as a whole. Chang Huang (1527–1608) noted that making the land tax the sole assessment base drove down the value of land, forcing many people to give up landowning and seek other pursuits.[95] Small taxpayers, who might have been able to afford one year's personal service in every ten, found that they could not meet the new annual service payments. Large landowners managed, through influence, concealment, and bribery, to reduce their liabilities. In short, the reform did not reduce chronic inequities. Describing T'ai-ho in the 1590s, native son Kuo Tzu-chang (1543–1618) wrote that "the rich occupy extended stretches of land and pay no tax, while those so poor they don't own enough land to stick an awl into are burdened with excessive obligations."[96]

The ill effects of the Single Whip reform are probably part of the reason why, in 1598, some twenty years after its adoption, a meticulous resurvey of all agricultural land in T'ai-ho was at last conducted by the prefectural and county officials, with a view to ascertaining precisely who owned what. Native son Yang Yin-ch'iu (1547–1601), at the time surveillance commissioner (3A) of Kweichow Province, prevailed upon Tseng T'ung-heng, a respected scholar-official from Chi-shui County to the north, to compose an account describing the stern and exacting survey procedures that were used, with the happy result that "there are no more hidden *mou* in the countryside, or hidden taxes on the *mou*. No one can complain of unequal burdens. The T'ai-ho people say that this is the first time in a century that the fields have been measured correctly."[97]

.   .   .

In sum, it appears appropriate to conclude (1) that there existed in T'ai-ho throughout the Ming era a strong and distinct rural class system, an upper class of elite landowners and managers of material resources, and a lower class of dependents or menials; (2) that within the elite itself, there were ways to create and perpetuate inequalities in land ownership, despite the custom of partible inheritance; (3) that the rural tax-and-service system of early Ming was based upon those inequalities and could not have been instituted without them; (4) that from the sixteenth century, taxes and services came more and more under the control of managers of corporate lineage estates, rather than individual landowners; and (5) that the increasing availability of silver in T'ai-ho coincided with (it may or may not have been directly connected to) the development of corporate lineage estates, with their own permanent and inalienable endowments of (taxable) rice fields, safe from either sale or partition through private inheritance.

The origin of T'ai-ho's lineages, the story of how they emerged in the sixteenth century from a looser set of common-descent groups, is the subject of chapter 4. Material resources and the changing ways in which they were regarded and managed play important parts in the story of T'ai-ho's kinship organizations and their evolution. But so did demography and family formation, and I take up those latter topics next.

CHAPTER 3

The Demography of Family and Class

THE DATA

The written works of the T'ai-ho literati are full of short pieces that fall generally under the category of obituary or necrology—that is, commemorative accounts of the lives of dead friends, relatives, and neighbors and their wives. I have found about five hundred obituaries written on behalf of T'ai-ho people. They come in several genres, most of them related to the funerary cult. Most common was the *mu-chih ming,* a life account chiseled in stone and placed underground near the grave of the deceased. A bit less common was the *mu-piao,* a life account, also engraved on stone, that was exhibited in the open air so that people could read it. (Many people were honored with both forms of inscription.) There are also available a number of *hsing-chuang,* or "draft necrologies," usually very detailed, done by family members or other intimates and given to writers of tomb inscriptions to use as source material. There are several minor genres, like eulogies (*ai-tz'u*), appreciations (*tsan*), and biographical accounts (*chuan*). Many of these accounts state just how the necrology came to be written.[1] Copies of all these documents were kept by their authors and were later included in their collected literary works (*wen-chi*), which makes it possible to read them now. By this means, even a *mu-chih ming,* interred as stone, became quasi-public in its paper copy and thus available to interested readers.

Chinese necrologies are fairly rigid in their form, and as a rule they provide (1) a list of immediate ancestors; (2) a list of a man's wives and concubines or the name of a woman's husband; (3) a list of children and grandchildren, usually by name; and (4) date of death and an age reckoning in *sui,* although many accounts give birth and death dates to the exact day.[2]

All these sources constitute very interesting data with which to explore social questions—but how good are the data? They are surely useful, although there are errors and pitfalls to watch out for. Some errors and omissions can be corrected easily if, for example, two or more accounts exist for the same person or if several members of the same immediate family each have an account written for him or for her. A serious pitfall that can rarely be corrected for is the common habit of ascribing to the principal wife the children her husband sired by other women. Also, *sui*-ages are sometimes found to be wrong when compared against exact dates, when exact dates are given; but the *sui*-age is usually all there is, and one can do nothing but accept it.

There is also a problem with children, in that children who died in infancy or early childhood may not be listed in the epitaph of the mother or father. The word *shang,* meaning "to die in infancy," sometimes flags a given child in the necrology of its parent; and sometimes a child is noted merely as having "died early," a statement without exact meaning. Usually, however, children listed in their parents' epitaphs were only those who survived at least into early adulthood. Thus one cannot use the epitaphs, except in a few isolated cases, to get any idea about infant or child mortality. (For example, we happen to know that Liang Ch'ien [1366–1418] lost a son aged three and a little daughter who died at an age just short of two, because he wrote touching little epitaphs for them. Yet Liang Ch'ien's own epitaph, composed by Yang Shih-ch'i, omits them completely and lists only the four sons and two daughters who grew to adulthood.)[3]

A hundred or so T'ai-ho men are credited with having authored literary collections—four of them in the Sung, four in the Yuan, eighty-eight in the Ming, and eleven in the Ch'ing. I have been able to gain access only to nineteen, all of Ming date. Most of the rest are probably now lost. So I have constructed a T'ai-ho population out of what I could find in the writings of the T'ai-ho authors of the Ming, plus everything I could find in the way of obituaries written for T'ai-ho people by non-native authors.[4] The total comes to 508 men and women.

The appropriate first step is to arrange these 508 people in chronological order. The earliest known was born in 994, and the last known died in 1888; but most of the people lived in the Yuan after 1279 and

Ming (1368–1644). Table 1 places everyone in birth cohorts. Starting with the year 1250, when information starts to get plentiful, the people have been arranged in twenty-five-year groups based upon their year of birth.

Immediately evident from this breakdown is a strong clustering in the returns, with two peaks, a larger one for people born in the years 1350–74 and a smaller for people born a century later, 1450–74. These peaks reflect the active years of the more prolific T'ai-ho writers. I should like first to confine my discussion to those people born in the Yuan and Ming (1279–1644), next to profile a few features of the whole Yuan and Ming population, and last to give special attention to the fourteenth- and fifteenth-century maxima, because these coincide with known changes in bureaucratic recruitment rates and with stages in the development of formally organized lineage systems.

The obituaries give us natural families, not the complex households into which natural families were often enfolded or the fiscal households that appear in the tax-and-service registers. In the population in table 1, there are 353 men and 111 women whose obituaries give information about their children. The progeny of the men ranged in number from zero to thirteen, and that of the women from one to eight. The average father had 4.58 children, and the average mother, 3.93. The difference reflects, of course, the polygyny or remarriage of the fathers.

SEX RATIOS

The obituaries list sons and daughters. The ratio of sons to daughters is a topic crucial to explore because of its significance for population growth or decline and for social structure. What sort of ratio should one expect to find? Other things being equal, a random distribution of human births should approach 104:100, and since infant survival rates favor girls, an adult population should either favor females or show something close to parity.[5] The T'ai-ho ratios show nothing of the sort. Counting up all the children of T'ai-ho fathers born 1279–1644 gives 985 boys and 555 girls (177:100). For T'ai-ho mothers, the total is 281 boys and 155 girls (181:100).

These ratios are so lopsided as to appear insane. Was female infanticide responsible? Kiangsi in the Ming and later was notorious for its practice of female infanticide. In 1526, it came to the attention of the court in Peking that "many female babies in Kiangsi are not raised"

TABLE I
T'AI-HO BIRTH COHORTS

Year of Birth	N (Males)	N (Females)
(994–1249)[a]	8	7
1250–1274	9	1
1275–1299	12	2
1300–1324	22	6
1325–1349	39	17
1350–1374	93	19
1375–1399	75	11
1400–1424	12	8
1425–1449	16	3
1450–1474	36	15
1475–1499	32	9
1500–1524	21	15
1525–1549	11	3
(1550–1624)[a]	5	0
(later)[a]	1	0
Total	392	116

[a] Arranged in 25-year groups, except for dates in parentheses.

(*pu chü*), with the result that boys coming of age often failed to find mates and so resorted to litigation or to kidnapping widows. The court ordered the censorial authorities to "make strict the former prohibitions on infanticide."[6] A casual comment by an outsider, Chu Kuo-chen (1557–1632), began with the phrase "Kiangsi people are fond of drowning girls," and then went on to relate a gruesome anecdote about a commoner who drowned four girls and buried them, only to have to keep reburying them because their arms and legs kept protruding from the soil.[7] T'ai-ho writers were themselves extremely reticent about infanticide. The only mention of it I have found is in Ou-yang Te's epitaph for his in-law K'ang I-sung (1464–1524), which relates how K'ang's father urged him and his brothers to adhere to Chu Hsi's *Family Rituals* and not drown daughters, as a result of which seven daughters were saved.[8] Female infanticide was still enough of a general problem, however, that in 1575 the Chi-an prefect issued a prohibition against it.[9] It seems safe to conclude that female infanticide was practiced in T'ai-ho, but at what rates? How much of the lopsidedness of the local sex ratio can infanticide have been responsible for?

A number of estimates for sex ratios in pre-1949 south China populations practicing female infanticide are available. George W. Barclay gives 106:100 (106 males for every 100 females). Michael Marmé suggests 108.7:100. Edwin B. Moise offers 110.7:100.[10] If one were able to make an actual head count of adults in Ming T'ai-ho, the ratio would, in all likelihood, be more like 110:100 than 176:100.

If the 176:100 ratio does not reflect a countable reality in a straightforward way, it may well reflect a social reality of a different kind. If one counts, say, all the sons and daughters of the sixteen Ming emperors, one finds a total of one hundred sons and seventy-six daughters, for a ratio of 132:100, which is also badly lopsided.[11] Closer to home, the 1610 salt tax for T'ai-ho County was imposed upon a population of 49,921 males (ages 15–59, *jen-ting*) and 26,452 females (*fu-nü-k'ou*, presumably of the same age range)—a sex ratio of 189:100, which is remarkably close to what the T'ai-ho obituaries show. Whatever was going on, it seems to have infected the Ming imperial house and those in T'ai-ho capable of paying salt tax.

One possibility is, of course, a simple failure to report girls, which would explain the shortage of daughters. How can one tell if that is the case? One way to check is to compare sex ratios to family size to see whether small and large families report their daughters differently. In fact, there is a big difference. When the entire population is considered, the sex ratio in fathers' families with one to five children is 220:100 (535 boys, 244 girls), and in families with six to thirteen children the ratio is 145:100 (499 boys, 343 girls). Simple negligence in reporting should have shown a more even distribution across family sizes. The larger T'ai-ho families had boy-to-girl ratios that approached those of the families of the Ming emperors.

Another way to check is to isolate and compare all families, irrespective of size, that report either all boys and no girls, or all girls and no boys. If girls are merely being omitted by the composers of the obituaries, then this exercise should help detect it. The expectation is that the number of zero-boy families should, other things being equal, be comparable to the number of zero-girl families. However, the data in table 2 clearly indicate that there are far fewer zero-boy families than zero-girl families: nearly thirteen times as many families report no daughters as report no sons.

Surely, some of this lopsidedness must be attributed to the simple neglect of the writers to list in the daughters (some epitaphs state that a man had no sons, but no epitaph ever states that he had no daughters). However, some of it must indicate that there were families that actually

TABLE 2

SINGLE SEX FAMILIES

	N Zero-Girl Families	N Zero-Boy Families
1 child	24	3
2 children	25	3
3 children	13	1
4 children	11	0
5 children	11	0
6 children	3	0
7 children	3	0
Total	90	7

had no daughters, or none they wished to report. One is tempted to throw out all these single-sex cases as flawed evidence, but the sex ratio derived from the gabelle leads one to suspect that many, if not all of them, must in some sense be genuine. The seven families without sons are probably reported correctly; in all but one case, the father in question adopted a male kinsman as his heir. I see no compelling reason to subtract all children from single-sex families from the grand total in table 1, so perhaps the evidence is best left just as it is, on the grounds that much of it may indeed represent something real, if not strictly demographic.

Unquestionably, there is a major problem of unaccounted for daughters here, but the practice of infanticide can explain only about 10 percent of it. If we accept the proposal that an actual Yuan-Ming head count, reflecting female infanticide, would show a real male:female sex ratio of 110:100, then to match 985 boys we need to find some 886 girls. But only 555 girls are reported. That leaves 331 missing daughters. Some, but not all, must have been omitted inadvertently. What can have happened to the rest? Plain-language evidence may offer some guidance.

WIVES, CONCUBINES, AND MAIDS IN T'AI-HO

There are available 114 epitaphs written for T'ai-ho women. All were written for principal wives, usually the husband's first wife. (Law and custom permitted only one wife at a time. A man could marry a second wife only if the first died or was divorced. Concubines and maids ranked below wives and could be acquired at any time.)

The evidence from the epitaphs indicates that, while wives were expected to bear sons, it was even more important that they possess managerial and interpersonal skills and altruism and that they put these characteristics to use within the circle of the family.

It was hard going for a wife without sons, but such a wife could keep her status if, like Ch'en Tou (1369–1409), who lost her only son in infancy, her cooking and tailoring and service to her husband's parents were superior and if she helped buy a concubine for her husband so that his line might continue.[12] Two of Ch'en Tou's brothers were imperial officials. Her common-descent group, the Willow Creek Ch'en, later prided itself on the excellence of its daughters. "Our family," boasted Ch'en Ch'ang-chi in the sixteenth century, "has produced many notable girls, who have married the great talents in the best families, and have had outstanding men as sons."[13]

A good wife did some or all of the following things: gave her sons their first lessons in the Four Books; gave aid and counsel to her husband and sons; managed the family budget, including debts and loans; extended the fields and gardens and fixed and enlarged the housing; managed the household bondservants with efficiency; conciliated her sisters-in-law; managed banquets and funerals; arranged nursing for motherless infants; arranged marriages; supervised property division among heirs; and, if her husband died young, protected the property rights of her sons by resisting pressures to remarry.

Just what the better class of T'ai-ho men expected of their principal wives was spelled out by Wang Chih (1379–1462). Wang Chih edited a continuation (now lost) of a well-regarded reader for women, for which he wrote the following interesting preface:

> The rise and fall of families is intimately connected to the presence or absence of virtue in the women [the men marry]. That is why we must have concern for how women are taught.
>
> Chu Hsi [1130–1200] established the method for elementary texts when he collected examples of good words and fine actions of the great men of the past. In the Yuan era, Hsu Hsien-ch'en [Hsi-tsai] selected out of the classics and histories good examples for women, and he edited these into a text called the *Book of Female Teachings*. That text gives a good picture of how to be a proper daughter, wife, and mother. Wu Ch'eng [1249–1331] said that it deserved to rank with the elementary texts [edited by Chu Hsi] and should circulate right along with them.
>
> So Hsu did a good job, but I have been impressed by the *Book of Changes,*

where it says that superior men develop virtue by widening their knowledge of the words and deeds of the past. Superior men, as we know, are people who put prime value on such knowledge, but they have the advantage of teachers and classmates and intellectual exchange. Obviously, you can't develop virtue if you're isolated and knowledge-poor. Yet the women's quarters are isolated; what is said inside doesn't leak outside, and what is said outside doesn't get inside. Unless there is a text available, it is hard for women to broaden their horizons and increase their knowledge so that they can establish their virtue and refine their actions.

In moments when I have been free of official duties, I have copied extracts and brought together new material not to be found in Chu Hsi or Hsu Hsi-tsai. Of this I've made a book.

Scoffing at my effort, a friend said: "Women are supposed to be soft and yielding, not hard and assertive. It is a bad woman who makes a slave of her husband, defies her in-laws, and fights her neighbors. She will bring on disaster for sure. You can't let her live with you. Yet here you take the hexagram *k'un* [female] from the *Book of Changes* and you gloss it to mean 'hard and square.' Surely that's going too far."

"*K'un* is the opposite of *ch'ien* [male]," I replied. "It is the mother of all things. What is female virtue to model itself on if not the hexagram *k'un*? Softness and yielding are correct as the 'substance,' but hardness and squareness define how that substance materializes as 'function.' Herein lies the key to handling things both in normal times and in times of crisis. With hardness, [women] can hold firm in the face of threat. With squareness, they can fix their determination and never waver. This is the fulfillment of the 'substance' of softness and yielding, because those words really mean that [women's] minds should be free of violence, that they should not inflict their anger on others, that they should be courteous and forbearing, and never vicious or abusive. Women must have the virtue of hardness and squareness, because when they are weak and swayable, others can control them. The ruin of men and the fall of families results when [women] go along with [bad schemes], or do nothing.

"You have the wrong idea of hardness in mind. The hardness I have in mind is a good hardness. Wise people know how to choose good and avoid evil; everyone is endowed with [the rudiments of] hardness and softness and resistance and compliance because everyone has received the same matter-energy of Heaven and Earth. So when I teach women these things, I'm just guiding them in the light of what they possess already. How can you say I'm going too far?"

My friend couldn't argue with that, so I have restated my point here, to serve as a preface to the book.[14]

Wang Chih's text-writing project provides an important clue to the problem of the missing females. Whether Wang's educational effort was a success or not, it is clear that the role of principal wife was a demanding one. It was a challenging responsibility that not every daughter was prepared either by nature or by training to fulfill, no more than every son was equal to the demands of a career in bureaucracy. It is quite possible that many of the missing daughters were girls whom their parents or relatives, for one reason or another, were unable or unwilling to match to a suitable husband as his principal wife.

Indeed, when daughters *are* accounted for in the epitaphs, it was usual for the writers to give their husbands' name, or to say that they were promised to someone, or that they had married into "famous lineages," or that they were young and still at home. That obituaries seem to list married or marriageable daughters only and omit mention of any others is another clue.

Marrying off a daughter as a principal wife could prove difficult and expensive. For example, there was the case of Yang Tzu-p'ei (1391–1458), who had four sons and one (listed) daughter. A local man, though poor, had presented gifts with a view to marrying that daughter, and a marriage agreement had been made. Then later, for some reason, the suitor changed his mind and backed out. Outraged, Yang charged the fellow with breach of contract and took him before the magistrate. Yang won his case, but he ended up having to pay all the marriage costs himself.[15]

There was also the case of Madame Tseng (1341–1422), who had a similar problem with one of her four daughters—a suitor who could not afford the customary bridal gifts. She had to give the fellow a subvention so that the marriage could go through in proper style.[16] In another example, when Tseng Yü-hung (1521–88, no relation to Madame Tseng) was a rising star on the examination track, an unnamed powerful person tried to engage his daughter to Tseng; however, Tseng was already engaged, and it was remembered as an excellent mark in the dossier of his life that he indignantly refused to break the earlier engagement. Later, he himself undertook to find mates for the sons and daughters of a deceased brother, fearing that the job would be too hard for his father to handle.[17] In fact, a major family responsibility, often mentioned in the accounts, was finding marriage partners for orphaned relatives, male and female alike.

Although the above evidence could be extended by further examples, the point can simply be made here that a first-class marriage was not easily arranged, and the evidence shows how, generation after generation, pools of unmarried or unmarriageable women might have formed. But because no one wrote epitaphs for such women, or even discussed the issue in a general way, one has to imagine an invisible but by no means small class of luckless T'ai-ho females spared the awful fate of infanticide but unable to become first-class wives because of the poverty of their parents, the inability of their parents to find mates for them, the death of their parents, broken engagements, or their own unsuitability for the role. What can have become of such women?

Some must surely have been sold into bondage as maidservants or concubines. Again, no one wrote obituaries for such women. And while maids and concubines, as did all women, kept the surnames of their fathers, no T'ai-ho maid or concubine can be traced to any specific family, common-descent group, or lineage. A few stories concerning the concubines of T'ai-ho men can be found, however. Yang Shih-ch'i's wife Yen Hsiu died in 1425 at the age of forty-seven, and her epitaph, composed by Yang himself, ascribes all his children, four sons and four daughters, to her (a fifth daughter, who died in infancy, is ignored by Yang here). While Yang was on duty in Peking as grand secretary, Mme Yen spent most of her time looking after things in T'ai-ho, and rumor had it that the third son, Yang Tao (later vice minister of the Court of Imperial Sacrifices, d. 1483), was actually the son of Yang Shih-ch'i's housemaid, a woman surnamed Kuo. Gossip has it that housemaid Kuo was an abused and beaten-looking creature:

> When Yang Shih-ch'i was grand secretary, his wife had already died. He had but one maid to handle his sash and comb. One day the imperial palace women invited the wives of the high officials to come to court. When the empress heard that Yang had no regular wife, she ordered her servants to summon his maid. When she saw how lowly and ragged the maid was, she had her combed and rouged, dressed her in jewelry and robes, and sent her off, with the laughing remark: "Master Yang won't recognize her now!" The next day she had the authorities confer a title upon her, as per regulation [for the regular wife of a grand secretary].[18]

Grand Secretary Ch'en Hsun's (1385–1463) principal wife was Tseng Ching (1387–1431). She gave birth to two boys, who, unfortunately, died as infants. Ch'en was a Han-lin compiler in Nanking at the time. Madame Tseng returned to T'ai-ho, and a few months later, in the fall of 1422, Ch'en acquired a concubine surnamed Mo, who was not a native of T'ai-ho but a young woman left stranded in Nanking by the sudden death there of her brother, an assistant instructor. Ch'en soon fathered one son by concubine Mo (and, immediately thereafter, another by wife Tseng). Reportedly, concubine Mo and wife Tseng got along well together. When wife Tseng died in 1431, however, Ch'en Hsun did not promote concubine Mo to the status of principal wife.

Instead, he kept her as concubine and married as second wife a T'ai-ho woman, Kuo Miao-chih (1413–49, of Kuan-ch'ao, township 31). She produced only a daughter, who died before she could be married. Thus even having produced a first son did little for concubine Mo.[19] Ch'en Hsun never raised her to the rank of principal wife. In fact, aside from the empress's joke on Yang Shih-ch'i, there is not a single example of a concubine being promoted to wife in the available T'ai-ho data.

Ch'en Hsun is rumored to have had some strong feelings about wife-concubine relations. There is a vivid anecdote about that:

> Kao Wen-i [Kao Ku, later a grand secretary] had no sons, and so he took on a concubine. But his wife was jealous, and she got between them and wouldn't let him approach her.
>
> One day Academician Ch'en Hsun paid a visit, and while he and Kao were discussing this problem, Kao's wife, who was listening in behind a screen, suddenly burst forth, screaming and cursing. Feigning anger, Ch'en lifted the table and rose. He hit Kao's wife with a stick until she fell to the floor and couldn't get up, and he kept on hitting her, until finally Kao Ku interceded. Ch'en then admonished her: "You don't have a son, and you can be legally divorced. But Kao hasn't divorced you. He's set up a concubine. And you're cutting off his line of descent by getting between them. If you don't stop, I'll report this in a memorial to the court, where you'll be prosecuted without mercy!"
>
> After that, the wife's jealousy abated. Thanks to Ch'en's anger, there was eventually born Kao Huan, who later became a secretariat drafter.[20]

To come back to the problem at hand, it appears that T'ai-ho men of means and influence acquired maids and concubines, at least in some cases, in order to sire male heirs by them. In this connection, the suspicion arises that some proportion of the daughters unaccounted for in the parental obituaries—specifically those daughters who lived to become adults but never underwent formal marriage ceremonies, and so "disappeared" into the anonymity of the maid and concubine class—reappear in the obituaries of the men of the next generation, now listed among their consorts because they were the bearer of one or more of the men's children. (Some epitaphs make a clear distinction of rank between a man's wives and his concubines and carefully point out which women produced which of his children. Many epitaphs, however, simply list all the consorts without indicating rank and without assigning any of the children to any mother in particular, so that one is never certain whether a given extra consort is a second wife, a concubine, or an exconcubine promoted to wife.)

To conclude, then, social-class distinctions imposed upon each generation of T'ai-ho daughters must be considered an unquantifiable but major force, which acted in some powerful way to help produce T'ai-ho's terribly lopsided sex ratios. Of all the T'ai-ho women born into respectable station and spared infanticide, one may estimate that only some 60 percent ended up as principal wives, so managing to preserve their social station. Upwards of 30 percent could not stay in the station into which they were born and were pushed out, or socially downward, into concubinage or servitude.

THE PROBLEM OF UPPER-CLASS
POPULATION GROWTH

At this point, I should like to make the assumption that any man or woman in T'ai-ho whose relatives or descendants went to all the trouble and expense of securing a written obituary to be engraved on stone from one or another high ranking scholar-official must in some sense have been socially respectable and, as such, a member of what I propose to define as T'ai-ho's upper class. This group included rich and poor people, people whose lives were serene, people whose lives were filled with distress, people with good educations, and people with only minimal educations; but they all shared some recognized genealogical identity, and they are all described as having performed effectively at some time in their lives some sort of *management* role—if not as officials then at least as landowners, teachers, family managers, or as parents of successful children. Not one was a servant, a clerk, a maid, a bondsman, a craftsman, a small trader, a tenant farmer, a porter, a hired worker, or anything that smacked of the proletarian, the menial, or the servile.

The first thing to be noted of this upper class, so defined, in connection with the question of its population growth, is that the men often had more than one consort, because they remarried on the death of a principal wife or because they bought concubines or both. (The sex ratio of upper-class parents in the Yuan and Ming was 68:100.)

Was it the case that the more consorts an upper-class male acquired, the more children he had? Surprisingly, perhaps, this is not quite what a study of the issue shows. The results are interesting. For 336 fathers and 1,540 children born in the Yuan and Ming periods, the proposition that having more consorts leads to having more children holds true—to a point (see table 3). However, the T'ai-ho data also bear out Gary Becker's axiom that the more wives a man has, the fewer children each

TABLE 3
POLYGYNY AND FEMALE FERTILITY

	N (Fathers)	N (Children)	Average N children per consort	Completed family size	Marginal productivity per consort
1 consort	208	864	4.15	4.15	4.15
2 consorts	101	546	2.70	5.41	1.26
3 consorts	21	102	1.62	4.86	-0.55
4 consorts	6	28	1.17	4.67	-0.19
Total	336	1,540			
Average				4.58	

wife will produce.[21] But there is more. It may be a quirk caused by the limitations of the T'ai-ho data, but there is a remarkable illustration here of the mutual behavior of not one but three productivity curves. The *average* productivity curve steadily declines as more consorts are added. The *total* productivity curve rises until it reaches the second consort, where completed family size achieves its maximum, and then it too declines. The *marginal* productivity curve (which rates each new consort's contribution to the completed family) shows the maximum impact of the first, the lesser impact of a second, and the increasingly negative contributions of the third and a fourth (the first consort contributes 4.15 children, the second 1.26, the third takes away .55, and the fourth takes away a further .19).[22]

One might also ask whether, judging from the numbers and sex ratios of their children as supplied by their obituaries, T'ai-ho's upper class was capable of reproducing itself over time, and if so, at what rate? In other words, if everyone born in the Yuan and Ming (1279–1644) is considered and the absence of upper-class in-migration is assumed, did T'ai-ho's quality population expand in size? It is an important question.

To help answer it, I have modified the inputs to a simple equation used by Nathan Keyfitz to answer the related question of how one determines the annual rate of increase in a population with a given average family size.[23] The procedure is to find the mean age of women at childbirth and use that as the nth root of that proportion of the average family represented by females who grow up to bear children. The result gives an annual average growth rate. As was noted earlier, however, there is a shortage of obituaries for T'ai-ho women (there are three times as many epitaphs for men as there are for women), and the obituaries suffer from the common custom of ascribing all children to the principal wife, whether they were really hers or not. Therefore it is preferable to identify families from the men's epitaphs, not the women's, and to calculate the reproduction rates of the men rather than of the women. The rephrased question, then, is whether annual reproduction rates, taken from the men's point of view, led to an expanding, a shrinking, or a stable upper class in T'ai-ho.[24]

The great problem in the average father-centered T'ai-ho family was its large surplus of listed boys relative to listed girls (985 boys and 555 girls of the Yuan and Ming). Eighty-nine of the above boys are reported as having "died early." The exact meaning of this phrase is unclear from the sources, but let us assume arbitrarily that half (approximately 45) of them died before marriage, or before having children. That leaves 940 boys. Thirteen girls "died early." Making the same assumption for them leaves 548 girls.

The result is an excess of 392 boys, who could not have found quality mates in T'ai-ho (where almost all marriages were contracted) and must therefore have been unable to reproduce themselves, at least at the same social level into which they were born. (Elite genealogical identity and pride, and good family management, required upper-class wives; and, as stated earlier, there is no evidence that any concubine was ever promoted to the rank of wife.) Thus only 548 of the 940 boys can have married "good" wives, if they married at all. (Meanwhile, the proportion of the 548 girls who married "good" husbands and bore children must have been close to, if not exactly, 100 percent). For 336 fathers of the Yuan and Ming, the average family size was 4.58. Adapting Keyfitz's procedure, then, we should multiply 4.58 by .37 (the estimated proportion of all the children of the average family which consists of boys able to marry first-class wives). The result is 1.69.

The next step is to calculate a mean age of women at childbirth and use that as the nth root of 1.69. How old were T'ai-ho women at the time of the birth(s) of their children? The answer to that has to be painfully figured out by matching cases where epitaphs of mothers, fathers, and their children are available. I found fifty-five instances where a woman's age at childbirth was known; these ages range from 16 to 44, and the average age comes out to be 26.5. The 26.5th root of 1.69 is

1.0200, which means that, over the very long term (1279–1644), the elite, upper class of T'ai-ho people could have expanded at an annual rate of 2 percent, which is very high. It implies that the upper class was capable of doubling its size every seventy years at the least.

Given the patriarchal family order of T'ai-ho, it may be preferable to consider the growth rate from the men's point of view. The ages of 106 men are known as of the time one or more of their children were born. These ages range from 16 to 49, and the average is 30.9. That still gives 1.0171, meaning a growth rate of over 1.7 percent a year. (These rates are only somewhat less than recent *total* population growth rates in parts of the present-day developing world).[25]

While capable of such growth rates, T'ai-ho's upper class could not have exploded at a rate of nearly 2 percent a year for very long. It is absurd even to suppose that a county of limited size and resources like T'ai-ho could have supported such growth. One remedy was, indeed, emigration, a topic I should like to address in a moment. But the function of two other remedies—infanticide and downward social mobility—should now be quite apparent. Every generation, the socially pedigreed class of T'ai-ho people engaged in behavior that had the effect of reducing excessive numbers, so that it did not, in fact, grow at a rate approaching 2 percent a year, even though in theory it was capable of doing so. For purposes of social reproduction at the elite level, the average elite family size of 4.58 was an illusion.

What was the purge rate? In spite of the risk of giving a false impression of numerical exactitude, the issue invites numerical exploration. Let us go back to the population of 940 boys and 548 girls, defined as those who survived long enough to marry and bear children. The sex ratio of this population is 172:100, which, as explained earlier, cannot reflect demographic reality in the strict sense. If, given female infanticide, the "real" sex ratio was 110:100, then the "real" population must have consisted of 940 boys and 855 girls. However, only 548 girls are accounted for, so the remainder (307) of them must have disappeared into the maid or concubine class, where their contribution of children to their masters' families was minimal, as indicated earlier.

The effect of this was to create a sizable population of unmarriageable males. Of the 940 males, 392 cannot have found first-class brides.[26] As social detritus, these 392 males were joined by 307 luckless females, creating a total cast-off population of 699. If we divide that figure by the number of fathers, 336, the result is a "family" whose average number of children is 2.08.

It is, of course, a "ghost" family. It is the elite family that could have been but never was. It is impossible to say to what extent such ghost families were real at some lower social level. Some of the girls were re-absorbed into elite families as maids or concubines (however, only 33 of 289 extra consorts are specifically noted as having been concubines, and nothing at all definite is known of working maids). Some of the males must surely have joined the large army of Kiangsi sojourners and émigrés who plied their crafts and trades in many different parts of China in the Ming.[27] At all events, the sex ratio of this notional family is 128:100, much more favorable to females than the elite sex ratio.

The ghost family is an offscouring of the elite families. Its creation, generation after generation, is one major reason why the T'ai-ho upper class did not, in fact, expand at a 2 percent annual rate through the Yuan and Ming periods, a rate that in theory it was quite capable of achieving.

Because of the drag it exerted, the latent demographic power of the ghost family should somehow be subtracted from that of its elite parent. One possibility might be to subtract its potential growth rate. The total of cast-off (or émigré) children comes to 699; .78 of the boys "marry" all the girls (multiplying 2.08 by .78 gives 1.62); and, again using 30.9 as the nth root, the annual rate of increase comes to 1.0157. This "ghostly" rate, subtracted from the elite rate of 1.0171 obtained above, leaves a remainder of .0014, or .14 percent. Indeed, something that low may well have represented the real rate of increase of the pedigreed class of T'ai-ho over the very long run, that is, for the whole period 1279–1644.

THE DEMOGRAPHIC BEHAVIOR OF
THE T'AI-HO ELITE IN THE MING

To return once again to table 1, there are two periods a century apart where the obituaries bunch up. One is the quarter century 1350–1374. The other is the quarter century 1450–1474.

These two cohorts lived and reproduced in periods of Ming history that were different both in the constraints they imposed and in the op-portunities they provided. The first cohort helped rebuild and repopu-late T'ai-ho after its devastation in the civil wars of the 1350s and 1360s. A few of its children reached the very highest positions in Ming imperial government. Hundreds more availed themselves of unusually favorable opportunities to become officials and government teachers at

TABLE 4
REPRODUCTION RATES, EARLY AND MID-MING

	N (Fathers)	N (Consorts)	N (Sons)[a]	N (Daughters)[a]
1325–1399	179	255	571 (−55)	357 (−7)
1425–1499	82	125	234 (−15)	104 (−1)

[a] Numbers in parentheses are those who "died early."

every level. (As the next chapter will note, this cohort was also heavily involved in researching and compiling the genealogies that became the founding documents, so to speak, of T'ai-ho's pedigreed common-descent groups.)

The second cohort faced new challenges. The rate of bureaucratic recruitment declined by half. Opportunities for local estate-building, available earlier, shrank as well. This cohort's children contributed to the social anomie that people said infected T'ai-ho, as well as Kiangsi generally, in the Hung-chih period (1488–1505) and later. People emigrated in some number. They also spearheaded the founding of organized, property-holding lineages, which were an evolutionary step beyond the more loosely ordered common-descent groups of a century earlier. Did these cohorts share the same "demography," as outlined above? Or did demographic change accompany changing general conditions?

I would propose to enlarge both groups by adding birth cohorts on either side, thus creating seventy-five-year groups, 1325–1399 and 1425–1499 (see table 4). These correspond roughly to early Ming and mid-Ming. Men whose obituaries provide information about children number 179 for the first group, and 82 for the second. The numbers in parentheses in table 4 are those said to have "died early."

Subtracting half the "died early" cases as before and calculating in the same way as was done above for the whole Yuan and Ming population, we find that there were indeed measurable differences between these historically distinct cohorts. While the early Ming cohort, born in a time of opportunity, was nominally capable of expanding at a yearly rate of 2.2 percent, the later cohort, born in a time of reduced opportunity, had a nominal rate of growth of only .7 percent, a dramatic decline.

A comparison of the sex ratios of the children of the two cohorts

(154:100 for the early cohort and 219:100 for the second) shows that while both groups pruned excess children, the elite families of the fifteenth century acted in such a way as to push their children down the social ladder, or encourage them to emigrate, at a significantly higher rate.

In the early Ming, female reproduction rates were comparatively high; on average, each consort produced 3.51 accounted-for sons and daughters who lived to become adults. The fifteenth century witnessed a dramatic decline, as each consort produced only 2.63. Meanwhile the fathers acquired consorts at about the same rate in the fifteenth century as they had in the fourteenth (1.42 in the earlier period, 1.52 in the later).

· · ·

The above computations relating to elite family formation and its inevitable by-product, social downloading, help explain a number of instances of family behavior discussed in plain language in the obituaries. Whether elite society was expanding, as in the fourteenth century, or shrinking its size, as in the fifteenth, it still extruded, or was forced to extrude, great numbers of its children. The experience was not pleasant. In the fourteenth century, good people sometimes intervened to try to prevent its happening.

For example, there was Liu O (1295–1352), of the Chu-lin Liu of township 38. It was said that a malignant ghost was spreading disease. The parents of one of the Chu-lin Liu families died of the disease, leaving three orphans and unpaid taxes. The tax collectors decided that proceeds from the sale of the three orphans into bondage should be used to clear the account. Liu O went before the T'ai-ho magistrate and made a dramatic plea:

> Long ago, our ancestors held the highest positions at court. But now some descendants have fallen into difficulties. They have no food or shelter. They are destitute. They've become slaves to others. This distresses me no end.
> It is up to the magistrates to ensure that abuses are stopped, that social custom is restrained, and that compassion is extended. As we know, righteousness means suppressing abuse, decorum means restraining custom, and benevolence means extending compassion. All three are fundamental principles of imperial administration, and those who rule the people cannot ignore those principles. We common folk are no more than baby birds trying to fly without feathers when the magistrates don't give us protection!

Liu O then burst into tears, and the magistrate was moved to compassion. He remanded the three enslaved orphans to Liu O's care, and Liu O raised them and arranged marriages for them.[28]

Things did not turn out this well for Ch'en Meng-hsing of the Willow Creek Ch'en of T'ai-ho city. A one-time *sheng-yuan* (county student) expelled for a rules violation, Ch'en died a depressed and broken man in Nanking in 1390, when he was thirty-four. His only son, orphaned young, could not study. He became a small tradesman of some kind and eventually died without heir.[29] Such for him was the cost of downward social mobility.

Servitude was certainly a possible fate for the downwardly mobile. Escape from servitude is the theme of the celebrated story of P'eng Hsu (1381–1430) and his mother, Liu Ling (1365–1432). She was from neighboring Wan-an County, and her husband's family were Moon Pond P'engs of township 56 in T'ai-ho.

Pieced together from several sources, the story goes like this. Liu Ling's husband died in 1390. He had been a *li-chia* (tax community) chief for his part of T'ai-ho, and he died in serious arrears with his tax payments, for which his kinsmen became responsible. Accordingly, little P'eng Hsu's uncle, a man who "ran after the properties of widows and orphans," seized the child's inherited property and, at least for a time, placed him in bondage as a household slave (*p'u-li*). At length Liu Ling fled with her little son to her father's house, and there she personally supervised the child's primary education. Later she sent him to live with his paternal cousin and her husband, Hsiao Yung-tao (1359–1412), a minor official and an expert in the *Book of Documents*. P'eng Hsu went on to have a minor career of his own. He entered government through the recommendation channel and ended up as an archivist (9B) in the northern imperial college. P'eng Hsu's gratitude to his mother knew no bounds. Eventually, he moved her back to the P'eng settlement in T'ai-ho and saw to it that she was honored and well cared for in her old age.

It is interesting to see in this example that, while some family-centered institutions and values speeded downward mobility, a countervailing set of institutions and values were sometimes activated to create a rescue net. Here, the indebtedness and early death of P'eng Hsu's father set the conditions in motion that propelled the little fellow right down the social slide. Liu Ling could perhaps have made things easier for herself if she had simply abandoned her son and remarried. Instead, she chose to protect her son. She wove and sold cloth to help pay off her husband's debts, while she and her child resigned themselves to "living in a bare room, with a ragged coverlet and a tile lamp [as their only possessions]." Her father's family, the Liu of Wan-an County, played an important role in the rescue, as they put up or "boarded" (*kuan*) P'eng Hsu and later hired him as a primary tutor. It was said that P'eng Hsu could have earned more as a tradesman or accountant than as a tutor, but his mother made him study and teach the Confucian classics. She knew the *Analects* and the *Classic of Filial Piety* and taught these orally to her son.[30]

It may be noted that the Moon Pond P'eng, who tried to enslave one of their own, were not a poor and obscure bunch but one of the most prominent common-descent groups of T'ai-ho. One can also see the value in one's marrying not just any girl, but a girl of quality, partly as insurance against the ever present possibility that social disaster might engulf one's sons.

However, to accept boarding (*kuan-ku*) at someone else's expense, as P'eng Hsu did in his mother's family, was to accept a status of dependency, and that was not necessarily a good situation for a boy to be in. For example, when Ch'en Hsun was fifteen years old, he declined the kind offer of an uncle to accompany him as a student to the home of a certain K'ang family in the T'ai-ho countryside, where the uncle had accepted a teaching position. Ch'en Hsun declined because the K'ang would have had to feed him, and he did not want to be "treated lightly by people," as he would have been had he accepted the dole.[31] Even hired tutors, like Ch'en's uncle, were in a socially delicate position because of a tendency on the part of their employers to treat them as though they were laborers or servants. As highly regarded a local teacher as he was, Hsiao Ch'i (1325–96) experienced this problem. When he taught in the Lo family school in T'ai-ho city, a matriarch, Madame Liu (1324–1400) had to warn her sons not to ignore or humiliate him. She gave Hsiao Ch'i some face by seeing personally, morning and night, to the preparation of his meals.[32]

It is evident that T'ai-ho's patriarchal families were often torn between a practical desire to rid themselves of their weaker members and a moral obligation to go to all lengths to provide for their welfare. Yang Shih-ch'i and Wang Chih and the other epitaph writers were intent upon praising those few who acted on their moral duty to prevent the downward mobility that the statistics show to have been so very common.

Some of the writers, indeed, had personally experienced the threat of social extinction in their childhoods. Yang Shih-ch'i is a case in point.[33] Another is Wang Chih, who gives interesting and detailed testimony about how his step-grandmother, Madame Li, intervened to save him (and his sister and brother) from the predatory designs of his male kinsmen, members of the socially prominent Ao-chieh (Hollow Street) Wangs of T'ai-ho's western suburb:

> Madame Li certainly helped us Wang. She raised me and my brother long enough to let us continue the sacrifices to our ancestors, and thanks to her, our ancestors buried below can rest in peace. What she did for us can hardly be repaid. I cannot forget that. That is why I must now write about her, so our posterity will know.
>
> Madame Ch'en was the first wife of my grandfather [Wang Chu-t'ing, 1317–83]. After she died, he married Madame Li. My mother, Madame Ou-yang [1349–84], served Madame Li faithfully, and they worked together harmoniously to manage the family, so that my grandfather and my father [Wang Po-chen, 1342–1416] were not burdened with domestic duties and could spend all their time in literary pursuits.
>
> Then my grandfather died, and a year later my mother died. There were no maids in the house. My brother and I were young [Wang Chih was five], and Madame Li was the only person we could rely on to stay alive. She looked after us carefully, as though we were her own children. She fed and clothed us and kept us from doing foolish or dangerous things.
>
> When I was five or six *sui,* she had me study under tutor Tseng Chung-chang. I used to shirk my studies, and she would cry angry tears and say: "The job of you Wangs has always been to study, but you shirk! Do you want to become a small man?" Every evening she would remind tutor Tseng to come by at daybreak to make sure we got to school. It was as though she felt she couldn't do enough to show her care and her worry for our futures.
>
> Careful as she was of us, we still hadn't encountered serious troubles.
>
> My father [at the time a bureau secretary (6A) in the Ministry of Works], after mourning leave, returned late to duty, and for that infraction he was ordered exiled to An-ch'ing [in present-day Anhwei Province, where he remained, ca. 1388–98]. A Wang kinsman then got the idea to seize his personal property, and suddenly Madame Li was faced with more trouble than it appeared she could handle. First the kinsman tried cajoling her: she could stay and be fed in his house and live with his mother. But Madame Li replied: "I'll just stay in this poor house and raise my young grandchildren. I won't go, even though you say you'll take care of me." That was the end of that ploy.
>
> Now it happened that there was a widow in our common-descent group who fell for that kinsman's false promises. He got hold of her dead husband's deed and sold all the property [she was holding in trust]. Finally, she died homeless, and her grandson fell victim to hunger and cold. People then came to see that my grandmother was extraordinarily farsighted.

When his first ploy failed, the kinsman seized the old home of my grand-father's younger brother and sold it. He also claimed that a certain garden of ours was partly his possession. He divided it up. Then he invited a bunch of bad people to buy cheaply [the topsoil rights?], and he had them bring their tools and come work it. Someone objected to all this, and he struck and killed him. But Madame Li spoke up and said: "I'm just an old Wang widow, but when your uncle and older brother were alive, you never said anything about that property, and yet now you and those slaves [*nu-pei*] just seize it. I'm going to be buried there when I die, so if you want that land, you'd better kill me first. As long as I'm alive, I won't let you have it!" When they all heard that, they put out their tongues in shock, and in the end, they backed off. So the garden was saved.

Our ninth generation ancestor was buried in a safe place. Everybody con-sidered the site geomantically good. The P'eng, a powerful common-descent group of our county, were trying to find a place to bury a father of theirs, and they were offering a high price for a site good enough to bring wealth and status to the dead man's descendants. At that time, my father was still in exile. My brother and I were in prison in the provincial capital, because of an accusation made against us. Our kinsmen, eager for the money, wanted to exhume [our ancestor] and sell the tomb site to the P'eng; but they were afraid of Madame Li, and so they made the argument that the tomb site was in fact no good, given that none of the Wang families was doing well, with three men presently in exile in army garrisons, and two grandsons under indictment, with who knows what disaster in store for them. But that argu-ment did not impress our step-grandmother, who forbade them to sell the tomb site.

Finally they sent a dull-witted fellow to go to Madame Li, to tell her that everyone's mind was made up, that she had no sons or grandsons and had no business stopping the sale.

At that time, my son Wang Tzu [1397–1458] was born. Madame Li held him on her knee as she replied: "Four big Wang families [*fang*] descend from that ancestor. Three of them want to sell. But that leaves us. If our sons and grandsons never return, there is this great-grandson here to serve as master of the tomb, and he'll never let it go. You people are violating the principle of Heaven!"

She placed the child on the floor, grabbed a stick, and drove the fellow away. When the P'eng heard about the dispute, they decided it would be wrong to continue to try to buy the site, and that is how the site continues to be ours to the present day. We Wang had declined in those days, and except for Madame Li, we could not have survived our troubles.[34]

Wang Chih went on to make the very same point, about how important it was for women to be "hard and square," that he made in the preface to his sourcebook for women.

Wang did not mention here that when he was twelve years old, he was sent away to Lu-ling County to live with a maternal uncle, a professional tutor, who "fed and taught" him for two years. Nor did he mention that when he was five and had just lost his mother, Madame Li needed help at once; and so a child-bride (Madame Ch'en, 1377-1458, of the Willow Creek Ch'en, and a relative of Wang's dead grandmother) was brought in nominally as a wife for Wang Chih but principally for her skills in weaving and tailoring.[35]

Wang Chih spent most of his adult life as a high official far away in Peking, but even from that distance, he tried to redirect Wang family strategy—away from predation on the weak and toward a new goal of social welfare for all. His oldest son, Wang Tzu, grew up to become a government Confucian instructor, but Wang Chih had four other sons, who took turns living with him in Peking. Using those sons as agents, he was able to keep a hand in family management back in T'ai-ho. By 1450, that family was a large one; Wang guessed that it contained "over a hundred" people of high and low status.[36]

In Peking, Wang lived with concubine Ch'iu. His wife Madame Ch'en stayed in T'ai-ho until her sons grew up. At one point, there were so many dependents that some of them were going to have to move out, but Madame Ch'en saved the day for them. In her epitaph, Wang Chih wrote that she "sold all her own jewelry and utensils to buy paddy at the west wall [of T'ai-ho], and then day and night she allotted farming tasks to the male and female slaves or bondservants [t'ung-pei] and to the older sons who were capable of farm work, and with Heaven's help there was enough food [to keep the family together]. Thanks to her direction, my sons to this day provide for themselves by working at farming."

. . .

Another case from the early Ming era centers upon Liang Hun (1370-1434) and his wife, Madame Liu (1369-1432). In their case, cooperation among intermarried common-descent groups created a social safety net for as many as five weak orphans, who might otherwise not have survived. It must be emphasized that examples of this kind (there are many other early Ming instances of it) must have been exceptional and thus worthy of comment by the local literati. In view of the implications of the statistics, such cases cannot have been the rule. Yet they serve to illustrate very dramatically the relentlessness of the pressures that created downward mobility in T'ai-ho.

In 1393 or 1394, Investigating Censor (7A) Ch'en Chung-shu, a Willow Creek Ch'en, died, unexpectedly and destitute of personal property, in his early 40s in Kwangtung. His wife had already died several years before. Thus his son Ch'en Shang (aged fifteen or sixteen) and his daughter became orphans. His younger brother Ch'en Chung-heng (1354–1413) refused to concede them a share in his personal estate. He owned a nice house and substantial farm property near T'ai-ho city, but his own four sons wanted it all for themselves. So censor Ch'en's grieving orphans were placed "in a condition so wretched that few people could have borne it"—and it is left to the imagination whether that meant beggary or enslavement or what. Then fortune smiled. Ch'en Shun-chih (1344–1426) was the older sister of Ch'en Chung-shu and Ch'en Chung-heng, and she was Liang Hun's mother. She imposed it as a moral obligation upon her son to step in and help raise her brother's orphans.

The Liang also owned farm property near T'ai-ho city, so there was a resource base to help support their social work. (Liang Hun was no stingy manager. He rented some of that land to unnamed in-laws, who suffered some untimely deaths and so fell behind in their rent payments; but he forgave the debts, and even signed over some of the land because the renters were a Confucian [*ju*] family that had fallen temporarily on hard times.)

Liang Hun was able to raise Ch'en Chung-shu's orphan daughter and eventually to marry her to a good boy of the Yen family. The other orphan, Ch'en Shang (1378–1413), soon proved a brilliant success. In 1411 he achieved his *chin-shih* degree and had just begun his official career when he, like his father before him, died young, leaving behind, just as his father had done, two young orphans, a boy (Ch'en I) and a girl, and no property. Again, they and their mother faced beggary. Someone made an appeal on their behalf to investigating censors, who interrogated Ch'en Chung-heng about the matter and forced him to allot them "a tiny plot where they could stay." At some point Ch'en Shun-chih also stepped in and again got her son Liang Hun to help take care of them. Later she also arranged the orphans' marriages. She married Ch'en I to her own granddaughter, née Liang. So here were two generations of Ch'en orphans that Liang Hun and his wife and mother helped raise.

Liang Hun also took in and helped raise and teach an orphaned paternal cousin, Liang Chiung (1384–1429). In fact, Liang Hun's wife, Madame Liu, did most of the nurturing, and she also took care of her aging mother-in-law, Ch'en Shun-chih. She had a staff of maidservants (*nu-pei*), whom she was recalled as having managed with skill. It was

her third daughter who was married to orphan Ch'en I. They all lived
in T'ai-ho. As the male orphans grew old enough, the women sent them
for their education to wherever Liang Hun happened to be at the time
as an instructor in county schools in various far-flung parts of China.

In addition to Madame Liu, Liang Hun had another woman, probably a concubine, who lived with him when he was away from T'ai-ho.
Between them, Liang Hun fathered four boys and four girls. The girls
were given good marriages (although the youngest was married to
Grand Secretary Yang Shih-ch'i's oldest son, a real estate entrepreneur
who died in prison on charges of extortion and murder in 1444). One
of Liang Hun's sons, Liang Li, was taken by recommendation into government teaching and ended his career as instructor second class in the
imperial college. All the orphans did quite well. Liang Chiung went
on to achieve a *chin-shih* degree and was a bureau director (5A) in the
Ministry of Justice at the time of his death. Respectable marriages were
arranged for all the girls. Ch'en I's son Ch'en Yen became a county Confucian instructor. Altogether, this was a very successful social rescue operation.[37]

. . .

If the figures derived from obituaries of people born in the fifteenth century provide anything like an accurate view into elite social processes
in T'ai-ho County, they show that while the rates of reproduction went
down, the rates of downward or outward mobility went up. Moreover,
the stories of social rescue that one often encounters in the epitaphs of
people born in the fourteenth century are vanishingly scarce in the epitaphs of people born in the fifteenth. It was men born in the fifteenth
century who took the lead in the founding of the organized lineages
that became prominent features of the social landscape of T'ai-ho in the
sixteenth century and later; and while lineages had welfare functions, it
is impossible to tell whether they were more effective, or less, as inhibi-
tors of social disaster than the informal interfamily networks that
they seem to have replaced.

It is interesting that the few social rescue stories of this later era
should center upon travelers and émigrés—upon people down on their
luck and far from their native county.

Wang Ch'iu (1445–1507) was a grandson of Wang Chih, and his
second wife was Jen Lien-chen (1454–1526), youngest daughter of Jen
Heng (a provincial degree holder from T'ai-ho city who ended his career as a county magistrate in Fukien). Around 1500, Wang Ch'iu was

serving as an office director (6B) in the Court of Imperial Entertainments in Nanking, and Jen Lien-chen stretched his small salary to help
pay for entertaining visitors from back home in T'ai-ho; for a tutor for
their five sons; for board and school supplies for some other boys
who came to study with her sons; and for charity to locals in straits.
She helped poor Hsiao Jou. "Hsiao Jou had come [from T'ai-ho] to the
Ministry [of Revenue in Nanking] accompanying a tax shipment," her
epitaph reads. "But his comrades had abandoned him because he was
sick, and so he came crawling [to Wang's house in Nanking]. Wang
was away in Peking at the time, and the gatekeeper wouldn't let him
in. But Madame Jen, when she was told, frowned and said: 'He's sick
and so far from home, and he has nowhere else to go.' At once she had
him housed nearby, and fed and medicated him until he got well and
then gave him money enough to return home. People admired her for
that."[38]

There was also Lo Fu (1438–1507), a T'ai-ho man who also lived in
Nanking, where he was registered with a naval guards unit and served
as something of a one-man social welfare agency for failing elites from
back home. The early deaths of his two brothers left him the task of
supporting their widows and one orphan daughter. He also supported
his sister and her husband, who lived with him. Plus there came indigent
kin from back in T'ai-ho. People said his kitchen was always busy, with
maids and servers constantly running about under his personal direction. His T'ai-ho neighbors in Nanking reported that he took in two
generations of orphaned cousins, plus a distantly related orphan boy
from back home, plus a destitute friend and his little daughter. The
friend soon died, and Lo made it his responsibility to marry the daughter off. His neighbors also reported that a certain Hsiao Hsin owed him
money that he could not repay by any means other than selling him
his daughter; but Lo Fu indignantly refused and forgave the debt altogether.

Lo Fu was obviously well off. Where his income came from is a
complete mystery because his grandfather had been exiled to Manchuria early in the Ming for the offense of "discussing national affairs as
a mere commoner" and had returned home to T'ai-ho in his old age.
His father moved to Nanking under military registry, but because he
was a noted tutor in the *Book of Changes,* his commander excused him
from duty. Lo Fu himself was no more than a *sheng-yuan* who had
failed five times to get his provincial degree. Eventually his son, Lo

Feng, achieved his *chin-shih* degree in 1496 and went on to have a moderately successful official career.[39]

EMIGRATION

There is no doubt that emigration drew off some substantial percentage of the excess population of T'ai-ho. The numbers cannot be counted. It is possible, however, to catch certain glimpses of the process.

There are signs that T'ai-ho began to send out émigrés in early times, when it was still attracting new settlers. There were, for example, successive generations of Wus who moved from T'ai-ho to Kwangsi in the thirteenth century.[40] In Kwangtung Province, five of forty Hakka surnames claimed ancestors who were T'ai-ho people in Sung, Yuan, or Ming times, and these include émigrés from such well-known common-descent groups as the Hsiao of Nan-ch'i and the Lo of Ch'üeh-ch'eng (which in T'ai-ho are never flagged as being Hakka).[41]

Early in the Ming, three brothers of the Liu of K'an-ch'i Ward (township 63) moved away to make new homes for themselves in Yen-t'ing County, Szechwan.[42] Wang Chih's distant kinsman, Wang Tsai (1314–90), was a government instructor in Kan-chou in southern Kiangsi, and he decided to settle there permanently. Wang Chih's maternal uncle, Ou-yang Huai (1357–1444), moved from T'ai-ho to the market town of Yung-ho across the border in Lu-ling County, where he was attracted by an offer to board as a live-in son-in-law to a local resident. Ou-yang made a career as a private tutor in classics and calligraphy.[43] Yang Yun-wen died in office as magistrate of Ch'ang-yuan County, Honan, in the 1370s. His young son, rather than returning home, took up registry there, and two descendants of these ex-T'ai-ho Yang later became local government students in Ch'ang-yuan.[44] Sometime during the Ming, various Chiangs, Ch'ens, and P'engs emigrated to Hunan Province, where they became founding ancestors of lineages that by Ch'ing times (1644–1912) had achieved national prominence.[45] A study done long ago shows that, in fact, at least some fifty-four émigrés from T'ai-ho moved west to Hunan, as part of a large outflow of Kiangsi people, mainly in the early part of the Ming period.[46]

Military exile created a certain amount of early Ming emigration. A few ragged original records remain of twenty-two T'ai-ho convicts who were exiled to garrisons in Manchuria in 1392; twenty-one of them died there.[47] But some exiles found permanent homes in Manchuria—

the Liu at the Fu-chou guards, and the Hsiao at the T'ieh-ling guards, for example—and they are regularly referred to, even in the late Ming, as T'ai-ho people registered in Fu-chou or T'ieh-ling. Their T'ai-ho connections were never completely cut.[48] Whether or not the rate of emigration increased in the middle years of the Ming dynasty is hard to say. In any event, it surely continued. The T'ai-ho County gazetteer, in its list of native sons who qualified themselves for official position, begins to note from the Ch'eng-hua era (1465–87) onwards significant (and increasing) numbers of one-time natives who achieved their provincial (chü-jen) degrees in provinces other than Kiangsi, or who entered the imperial colleges as sui-kung (annual tribute) from county schools in various parts of China.

It is also clear that the T'ai-ho émigrés of the fifteenth century and later found two new and undeveloped frontier regions in China to settle in and exploit. One such region was the far south of Kiangsi where, earlier on, Wang Tsai had gone. An official report of around 1530 describes southern Kiangsi (Nan-Kan) as having long acted as a magnet for people from Chi-an Prefecture, because paddy and mountain land were available, and newcomers might reap profits from rice, indigo, timber, and charcoal production.[49] "Kan-chou has a lot of high-grade fields and idle soil," wrote Ch'en Ch'ang-chi, probably sometime in the 1540s. "The taxes there are light, and the people are few; whereas in Chi-an the fields are low-grade and the imposts are heavy, and the population is thick, but production is thin. As a result, many poor people take their families and kin and find work in Kan-chou, and they never return."[50]

From 1563 to 1564, Hai Jui (at the time magistrate of Hsing-kuo County, T'ai-ho's neighbor to the east) also noted that the population of Chi-an Prefecture was dense, that land and commercial opportunity were scarce, and that therefore many people were leaving the province altogether. He argued that more people would migrate within the province if it were not so hard to do so legally.[51] Despite the difficulty, there were at least twenty-eight T'ai-ho men who emigrated to southern Kiangsi, entered county schools in that region as sheng-yuan, and qualified themselves as officials in the Hung-chih, Cheng-te, and Chia-ching eras (1488–1566). Around 1568, an official complaint was voiced that Hsin-feng County, about a hundred miles south of T'ai-ho, had in effect been seized and occupied by emigrants from Wan-an and T'ai-ho, even though they could not legally register there. It was asserted that most of the shopkeepers were outsiders and that 70–80 percent of the land was in the hands of outsiders as well.[52] Some Hsin-feng earnings were repatriated to T'ai-ho: the Kuo lineage temple in Ch'e-t'ien Ward (township 60) was funded in part from the proceeds of fields owned by kinsmen down in that county.[53]

The other region that attracted T'ai-ho émigrés was extreme northwestern Hupei, about five hundred miles away, a turbulent and violent frontier zone in Ming times.[54] A massive emigration of Kiangsi people into all parts of Hupei was underway in the fifteenth and sixteenth centuries.[55] T'ai-ho émigrés concentrated in a few counties near the Shensi and Honan borders. Representatives of at least twenty-one T'ai-ho lineages settled in there, and soon at least fifty men from these émigré lineages achieved *chü-jen* degrees or entered the imperial colleges. By the 1570s, Liang Ju-hsiao and his son had organized in Yun-hsi County, near the Shensi border, a replica of the Liang lineage back in T'ai-ho, with its own endowed ancestral temple and school. Fourteen of these transplanted Liangs became *sheng-yuan* and eventually Ming officials.[56] South of Yun-hsi, in Chu-shan County, Ou-yang Jen made similar kinds of arrangements, and the Ou-yang lineage there, like its parent back in T'ai-ho, came to be regarded as an unusually large one. Ou-yang Te (1496–1554) certainly considered these émigré Ou-yangs as kin; he once wrote them a letter congratulating eight of them for qualifying to take provincial examinations and scolding the others for their squabbling.[57]

BONDAGE

While it can be stated with certainty that the sale of persons took place in T'ai-ho and that the upper class placed certain of its children in bondage, there is no way to tell whether these unfortunate males and females were then exported from their native county, or whether they were kept in family service somewhere in T'ai-ho itself. Was T'ai-ho's servile population a population of strangers? It is impossible to know. Judging from the few known surnames of individual bondsmen (Lin; Yang, meaning "sheep"), it appears that at least some were strangers to the county.

It is also unclear to what extent people in bondage reproduced. Nor is it clear whether bondage was hereditary, life-long, or for a stipulated term of years. It was surely a persistent institution, at least in a mild form, as witnessed by the "hereditary servants" of eighteenth-century T'ai-ho and the occasional field slaves observed there in the 1930s.[58] In

Ming times, bondage was often mentioned in the obituaries of men and women of T'ai-ho's upper class as a troublesome issue in family management.

It was felt to be best when family servants were kept under benevolent but very strict control. It was stated, for example, of Hsiao Ch'uan (fl. 1540s, of Nan-ch'i, township 59) that "he didn't flog his slaves when they made sly excuses for their misbehavior; he would have them flogged for serious offenses, but then he would dismiss such incidents from his mind and forget that they had ever occurred."[59] Yang Yin-ch'iu's wife, Madame Liang (1548–95), "carefully kept [the family quarters] locked and bolted. When she collected woven hemp cloth from the female slaves [nü-nu], she would issue them raw hemp, grain, and vegetables. When [doling them food] from the jar, she would give them orders and examine them. 'Who in the world eats without working?' " she would ask. As manager of a large family in T'ai-ho (her husband, an official, was absent), Madame Liang "forbade the slaves to overstep the bounds and flout the family rules, but she would reward the hardworking ones and cherish those who showed a willingness to reform. Whenever the other wives thrashed the slaves too hard, she would weep and scream in an effort to stop the violence, on the grounds that slaves were, after all, human beings."[60]

There existed a certain sense of moral responsibility for the welfare of faithful bondservants. For example, there came a point in the life of Liu Sui (1455–1533, of Liu-chia-kang, township 61) when he became poor. Yet despite his reduced circumstances, he "could not bear to abandon his slaves and have them go into the service of others"; and his servants were, reportedly, grateful for his determination to keep looking after them.[61] Hu Chih's mother, poor as she was, kept two bondspeople, a man and a woman, both of whom were old and thin and had no other place to go.[62]

Slaves in T'ai-ho were ordinarily assigned menial work as house servants and as field hands, but sometimes they, like eunuchs in the palace of the later Ming emperors, won the confidence of their masters and by degrees encroached upon matters of family government and made themselves "powerful" (hao) in the process. The T'ai-ho gazetteer of 1579 issued a general warning about this matter. "Villainous slaves of the hereditary families are swallowing their masters and mistreating their helpless heirs," it stated. "This has created an atmosphere of growing insubordination and rebellion that numerous prosecutions and punishments have been unable to stop."[63]

Indeed, sixteenth-century obituaries yield examples of what appears to have been an increasing aggressiveness on the part of T'ai-ho's bondsmen. In Kuan-ch'ao Ward (township 31), Kuo Ch'i-shih (1496–1573) was nearly ruined in some unspecified litigation in which "powerful slaves" brought "false" testimony against him.[64]

For reasons unknown, one or more "powerful slaves" nearly beat to death the elder brother of Chang T'ing, a sixteenth-century T'ai-ho geomancer and physician. Chang T'ing was forced to sell personal property in order to finance legal prosecution of the offenders.[65] On Hollow Street in T'ai-ho's western suburb lived Wang Jui, a sixteenth-century descendant of Wang Chih. Wang Jui was a merchant and part-time litigator. Among the component families of the Wang lineage, a "powerful slave" was bullying his young master. The young master complained to the lineage head (tsu-chang), and when the head did nothing about it, Wang Jui took it upon himself to arrest the slave, flog him before the Wang ancestral temple, and charge him at the county yamen. "There is no need to thank me," said Wang Jui to the grateful young master. "My thought was to prevent the downfall of the Wang lineage, and that I succeeded in doing."[66]

In Moon Hill Ward (township 32), Tseng I-ch'ing (1538–87) perceived that local custom had degenerated, with "sons selling their fathers' estates, slaves stealing their masters' properties, and the strong eating the flesh of the weak." He further noted that "in some of the old families of [T'ai-ho] city, the clothing of the slaves is as fine as that of the kinsmen themselves." Tseng thought the fault for that lay with the kinsmen. He enforced the appropriate status differences on his own estate and disciplined the menials, so that "none of them dared wield power, or disorder the family rules."[67]

In the mid–seventeenth century, with the collapse of Ming rule in China, the upper class faced widespread and serious retaliation for the downward social mobility that its demographic behavior had for so long encouraged. For a long time, the elite people of T'ai-ho had exacerbated the situation by extending to their servile population a dangerously contradictory combination of privilege and repression, of empowerment and punishment. The same or worse was the case elsewhere in Chi-an Prefecture. In Yung-feng County, both slaves (nu-p'u) and tenant farmers (tien-hu) organized themselves into groups called "small compacts" (hsiao-yueh) and revolted against their masters.[68] In the period from 1645 to 1648, "tenants and powerful slaves" (tien-k'o hao-nu) in Lu-ling, An-fu, and Yung-hsin Counties went on rampage under the leadership of "leveler kings" (*ch'an-p'ing wang*) who threatened to "level master and slave, noble and base, and rich and poor." They forced their way into the great residences, looted the storehouses, and put on finery. They tied and flogged the owners and then made servants of them. "We are all men," they reportedly said. "Why do you call us slaves? We'll reverse that from now on."[69]

T'ai-ho County suffered the destruction of a murderous outlaw by the name of Liu Chin (or Ching), described as a former slave (*p'u*) of an unnamed great local family. He was captured late in the Ming, and the magistrate was going to execute him; however, certain T'ai-ho men holding official status (*shen-shih*) took bribes from Liu Chin and effectively interceded on his behalf. Some local people protested. The magistrate's answer to them was that Liu's followers would exact fearful revenge: "If he dies, there will be a rising and certain disaster for you T'ai-ho people. We don't want war out in there in the cantons."

In 1645, in the civil wars of the Ming-Ch'ing transition, "poor people" in the eastern cantons conducted food riots, and "powerful slaves [*hao-nu han-p'u*] resisted their masters, formed gangs, and did bad things." In 1649, exslave Liu Chin and his forces seized and occupied the city of T'ai-ho for several months, until Ch'ing troops drove him out. In 1653, finally, Liu Chin was captured in the mountains along the Hunan border and executed.[70]

•   •   •

It is time for a brief recapitulation. Just as the "economy" of T'ai-ho County in the Ming period is unknowable, its "demography" cannot be known either. What can be discussed are the changing styles of resource management by local elites and the demographic processes that affected those same elites. It is impossible to talk about T'ai-ho County in the Ming without becoming constantly aware of the presence of a robust two-class system there: an upper class of "managers" of various sorts who bore genealogical credentials and a lower class of menials, maids, concubines, bondservants, field families, laborers, small traders and the like who were without genealogical credentials. In the Ming, upward mobility from the lower class was unheard of. "Powerful slaves" were still slaves. (The lower-class revolts of the late Ming may have loosened things a little—they did elsewhere in China—but little is known of T'ai-ho County in the Ch'ing.) Downward mobility from the elite into the lower class was, however, a perennial possibility.

One may ask whether the demographic profile of the T'ai-ho elite can be understood as a local example of a much wider phenomenon. It has recently been shown that the results of studies of Chinese microdemography can in some respects be generalized to the region and nation and can lay groundwork for revising accepted notions of the larger trends of China's population history.[71] Almost all of the work that has been done centers on the late Ming and Ch'ing, however, and uses lineage-kept genealogical records rather than county epitaphs as source material. In an earlier paper, I showed that T'ai-ho mortality rates (lower in the fifteenth century, higher in the sixteenth) mirror those given for south China generally in a 1973 study by Michel Cartier.[72] But a great deal more work needs to be done in demographic study for the Sung, Yuan, and early Ming periods, and there is as yet little available on the regional or national scene to which to link the microdemography done in this chapter.

What can be emphasized here are connections between the demographic behavior of the upper class and other developments inside T'ai-ho over the course of the Ming. The expansion of the upper class (as shown in the male cohort born 1325–1399) coincides with a loving appreciation of the local landscape, the building or rebuilding of landed estates, the formation or reconstitution of common-descent groups, unusually high rates of recruitment into Ming government, and, as will be noted in part 3, a strong sense of county patriotism among T'ai-ho men inside Ming government itself. The contraction of the upper class (as seen in the cohort born 1425–1499) through increased rates of downward mobility and emigration coincides with a loss of interest in local landscape, the creation of powerful lineage institutions in place of the looser common-descent groups of the earlier period, an abrupt decline in the rates of bureaucratic recruitment, and, for the literati, the adoption of new intellectual orientations in which pride in one's native locality had no place.

CHAPTER 4

Patrilineal Groups and Their Transformation

Upper-class society in southern China, certainly in its T'ai-ho version, was not so much a society of individuals, or of families in the nuclear sense of that word, as a society thick with larger patrilineal structures. These structures did not emerge haphazardly. They were consciously and deliberately organized. Moreover, their history, which can be traced through the course of the Ming dynasty, clearly indicates that they underwent a qualitative evolutionary leap in nature and in function.

The majority of T'ai-ho's patrilineages were founded (or refounded) early in the Ming as "common-descent groups," as part of a determined effort to identify an upper class and to justify its existence in the light of the moral values of Confucianism. Later, in the sixteenth century, some of T'ai-ho's common-descent groups underwent a further transformation: into large and corporate "lineages," with special endowments of buildings and property, and institutions for the control and discipline of their memberships.[1] The purpose of this chapter is to explore the questions how and why the people of T'ai-ho felt it essential to their identity and their welfare to make the exceptional efforts and pay the high costs necessary for the development of extrafamilial social organizations of the above kinds. What was the point of it all?

THE FORMATION OF COMMON-DESCENT GROUPS

Patrilineal groups of one kind or another had long been a feature of the local social landscape. They had existed in T'ai-ho in the Sung (960–

1279) and Yuan (1279–1368). But T'ai-ho was very badly battered in the civil wars that engulfed south China in the 1350s and 1360s. After around 1370, when order was finally restored and Ming rule established, people began slowly to rebuild their homes and their lives. They also tried to reassemble what they could of the records of their genealogies. If the large quantity of early Ming testimony to these endeavors is any guide, creating (or re-creating) a genealogically credentialed society was for some reason a critically important component of local postwar social reconstruction. Local people were strongly encouraged to gather whatever they could of written evidence and oral tradition about their ancestors and to organize this information into books or files (*p'u*). What was going on?

The evidence available to answer this question consists of a large number of detailed prefaces and colophons to genealogical books which have since been lost, or are unavailable. In addition, there is often considerable genealogical information to be found in the obituaries of individuals. Altogether, these references provide information about 141 genealogically distinct common-descent groups, large and small (not counting local branches).[2]

The stories that these genealogies provide shed some light on the settlement history of T'ai-ho. It turns out that ninety-six common-descent groups considered themselves immigrants: forty-three from other parts of Kiangsi Province, and smaller numbers from the Nanking area (twenty-five) and from Hunan (twelve). The immigrants often arrived in T'ai-ho during times of national turmoil: thirty-four came in the tenth century, and forty-eight in the thirteenth. Only two came in the fourteenth century, at the time of the Yuan collapse; and it is clear that T'ai-ho was full in Ming times, no longer attractive to new settlers, and indeed it became an exporter of population rather than an importer.

The original immigrants, as recalled by their upper-class descendants many generations later, turn out to have been minor local officials in many instances (forty); they came to T'ai-ho, liked what they saw, and decided to stay. Six others were military officers; two were medical practitioners; two were geomancers; and two others moved to T'ai-ho as uxorilocal husbands in families already established there. A large number (thirty-two) of founding ancestors are known by name only, without any further description at all.

It would be inadvisable to accept any single founding story as historical fact. The reconstitution of common-descent groups in early Ming

T'ai-ho was undertaken in an atmosphere of competition for social prestige, even while it was part of a high-minded Confucian sociomoral cru-
sade. And hard evidence about founding ancestors often proved vanishingly scarce. In twenty-one cases, the compiler asserted that the family
genealogy had been lost or destroyed in the civil upheavals of the mid–
fourteenth century; in another twenty-one cases, the compiler stated
that his was the first attempt ever to draw up any kind of genealogy for
his common-descent group.

Anecdotes show just how hard it could be to preserve or find any
evidence at all about one's ancestors. In 1384, Lung Chih-yun showed
Hsiao Ch'i six dedicatory poems and descriptions written by local literati, which were all that remained of what had been, before the wars, a
large family library. Hsiao Ch'i knew something about five of the six
writers, and he wrote down what he knew in a preface to the tiny file
of papers.³ In 1366, Liu Sung (1321–81) happened to find in a wine-
shop in the prefectural city of Chi-an an old official recommendation
written ten years earlier for a friend, Kuo Yü-ch'ing, authorizing him
to take the provincial civil service examinations—which he later failed.
Liu retrieved the old paper and gave it to the Kuo family, as something
they would surely cherish. In his colophon to this document, Hsiao Ch'i
speculated that his own lost papers had probably been put to use somewhere as lids for medicine jars or as towels to wipe up dirty tables.⁴

The Lo of Tung-ch'an Lane inside T'ai-ho city still treasured a deed
for a sacrificial field, dating to the early twelfth century. The old deed
was a chance possession and their only concrete link to the past.⁵ The
rest of their past was reclaimed from an elder who recited from memory
what he knew of the family's genealogy. The Tseng of Nan-ch'i Ward
(township 4) also had nothing but the oral testimony of old people to
rely on when they drew up their genealogy early in the Ming.⁶

Chou Shih-hsiu recounted how when his family was forced to flee
local violence in 1360, his father packed the family genealogy, together
with an imperial patent of Sung date that had been issued to an ancestor,
into a silk bag which he attached to a carrying pole.

His idea [wrote Chou] was that in case of emergency, he would abandon the
pole, grab the bag, and hide. But the pole bearer knew nothing of this. Ar-
riving at a place called Fen-shui, the bearer got tired of the weight. Guessing
that the bag contained paintings, he said: "Our lives are in danger; why am
I carrying paintings?" So he detached the silk bag and threw it away. Ten *li*
further on, someone noticed that the bag was missing, and the bearer replied

truthfully when asked about it. At once they went back to get it, and though they searched for over a month, the bag was never found. My father got sick with grief and anger and died.[7]

Early in the Ming era, fearing imminent confiscation of his properties by the local officials, Tax Captain Hsiao Yen-ming of Chang-ch'iao (Camphor Bridge Ward, township 41) hid the family genealogy in a monk's cell in a local Buddhist temple; but when the panic was over, the genealogy had disappeared. It seems someone had stupidly mistaken it for an old calendar and burned it. A nephew was later able to reconstruct seven generations using his father's recollection of what the genealogy had contained.[8]

A sixteenth-century writer explained that throughout Chi-an Prefecture (of which T'ai-ho was a component county), big and old families treasured their genealogies as much as emperors treasured imperial seals; but he noted that few of those genealogies were deep, and people were considered fortunate if they had even one or two bits of hard evidence that linked them back to the Sung or Yuan.[9] Indeed, all the Ts'ai family had by way of evidentiary link to its past was a very truncated genealogy inscribed on an uncle's tombstone.[10] The Hu of Ho-ch'i Ward (township 65) had lost their genealogy in the late Yuan wars, but had better luck than the Ts'ai because they were able to reconstruct ten generations based on epitaphs and other evidence.[11]

The doubtfulness of the evidence that some common-descent groups advanced to establish their ancestry is particularly striking in the case of the Liu of Sha-ch'i (Sand Creek Ward, township 22). One commentator states that Liu Ching-an hid the family genealogy behind a wall when Sha-ch'i Ward was overrun in the late Yuan wars. When he retrieved it, he found it had rotted, and so he had a student-boarder (*kuan-jen*) reassemble and recopy it.[12] The story sounds straightforward enough — but a later commentator contradicts it. He states that the original genealogy was lost altogether and that evidence of the Liu past was uncovered only in 1410, when a nephew of Liu Ching-an's unearthed several dated dedicatory inscriptions in the ruins of one of the family's old buildings.[13]

It must be emphasized, however, that there was a crucial, almost essential, *public* dimension to the compiling of genealogies, which at first sight would appear to have been purely family-centered documents. Men who prepared their families' genealogies certainly felt some compulsion to show them to respected outsiders, and to secure their favor-

able comment and endorsement. Early in the Ming, the best way for the
compilers to achieve this was to take their genealogies to the capital of
Nanking (after 1421, Peking) and have one or more of the native sons
of T'ai-ho who were serving there as high-ranking imperial officials
write the endorsement. To have one's genealogy read and approved by
one of these eminent native sons was, in effect, to be granted a kind of
ticket of admission into an emerging T'ai-ho social elite. Wang Chih
wrote endorsements for the genealogies of seventy-four common-descent groups of T'ai-ho; Yang Shih-ch'i wrote sixty-three, and Ch'en
Hsun (1385–1462) forty-five (other writers wrote forty-seven). Some
compilers secured endorsements from more than one of these high officials, so there is some overlap in the numbers.

What did it mean to be admitted into a T'ai-ho social elite? Why was
an endorsed genealogy a requirement for admission? These questions
evoked much discussion. Researching family history partly served practical and psychological needs. As Yang Shih-ch'i noted in his preface
to the genealogy of the Lo of Shu-yuan (Academy Ward, township 1):
"There is no descendant who does not desire to trace his origins, to
discover where he came from, and record it, weaving in as he does so
his thoughts for his own descendants."[14] "Why compile a genealogy?"
asked Yang in a preface to another genealogy.

> The aim is to make clear one's roots and origins, and to discriminate between
> those close and those distant. It's like a tree, whose branches and twigs
> spread everywhere, even though all originate in the same main stem. Like-
> wise the kinfolk in a family. They share the same matter-energy, but they
> become once and then twice removed, and then they fall outside the mourn-
> ing grades, until finally they become as separate and distant as strangers. Yet
> they all descend from one man's body. So how can one not compile a gene-
> alogy that embraces everyone, from the original man to the strangers?[15]

The arboreal metaphor was never far from the commentators' pens.
According to Ch'en Hsun, a long family line "is like a tree on a great
mountain, or in a broad valley. Its roots are deep. The trunk, limbs,
branches, and leaves proliferate and spread, shading many a mound
and gully."[16] A good ancestor leaves behind him a legacy (*tse*), which,
wrote Yang Shih-ch'i, "is like a great tree on a high mountain, growing
deeper the longer it is blasted by wind and sun and snow. The leaves,
branches, and trunk may be battered to nothing, but if the roots survive, the tree will grow again with vigor when one day a milder climate
returns."[17] And how is it that the great junipers and southernwoods
branch so densely, reaching the clouds and giving shade from the sun?

They have deep roots. "Now," continued Yang, "suddenly risen families prosper in the morning and wither by evening. They burst forth, and as rapidly decline, because they lack such roots. And what are those roots? Virtue and goodness, that is all."[18]

History's painful lesson for T'ai-ho was that one could not place trust in material legacies like land or money to perpetuate one's line. The writers insisted that a family legacy had to be planted in different soil, soil whose main constituent was Confucian education. It was not wealth, not high office, but education that perpetuated a patriline. Without education, no one could write a genealogy, update it, or transmit it down the generations. Wang Chih insisted that as long as its members kept up a tradition of study, a descent line could survive financial ruin and continue forever.[19] Yang Shih-ch'i wrote that a branch of his own line had survived the loss of its considerable wealth in the late Yuan wars because its true inheritance lay in education, not in property.[20] He approved the pending marriage of a junior kinsman with a girl of the Wang of Shan-tung Ward (township 44) because those Wang, though undistinguished, were an old and good family. "In the future when my descendants discuss marriage," he counseled, "they need only seek out honest and dutiful families, no matter whether they are rich or poor. Marriages may be contracted with families of impoverished students or landowners, provided that they are virtuous and good people."[21]

Confucian education helped encourage evidentiary honesty in genealogical research, which was in turn useful if one wanted one's pedigree endorsed. If a family could not trace its line of descent back any further than the great-great-grandfather, then, reluctantly, it had to begin the pedigree there. "It is the acme of unfiliality," wrote Wang Chih, "to make false assertions about the identities of one's ancestors."[22]

Genealogy, then, afforded sure knowledge of personal identity. It was a form of psychic insurance against unpredictable personal tragedy. Yuan Pen-ch'ien lost both his parents when he was only a baby, and was raised by a grandmother. "What let him know where his ancestors came from, and who his kinsmen were, was the existence of a genealogy," wrote Yang Shih-ch'i. "So we see why a genealogy is essential."[23]

A living man will one day become an ancestor himself and will do well to think how best to build the kind of legacy that will inspire his descendants to remember him. But an excellent thought like that can never arise unless a man lives already in a society where ancestral accomplishments are customarily recorded and are therefore known. And when a living man reads about his ancestors, "he will," wrote Yang

Shih-ch'i, "realize in shock how short he himself has come, and he will begin thinking about how to improve himself, so as not to leave shame to his own descendants. Any man's descendant who is eager to do good will understand this feeling . . . which is why the making of a genealogy is no small affair."[24]

Such thoughts, guided by genealogy, helped generate good social order through the whole county of T'ai-ho. Public virtue grew from seeds that germinated in the rich soil of private, family-centered descent lines. Ch'en Hsun argued that genealogical record keeping ignited generosity, filial piety, and fraternal submission in this and that family; and that these virtues then, by extension, engendered righteous commitments over larger and extrafamilial social fields.[25] "Indeed," exclaimed Yang Shih-ch'i, "a genealogy is something the benevolent man puts his mind to. A *shih* [an aspiring leader] carries out benevolence first in his family, and when after that he extends it to his locale and on to the whole realm, it is by way of an extension from his family."[26]

The honest and sincere endeavors of all the hundred or more pedigree compilers of early-fifteenth-century T'ai-ho thus had the cumulative aim of shaping a local social order whose fine qualities, in the testimony of its own native sons, stood second to none in Ming China. Yang Shih-ch'i had seen other parts of Ming China. When he compared them to his native T'ai-ho, their defects struck him forcefully. So he commented in an inscription he wrote on request for the Stone Hill Academy, a family school maintained by the Stone Hill Hsiao of township 10. Yang described the Hsiao genealogy and discussed the history of the school. Following that, he rejoiced in the T'ai-ho social order as a whole:

> I venture to say that what is estimable about the customs of our prefecture, something that other prefectures cannot match, is that here people devote themselves to righteousness, observe propriety, and value a steadfast sense of honor. No matter how poor people become, they never cease studying the classics. No matter how low they fall, they can still recite from the *Classic of Filial Piety* and the *Analects* and grasp their general meaning. There is a school on every city street and in every rural valley. Whenever the rich and those of high status encounter a *shih* wearing the scholar's robe, they always greet him respectfully and don't dare slight him.
>
> And it is here that hereditary patrilines are especially esteemed. If [a man whose] patriline is of low origin achieves wealth and status, people will not accept him as an equal; and that man, for his part, will not dare place himself above others on account of his wealth and status. That is how customs are in my home area.

How do I know these customs are rare? I have traveled up the Yangtze to Hunan. I have been to Hupei, and through the Huai region, several thousand *li* altogether. There have been times when I've gone several days without see-ing any sign of a school at all. I've seen how people live in such places. The simple people fish and farm; the smart ones profit as merchants. The rich and powerful who are the local elites do not devote themselves to the clas-sics or respect the robe-wearing *shih* or discriminate among the hereditary patrilines.[27]

Nonetheless, the new wave of genealogy writing that Yang Shih-ch'i's many endorsements encouraged was not universally welcomed. Indeed, Hu Kuang (1370–1418), a colleague from Chi-shui County, about thirty miles north of T'ai-ho, is reported as having strongly disapproved of it:

Hu [Kuang] hated to preface genealogies for people, because most of them were clapped together and unreliable. But Yang [Shih-ch'i] prefaced genealo-gies for more than fifty families, more than any other literatus had ever done before. Hu Kuang's strictness edged toward righteousness, and Yang's gener-osity toward benevolence. But Yang's writing was appropriate to his high position. He lived to great old age, and he enjoyed an era of peace and pros-perity, which was truly a happy juncture in world history. Those who chose a parsimonious view of things [in times such as that] are hardly worth taking seriously.[28]

Thus Yang Shih-ch'i and his T'ai-ho colleagues, occupying some of the Ming dynasty's highest positions in the early and middle decades of the fifteenth century, made it their extraofficial duty to get to know people from their home county and to lend their prestige and authority to the formation, or reconstitution, of a society of certified common-descent groups, whose claims to ancestry were based as much as could be managed upon whatever facts could be ascertained from research into old documents and inscriptions and from interviews with elders. The outcome of these efforts was, as Yang Shih-ch'i noted, a *hierarchy* of such groups, and a group's place in the hierarchy depended upon whether it had a deep and well-founded genealogy featuring notable an-cestors or only the shallowest of descent lines without notable ances-tors. There was never any intention of making all common-descent groups equal.

The elite descent lines of T'ai-ho were tagged with a variety of spe-cial labels: "old families" (*chiu chia*); "hereditary families" (*shih-chia*); "robe-and-cap lineages" (*i-kuan chih tsu*); "office holding lineages" (*kuan-tsu*); "scholar-gentry lineages" (*shih-tsu*); and the like. Ch'en Mo (Yang Shih-ch'i's uncle and tutor) noted that common people did not bother to keep genealogical records, so it was the *shih-ta-fu* (scholar-official elite) who kept and updated such records "over a hundred or a thousand years, and [wrote down their descent lines] on sheets of paper."[29]

Even so, very few such elite descent lines persisted intact over very many generations, as Yang Shih-ch'i explained:

> What the world styles old families are those whose ancestors were noted in their time for their great merits, their virtuous righteousness, or their literary study. They are found in the dynastic histories, or in the written works of great men and literati. When posterity reads about them, it always wonders about the fate of their descendants. It turns out that scarcely ten of a hundred have any descendants left. Of those ten, only two or three have good descendants who haven't shamed their ancestors. Is this because the original legacy was poor? Or is it because the descendants themselves were unequal to the task of carrying on? In either case, it must be that Heaven didn't protect them.
>
> In our county [of T'ai-ho], there once were easily several tens of surnames that were "old families" based upon merit, virtue, or letters achieved in good times. Then came troubled times, and their descendants died out, or they scattered, roiling like waves or curls of smoke, with the result that many people nowadays who are good and conscientious and do not shame their forebears don't realize that they are actually the descendants of an [illustrious] ancestor.
>
> The P'eng surname of Yueh-ch'ih [Moon Pond Ward, township 56] is the only one known to have lived together more than ten generations, with old and young in rank-order day and night, and who do things together as a group, so that everyone acknowledges that they are the descendants of a certain definite ancestor.[30]

·   ·   ·

The high-minded view of T'ai-ho's common-descent groups that Yang Shih-ch'i and his colleagues championed was often blind to the vulgar (*liu-su*) thoughts and behavior of the real world. From the far-away aerie of Peking, local society's blemishes were sometimes hard to see, which favored a clearer perception of its better tendencies. Occasionally, however, there were rude surprises. One day, Wang Chih happened to mention to Yang that he had endorsed a genealogy submitted to him by Yang Meng-pien, a very rich man from township 43. In it, Meng-pien claimed descent from a line in Yang Shih-ch'i's genealogy that Yang Shih-ch'i knew to be extinct. Wang confessed that he had simply taken Yang Meng-pien at his word. Yang Shih-ch'i knew of those Yangs, and he knew that in fact they had lost track of their descent. He wrote a note to that effect for insertion in his own genealogy so as to discourage any future attempt on their part to interlope.[31]

Lineage interloping was a problem in T'ai-ho. It was a problem because of the very prestige hierarchy that Yang Shih-ch'i and others favored. One learns about interloping mainly in those instances where
it was foiled. For example, in 1420, two members of the Ch'ing-ch'i
Ch'en descent group of T'ai-ho city passed their provincial exams and
then decided for the first time to compile a genealogy. On the basis of
surviving evidence, they could trace themselves back no further than a
great-great-grandfather, a government medical teacher. However, they
believed they were an offshoot of the Liu-ch'i (Willow Creek) Ch'en, a
line with a long and distinguished pedigree, but they had no proof for
that belief. Intimidated no doubt by the opinions of Yang Shih-ch'i and
the others in questions like this, they contented themselves with the
meager results of their research and a lowly place in T'ai-ho's prestige
hierarchy of common-descent groups.[32]

Similarly, the high-level climate of opinion that insisted upon concrete evidence persuaded Liu I (1361–1429) to start his genealogy four
generations back instead of intruding upon the Chu-lin Liu, a very distinguished kin group to whom he thought he was related. Yang Shih-
ch'i commented:

> Our area is noted for its generations of classics students who wear the cap
> and robe. As Liu I himself knows very well, many of them can record no
> more in the way of a pedigree than he, so he can have no regrets [about the
> shallowness of his own]. He has set his family in line with [the good cus-
> toms] of the area, and from this promising start onwards, there will surely
> be no end to [the good things that] the minds of the benevolent people and
> gentlemen [of his family will focus upon].[33]

It was often tempting for representatives of established elite lineages
to admit into their genealogies interlopers of the same surname who
were rich and wanted to buy social prestige. The temptation must often
have been yielded to. Rebuffs may have been rare. It is clear that they
were occasions to celebrate. Thus the Kuo of Kuan-ch'ao Ward (township 31) "refused to record [in their genealogy] unrelated people of the
same Kuo surname, even if they happened to live in Kuan-ch'ao; and if
a member without male heir adopted someone suspected of being nonkin, he was simply recorded as having died without issue. They rejected
unrelated people, even if they were rich and noble. They admitted all
relatives, even if they were humble and poor."[34]

Chou Shih-hsiu recalled how his father once had angrily refused
to sell an imperial patent issued to an ancestor to someone who bore
the Chou surname but was unrelated.[35] Chou Shih-hsiu's family lived in

Yang-kang Ward (township 55). The would-be interloper was a Chou of Ta-yuan Ward (township 33). The Ta-yuan Chou were rich but lacked a deep pedigree. They later decided they were related to the famous Neo-Confucian thinker Chou Tun-i (1017–73). They went so far as to add his biography to their genealogical file. Liu Sung wrote a colophon to their file in which he said he saw no proof of such a relationship and said he doubted truth of the claim.[36]

It appears there was abroad in T'ai-ho a general attitude of skepticism about the assertions people made about their descent. "Vulgar people," wrote Yang Shih-ch'i, "cling to their prejudices and accuse others of lying if they boast a distinguished ancestor, or of being the descendant of bandits if they do not. Yet while spurious claims do exist, most are definitely genuine."[37]

·   ·   ·

A descent group contaminant of a very different kind was the custom, common at least in the fourteenth century, of adopting children who were not kin. At least two of T'ai-ho's high literati personally experienced this problem.

When Yang Shih-ch'i was a baby, his father died, and his mother married Lo Tzu-li. At the age of five or so, Yang was excluded for no apparent reason from the Lo ancestral rites, and he burst into tears. Only then did his mother tell him that he was not a Lo at all, but a Yang. As a child of six, as he later recalled it, he fashioned his own little ancestral altar, where he secretly burned incense before the tablets representing his father, grandfather, and great-grandfather; eventually Lo Tzu-li, his stepfather, discovered what he was doing and was so moved by the child's devotions that he took the necessary legal steps to restore Yang Shih-ch'i to his original surname.[38] The grandfather of Liang Ch'ien (1366–1418) had been adopted into the Chung family, and Liang Ch'ien was Chung Ch'ien until, as an adult, he himself got his original surname officially restored.[39]

Surname restoration was not so easy. An adopted child certainly felt moral obligations toward the family who had borne the expense of raising him. Ch'en Ts'ung-lung, for example, was really Kuo Ts'ung-lung. But it was the Ch'en, an "alien" patriline, that had raised him, admitted him to its sacrifices, educated him, and given him his name and identity. Was it not ungrateful of him, then, to want to restore his surname to the original Kuo? Chou Shih-hsiu thought not. By restoring his original surname, he was removing himself as a source of disorder (*luan*) in his adopted descent group; he was really making the Ch'en line pure and uniform (*ch'un-i*) once again.[40]

Liu Sung's brother Liu Yeh (d. 1386) described an even more tangled case:

> There were sixteen local [T'ai-ho] men whom the county magistrate rec-ommended as refined talents [*hsiu-ts'ai*] and sent to sit for the provincial exams in 1382. Liu Ssu-te was one. He and I shared the same surname, so I asked him his ancestry. "My surname is really Fu," he said in tears. "When I was a child, I lost my father. My stepfather Liu taught me and got me es-tablished, so I took his surname. I'm aware of my obligation to continue the ancestral rites, and I want to restore the Fu surname, but I'm afraid that would show ingratitude for my education. Yet by keeping the Liu name, I'm forgetting my origins. What am I to do? Moreover, my father was a live-in son-in-law to the Hsiao, and he inherited the Hsiao ancestral rites. Now that he's dead, I venture to think that there is no one to succeed him in continuing those rites. What am I to do about that?"[41]

Liu Yeh urged him by all means to restore his original surname.

The adoption of nonkin is hard to account for as a strategy aimed at strengthening the descent group. Perhaps it was felt that the descent group was somehow better served by a capable outside adoptee than by a kinsman, but the available literature contains no explicit statement to that effect. Indeed, it may have been the case that when nonkin were adopted, it was for reasons having to do with the nuclear family and not the descent group as such.[42]

At all events, the high literati of T'ai-ho invariably championed the purity of blood in the common-descent group, and they always urged adoptees to restore their surnames (*fu hsing*) in the strongest possible terms.

.   .   .

As of the mid–fifteenth century, then, pushed from below by socio-psychological need and local social competition and given refined shape from on high by its great social arbiters, T'ai-ho evolved in the direction of a well-ordered society of patrilineal common-descent groups, their pure-blood identities established on the basis of honest research into known facts, and their place in the local hierarchy of common-de-scent groups assigned according to the depth of their genealogical roots and the good reputations of their ancestors.

The reconstituted common-descent groups of T'ai-ho regularly iden-tified themselves with, and sometimes seem to have controlled outright, a city sector or rural ward, which became for them what David Johnson has styled a "choronym." The choronym was regularly featured in the title of the genealogical book that was the descent group's constitutional charter (consisting of its body of rules, its history, and its membership roster). Thus we have the Ch'ing-ch'i (Clear Creek) Ch'en, the T'ao-yuan (Peach Spring) Hsiao, the Nan-ching (South Path) Hu, and on and on. Though the genealogical books were always compiled by kinsmen, it does appear that it was advisable for groups to obtain the recognition of at least one outsider who was *not* a kinsman, by way of a detailed written preface or other written token of acknowledgment, in order to be accepted into the larger family of T'ai-ho common-descent groups.

Thus constituted and recognized, the common-descent groups of T'ai-ho were expected to serve as bulwarks against social decay. A crucial weapon in the fight against social decay was the very information that the groups collected, stored, updated, and transmitted. Yin Ch'ang-lung (ca. 1369–ca. 1417) made that point clear. What happened when information about descent was lost or falsified? Two things. When people rose from low and obscure origins to wealth and status, they often felt shame for their real ancestors and found ways to go by some different surname. On the other side of the coin, hapless people of powerful and famous pedigree fell into bondage because their closest kin were ashamed to have them near. Sons began to divide their inherited property while their parents were still alive; people began looking upon their living kin as strangers; no announcements about marriages or funerals were circulated; and no aid was extended to the poor and distressed.[43]

In other words, in the absence of accurate descent reckoning, what resulted was meanness, strife, rootlessness, and social isolation. What resulted was, generally, social decay. Thus the practice of conscientious fact gathering about one's *own* line of blood descent constituted the very gateway into the great arena of collective moral and social order for T'ai-ho, and for China as a whole. The inward looking exclusivity of cherishing pure blooded descent was understood to create, almost as though by magic, *generalized* social order. Genealogy was absolutely essential to the formation of the common-descent group, and it was precisely the common-descent group (rather than the nuclear family or the individual) that made possible the expression in the real world of Confucian social and moral values.

FROM COMMON-DESCENT GROUPS TO LINEAGES

Sixteenth-century sources afford a quite different impression of the social landscape of kinship systems in T'ai-ho County. For one thing, the
native sons of the sixteenth century whose collected works survive were
never as highly placed as officials as their fifteenth-century counterparts
had been, and their knowledge of T'ai-ho society was less comprehensive. Ou-yang To (1487–1544) admitted outright that he spent too
much time in official duties to learn much about T'ai-ho society.[44] The
constant stream of T'ai-ho visitors—taxpayers, bureaucratic hopefuls,
lower ranking colleagues and the like—that had come to Nanking or
Peking and paid courtesy calls on the likes of Yang Shih-ch'i or Wang
Chih and asked them to preface a genealogy or write a special message
had pretty much dried up by the sixteenth century.

Yet the quantity of information, though diminished, is still substantial; and the information conveys a picture of a society where the common-descent groups have gone beyond data collecting and recognition seeking to develop a truly corporate existence, with collective
assets in land and rice and silver, and disciplinary powers over their
memberships. There are twenty-four known examples of this transformation.

Some prefacing of genealogical books still went on in the sixteenth
century. Some prefaces were new, but many were for updated versions of genealogies whose main texts had been assembled a century
before. Thus the rate of admission of new common-descent groups
into the elite society of T'ai-ho had clearly slowed; of the 141 groups
known, only 22 are mentioned for the first time in the sixteenth century
or later.

Patricia Ebrey and James Watson draw a useful definitional distinction between "descent groups," which have few corporate activities,
and corporate "lineages," which have many. In T'ai-ho, the groups represented by these designations are clearly consecutive stages in an evolutionary development. The fifteenth century featured the formation of
descent groups, by way of evidentiary research undertaken by members
and endorsement supplied by outsiders. In the sixteenth century, some
of these descent groups evolved into lineages. Lineage creation entailed
at least four new phenomena: (1) a downgrading of the importance
of indisputable evidence for establishing distant kinship connections;
(2) the construction of elaborate temples in honor of original founding

ancestors; (3) the creation of new means of finance for intensified ritual and other activities; and (4) the elaboration of regulatory and judicial mechanisms within and among the corporate kinship groups.

· · ·

Interesting examples exist to show that the rules of evidence insisted upon in the fifteenth century were no longer strictly followed in the sixteenth. This dispensation opened the way to the formation of some new and very large kinship conglomerates.

Two K'ang descent groups of T'ai-ho were the Chueh-yü K'ang of township 52 and the Lei-kang (Thunder Hill) K'ang of township 62. The founder of the Chueh-yü K'ang group had originally emigrated from Nanking to T'ai-ho in the Sung period. Sometime after that a branch had moved to Thunder Hill, following which, supposedly sometime in the twelfth century, one K'ang Chung-yen moved from Thunder Hill to Chueh-yü Ward as a live-in son-in-law to the Chueh-yü Chou. K'ang Chung-yen's descendants kept their original surname and stayed and multiplied in Chueh-yü.

Hu Chih (1517–85) knew these K'angs. Several of their junior members helped him organize a community compact (*hsiang-yueh*) in their part of T'ai-ho, "where the land is flat, and the great surnames live dispersed about like chesspieces." One day Hu Chih made a personal visit to the K'ang home in Chueh-yü. "Their old, high-roofed residences sit [as densely crowded together] as the scales of a fish or the teeth of a comb," he wrote. "In the crowd of greeters you could spot the elders by their thick eyebrows, white hair, tasseled caps, laced shoes, and attentively reverential air. The excellence of the younger men you could tell by the way they invited me to sit, and brought a basin, moving neither too fast nor too slow."[45]

The K'ang genealogies had all been destroyed in the late Yuan wars, and proof that the Chueh-yü and Lei-kang K'ang were kin had disappeared. Earnest research efforts by men of both groups early in the Ming had failed to find any evidence for the presumed connection. Accordingly, Lo Ch'in-shun's (1465–1547) preface to the Thunder Hill genealogy relates a wholly different founding legend from that of the Chueh-yü and makes no mention of any possible link at all.[46] Yet in this same sixteenth century, while some K'ang fed Lo Ch'in-shun one story, some other K'ang fed Yin T'ai (1506–79, of Yung-hsin County, west of T'ai-ho) another story altogether. In this latter story, the Thunder Hill and the Chueh-yü groups merge and become the T'ai-ho K'ang. Yin T'ai explained: "people [nowadays] hold ancient study in high regard, and excellent students from both K'ang groups, who had been doing well [as *sheng-yuan*] at school, felt badly that because their genealogy was not in order, it was impossible for them to teach and inspire the various family heads. So they consulted with all the elders and compiled a joint and expanded genealogy, with the first T'ai-ho ancestor as [founder] of one permanent great descent line [*ta tsung*]."[47] Thus when missing evidence threatened to frustrate a wave of enthusiasm in favor of lineage merger, the difficulty was simply swept aside. This particular merger joined two groups of approximately equal prestige and strength.

Likewise, the sixteenth century saw the coming together of the many scattered Teng people of T'ai-ho. They lived in at least three different localities there. Earlier on, Teng Ting (d. 1504) contributed from his own official salary to try to organize his kinsmen into a commune, a project that, "due to exhaustion," he eventually had to give up. Nor was he able, though he tried, to revise and update an earlier Teng genealogy. Later, his third son failed at the same task. Perhaps the problem was lost data. Finally in 1533, three Teng juniors who were *sheng-yuan* (county students) completed the genealogical revision with the advice and financial support of some of the Teng elders. This was the first complete genealogy ever done for the Teng, who had already been living some twenty generations in T'ai-ho. The genealogy was printed, and one of the juniors asked Lo Hung-hsien (1504–64) for a preface. Lo was a renowned official and Confucian thinker, but he lived in Chi-shui, two counties to the north; and he made no attempt to verify the accuracy of the research that he endorsed.[48]

Similarly with the Ch'ens. In the fifteenth century, there were at least four distinct common-descent groups of the Ch'en surname in T'ai-ho, each with a founding story completely different from that of any of the others. Of these, the Willow Creek Ch'en were the largest and most distinguished. Grand Secretary Ch'en Hsun was a Nan-liao Ch'en; and as he explained in a message to a friend of his who was a Willow Creek Ch'en, the two common-descent groups were unrelated. The Willow Creek founder had immigrated in the tenth century, whereas the Nan-liao founder had come in the early Yuan, three centuries later; and the two groups had no common ancestors.[49] Nothing could be more clear-cut than that. Or could it? Around 1570, Ch'en Ch'ang-chi, a Willow Creek Ch'en, offered an extended argument (which, strangely, he placed in an obituary for a grandmother, née Lung) that in fact the Nan-liao and Willow Creek Ch'en *were* the same, if one went far enough back in history. He asserted that Ch'en Hsun had been very reluctant to declare the two Ch'en as separate groups. "Many of the old families and great houses of our county trace themselves to ancestors who lived in the Chou or Han," he insisted, "and surely they're not the only ones who descend from an historically verifiable original ancestor."[50] So, another merger.

The Kuo case shows how kin-group unions might involve more than two parties and thus grow to enormous size. In the fourteenth century, Liu Sung found the descent record of the Kuo of Kuan-ch'ao (township 31) a confused jumble of fragments, full of gaps and copying errors.[51] Early in the fifteenth century, Liang Ch'ien reviewed the corrected record and noted that it had been improved in the light of new evidence.[52] A few decades later, Ch'en Hsun (whose second wife was a Kuan-ch'ao Kuo) wrote a detailed preface to a newly revised genealogy in which, miraculously, all the evidence fit without gap or doubtful link. (Here the acknowledged problem was that certain outsiders of the Kuo surname were trying to insinuate themselves into the Kuan-ch'ao pedigree.) The founding story, related for the first time publicly by Ch'en Hsun, now had it that the Kuan-ch'ao Kuo were all descended from an official who had made his home there in 878, in the time of the Huang Ch'ao rebellion. His four sons had all moved south to Wan-an County. Then a great-grandson of the second of them had migrated back to T'ai-ho for good, thus becoming the first Kuan-ch'ao ancestor.[53]

The greatest scion of the Kuan-ch'ao Kuo was Kuo Tzu-chang (1543–1618), an important Ming provincial official and writer. By his own testimony, he had a leading hand in establishing linkages among several large Kuo lineage branches (descendants of the settler of 878), by way of making exchanges of genealogical information. Kuo stated that, altogether, the original founder had produced some eight thousand male descendants as of the year 1600.[54] In a letter addressed to the heads of the "five" Kuo lineages, Kuo Tzu-chang said that they currently numbered some "several myriad" people altogether.[55] The number five somehow stuck. Despite the number five, Kuo never enumerates any more than four, two in Wan-an County and two in T'ai-ho. He never mentions the Kuo of nearby Ta-kang (township 29 in T'ai-ho), who had in Ch'en Hsun's time laid a vague claim to descent from one of the four ancient Kuo brothers but were no longer making that claim in the sixteenth century.[56] Nor does he mention the Kuo of Kao-p'ing (township 61 in T'ai-ho), who had made an equally vague claim to the same descent in the fifteenth century and were still making it in the sixteenth.[57]

(The Ta-kang Kuo, themselves a huge group in the fifteenth century with some eight local branches and three thousand undistinguished descendants, boasted that they were the oldest and largest of all the Kuo in T'ai-ho.)

The Kuo case shows (1) that acts of recognition of kinship connections among already large lineages could create huge aggregations, "several myriad" in the Kuo case and (2) that there was some picking and choosing as to just which lineages of the same surname were to be admitted into the aggregation. There are at least three other T'ai-ho examples of Kuo-style lineage conglomerates. The purposes behind their formation is not entirely clear. At the very least, these unions absorbed educated talents and created wider opportunities for social interaction.[58]

·   ·   ·

Besides mergers and unions, another kinship enterprise of the sixteenth century was the construction of elaborate temples to original founding ancestors. This was new. The orthodox cult of ancestral piety that T'ai-ho people observed in the fifteenth century restricted itself to modest shrines to immediate forbears rather than lavish temples to distant founders of unknown or doubtful identity.

However, there was a time in T'ai-ho, in the poorly known era of the Sung and Yuan, when it apparently was not rare for the richer lineages or common-descent groups to consign the guardianship of their ancestral cults to Buddhist or Taoist temples. As Liu Sung pointed out, people had once felt churches to be safer and more stable than lay families as protective institutions. The Yueh of Ho-ch'i Ward (township 65) had once entrusted its ancestral cult to a nearby Buddhist temple.[59] In the late thirteenth century, the Tseng of Mei-shan (township 3) delegated the management of their cult to a local Taoist temple; they also had cast and installed there a bronze image of the Jade Emperor, the Taoist god coeval with Heaven and Earth, as their lord and family guardian.[60] Yang Shih-ch'i's genealogy, lost in the late Yuan wars, had once been cut into stone and kept in a Taoist temple as well.[61] Thus in a way, the sixteenth-century construction of ancestral temples, though under lay rather than religious auspices, represents a revival of a lavish tradition of much earlier times.

At least a dozen examples of sixteenth-century temples built in honor of original founding ancestors can be found in the literature. The Ch'en of Willow Creek built one of them:

In 1541, Ch'en Te-ming, who had been assistant surveillance commissioner [of Shantung Province, 5A], and Ch'en Te-wen, [vice director, 5B, in the] Ministry of Works, conferred and said: "In antiquity, high officials used to have hereditary temples, and the completion of families used to require their producing hereditary officials. So far, we have not been able to gather the lineage together for seasonal rites in honor of our founding ancestor. That is a dereliction of propriety, and is tantamount to neglecting all our ancestors."

In 1557, a tract of land in T'ai-ho near White Crane Mountain was bought, and on it the kinsmen built a main hall, covered walkways, a shrine, and a repository for archives. It was all very impressive looking.[62]

Ch'en Te-ming, who had died by the time the temple was built, is reported as having been uneasy over the prospect that the enlarged ancestral cult would attract interlopers. He wrote: "Our founding ancestor held no higher an office than that of case reviewer. His family's income was less than middle-rank, and he settled in T'ai-ho in order to escape the upheavals [of the tenth century]. He was loyal and filial. His descendants have continued the sacrifices ever since. Unfortunately, more and more people who are not his descendants have insinuated their way into those rites."[63]

Lung Tsung-wu (1542–1609), an official exiled to Kwangtung, directed that miscellaneous income from his personal property in T'ai-ho be saved up to buy land and materials to enlarge the temple in honor of the original Lung founder, who had migrated to Kan-chu Ward (township 54) sometime in the Sung. Management of the temple and its fund was to rotate annually among the five branches (p'ai) of the Lung lineage. All the many Lung celebrants could now be accommodated. After Lung Tsung-wu died, his son asked Tsou Yuan-piao to write the dedicatory inscription.[64]

Tsou Yuan-piao (1551–1624), a native of Chi-shui County, thirty miles north of T'ai-ho, was a latter-day adherent of the Wang Yang-ming school of Confucian thought and one of the most noted imperial officials of his day, which is why he was asked to write commemorative inscriptions for the Ch'en and Lung lineage temples. Orthodox Neo-Confucianism did not countenance such temples, but now there was a new dispensation, as Tsou explained:

Chu Hsi [1130–1200] . . . stated that sacrifices should be made only to the last four generations. It isn't that he didn't want [to go further; he understood that] there was a restriction, and he didn't dare. Nowadays, everyone has been thinking about those whom their ancestors descend from, and everyone has begun sacrificing to those distant ancestors. It is quite all right to do that, provided one does not neglect one's near kin in the process.[65]

Tsou Yuan-piao made a personal visit to the Hsiao lineage at South Creek Ward (township 59). There the Hsiao settlements were spread out over several miles, and until recently, the Hsiao had maintained separate ancestral cults. A retired minor official, Hsiao Yuan-kang (1531–1610+), had built a big new temple in honor of the original local ancestor and created a common cult for all the Hsiao kinsmen. Tsou Yuan-piao appeared before the first grand congregation of Hsiao and delivered them two remarkable short speeches, first before the elders, then before the juniors:

> Do you all realize how righteous your original ancestor was? You Hsiao descendants are numerous and important, and that original ancestor is the one who gave rise to you all. Today, after the passing of many generations, you've gathered the lineage in order to reflect upon your origins.
> I've heard it said that if there is a root, then there is a time before that root emerged. There is an origin to the root, a beginning before the beginning. That's how we should think about beginnings.
> How should we conceive the situation before the beginning? There was somebody who existed naturally of himself, who accomplished things without action or intention. Things done by action always decay in time. Things done intentionally always dissolve. Those are the conditions under which you now celebrate your founding ancestor. And surely the same principle applies to this very assembly. Hsiao [Yuan-kang] leads you in this because he cannot contain his sincerity within himself. You, the lineage, respond to him for the very same reason. Only a breath of air lies between your founder and you here now. (Here the elders said: "So it is!" Then I went before the juniors, and I said):
> When people are physically strong, their pneuma circulates freely and their pulse is vigorous. But when there is any blockage, these stop. The same applies to men who harmonize their lineages. Thanks to [Hsiao Yuan-kang], your descent group has a freely circulating pneuma and a strong pulse. He went away [as an official], and he made an excellent reputation wherever he went, and when he retired home, he devoted all his thoughts to his ancestors. You see how a benevolent man cleaves to his learning!
> It is the responsibility of you all to continue in his footsteps. When you enter this hall, you must lead the congregation of kin by means of filial intentions so keen that you make it look as though [the ancestors] were actually present. If you don't make [Hsiao Yuan-kang's] mind your mind; if you don't reflect upon where your bodies come from; if you don't firm up the roots and nourish the branches—then you will come to a standstill, and you won't even be able to regulate a three-family market, let alone the realm and the state, and no one will acclaim you. So you must strive. Benevolence in the realm and in the state begin in the family.

(The elders leapt up and said: "What you've said is exactly right. We'd like you to write it up for engraving on the back of the stela [commemorating the building of the new temple]." So afterwards I wrote it up as they asked. The contributors and dates of construction are recorded elsewhere).[66]

•   •   •

The construction and upkeep of large lineage temples entailed high costs. Lung Tsung-wu's contribution included, aside from income from his own fields, a donation of a thousand taels of silver. The Willow Creek Ch'en financed the building of their temple by laying periodic assessments in silver upon each constituent family (*fang*), the amount varying according to the number of able adult males (*ting*) in each. Several "honest men" from the Hou-chieh (Back Street) branch were put in charge of the fund, which was lent out at interest and, after a few years, yielded earnings of "over a thousand [taels of] silver." It was interest earnings on silver loans that paid construction costs for the temple.

The Kuan-ch'ao Kuo lineage (in the sixteenth century, before Kuo Tzu-chang's time) collected money from their kinsmen and bought new "constant harvest" fields. Income from these collectively owned fields allowed them to raise the frequency of their ancestral rites from once to three times a year. (Unspent funds, controlled by the officers of the ancestral hall, may have been loaned at interest.)[67]

The Tseng of Yueh-Kang (Moon Hill Ward, township 32) built a temple at a former homesite on Sandalwood Lane in T'ai-ho city, as well as another in Moon Hill itself, in honor of the recent founder of that subsettlement. Rental income from collectively owned sacrificial fields funded annual birthday celebrations for the Moon Hill founder and his four wives.[68] The distantly related Tseng of Shang-mo (township 28) found their ancestral temple in disrepair and the rents from their sacrificial fields undependable, and so they levied contributions on thirty-one kinsmen. The temple was then repaired and enlarged, and more fields were purchased. A list (not preserved) was made of the donors, the fields, and the rental income amounts.[69]

One subbranch of the huge Wang lineage of Nan-fu (township 61) funded their joint ceremonies by imposing graded assessments in silver upon each of their 221 adult males, with further amounts to be paid on any of several special occasions, such as reaching age fifty *sui,* or upon the birth or marriage of an eldest son. Sixteen junior kinsmen controlled the fund and made interest-bearing loans from the surplus.

In addition, the subbranch received yearly 26 piculs from rents on sacrificial fields nearby, and a further 123 piculs from sacrificial fields they owned a hundred miles south, in Hsin-feng County, in southern Kiangsi.[70]

One could go on and list further examples of this kind, each differing in its details, but the main point in each such case is clear: that in the sixteenth and early seventeenth centuries, T'ai-ho's common-descent groups were acquiring a self-sustaining economic base that was controlled by a joint board of managers. Lineage property was in most cases taxable, but it was removed from the reach of individual ownership and inheritance. In some instances at least, joint lineage income served social welfare needs. The ancestral temple built by Chang Ssu (1465–1542, of Hou-tung Ward, township 5) had attached to it fields whose yield supported, in addition to sacrifices, a grain fund of a thousand piculs that was lent interest-free to poor kinsfolk. Those too poor to repay even the principal were placed on permanent dole, which was funded from the rent income on forty *mou* of fields especially set aside for that purpose.[71]

Thus the resource base of some T'ai-ho lineages, like the Kuan-ch'ao Kuo and the Nan-fu Wang, extended well beyond the borders of T'ai-ho itself, forming sort of a low-level colonial order, with its home base in T'ai-ho. However, it was also true that certain other T'ai-ho lineages were but constituent units in giant lineage conglomerates based outside the county. For example, from 1636 to 1638, toward the very end of the Ming era, Li Pang-hua (1574–1644) of Chi-shui County, a high official, built a great temple in the prefectural capital of Chi-an for all the Li everywhere who considered themselves descendants of a certain prince of the T'ang imperial house. T'ai-ho Lis were included. Li Pang-hua left instructions that the management of this temple and its funding should rotate among all the component Li lineage branches. He said that he chose Chi-an city because it would be easiest for large numbers of scattered relatives to gather together there.[72]

.   .   .

Finally, it needs to be pointed out that the corporate lineages that were being established in sixteenth and early seventeenth centuries in T'ai-ho took on judicial and penal functions that were not within the competence of the descent groups typical of the earlier part of the Ming.

For example, the Lung of Kan-chu Ward made their new ancestral temple not just a ritual center but also a venue for lectures on ethics and law, and a court of first instance for the adjudication of disputes among the kin.

When the Chou of Ch'i-t'ien (Lacquer Field Ward, township 51) enlarged their ancestral temple in 1570 in order to accommodate their growing population, they also instituted regulations threatening punishment for those who were lax in their ritual obligations and for those who oppressed and mistreated their poorer and weaker kin.[73] The Hu of I-ho (also in township 51) organized a "family compact" (*chia-yueh*) with an elder in charge of enforcing discipline through it.[74]

In order to suppress a wave of unruliness among his relatives, Tseng Hsin (1445–1530, of Shang-mo Ward, township 28) drew up a set of "family rules" (*chia-fan*) and had "two or three good juniors" help him admonish those who broke the rules and penalize them for misbehavior. These rules he submitted to the provincial censorial authorities, who reviewed and endorsed them and directed the prefectural and county officials to enforce them in case of appeal.[75]

About a century later, Kuo Tzu-chang (1543–1618) compiled a list of "family instructions" (*chia-hsun*) for the Kuan-ch'ao Kuo lineage. These were aimed at correcting certain disorders that he believed arose from invidious income differences among the component Kuo families. According to Kuo Tzu-chang, the lineage was suffering discord because "the rich and noble use their status to act arrogantly toward the poor and humble, while the poor and humble rely on their greater numbers to abuse the rich and noble." Affluent Kuo were dissipating themselves in drunken socializing with male and female opera performers; poor Kuo were drifting into gambling and thievery. Scheming kinsmen were cheating dissolute heirs out of their rightful inheritances. To remedy these disorders, Kuo Tzu-chang directed the lineage head (*tsu-chang*) to conduct bimonthly meetings with all the family heads (*fang-chang*) in the ancestral temple. Warnings and beatings were to be administered. If all else failed, malefactors were to be disowned and handed over to the county authorities for imprisonment.[76]

INTERLINEAGE ORGANIZATION:
THE COMMUNITY COMPACT

In the sixteenth century, and with the encouragement of imperial government, T'ai-ho's lineage leaders undertook to organize regional federations—the higher-order interlineage alliances known as "community compacts" (*hsiang-yueh*). In T'ai-ho, the first term in this expression (*hsiang*) was the same as the word for "canton," the mostly functionless territorial units into which the townships were grouped. The formation of community compacts in T'ai-ho was in fact based upon the cantons and breathed new life into at least some of them.

The earliest major example was a compact created in and for the canton of Yun-t'ing. In 1531, Lo Ch'in-shun, who had resigned from office and was living at home in Hsi-kang (West Hill Ward, township 28), joined together with Tseng Hsien of Moon Hill and several others and drew up a compact that appears to have comprised the entire area. Since a total of seventeen "elites" (*shih-ta-fu*) attended the organization meeting, held at a Buddhist temple, it looks as though all but one of Yun-t'ing's eighteen townships were represented. The conferees agreed upon a set of regulations. The regulations were later printed up into a pamphlet, together with Tseng Hsien's address to the session and poems by all. The regulations, now lost, are known to have included a reform of burial customs, a perennial source of litigation. What prompted the meeting and the compact was a sense that the old social order, which had worked well in the fifteenth century, had begun to unravel sometime during the Hung-chih era (1488–1505)—as evidenced by rising rates of idleness, luxury, and crime—and that measures had to be taken to reverse the disastrous course that society seemed to be taking.[77]

As the old tax-and-service system came to be replaced by the silver-based Single Whip regime in the latter part of the sixteenth century, the Chi-an prefectural officials sought to co-opt the lineages and the community compacts and make them part of the new tax mechanism. In 1577, the prefecture urged all nine counties (T'ai-ho was one) to organize community compacts as a means toward comprehensive social reform.

New compacts were formed in at least three of T'ai-ho's six cantons. In Yun-t'ing Canton, the compact of 1531 had in the meantime dissolved. Tseng Yü-hung (1521–88), retired from office and living at home in Moon Hill, issued a circular which succeeded in getting it revived. The circular read:

> Our canton consists of eighteen townships and nearly fifty wards. Here, earlier generations plowed and studied, valuing hard work and frugality, and observing decorum and righteousness. People despised laziness and profligacy. Thieves and traitors did not exist. This you—fathers, sons, and brothers—have all heard.
>
> But starting in the Hung-chih era [1488–1505], customs decayed from that

standard. That's why in the Cheng-te and Chia-ching periods [1506–66], two of my kinsmen who were retired officials took the lead, and Lo Ch'in-shun presided, and they met in the Nan-t'ai [temple], and what they came up with was called "Improving the Canton." This you fathers, sons, and brothers all know.

Alas, since then, the old and experienced men have died. Then in 1561 came roving bandits, and they inflicted grave damage. In the aftermath of the killing and destruction, there was no time for decorum and righteousness, with the result that our customs have been declining, litigation has been mounting, and more bandits keep appearing. This you are all painfully aware of, and angered about.

Since leaving office, I too have seen and been distressed by these things, but fortunately the authorities have called for the formation of community compacts throughout the nine counties. We must heed these wise instructions and urge each other to take action. May you fathers of the canton take note![78]

At the same time that Tseng Yü-hung tried (and, apparently, succeeded) in reviving the community compact in Yun-t'ing in southern T'ai-ho, another official, Hu Chih, temporarily retired and living at home, helped organize a first-time compact for the cantons of Hsin-shih and Kao-hsing, in western T'ai-ho.

Hu Chih's home was in I-ho Ward (township 51) in Hsin-shih Canton. The new compact, taking in the two cantons, was called the Ch'iu-jen (Search for Benevolence) Compact. Organizers and participants are known to have included, besides the Hu of I-ho, the unrelated Hu of She-pei Ward (township 51); the Chou of Ch'i-t'ien (Lacquer Field Ward, also township 51); the K'ang of Chueh-yü (township 52); and probably also the Yueh of Ho-ch'i (Grain Creek Ward, township 65).

The Ch'iu-jen compact was elaborately organized, and it acquired something of a permanent institutional base. The Chou of Lacquer Field funded the building of a special meetinghouse in a scenic location. A Confucian study society was formed there; community sacrifices to the soil and grain gods were held; and a community militia (t'uan-chieh) was assembled for defense against wintertime bandit raids. The aim of the community compact proper was to encourage reform of degenerate customs and bad behavior among the young men—in particular, the "several hundred" on stipend as boarders (kuan-ku) in the schools operated by the great lineages of western T'ai-ho.[79]

There is no particular reason to suppose that T'ai-ho's community compacts survived the upheavals of the Ming-Ch'ing interregnum of the middle and late seventeenth century. At least, there is no evidence that they did. For one thing, there were no more native sons successful enough in office, and zealous enough as Confucian thinkers, to give ex-tralineage organization at the cantonal level the spark and the push and the literary celebration that it seemed to require for its success. No T'ai-ho native in Ch'ing times ever achieved the national eminence that men such as Lo Ch'in-shun, Hu Chih, Tseng Yü-hung, or Kuo Tzu-chang did in the Ming; and the presence of such high elites as organizers and participants seems to have been required to ensure that the compacts fulfilled both the needs of the state for security and revenue, and of local society for moral reinforcement.

But patrilineal systems survived, at least in some form. As late as the 1840s, many of the old T'ai-ho patrilineages, already well known in Ming times, were still very much alive and active—cheating on their taxes, oppressing their poor relatives, encroaching upon each other's grave sites, and selling their genealogical credentials to interlopers.[80]

. . .

One is curious about how the story of patrilineages in Ming T'ai-ho compares with that of other parts of south China. Is the T'ai-ho story recapitulated elsewhere? Did what Timothy Brook has aptly called an "aristogenic" order—a corporate, kin-based upper class—also charac-terize other local societies in south China in late imperial times? It ap-pears that the answer to both questions is, generally, yes.

The compiling and prefacing of genealogies were activities well un-der way in parts of south China, Chekiang Province especially, in Yuan times, if not before, so T'ai-ho got into this game a bit late. Other coun-ties, such as T'ung-ch'eng in Anhwei and Han-yang in Hupei, were newly settled in the early Ming era, so genealogy compiling started later than it did in T'ai-ho, in the sixteenth century in the case of T'ung-ch'eng. Once created, however, local societies of aristogenic com-mon-descent groups became extraordinarily stable and durable. As in T'ai-ho, these groups often evolved further into corporate, endowed, rule-bound "lineages"—in the seventeenth century in T'ung-ch'eng and in the late eighteenth in Wu-hsi in Kiangsu.[81] In short, the developmen-tal cycle discernible in T'ai-ho in the Ming seems also to have been spun out, at one time or another, in other south China counties.

Wherever an aristogenic society was founded in the counties of south China, it was part of what Robert Hymes has called the creation of a "localist strategy," a major historical change that dates from the twelfth century, wherein a previously national elite decided to distance itself from the uncertainties of too close a tie to the capital, and develop new sources of security, identity, and livelihood for itself at home in the south China countryside.[82] There, survival and continuance were no longer so closely dependent upon success in bureaucracy. Key to the long-term survivability of the south China patrilines as local elites was what William Rowe has described as their "constant flexibility and innovation."[83] And the T'ai-ho record confirms that. Not only did the T'ai-ho aristogeny as a whole evolve in terms of its corporate organization but also members individually contributed to its continuation by constantly adapting themselves to new opportunities and constraints — to commerce, moneylending, landowning, land managing, tutoring, or degree winning and officeholding — and by pledging some good part of their income, energies, or prestige and influence to the welfare of their own kinship groups, certainly, and at times to the welfare of the larger society of such kinship groups as well.

CHAPTER 5

Pathways to Ming Government

For the young men from the city and countryside of T'ai-ho seeking employment, and every one of them sought employment of some kind, government was, without question, the firm of choice.

Not that government necessarily paid well. For the lowest civil service grade, *wei ju liu,* or "not yet in the current," the annual salary was thirty-six *shih,* about enough to feed a family of ten or twelve when paid in full. However, other living expenses besides food had to be met as well. A son or younger brother successful in the quest for office could sometimes find himself in serious debt. Yet while it was possible to earn much more in estate management or commerce, no other career could offer what Ming bureaucracy could offer: status; honor; extrastatutory income from gifts and other emoluments; literary fame; the opportunity to meet the best minds and talents of China; certain service exemptions; authorization to wear the caps, robes, sashes, and silk badges of a select elite; and a chance to immortalize oneself and honor one's ancestors, to right wrongs and create benefits for the great masses of China, and to leave one's mark in the annals of civilization. Many young men from T'ai-ho, and from all over Ming China, devoted their lives to the goal of one day becoming civil officials.

The aspirants were many, but the available positions few. Regular civil service officials held one of eighteen ranked positions, from 1A at the top down to 9B, plus the rank *wei ju liu* (actually the nineteenth grade) at the bottom. Exactly how many such positions were open, or filled, at any one time is impossible to say, but some total figures exist, supplied by grand secretaries who were probably privy to reliable information. Wang Ao, grand secretary from 1506 to 1509, counted 20,400 civil positions; Chu Kuo-chen, who held the same position from 1623 to 1625, reported 24,683 (1,146 in Peking, 558 in Nanking, and 22,709 in the rest of the realm).[1] The mandarin segment of civil government (that is, excluding some 55,000 clerks) thus had about the population size of a small city.

T'ai-ho produced at least 1,668 men who qualified themselves for official position during the 276 years of the Ming era. An explanation is in order as to exactly what that figure means. It means that on the basis of the earliest extant county gazetteer, that of 1579, and later gazetteers of the Ch'ing period, it is possible to identify, by address and by the year or reign-period of their qualification, 1,668 men. The true total must be somewhere around 2,000 because (1) 229 men are listed in the gazetteers without date, or by name only, and cannot be further identified; (2) data for the years 1580–1644 is incomplete; and (3) easily dozens of men identified as men from T'ai-ho County, Kiangsi, appear as local officials in gazetteers from other parts of China but are otherwise unknown. A national roster of officials dating to the 1630s lists eighteen men from T'ai-ho, but only four of them are listed in the T'ai-ho gazetteers; and since this particular roster omits all government teachers and princely officials, perhaps twice as many T'ai-ho men actually were in office at that time.[2] Although 1,668 is unquestionably an undercount, they are men whose identities (and, in many cases, lives) are known for certain, and it is with them that I wish to deal here.

T'ai-ho was but one of over a thousand counties (*hsien*) in Ming China, and it was a matter of great local pride that it succeeded as well as it did, especially in the fifteenth century, in placing so many of its men in imperial government. As many as 1,668 men are known because the magistrates and their assistants at county headquarters kept a perpetual list of all the locals who qualified themselves for office. It must also be emphasized that the common-descent groups and lineages endeavored to do the same thing for their members. The channel through which a man qualified himself for office and the highest post to which he rose in his official career became integral parts of his personal identity, and a proud entry in the genealogical records, where ancestors' offices, real or honorary, were invariably mentioned. If a dead person had ever held an office, the headline on his engraved tombstone inscription always stated it.

Besides gravestones (especially the *mu-piao,* whose whole text was in view for anyone to read), small monuments to deceased native sons who had been officials could be found all over T'ai-ho city and the countryside, more than two hundred of them by late Ming times, singly or in various family or other groups. In addition there were two great temples built and maintained at imperial government expense, one in memory of Grand Secretary Yang Shih-ch'i (1365–1444) and the other in honor of Ou-yang Te (1496–1554), who had been a minister of rites and a renowned exponent of the thought of Wang Yang-ming. All this shows that Ming bureaucracy made a strong and shaping imprint upon local society. Participation in that bureaucracy helped to define the local elite and contributed to the formation of a local hierarchy of prestige, not solely because of the downward force exerted upon those who were not in the bureaucracy but also because of the inducements participation offered to encourage men to rise up.

.   .   .

The 1,668+ officials T'ai-ho County produced in the Ming provide an opportunity to explore the larger world of Ming bureaucracy, particularly with respect to such issues such as the significance of the different channels through which it recruited its manpower; how the experience of having come up through a particular channel affected one's career prospects; and how these things changed over the course of the Ming.

The channels of recruitment were several, the differences among them wide; and which path one took had certain consequences for one's personal status and identity, in life and afterwards.

Around the year 1600, Kuo Tzu-chang (himself an eminent official) wrote a preface to the genealogy of the Hsiao lineage of Huang-kang (Phoenix Hill Ward, township 25), who were not a particularly distinguished bunch. In it, he listed by name and by path of entry all Hsiao who had by that time become Ming officials: two men who had won the highest degree, the "metropolitan" degree (*chin-shih*); fourteen men who held the "provincial" degree (*chü-jen*); seven men who had achieved office by way of "recommendation" (*chien-chü, cheng-pi*); twelve men who had taken one or another "tribute" (*kung*) route through one of the two imperial colleges; three more who had taken other routes through the college; and four men who had been promoted to officialdom from the ranks of the national clerical service (*yuan, li-yuan*).[3] That makes forty-two in all (fifteen of them are missing in the county lists). The Huang-kang (Phoenix Hill) Hsiao men were scarcely visible in the great aggregate of Ming bureaucracy; yet it was men like them who constituted the great mass of Ming bureaucrats and made the greatest contribution to establishing the whole presence of the bureaucracy in the life of the nation.

But just what did having entered through these different channels mean to the individuals who followed them? What larger strategic purposes did the Ming state have in mind when it established this and that track for its new recruits? Why so many tracks? (The Phoenix Hill Hsiao genealogy shows five broad categories.) These are complex questions. It seems most convenient to discuss these tracks, and to give some account of the men who entered upon them, principally in order of the kinds of pools of eligibles that each track drew upon and secondarily with respect to each track's relative prestige. Through a given track one was said to "graduate" (*ch'u-shen*), and each path created its own special "credential" (*tzu-ko*)—to use the official jargon of the time. The pool of potential recruits through the recommendation channel was for a while the largest of all, and I would like to discuss it and its place in the scheme of things first.

RECOMMENDATION (*CHIEN-CHÜ*)

The recommendation route into Ming government was an important channel of opportunity for roughly the first century of Ming rule; its prestige value was extremely variable, and it drew men up directly into government from the population at large. Recruitment by recommendation was a favorite tool of the dynasty's founder, Ming T'ai-tsu (the Hung-wu emperor, r. 1368–98). Local officials everywhere were required actively to hunt out the best and most promising men from the population at large and nominate them for employment. Typical categories under which searches and recommendations were made included "those worthy and good, square and upright"; "those possessing talent and virtue"; "those versed in the classics and refined in behavior"; and so on. After having been screened by the personnel authorities in the capital, the nominees were then assigned either to administrative positions or to government teaching positions. Not everyone passed the screening, as T'ai-ho man Tseng Ts'un-shan found out; recommended for talent at the age of forty-nine, perhaps sometime in the 1430s, he came to the capital, got nothing, and so went back to T'ai-ho empty-handed.[4] (Overall rejection rates are unknown.)

The recommendation route was an important channel of opportunity for roughly the first century of Ming rule. Some 416 known T'ai-ho men were selected for service through this channel from the inception of the Ming down to the closure of the channel early in 1459.

During Ming T'ai-tsu's reign, recommendation was mainly a means for recruiting new administrative officials (of 123 T'ai-ho men so recruited during his reign, 70 percent entered administration). From the Yung-lo era (1403–24) onward, however, priorities changed, so that nearly 75 percent of the recommendation men (212 of 287) were taken into government teaching service. (After recommendation was shut down in 1459, the task of supplying teachers was shifted to the *chü-jen* and the *sui-kung,* or county students sent as "tribute" to the imperial colleges.)

As administrators, T'ai-ho's recommendation men ended their careers in posts with the median rank of 8A; that is, half achieved posts ranked 8A or higher, and half 8A or lower. A typical 8A post was that of county vice magistrate. Thus while a handful of recommendation men did well, it is evident that the dynasty used that channel principally as a means of recruiting manpower for the very lowest levels of civil bureaucracy.

There was a time very early in the Ming when even those recommended for government teaching posts could hope to advance into the higher levels of civil bureaucracy. Early in the Ming, promotion chances were not as fixed and predictable as they later became. A good example of what was possible early but not later is provided by T'ai-ho's most famous native son, Yang Shih-ch'i, originally recommended and appointed a lowly county-level assistant instructor of *wei ju liu* rank, who eventually ended up at the very top of the civil service as grand secretary and became one of the great statesmen of the early Ming dynasty.

Though recommendation led only to the lowest administrative posts, or to the backwaters of the government teaching service, its abolition constituted a serious setback for many young men of T'ai-ho. The cumulative figures make that clear. From 1400 to 1464, an average of ten T'ai-ho men entered government through all channels every year. From 1465 to the end of the dynasty, however, the annual average dropped by half, to five men per year. Thus when recommendation ended, the other channels did not expand commensurately.

From a national standpoint, the diminution of official opportunity in T'ai-ho was surely justifiable, given the fairly constant size of Ming government and the competition of men from some 1,145 county-level units like T'ai-ho all across China. In the Hung-wu era (1368–98), when far more T'ai-ho men entered office by the recommendation path than by any other, the *total* annual average of new recruits through all channels was only around six per year. Thus over the years 1400–64, T'ai-ho's rate of ten per year was excessive, and what happened after 1464 was something on the order of an equitable downward readjustment.

It is no accident that so many T'ai-ho men entered government in the first half of the fifteenth century. Several T'ai-ho men occupying the very highest central posts in Ming government saw fit to extend patronage and protection to their county compatriots. The greatest patron was Yang Shih-ch'i. When Yang died in office in 1444, his place as grand secretary was assumed by a T'ai-ho protégé of his, Ch'en Hsun (1385–1462). In 1451, Ch'en was joined as grand secretary by yet another T'ai-ho man, Hsiao Tzu (d. 1464). T'ai-ho man Wang Chih (1379–1462), earlier a grand secretary, and long influential, in 1443 became minister of personnel. The grip of a handful of men from one county in China on the controlling levers of Ming government was quite extraordinary.

It could not last; and indeed, it did not survive the great palace coup of 1457, a critical event that has been well described in Philip de Heer's *The Care-Taker Emperor*.[5] Grand Secretaries Ch'en Hsun and Hsiao Tzu and Minister of Personnel Wang Chih were all dismissed in the aftermath of that coup, which restored Ying-tsung to the throne and inaugurated the T'ien-shun reign-period (1457–1464).

In fact, the presence of too many T'ai-ho men in government, and the recommendation channel through which so many of them came into government, came under political attack not long after the death of Grand Secretary Yang Shih-ch'i. In 1451, for example, the emperor was prompted by the censorate to order more stringent screening procedures at the provincial level for new government teachers coming up through a too wide recommendation route.[6]

In 1453, censors broadened the attack on the route by making a case of Grand Secretary Ch'en Hsun's distant cousin, T'ai-ho man Ch'en Yung (1400–56). The allegation was that cousin Ch'en Yung had attended the T'ai-ho County school as a registered student, or *sheng-yuan,* but had been expelled for poor performance. After he was expelled, he took up tutoring for a living. In 1430, an assistant instructorship opened up in Ch'ang-chou Prefecture, in what is now Kiangsu Province. From Ch'ang-chou an emissary was sent to T'ai-ho with a gift and an invitation for Ch'en Yung to assume the position. Not by coincidence, surely, the chief instructor (rank 9B) in Ch'ang-chou was none other than Ch'en Yung's brother-in-law, Yü Hsueh-shih.

Ch'en Yung first proceeded to Peking, where the recommendation was viewed favorably by the Ministry of Personnel, and then he was duly appointed. A friend got Wang Chih to write Ch'en a personal message, a kind of testimonial and letter of introduction.

After completing his nine-year term, Assistant Instructor Ch'en went again to Peking, this time for the required review and evaluation of his performance. A pleasant surprise! The Ministry of Personnel took him out of educational service and placed him in administration, as first a probationary, then a regular, investigating censor (7A).

In 1446, Ch'en's work as censor was favorably reviewed, and he was promoted to assistant surveillance commissioner (5A) of Chekiang Province. His work there involved overseeing tax shipments and directing antibandit militia, and for effectively discharging those tasks, his salary was raised.

On April 2, 1453, he was promoted to administration commissioner (2B) of Fukien Province, surely for him the capstone of an unexpectedly successful career as a recommendation man. But it was not to be. On April 9, the roof fell in on him. Lin Ts'ung, chief supervising secretary of the Office of Scrutiny for Personnel, an alert watchdog in such matters, blocked the appointment on the grounds that Ch'en Yung was an expelled *sheng-yuan* who had become an assistant instructor through special connections; that as a government teacher he should never have been brought into administration; and that he was too shallow a personality to manage successfully the new task assigned him. Grand Secretary Ch'en Hsun was unable to help him; he was forced from government, and he died three years later.[7]

It was one thing to try to confine recommendation men to low teaching posts; but there was in addition a desire on the part of some Ming officials to get rid of the recommendation channel altogether. In 1456, in a long brief he composed for the emperor, Grand Secretary Ch'en Hsun tried to hold together the crumbling status quo on behalf of his fellow locals. He explained to the emperor that T'ai-ho County was heavily populated and that it lacked enough commerce, crafts production, or farmland to occupy all its young men. Consequently, as many as 20 or 30 percent of its men made their living as primary tutors in the classics in family schools all over China. Given the tight quota restrictions on the provincial examinations, only a handful could ever hope to pass, which was why so many sought recommendations to become government assistant instructors. It was most unfair, argued Ch'en, that so many in government hated these men and considered them "filth" (*fen-t'u*), when no less a man than Yang Shih-ch'i had risen precisely through that route. Actually, confided Ch'en, the issue was not just a supposed surfeit of recommended assistant instructors from T'ai-ho; the real issue was that all the other officials out there hated everyone from T'ai-ho, himself included.[8]

The specific issue that prompted Ch'en Hsun's brief was the question whether newly recommended assistant instructors should go directly to the Ministry of Personnel (where Wang Chih was then minister) for evaluation and assignment, or whether they should be tested first at the Han-lin Academy, where, presumably, a large number would be weeded out. Ch'en demanded that they go directly to the ministry. The emperor had already ruled in Ch'en's favor on this issue a year earlier.[9] This time he responded to Ch'en's plea with a wave of the hand. He told Ch'en it was just too minor a matter to be so suspicious about.

But Ch'en Hsun's suspicions were on target; and when recommendation was abolished in 1459, the official justification was that the recommendees were ambitious men of inferior quality.[10] It may have indeed been the case that the pool of good young free-lances suitable for recommendation as teachers had dried up as more and more youth sought to enroll in the county Confucian schools (*ju-hsueh*) under the liberalized quotas that were in place by the mid–fifteenth century.

CLERICAL PROMOTION (*LI-YUAN*)

Recommendation, while it lasted, was used to recruit men from the population at large, not from the special pool of county students (*sheng-yuan*). The only other channel into regular bureaucracy for which the *sheng-yuan* did not serve as the recruitment base was the *li-yuan* channel, which drew from the body of government clerks. In the early sixteenth century, a total of some fifty-five thousand clerks were reported to have been employed at every level of government; their jobs are specified in detail in chapter 7 of the *Ta Ming hui-tien* (Collected ordinances of the Ming) of 1587.[11] The rule was that after nine or so years of satisfactory service, clerks were promotable to the lower (7B or below) grades of regular bureaucracy, just where depending upon the rank of the office they had served their clerkships in.

The T'ai-ho gazetteers list 109 men who were *li-yuan*, which is an undercount (missing, for example, are the four *li-yuan* produced by the

Hsiao lineage of Phoenix Hill). The civil service ranks that T'ai-ho's 109 listed *li-yuan* achieved range from 5B to *wei ju liu*. The median position they achieved ranked 9B, which is the worst for any of the recruitment channels.

The *li-yuan* credential was not held in respect. The Yung-lo emperor placed the entire category under official discrimination in 1411 by refusing to appoint a *li-yuan* nominated for the 7A post of censor because, he insisted, all *li-yuan* were simply after personal advantage and knew nothing of moral right or of the "big picture" (*ta-t'i*).[12] In 1428, the Hsuan-te emperor ordered a selective purge of officials holding the *li-yuan* credential and denied promotions to the rest. He also ordered a partial purge of *li-yuan* "with cap and belt on half salary awaiting official appointments." The *li-yuan* struck him and the upper echelons of the bureaucracy as often "crude" (*pi-wei*) in appearance, corrupt, or insufficiently literate.[13]

Waiting lists of clerks qualified for official appointments could grow long. Occasionally, government showed such men a bit of compassion. An official of the Ministry of Personnel indicated in 1495 that there existed a backlog of 33,900 and that the usual wait for all these men was thirteen or fourteen years, by which time many were no longer employable. His suggestion was to grant all of them retirements "with cap and belt," that is, with the status of retired officials.[14] In 1571, the Lung-ch'ing emperor lifted the native-place avoidance rule for the very lowest civil service posts (including that of granary commissioner, 9B, a typical *li-yuan* slot) because many men that low in the hierarchy simply could not afford the out-of-province travel and relocation costs.[15]

But the stigma remained. In 1576, the young Wan-li emperor, or someone acting in his behalf, denied a request from the Ministry of Personnel to promote a *li-yuan* from assistant magistrate (9A) to magistrate (7A), on the grounds that no exclerk was qualified enough.[16] Before 1469, it had been the rule to punish government students who failed or misbehaved by expelling them and forcing them to take government clerkships (though, somehow, Ch'en Yung escaped that rule). This was reckoned an effectively humiliating punishment because of the "status difference" (*ti-wei hsuan-ko*) separating students from clerks. Yet certain students, who were seen as evil, considered such demotion an opportunity. Some young and bright students reportedly flunked deliberately in order to get jobs as clerks. That had to stop, and so the emperor ruled that thenceforth the students would simply be expelled rather than be made clerks.[17]

Thus the *li-yuan* constituted something of a despised subcaste in the bureaucracy, morally and intellectually tainted by their training and their experience as clerks, consigned to the lowest positions, and liable to have their individual merits overriden by their caste stigma in promotion cases.

Some T'ai-ho people clearly shared these official attitudes. Yang Shih-ch'i's mother was one. In the 1380s, Yang Shih-ch'i was a poor boy, and as he remembered it all many years later, a neighbor who was doing very well as a clerk had liked and pitied young Yang and had sent a servant to ask his mother if he could take him on as an apprentice. Yang's mother had resolutely refused and insisted that her son continue his Confucian studies.[18] Young Wang Ching-hsien (1365–1420, from Yung-chiang Ward, township 49) was asked to fill a vacant clerkship by the T'ai-ho County magistrate. His mother, too, refused to let him accept, poor as the Wangs were at the time. The magistrate was impressed and appointed Wang a government student.[19] Obviously, status anxieties preyed upon these exemplary mothers of T'ai-ho. It seems that the decision to direct a boy into a clerical job was made early in his life, the price of that decision being his having to give up further Confucian education.

T'ai-ho's *li-yuan* list provides home addresses, which show that the 109 *li-yuan* came from fifty-seven different families, with none producing more than six. Even the most prominent and successful of T'ai-ho's lineages produced a few. But twenty-six came from obscure families, many with city addresses, whose only "output" during the Ming was that one single *li-yuan*.

One of the very few *li-yuan* mentioned individually in the literature is Hsiao Ssu-ching of Yen-chuang Ward (township 64). He was a prefectural clerk sometime during the Yung-lo era (1403–24). When his term expired, he went to Peking for reassignment and was made a document handler for General Chang Fu, earlier a top Ming commander in Vietnam. Following that, he was sent to the Ministry of Justice to learn its document system, and after a year at that, the Ministry of Personnel finally appointed him a vice magistrate (8A) in Hunan. Wang Chih, at the time a Han-lin official, knew Hsiao and had once visited his home in Yen-chuang Ward. When Hsiao's brother was about to return home from a visit to Peking, there was a going away party. The guests wrote a collection of poems, for which Wang wrote a preface. Hsiao Ssu-ching seems to have lacked a Confucian education, but Wang said in his preface that although Hsiao knew law well, he was not legalistic.[20] It appears that despite all the official prejudice, Hsiao Ssu-ching socialized well with his official betters. If as a category the *li-yuan* were despised, as individuals they might be treated quite differently.

Hsiao Lung-yu (no relation to Hsiao Ssu-ching) is also listed as a *li-yuan*. In the Chia-ching era (1522–66), he ended up somewhere as a county vice magistrate. His immediate ancestors were wealthy city people. He became a clerk because his father died young, and he thought studying law would be the best way to establish himself. (He is mentioned in the literature because he later regretted that decision, preferring to involve himself in local philosophical circles.) His career was not distinguished. After a term of service as a government clerk, he paid a sum of money to the Ministry of Works, received a cap and belt indicative of official status, was put on a waiting list for an official vacancy, and went back home to T'ai-ho. There a kinsman of his stepmother's interested him in Wang Yang-ming's philosophy, and he became a member of a study circle that Hu Chih organized in 1549. Then for ten years or so he served as a personal aide to Lo Hung-hsien of Chi-shui County (north of T'ai-ho), who was one of the leading Confucian thinkers of his time. When the Ministry of Personnel finally informed him of a vacant vice magistracy, he was reluctant to take it: "All I'll be doing is running around, getting abused and humiliated for the sake of some tiny salary," complained Hsiao. "I know for sure [the higher officials] won't accept me, and I won't do what I'll have to do for them. Rather than cringe, I'd rather stay as one of your disciples, following in your footsteps, walking through the woods and valleys, discussing things, internalizing them, and getting something for oneself from that, as a way of repaying you." Urging Hsiao to go, Lo Hung-hsien advised him that a vice magistrate's job did not lie outside the Confucian Way and that Hsiao should accept the challenge, despite the hardships.[21]

COUNTY STUDENTS (*SHENG-YUAN*)

All the other recruitment channels drew in one way or another upon the *sheng-yuan*. Young men in T'ai-ho had available to them both the county school and the larger prefectural school in Chi-an. I have found no information about how the choice was made as to which school a young man should attend and no indication that the county school was in any way inferior to the prefectural school.

T'ai-ho's county school was established in 1370 with a teaching cadre

consisting of an instructor and two assistant instructors. All the instructors were local appointees until 1404, and the all the assistants were
local until 1438.

The original *sheng-yuan* quota was twenty. All twenty *sheng-yuan*
received stipends. The annual stipend was not ungenerous: ten *shih* of
rice annually, about enough to feed three people, plus certain service
exemptions for the student's family. (Starting in 1610, the stipend was
paid in silver, at a rate of .6 ounces per *shih*.)

T'ai-ho's first *sheng-yuan* class was selected by the local officials on
the basis of the recommendations made by the new teaching cadre,
made up of local men. According to Yang Shih-ch'i (never himself a
sheng-yuan), the first class of boys, aged fifteen or older, varied widely
in character: half of them got into trouble and came to a bad end, and
of the rest, only a few eventually became officials.[22]

By 1401, the original quota was doubled by the addition of a category called added students, who received service exemptions but no stipends. Ch'en Hsun later remembered that there had been forty *sheng-
yuan* in the T'ai-ho County school in the years he attended it, 1401–14.
He also recalled a further ten or so men who, though not *sheng-yuan*,
regularly had taken the provincial exams anyway.[23] To accommodate an
evidently growing population of exam takers without school affiliation,
a final ring of supplementary students was authorized in 1447, with no
quota restrictions. School rosters from the Ming have not survived, and
so the creation of an unrestricted student category makes it impossible
to know exactly how many *sheng-yuan* there were in all at any given
time; but indications are that the numbers swelled. By 1470, the T'ai-ho
County school was cramped, moldy, and falling apart, and a major rebuilding effort ended in the enlargement of the main hall, lecture halls,
library, student housing, and kitchen.[24]

In the early years of the Ming, and as late as 1404, new *sheng-yuan*
seem to have been recruited by recommendation of the instructors and
assistant instructors.[25] Even the students themselves could make recommendations. In 1401, an investigating censor came to T'ai-ho, and,
upon discovering that there were only sixteen added students instead of
twenty, ordered each of the stipend students to recommend one candidate. Stipend Student T'ang Liu (1367–1406) made an effective repre-
sentation on behalf of his nephew Lung Ts'an (1384–1447), whom he
wanted to take on in an informal master-disciple relationship.[26] Ch'en
Hsun was recommended by Stipend Students Hsiao Hsing-shen (1380–

1429) and Yü Hsueh-k'uei (1372–1444), the son-in-law and the son, respectively, of the older sister of Ch'en I-ching (d. 1410), a minor official who was in turn Ch'en Hsun's father's first cousin. They were all fond of the talented Ch'en Hsun (who would become top-ranked *chin-shih* in 1415 and later a grand secretary). Their recommendation was accepted, and Ch'en Hsun became an added student.[27]

Though sometimes called the bachelor's degree, *sheng-yuan* status was not strictly speaking a degree at all, as were the *chü-jen* or *chin-shih* degree, but an appointment. Teaching cadres and stipend students, early on, made recommendations, but they could not appoint new *sheng-yuan*. Appointments could only be made by administrative officials: the magistrate, the prefect, and, after 1436, the regional education intendants.

Ch'en Hsun spent four years as an added student, without stipend. His family was fairly well off under his older brother's management, and the expense was affordable. In 1403 there was an opening, and the teaching cadre wanted Ch'en to take the vacated position, which carried a stipend. "However," noted Ch'en's biographer, "the private regulation of the school was that all who filled such openings had to pay a large amount to recompense the man who vacated the slot; but Ch'en was ashamed to buy the stipend, and so he declined, on the excuse that he hadn't yet tried the provincial examinations, and dared not accept the offer just yet." After failing his first try at the exams in 1405, however, Ch'en did become a stipend student. He may have avoided the fee; at least, when he vacated his slot upon passing the provincial exams in 1414, he declined payment from any of the several men vying to assume the vacated stipend.[28]

How large were these unauthorized fees paid in order for an added student to become a stipend student? To whom were they paid? The answers to these questions are not clear, but the problem was national in scope. In 1456, it was noted at court that most provincial degree winners were added students, not stipend students, for the reason that stipends were awarded by bribe, not by merit.[29] In 1468, Supervising Secretary Ch'en Hao (a Willow Creek Ch'en, no relation to Ch'en Hsun) proposed that, since the charge was often made that youths who entered the county schools of China did so mainly in order to escape service obligations, it would be best to terminate all such exemptions. The Ministry of Rites considered Ch'en Hao's proposal but refused to recommend it, on the grounds that it would "violate the old system" to do so. The emperor agreed and endorsed the ministry's position.[30] Until the end of the Ming, hints of corruption continued to hover about the national Confucian student body.

Yet, early in the Ming at least, there were occasional expulsions of *sheng-yuan*. The case of Ch'en Yung has already been noted. The early rule that expelled *sheng-yuan* must become clerks was sometimes enforced. For some reason not stated, the censorial authorities expelled Tseng Shih-jung from the T'ai-ho school. "Everyone who knew Tseng" felt the expulsion to have been unjust. Yang Shih-ch'i consoled poor Tseng with the thought that becoming a clerk was perhaps not such a bad fate after all.[31] It was indeed a bad fate for Ch'en Meng-hsing (1356–90), a grandson of Yang's maternal uncle and tutor, Ch'en Mo. Young Ch'en was devoted to his grandfather and was a good student, but his classmates thought him unsocial and arrogant; and they hated him enough to engineer his expulsion. Owing to the recent death of his beloved grandfather, Ch'en Meng-hsing went into mourning and refused to take the provincial exams. His classmates argued that the death of a grandparent was not a valid reason not to show for the exams; their argument carried, and in 1389 Ch'en was expelled. He then went to Nanking to receive his obligatory clerical assignment, but a year later he died, of severe depression.[32]

As the *sheng-yuan* population expanded all over China in the fifteenth century and later, some court officials proposed to conduct wholesale purges of their numbers. There was a proposal in 1468 to abolish the unrestricted supplementary student category altogether. Ch'en Hao successfully argued against it. His point was that some localities (including, presumably, his own home county, T'ai-ho) had many more talents than forty, and it would be disastrous simply to cut them off. They should be tested rigorously, however, to make sure they were indeed qualified.[33]

That was not quite the end of the matter. In 1494, and again in 1504, the Hung-chih emperor demanded a national purge of aged, sick, and unqualified *sheng-yuan*. On the earlier occasion, some officials interpreted the imperial order to mean the categorical abolition of all supplementary students. Certainly T'ai-ho was in an uproar. T'ai-ho County student Chou Shang-hua (1476–1520) wrote his friend Hu Hsing-kung (1469–1527) asking him what he thought of the impending purge. Hu Hsing-kung (who was Hu Chih's grandfather) was not a *sheng-yuan;* he could not afford it because he had to support his mother, wife, and four children on his income as a private tutor. Hu replied that the edict could not mean an all-out purge because in large counties (like T'ai-ho), with upwards of a thousand students, 90 percent of the students would be forced out, and many of the best of the victims would have to emigrate to smaller counties where they might successfully compete for the available quota slots. It was an abuse that so many of the *sheng-yuan* were sons of officials, and that their aim in life was simply to avoid service duties and raise themselves up from the common masses, but, according to Hu Hsing-kung, the fault for that lay with the education intendants who let them enroll. Hu urged the revival of the recommendation system, which had, after all, been aimed at commoners just like himself.[34]

One source of the problem of *sheng-yuan* inflation was that more than one official authority had the power to make appointments. Ch'en Hao raised this problem in 1468, but he could not get the court to agree that all appointment powers should be placed in the hands of the provincial education intendants (the counterargument was that the provincial administration and surveillance commissions had to help out because there were too many local schools for the intendants to manage unaided).

Ch'en Feng-wu (1475–1541, from T'ai-ho; no relation to Ch'en Hao or Ch'en Hsun) was intensely involved in just this issue, as education intendant in Hukuang and then Shansi, in the years 1504–10. Strict and conscientious, Ch'en reportedly expelled all irregularly appointed *sheng-yuan* from their schools. In a memorial of 1510, which the emperor approved, he acquired full control over the Shansi *sheng-yuan;* no other provincial-level official was allowed to interfere in appointments and evaluations.[35]

That seems to have been an exceptional arrangement. Nothing like that happened in Kiangsi Province, where T'ai-ho was located. Around the very time Ch'en Feng-wu secured his powers in Shansi, Kiangsi Education Intendant Li Meng-yang, owing to his great popularity among the Kiangsi *sheng-yuan* and his defiance of the attempts of other provincial officials to interfere with him or with the *sheng-yuan,* was put on trial and forced to retire in 1514.[36]

In the sixteenth century and later, it appears that a boy wishing to become a *sheng-yuan* had to qualify for appointment either by taking a test or by having someone influential nominate him. It appears that the teaching cadre no longer had a role to play in this respect. A case in point is Ch'en Ts'an (d. 1546), who declined an offer by his uncle (Ch'en Ch'ang-chi, who had just won his *chin-shih* degree in 1538) to recommend his appointment. "I have to make my own way," he insisted, "otherwise I won't have done it as you did it." Indeed, he soon got the *sheng-yuan* appointment on the basis of the high quality of his writing.[37]

Yang Tsai-ming competed in a boys' exam (*t'ung-tzu shih*) in 1528, when he was fourteen years old. The magistrate and education intendant both agreed on giving him the highest grade, and they appointed him a *sheng-yuan* then and there.[38] In 1483, when he was eighteen years old, Lo Ch'in-shun found himself one of "seven or eight hundred" T'ai-ho aspirants to *sheng-yuan* status; an exam was given, and Lo was one of the 25 percent who passed.[39] Kuo Tzu-chang's (1543–1618) father took him to take the *sheng-yuan* test when he was only twelve years old. The county magistrate, though impressed, advised his father to take him home and have him study some more. At age fourteen, Kuo took the test again, and, after passing further tests with the prefecture and with the education intendant, was accepted as a county *sheng-yuan*. Other T'ai-ho boys, Kuo's friends and later his official colleagues, passed those same exams: Yang Yin-ch'iu (1547–1601) at age ten; Lung Tsung-wu (1542–1609) at age fifteen.[40] Yet even exams were not free of a perception of corruption. Tseng Ch'iu-t'an (of Moon Hill Ward, township 32) took one such exam in the sixteenth century, and "when he saw that people were passed on the basis of bribes, he quit in indignation, and never came forth again. He studied in his family's library, never regretting having given up [an official career]."[41]

It should be noted that Kuo Tzu-chang was first appointed a supplementary student. He spent seven years in that category and graduated to added student upon passing an exam given by the education intendant. Two years later, he passed another exam and in the following year, 1567, was finally made a stipend student. Kuo was talented and energetic, but for lack of data, it cannot be said whether his progress through the *sheng-yuan* hierarchy was fast. Lo Ch'in-shun spent only nine years altogether as a *sheng-yuan*, but Lo was, when he started, four years older than Kuo had been.

Glimpses of student life in T'ai-ho are few and far between. The *sheng-yuan* of the 1390s are pictured working very hard at their studies. Yin Ch'ang-lung (ca. 1369–ca. 1417) "was very serious-minded and exceptionally intelligent, having benefited from the Ch'eng brothers' regimen of self-cultivation through seriousness. By day he studied for tests, and at night he stayed in the Tz'u-en Buddhist temple in [T'ai-ho's] City East, intoning texts by lamplight until midnight, then rising at the first bell at dawn."[42] Wang Chih recalled studying with junior members of the Tseng family of T'ai-ho's North Gate. He remembered how the boys' mother assigned them an empty room to study in and had a bondsman supply them with tea and lamps.[43]

There was periodic impromptu testing. Ch'en Hsun's is the only case known in detail. In 1402, the T'ai-ho magistrate set a poetry theme for the *sheng-yuan*, asking them to expound upon the lines "clouds follow the morning sun; the moon rises over the library." In 1403, a prose test was given in Chi-an Prefecture, on the theme "ending in seriousness." In 1404, Ch'en and three other students went again to Chi-an, where the assistant surveillance commissioner held a mock provincial exam. Another such official held an impromptu test in T'ai-ho in 1408. In 1409 and 1410, an administration vice commissioner came to the county and held tests for the students. In 1413, an assistant administration commissioner came and presided over an oral exam.[44]

Thus it seems the officials who tested the junior *sheng-yuan* were of lower rank than the officials who tested the senior *sheng-yuan*. Hierarchy among the *sheng-yuan* can also be seen in the fact that in 1408, by which time Ch'en Hsun had gained a reputation for the brilliance of his exams, he was appointed "school guest" (*shu-pin*) by the county instructor, with the responsibility of helping to teach the twenty added students.

There is no information available about student life during the period from the early 1440s to the sixteenth century, by which time the size of the T'ai-ho student population had ballooned from around one hundred (counting all three levels of students) to some many hundreds, perhaps a thousand. Some of the students led intense and complex intellectual lives which took them far from their original moorings in the strict need to meet examination requirements. So much can be seen from what Hu Chih tells of himself and his classmates during the years 1533–43, when he was a T'ai-ho county *sheng-yuan*. Some students actively engaged themselves in local issues; others conducted raging arguments over literary models and literary criticism; yet others formed philosophical groups for the purpose of exploring the new Confucian ideas of Wang Yang-ming. All of this activity seems distant indeed from student life a century and a half before.[45]

PROVINCIAL DEGREE HOLDERS (*CHÜ-JEN*)

The hope of all *sheng-yuan*—and it did not matter whether they were stipend, added, or supplementary students, all were equally eligible—was to pass the triennial provincial examinations for the *chü-jen* degree. Winners of that degree then proceeded in the following year to the national capital (Nanking until 1421, Peking thereafter) to attempt the metropolitan and palace examinations for the *chin-shih* degree, which was, by far, the best credential of all. But first, the provincial hurdle had to be cleared.

Over the course of the Ming, altogether eighty-nine examinations were given in the Kiangsi provincial capital, Nan-ch'ang. During the first century of Ming rule, T'ai-ho candidates did exceptionally well. After that, they did worse and worse.

It makes an interesting exercise to compare the performance of the T'ai-ho men to that of the average candidate, as far as the latter can be determined.

Over the course of the 276 years of the Ming dynasty, 555 T'ai-ho men, sometimes after several tries, passed the Kiangsi provincial exams (89 others achieved the *chü-jen* degree under other provincial quotas).

The triennial *chü-jen* quota for Kiangsi was set at forty in 1370 and was raised to fifty in 1425, sixty-five in 1440, and ninety-five in 1453, where it stayed for most of the rest of the Ming.

There were ninety-one government schools in Kiangsi: seventy-seven county schools, thirteen prefectural schools, and one subprefectural school. It was the main purpose of all of them to prepare *sheng-yuan* for the provincial examinations.

If everything had been equal, then no more than one or two candidates from any one school would have passed in any given year. At least at the outset, however, things were unequal, because under the forty quota, 30 percent of all the Kiangsi *chü-jen* were T'ai-ho men. Under the fifty quota, 12 percent were. Under the sixty-five quota, 10 percent were T'ai-ho men. But under the ninety-five quota, as the years wore on, T'ai-ho's advantage grew less and less; by around the middle of the sixteenth century, less than 1 percent of the Kiangsi *chü-jen* were from T'ai-ho, a figure that is right about where a pure law of equal opportunity would put it.

When the quota was raised to ninety-five in 1453, the unrestricted supplementary student category had already been six years in existence, and after that time, the supplementary students gradually increased T'ai-ho's *sheng-yuan* population to several hundred, perhaps a thousand. What chance, then, under these circumstances, did any one *sheng-yuan* from T'ai-ho have of ever achieving his goal of passing the provincial examinations?

It is possible to frame a crude answer to that question. Let us assume a population of one thousand T'ai-ho *sheng-yuan* of equal ability. Let us assume that an average *sheng-yuan* had a tenure of ten years, an assumption that gives him three chances at the provincial exams. There were ninety-one Kiangsi schools whose *sheng-yuan* were in the competition. The majority consisted of schools in counties smaller than T'ai-ho, so let us assume that the average body of Kiangsi *sheng-yuan* was five hundred, which gives a provincial total of 45,500. It is known that not all were certified to go to Nan-ch'ang in any given year. In fact, in 1456, more than 2,000 were. In 1534, more than 3,000 were. In 1558, there were more than 4,300 candidates, and in 1627, more than 5,300.[46] Thus, every three years, something like 10 percent of the provincial student body underwent the exams. Something on the order of ten T'ai-ho students, then, would have gone to Nan-ch'ang in any given examination year, or three hundred in a ten-year period. Thus the probability of a given T'ai-ho *sheng-yuan* even taking the exam was less than one in three (because some students took the exam more than once). The probability that any of the three hundred who took the exams might pass one of them, given a quota of ninety-five and a turnout of, say, thirty-five hundred each time, was something like one in thirty-six. Thus, the chance that any T'ai-ho student might take and pass the *chü-jen* exam was very small indeed, perhaps less than one chance in a hundred, assuming all had equal abilities and none was given special consideration. (Parameters and assumptions such as these, are, of course, always fair game for further experimentation.)

There is no doubt but that competitive pressures were intense. An official report of 1571 related news of a riot in the Kiangsi provincial capital of Nan-ch'ang by 40,000 (surely an error for 4,000) *sheng-yuan* who had just failed the exams. A rumor that one of the examining officials had played favorites fueled their outrage, and some sixty students were trampled to death in the melee.[47]

· · ·

Of T'ai-ho's 653 *chü-jen* (counting those who took their exams outside their home province), 201 (or about 30 percent) went on to pass the metropolitan and palace exams and become *chin-shih*. That left a residue of 452 men who failed one or more times at the national level but ended up on the so-called B-list as *fu-pang chü-jen,* men with a kind of second-class credential for office holding.

Chü-jen management was something of a continuing problem for central government. The Hsuan-te emperor (r. 1426–35) tried to push them all into government teaching. The Cheng-t'ung emperor (r. 1436–49) was at first willing to let those who did not want teaching posts to enroll in one of the imperial colleges, but later, in an effort to improve teaching quality, he forced all but the youngest (aged twenty-four or below) to take teaching positions.[48]

The T'ai-ho data show that, indeed, from early in the Ming down to the Ch'eng-hua era (1465–87), 70 percent of the *chü-jen* began and ended their careers as government teachers. But assignment policy changed, and from the Ch'eng-hua era on, 80 percent of T'ai-ho's provincial graduates ended their careers in administration rather than in teaching. This shift was effected in two ways: more of the men were sent to the imperial colleges for administrative training (where they were treated as a class apart from and above the regular tribute students); and *chü-jen* were regularly promoted from government teaching into regular administration. At least fifty-three T'ai-ho *chü-jen* benefited from the latter policy.

T'ai-ho men who qualified as *chü-jen* had much better careers than those who qualified as *chien-chü* or *li-yuan,* categories discussed earlier. As administrators, the highest bureaucratic ranks the *chü-jen* achieved range from 3A to 9B, with 6B being the median. (An example of a 6B post would be a subprefectural vice magistrate.) That compares very favorably to the medians of 8A and 9B, respectively, for officials holding the *chien-chü* and *li-yuan* credentials.

THE *CHIN-SHIH*

Fifty-six percent of the 201 men from T'ai-ho who achieved the *chin-shih* degree during the Ming dynasty did so after more than one try. This phenomenon is evident from a comparison of the median age at which men won the *chin-shih* degree with the median age of those who won only the *chü-jen* degree. The ages of thirty-two T'ai-ho *chü-jen* degree winners are known: they range from eighteen to forty-five, with a median age of twenty-seven. The known ages of ninety-one T'ai-ho *chin-shih* range from nineteen to fifty-three, with a median age of thirty-one.

The competition for the *chin-shih* degree was quite stiff, though only half as stiff as the competition for the *chü-jen* degree. Government set the triennial national quotas at between one hundred and four hundred, usually around three hundred, depending upon then current estimates of manpower needs at the elite levels of government. Usually, slightly less than 10 percent of the examinees passed each time the exam was given.[49] That compares to the 2 percent to 4 percent of Kiangsi *chü-jen* candidates who passed the provincial exams, and *chü-jen* pass rates elsewhere were comparable, or lower.

Within the general national *chin-shih* quota, government established regional subquotas in an effort to prevent any one region of the country from becoming too dominant. In 1436, for example, within an overall quota of one hundred, the ratio of southerners to northerners to people from central China was 60:30:10. In 1508, for a quota of three hundred, north and south absorbed the center and were then equalized at 150:150, a move which further diminished the chances of well-prepared candidates from a comparatively rich and populous southern province like Kiangsi.[50] There were yet further limits on how many men offering any one text as his classic of choice might pass. Thus T'ai-ho man Hsiao Luan (1399–1458, from South Creek Ward, township 59) failed the *chin-shih* exam of 1436 not because he wrote a bad exam but because he was one of too many offering the *Book of Documents* as his classic of choice to be tested on. As a B-list *chü-jen*, then, Hsiao was compelled to take a teaching post.[51]

Men from T'ai-ho fared extraordinary well at the national exams over roughly the first half of the fifteenth century. From 1404 to 1451, seventy-two T'ai-ho men passed the seventeen exams given. From 1454 to 1499, forty-five passed the sixteen exams given. But as the years rolled on, things got worse and worse for T'ai-ho, as of course they did also at the provincial exam level. From 1502 to 1550, thirty-four passed the seventeen *chin-shih* exams given. From 1553 to 1598, twenty-one passed the sixteen exams given. And from 1601 to 1642, sixteen passed the fifteen exams given. The fading visibility of T'ai-ho men on the national scene mirrors the declining fortunes of Chi-an Prefecture and of Kiangsi Province as a whole in the national competition, as men from the southeastern coastal regions gradually assumed complete dominance over them.[52]

But in the early fifteenth century, things were good indeed. In the examination of 1421, Yang Shih-ch'i was chief examiner. There were three thousand candidates, and the *chin-shih* quota was two hundred.

Seven T'ai-ho men made it. The B-list quota was three hundred, and nine T'ai-ho men made that. There were twenty-five hundred outright failures; of them, only four were from T'ai-ho.[53] In 1427, two thousand candidates, fifty (!) of them from T'ai-ho, gathered in Peking, hoping to make the one hundred quota set for that year. Six T'ai-ho men succeeded in achieving their *chin-shih* degrees. That year there was a B-list quota of 470, but how many T'ai-ho men made it is not stated.[54] These were, obviously, inordinate success rates for a single county, and there is no reason to suppose that they could have been sustained forever.

The bureaucratic careers of men holding the *chin-shih* degree were better by far than the careers of those who entered government service through other channels. The highest official positions obtained by *chin-shih* degree winners from T'ai-ho ran the gamut from grade 2A to 9B (one man demanded a prefectural instructorship, 9B, for personal reasons), with 5A as the median rank attained. (Vice prefect, assistant surveillance commissioner in the provinces, and bureau director in one of the six ministries in the capital were typical 5A posts.)

TRIBUTE (*KUNG*)

What happened to those who failed the examinations? It was the destiny of all but a tiny minority of *sheng-yuan* to fail repeatedly at the provincial exams. After repeated failures, many *sheng-yuan* just quit, but it was possible for some, through testing or through seniority or perhaps through bribery and special connections, to advance to the rank of stipend student. For county-level units of government like T'ai-ho, the number of stipend students was restricted to twenty. Stipend students were placed on a waiting list for the annual tribute (*sui-kung*) through which they were sent up one or two at a time either to the northern imperial college in Peking or to the southern one in Nanking. After 1441, the usual rule was for counties to send up one tribute student every two years; subprefectures two every three years; and prefectures one every year (Nationally, all schools sent up some 855 annual tribute students every year.)[55]

The plan, not always followed consistently, was for those sent up through the tribute channel to spend ten years as imperial college students (*chien-sheng*), then three years in job training (*li-shih*), usually as document drafters and checkers. At that point, the imperial college students were considered qualified for appointment to a range of low-level positions in administration, or as teachers in the national Confucian educational service. Actually, residency requirements for *chien-sheng* were often waived; and job-training stints were shortened or lengthened, depending on the size of the *chien-sheng* backlog and the current level of the government's need for the clerical work that the students performed.

Over the course of the Ming, T'ai-ho produced over 404 men who qualified themselves for office through annual tribute to either of the imperial colleges as *sui-kung chien-sheng*. What was their fate? Thirteen of them died before ever receiving an appointment. Eight retired unappointed, but with the cap and belt of official status. What happened to ninety-three of them, mostly of the Wan-li period (1573–1620) and later, is unknown owing to missing records. Of the remaining 290 men, 172 (60 percent) entered and remained in government teaching service, mostly at ranks lower than those of the *chü-jen*. Over half the *chien-sheng* who were appointed teachers were never promoted beyond the lowest rank of assistant instructor. Those 118 *chien-sheng* appointed to administrative posts eventually achieved offices whose ranks ranged from 4A down to *wei ju liu*. The median rank was 7A, clearly above the median ranks of the *li-yuan* (9B) and the recommendation men (8A), and just as clearly below those of the *chü-jen* (6A) and the *chin-shih* (5A).

·   ·   ·

I would like to take a moment to say something about government teaching because so many of T'ai-ho's *chü-jen* and *chien-sheng* were appointed to teaching positions, rather than to administrative ones. In fact, a total of 514 T'ai-ho men, recruited from virtually every pool except the *li-yuan*, spent their entire careers as government teachers. That constitutes 30 percent of all the T'ai-ho men who qualified themselves for office during the Ming, which is a substantial number and an important component of the collective experience of T'ai-ho society with the larger world of Ming governance.

Confucian schools were established in each of some fifteen hundred prefectures, subprefectures, and counties in China, as well as in a further number of military guards communities and regional princely establishments scattered about the realm. Just counting the regular civil units of government, there were, until the sixteenth century, some 5,244 teaching posts available: 1,564 instructorships and 3,680 assistant instructorships. (During the sixteenth century, some 612 assistant instructorships were abolished).[56]

The educational function of government was treated quite separately from administrative function, and the former lay distinctly beneath the latter in prestige. The highest local teaching post, that of prefectural school instructor, was ranked 9B, the same as the lowest regular rank in the administrative hierarchy. All other local teachers were ranked *wei ju liu* (effectively grade 19). The capstone of the teaching service was the imperial college staff, in Peking and Nanking, where there were altogether sixty-five positions, ranging from *wei ju liu* to 6A, for directors of studies. The college staffs were recruited mainly from *chü-jen* with good records as local teachers, but the deans (or rectors, 4B) were typically *chin-shih* appointees from regular administration, not former teaching officials at all. Rectors aside, government teachers were seldom promoted into administration. They were also issued insignia that displayed their inferiority to administrative officials at the same grade.[57]

Teaching may have been a respected function in Ming China, but that respect was clearly not shown in pay or prestige for the official teaching hierarchy. Out in the localities, government teachers were required to produce a given number of *chü-jen* per year and were penalized in various ways if they failed to do that.[58] Even early in the Ming, when education was not quite yet the dead-end service it eventually became, Yang Shih-ch'i noted that educational posts were considered "cold jobs" (*leng chih*), i.e., out of the bureaucratic mainstream, and were definitely not the first choice of the majority of T'ai-ho's ambitious young men.[59]

As much as 25 percent of the manpower of Ming civil bureaucracy was destined in fact to prepare *sheng-yuan* to become teachers of other *sheng-yuan*, who in turn prepared *sheng-yuan* yet elsewhere to become teachers to yet other *sheng-yuan*, and so on and on, in endless loops that, over time, snaked their way this way and that through the whole country.

·   ·   ·

To return to the *chien-sheng*, many of them were eventually appointed government teachers—to prepare *sheng-yuan* to pass the very provincial exams that they had, by definition, failed at themselves. It is little wonder their prestige was low.

Ming records are replete with expressions of concern about how to clear the huge backlogs of *sui-kung chien-sheng* awaiting their first official appointments. Little could be done about the matter. The T'ai-ho data, though thin, support the assertions of Ming government itself that the tribute students were old men by the time they at last became officials.[60]

There was, for example, Tseng Jen (1459–1543), from a prominent and successful lineage, the Tseng of Yueh-kang (Moon Hill Ward, township 32). Ou-yang Te remembered him well and wrote his epitaph. When Ou-yang Te became a *sheng-yuan,* at the age of fourteen (ca. 1510), Tseng was already fifty-one and well known locally as an authority on the *Book of Changes* in the orthodox Ch'eng-Chu interpretation, and he had already been a stipend student for some years. Though he always did well on the school tests conducted by the education intendants, he kept failing the provincial exams. Ou-yang Te shot right by him, achieving his *chü-jen* degree in 1516 (at the age of twenty) and his *chin-shih* in 1523. In 1523, poor old Tseng was sixty-four years old and still a county stipend student. Then in 1525, recalled Ou-yang,

> Tseng was placed first on the county *sui-kung* list, and [his classmate] Lung Chin was placed second. The tribute rule was to test two men from each county, with the better of the two getting the selection. The education intendant tested them, and decided that Tseng's writing was the better, and that therefore he should be selected for tribute. But Tseng declined, on the grounds that Lung Chin's writing was not necessarily worse than his own, and, besides, Lung was the older. [So grateful was Lung, of Kan-chu Ward] that he called Heaven's blessings down on Tseng in the presence of everyone, and that made Tseng famous: as "Master Tseng of T'ai-ho, who yielded his slot as *sui-kung.*"[61]

Three years later, Tseng himself finally got his reward and became a *chien-sheng,* at the age of sixty-nine. At some later date, he was made assistant instructor at a Confucian school in an educationally backward part of Kwangtung Province and was said to have done well there. He retired with enough vigor left to help enlarge his ancestral temple and lend grain.[62] He died at eighty-four. Lung Chin, old as he must have been, also lived long enough to be appointed an assistant instructor.

These appear to be extreme cases, but clearly the waiting time for those on the list of expectant *sui-kung* could at times be measured in decades. But there were ways to circumvent the bottleneck of the student tribute system; of these, purchase was by far the most common.

Purchase of *chien-sheng* status was known, euphemistically, as "regulation tribute" (*li-kung*). Central government openly established this purchase system for the first time soon after the security crisis of 1449, when the Mongols captured the emperor and held him hostage. It was reinstituted intermittently after that, at times when government found itself short of revenues. At least eighty-one T'ai-ho *sheng-yuan* took advantage of Ming fiscal crises to buy their way around the formidable logjam of the annual tribute system.

In 1517, a silver payment schedule was issued for those who wished to become *li-kung*. Stipend students were asked to pay 200 taels, added students 280, and supplementary students 340.[63] In 1537 these schedules were reissued and eligibility was extended to include failed *sheng-yuan* (price not noted). A price list of 1550 made official positions available to all *chien-sheng* who wanted to leap to the front of the waiting queue (a grade 7 post in the capital went for fifty taels, and one in the provinces for thirty).[64]

Sales of *chien-sheng* status were, to be sure, susceptible to terrible abuse; but sales offers seem to have been made mainly to men who were probably qualified anyway. Nevertheless, from the official documents and discussions recorded in the *Veritable Records*, it is clear that the *li-kung* were resented by their *sui-kung* classmates and heavily discriminated against by the upper classes of officialdom, and thus they constituted yet one more despised bureaucratic sub-caste, rather than a den of moneyed privilege.

The T'ai-ho evidence shows that, indeed, the *li-kung* were treated worse than the *sui-kung* were. Virtually all *li-kung* were appointed to low-ranking administrative positions. The median rank at which they ended their careers was 8A, marginally below the 7A median for *sui-kung*.

Who were the *li-kung*? It goes without saying that they came from wealthy T'ai-ho families. Interestingly, almost all of them came from academically successful families. Thirty-three *li-kung* were the sons or grandsons of prominent officials. It appears safe to say that, at least in T'ai-ho, the opportunities provided by the Ming state to buy preferment attracted not crass parvenus but the luckless or restless sons of the socially respected upper crust.

The lives of some half dozen T'ai-ho *li-kung* are known in some detail. One was Yang Ch'un-sheng of T'ai-ho city. These Yang were eminent and successful indeed, being descendants of Grand Secretary Yang Shih-ch'i. Yang Ch'un-sheng was the fourth of five sons of Yang Tso, who had won his provincial degree in 1525 and had ended his career a subprefectural magistrate (5B) in the 1540s.

Ch'un-sheng was bright, and his kin confidently expected him to succeed at least as well as his father had done. But as an added student in the T'ai-ho County school, he failed four times at the provincial exams, and so he paid a required sum and became a *li-kung*.

At the imperial college in Nanking, he proved an excellent student, and so was permitted to take the provincial exams for the southern metropolitan area that were held in Nanking. Three times he failed at those. At the age of forty-two, Yang had failed seven times in twenty-one years, and on the basis of examples he had read about in the Han dynastic history, he decided he could still achieve something worthwhile as a *li-kung*. How else could he even begin to satisfy the expectations his family had placed upon him? So he took "a substantial sum of money" and proceeded to Peking to buy a post from the Ministry of Personnel. His wife, Mme Tseng, a wholesaler in rice and salt back in T'ai-ho, provided the money. Alas, Yang died en route of a fever that same year.[65]

Wang I-chueh (1532–83, of Nan-fu Ward township 61) also had intellectual credentials in addition to money. His relatives included uncles who were *chü-jen;* officials; scholars; and devoted followers of the thought of Wang Yang-ming and Chan Jo-shui. Wang seems to have been a bit impatient. He became a *sheng-yuan* at age twenty-three, and three years later he bought into the Peking imperial college as a *li-kung*. At twenty-nine, he made a payment to the Ministry of Personnel and was then assigned the post of assistant office manager (8A) in the Directorate of Imperial Parks. After his nine-year term expired, he went home to manage lineage affairs and, from time to time, to attend Hu Chih's lectures on Confucianism.[66] His example shows how money could oil the frozen gears of official selection and placement.

For a favored few *sheng-yuan,* a special route into the imperial colleges was available: this was the *yin* (protection privilege) route, which one could take if one's father or grandfather had risen high enough in Ming bureaucracy. Upon promotion to a position ranked 3 or better, officials were permitted to nominate a son, sometimes also a grandson, for admittance into one or the other of the imperial colleges (in a few cases early in the Ming, the *yin* privilege led to a direct official appointment, bypassing the colleges).

Of thirty-four T'ai-ho sons and grandsons granted the protection privilege in the Ming, twenty-three eventually got official positions, all but one in administration. The median final position reached by these men was 7A, the same as that for the *sui-kung chien-sheng.*

In the colleges, the *yin* men were designated as *kuan-sheng,* or "offi-

cial students." It is apparent that, like the *sui-kung,* they could expect
to spend many years actually or nominally present in the colleges before
a post was assigned them. College matriculation dates are often known
from entries to that effect in the *Veritable Records.* The dates of first
appointments are sometimes known from other sources, mainly gazetteers. In the case of four men, both years are known, and these show
that these particular men spent from fourteen to twenty-nine years lan-
guishing as *kuan-sheng.*

On November 11, 1496, the emperor endorsed the petition of Chang
Ta (1432–1505, from Hsiu-ch'i, at T'ai-ho City West), at the time chief
minister (3B) in the Court of Imperial Entertainments in Nanking, to
have his son Chang Yin admitted into the imperial college under the *yin*
rules. So Chang Yin enrolled, and there he stayed, until 1525, when at
last he was appointed vice magistrate (8A) of little T'ai-p'ing County in
Chekiang Province, whose gazetteer notes, laconically, that "because his
salary came by inheritance, he tended to be insubordinate, and for that
reason he was [soon] dismissed."[67] (Other T'ai-ho *yin* men seem to have
bent better to bureaucratic discipline.)

•   •   •

This chapter has tried to sketch out the story of the experience of T'ai-
ho men with the world of Ming government, and the moment has now
come to offer some broader perspectives on issues that the discussion
has raised. One issue is the nature of Ming bureaucracy. Another issue
is regional and local competition for office. A third issue is the larger
implications for local society of the results of that competition.

The local T'ai-ho data reveal certain things about the nature of Ming
bureaucracy that might not be so easily found out by studying that bureaucracy from a purely national perspective. For one thing, the data
show the crucial importance of credentialing in recruitment and in promotion.

It is possible to see how credentialing—getting recommended, winning a degree, entering the imperial colleges, etc.—was not so much
an arbitrary creation as a cultural and institutional adaptation to the
mathematical laws of hierarchy.

To demonstrate that idea, one needs only to know the total size of
Ming civil bureaucracy (twenty to twenty-five thousand) and then to
estimate the number of hierarchical levels that it contained. A case can
be made for some five to nine levels; the choice is not crucial to the
essence of the matter. If five, then we place the emperor on level one; 12

grand secretaries and chief ministers, say, on level two; 144 other important central officials on level three; 1,728 provincial and prefectural officials on level four; and 20,736 local, educational, etc. functionaries on level five. (This configuration results from the choice of twelve as the average number of direct subordinates controlled by any immediately higher official.) The total number of men in this theoretical hierarchy comes to 22,611—very close to the actual size of Ming bureaucracy.

All things being equal, what are any one man's chances of promotion into a vacant higher-level position from a lower level in this theoretical bureaucracy? Exactly one chance in 20,736 for those on level five, one chance in 1,728 for those on level four, and so on up the ladder. There are some further features to be noted. There ten times as many men on the lowest level (20,736) than there are on all the other levels added together (1,885). The higher a person stands in the hierarchy already, the better his chances for (further) promotion are. If one assumes seniority to be the only qualification for promotion and an average career to be twenty years long, then a man on level five in this hierarchy will spend about 92 percent of his career there and 8 percent of it (or less than two years) on level four. (If level one, the emperor's position, were open to everyone for promotion on the same basis, then everyone would serve as emperor for about half an hour!)[68]

In this light, one can understand credentialing as an adaptation to the intractable realities of promotion in hierarchical systems. The Ming established a complex series of fast and slow tracks, and we have seen just what these were and have identified them as fast or slow on the basis of the median rank of the final post the men who entered them achieved. Demeaning as it may have been, slow-tracking was the method seized upon by a highly competitive society for justifying the lowering of the expectations of the vast majority of its officials and for reducing competition for scarce positions in the upper bureaucratic echelons. (It may also be noted that the *chin-shih* credential, which opened the fastest track, was itself differentiated into fast and slow tracks, depending largely upon one's final ranking [1–100, 1–300, etc.] in the palace examinations.)

Also at issue is the question of the places of Kiangsi Province, Chi-an Prefecture, and T'ai-ho County in the national competition for office. Ho Ping-ti's *The Ladder of Success in Imperial China* pointed out long ago how, with respect to the output of *chin-shih,* Kiangsi Province led the nation in the fifteenth century, only to lose out to Chekiang in the sixteenth, and to fall even further behind in the seventeenth. Ho's study, now a classic, also noted that during Kiangsi Province's fifteenth-century heyday, Chi-an Prefecture played an absolutely dominant role, both among Kiangsi prefectures and among all other prefectures in the realm; and that as Kiangsi's place among the provinces of China fell lower and lower, Chi-an Prefecture's place among the prefectures of Kiangsi did exactly the same.[69]

Ho professed himself unable adequately to account for the extraordinary socioacademic success of Chi-an Prefecture in the fifteenth century. It cannot be adequately accounted for here either, because (1) the question demands further research from a national perspective and (2) there were no prefecture-wide institutions through which common efforts toward turning young men into *chin-shih* might have been exerted. In addition, there was little sense among the prefectural elites that they were prefectural compatriots above and beyond all other possible modes of self-identification. The sense of county citizenship was stronger by far than any sense of being from the same prefecture or from the same province.

However, to continue Ho's paradigm of rise and decline in the output of *chin-shih*, it can be shown that as Kiangsi declined relative to the rest of China, and Chi-an declined relative to the rest of Kiangsi, T'ai-ho County also declined relative to the other eight counties that constituted Chi-an. *Chin-shih* degree winners from T'ai-ho were some 25 percent of the prefectural total from the time of the Ming founding down to the mid–fifteenth century; then their place declined slowly relative to that of competitors from the other Chi-an counties through the sixteenth century; finally it plunged to the 10–15 percent range in the first half of the seventeenth century—about where the principle of equal opportunity dictates it should have been all along.

Kiangsi men and Chi-an men of the sixteenth century were themselves aware of their declining place in the national scene, and Kiangsi man Lo Ch'i (1447–1519) thought he could explain it. He noted that when Szechwan Province bloomed in the Northern Sung, Kiangsi was obscure and far behind. Then later in the Sung, Kiangsi in turn burst forth all of a sudden. In the early Ming, Kiangsi was the cultural center (the *Tsou-Lu*) of China, but in later years it "lost sixty to seventy percent of its former fame," being regularly outperformed by other provinces. Lo's explanation was that the unpredictable motions of the cosmic process, the "spiritual energy [exuded by the] mountains and rivers" (*shan-ch'uan chih ch'i*), were responsible for these shifting fortunes. But he thought Kiangsi would some day rise again; one must just keep working hard, and wait.[70]

Finally, what does the competition for office in Ming civil bureaucracy reveal about the society of T'ai-ho, its common-descent groups and lineages in particular?

It is possible to identify T'ai-ho's more than 1,668 Ming officials with some 328 different common-descent groups and lineages.[71] If one considers each such lineage as a unit of production, competing against all the other units for the sale of its products to the Ming state, then one can see that success was by no means evenly distributed among the units.

The 328 units sort down into three or four giant firms, a hundred or so firms of middle to small size, and a huge number (204) of tiny operations, producing only one or two officials each over the whole course of the Ming. The biggest producer of all, by far, was the Ou-yang group, of Shu-chiang Ward (township 61), with 125 officials, including fourteen chin-shih. Next biggest was the Wang of Nan-fu Ward (also township 61), with fifty-eight officials, including four chin-shih. The three largest firms produced almost as many officials (236) as did the smallest two hundred and four (259).

When all 328 units are taken as members of a competitive elite, it is evident that T'ai-ho's elite was dominated by an oligarchy of unusually successful common-descent groups and lineages. And it bears keeping in mind that beneath this entire "oligopolized" elite lay a "gray" area of unknown size whose families produced no officials, though they tried; and a "white" area, again of unknown size, whose families never entered the competition at all.[72]

PART THREE

T'ai-Ho Literati in the Wider World of Ming China

CHAPTER 6

Colleagues and Protégés

The Fifteenth-Century World of
the T'ai-Ho Grand Secretaries

The question of how the people of T'ai-ho County fit themselves into the rest of Ming China must be considered in the light of the lives, thoughts, and often stormy careers of its leading literati—the very men whose writings provide the information that has made it possible to build the preceding series of changing local profiles of landscape, resource management, demography, and genealogy.

While landscape evaluation, social and demographic behavior, and bureaucratic recruitment rates changed over the course of the Ming, the wider intellectual and emotional preoccupations of T'ai-ho's literati changed also. Indeed, there took place a series of shifts in outlook so distinct that it is hard to imagine a member of one generation conversing easily with a member of another. There is little common ground between members of successive generations (between, say, Yang Shih-ch'i and Yin Chih) and virtually no common ground between widely separated generations (such as Liu Sung's generation in the early Ming and Hsiao Shih-wei's in the late Ming). In the sixteenth century, there were irreconcilable philosophical disagreements between two nationally prominent contemporaries, Lo Ch'in-shun and Ou-yang Te. The following chapters try to describe and explain these differences in a systematic way.

·   ·   ·

In the Yuan dynasty (1279–1368) for the first time enough becomes known of the details of the lives of T'ai-ho's "upper-class" men to allow us to begin to sketch a picture of how they thought, how they behaved, and how they placed themselves in the competition for fame and fortune, both in local society and in the broader landscape of China as a whole.

The atmosphere of Mongol-ruled China, certainly in the early to middle decades of the fourteenth century, and during the civil wars of the 1350s and 1360s, opened avenues for the expression of individual prowess, arrogance, conceit, and swagger.[1] In 1368, however, the new Ming dynasty made the radical regeneration and ethical remaking of the whole Chinese people its prime objective. Ming moral propaganda was intense, and Ming penal repression was unusually savage; and one can see signs of the effectiveness of the new Ming program for national psychobehavioral rectification in the new patterns that developed in the minds and thoughts of the men of T'ai-ho. Arrogance and conceit became dangerous in the extreme. A more cautious and more harmoniously interactive social style took their place.

The Ming founder had a liking for certain men from Kiangsi. They appeared to him talented, learned, frugal, unpretentious, and quick to grasp and conform to his vision of a new order for China.[2] The Kiangsi intelligentsia had no part in shaping the framework of Confucian ideas that rationalized the new Ming despotism; that was the work of men from Chekiang. But the ability of a few Kiangsi men, like T'ai-ho's Liu Sung (1321–81), to participate in it effectively certainly helped make it a success; and the good example set by Liu Sung also helped open the way to the later influx of Kiangsi men into Ming bureaucracy in the early part of the fifteenth century.

In the first half of the fifteenth century, T'ai-ho men entered Ming government in extraordinary numbers. From 1403 to 1457, more than 453 of them, or about ten men every year, entered bureaucracy through one or another of the available channels.

Atop this great surge stood T'ai-ho men Yang Shih-ch'i, Wang Chih, Ch'en Hsun, and Hsiao Tzu, who assumed the very highest positions in the Ming realm. They also helped their T'ai-ho compatriots in every way they could.

These T'ai-ho men, who were national leaders and beneficiaries of the Yung-lo usurpation of 1402, championed a distinct moral and social ethic. As long their leader, Yang Shih-ch'i, lived, they abjured individual conceit and assertiveness. They disliked uncompromising moral stances, and they did not pursue justice. When the Ming state abused one or another of their friends or protégés, they did not rally to his defense. Instead, they quietly commemorated his name and succored his survivors.

The T'ai-ho grand secretaries placed great value on their personal and social ties to other men from back home, and these they articulated as an ethic of collegiality and patronage. T'ai-ho men, they argued, deserved to be officials because they could be relied upon to be honest, hardworking, uncomplaining, and observant of regulations. The grand secretaries knew those men and could vouch for them.

It must be stressed that this was a new ethic. It was certainly not in evidence among the T'ai-ho men of the Yuan dynasty. It managed to last for half a century. Born in the palace usurpation of 1402, it came to a resounding end in the palace coup of 1457.

THE RISE OF T'AI-HO COLLEGIALITY: BLOODY NANKING, 1402

The Ming founder, T'ai-tsu, was succeeded as ruler by his grandson, the Chien-wen emperor, in Nanking in 1398. The new government at once undertook ambitious plans to remake China both politically and morally. One plan was to recentralize power by ridding the realm of the militarized princedoms the founder had recently created in the mistaken belief that, because they were ruled by his sons, they would serve reliably as a bulwark for his dynasty.

The Chien-wen government suppressed the weaker princedoms first, leaving the strongest (the princedom of Yen) for last. That was a strategic blunder. The prince of Yen, who was the new emperor's uncle, had time to prepare and take to arms. On July 13, 1402, after three years of civil war, the prince of Yen's army burst into Nanking. The Chien-wen emperor's palace went up in flames. No sure trace of the emperor was ever found again, though there were recurrent rumors that he had escaped. The prince of Yen, usurper, seized supreme power in Ming China. He ruled as the Yung-lo emperor until his death in 1424.[3]

The entry of the rebel prince into Nanking presented the civil bureaucrats of the Chien-wen government with a range of terrible moral and personal choices to make: whether to flee, to commit suicide, to resist—or to surrender to the usurper and join his government.

According to one source, 453 officials fled into permanent hiding.[4] Others had so closely identified themselves with Chien-wen national policy, or had been committed for so long to the idea of government as the crowning expression of the Confucian moral vision, that they felt compelled to make verbal defiance of the usurper the last act of their lives. The celebrated Fang Hsiao-ju, one of the moral architects of the Chien-wen order, was chief among these; but there were others, and it became a task of later generations to compile lists of their names and horrifying descriptions of their final moments. Friends and relatives of the protesters were also arrested and exterminated in some number. (One hundred and fifty-one kinsmen of Vice Censor-in-Chief Lien Tzu-ning were executed and another hundred or so exiled after Lien, his tongue having been cut out, wrote a defiant statement in blood on the floor in the usurper's very presence.)[5] The list runs on and on. The gestures of defiance and the cruel retaliatory slaughter create a cumulative picture of tragedy and horror with few parallels in history.

There were several T'ai-ho men serving in government in Nanking in the summer of 1402. None of them volunteered to join in this bloody public spectacle. However, one of them, Chou Shih-hsiu (1354–1402, from Chü-kang Ward, township 55), quietly committed suicide. Chou had come into government by way of recommendation as a "classics expert" and had been appointed first a county assistant instructor. Later he was made moral mentor (8A) to the prince of Heng and concurrently an assistant in the Han-lin Academy. It is likely that his sponsor was Fang Hsiao-ju.

Clearly the usurpation placed Chou in an impossible position. He had been friendly with the Chien-wen emperor. He had published works on Confucian ethics. He had warmly supported the failed policy of eliminating the armed princes. He had even gone so far as to argue that a prince's generals and officials must refuse to carry out any princely order that did not conform to ritual and law (li-fa). Had he chosen to live on, he could never have hidden all this or explained it away.

Quiet suicide was Chou's way out. (Unlike public protest, quiet suicide did not implicate one's relatives and friends.) On July 15, 16, or 17 (the dates vary), a few days after the fall of Nanking, Chou Shih-hsiu wrote farewell notes to his family, friends, and colleagues, walked to the prefectural Confucian school, and there hanged himself with a belt. The Yung-lo emperor, informed of the suicide, declined a suggestion to sentence Chou to posthumous execution. "He ate [his ruler's] salary, and he gave his all for him in return," Yang Shih-ch'i reports Yung-lo as having said.[6]

There were also rumors of a wider suicide pact. An unconfirmed but widely believed story had it that about the time of the fall of Nanking,

Chou Shih-hsiu and a half dozen others, Yang Shih-ch'i among them, vowed to commit suicide as a group but changed their minds; Chou was the only one brave enough to go ahead with it.[7]

Yang Shih-ch'i's behavior in Nanking in the summer of 1402 lends a certain perspective on the origins of the collegiality ethic that he soon came to espouse. Yang had risen in Ming service in much the same fashion as had Chou Shih-hsiu. Sometime in the late 1390s he was recommended and appointed a county assistant instructor. Then he left service. By some further recommendation procedure that is not clear, he was called to Nanking as an editorial assistant in the Han-lin Academy, just as Chou had been. There was a large literary project underway at the academy, under the general editorship of the Confucian reformer and moral visionary Fang Hsiao-ju; hence the need for bright young assistants.[8] Yang himself recalled, some years later, that he had been singled out for special praise by the general editor—whose name he declined to mention.[9] Of course it was Fang Hsiao-ju.

Then at some point the Chien-wen emperor had all the editorial aides go over to the Ministry of Personnel and take a written test. Yang remembered how the minister himself had read his test, ranked it number one, and exclaimed: "Here we have a usable talent who understands current affairs. His is not just a literary talent."[10] Yang was then given formal office as director of the disciplinary office (6A) to one of the Ming princes. In 1400, he was appointed a Han-lin expositor-in-waiting (6A).[11]

On July 13, 1402, the day that Nanking fell, twenty-six officials of the Chien-wen court, Yang Shih-ch'i among them, went to the headquarters of the prince of Yen and offered him their services.[12] On July 17, the prince—by then emperor—accepted. He soon made Yang Shih-ch'i one of an inner group of seven confidential palace advisers. In the coming years, this group would gradually assume formalized shape as the grand secretariat.

Thus the central enveloping circumstance in the formation of a collegiality ethic was a tainted moral-political act. Whether or not Yang Shih-ch'i actually made and then broke a pledge of suicide, he gave his loyalty to a usurper. The usurper soon made him an editor of the *Veritable Records* of the preceding Ming reigns. Acceptance of that duty required Yang Shih-ch'i's complicity in the official lie that the Chien-wen emperor had not been the founder's chosen successor, that both he and his reign had therefore been illegitimate. History was rewritten to expunge the four-year reign and the name Chien-wen from the record altogether. Every scholar-official who agreed to this line (i.e., anyone connected in any way with the government of the Yung-lo emperor) agreed to ethical castration. They could never seize the moral high ground. They could never radiate moral purity, as Fang Hsiao-ju had done. There would be no more Fang Hsiao-jus.

This diminution of moral authority and ideological zeal among the Confucian scholar-official class makes the Yung-lo usurpation of 1402 a major turning point in the history of the Ming. The effect of the coup was to close off further discussion of the future of China's civilization, to discourage any further attempts to reform its institutions from on high, and to discontinue as a major national goal the remolding of the minds of the people so as to make them conform to the sacred norms of the former kings of classical antiquity.[13] (When a visionary Confucianism returned to the scene in the sixteenth century, with Wang Yang-ming and his many followers from T'ai-ho and elsewhere, its aim was not to revamp the universe, as Fang Hsiao-ju and his circle had tried to do, but to inspire people to create ethical agendas within themselves.)

The Yung-lo court also moved quickly to suppress all original or creative scholarship on the Confucian texts. In this too, Yang Shih-ch'i took part. On August 28, 1404, the emperor met with his advisers to consider what to do about a private scholar from northern Kiangsi named Chu Chi-yu, who had come to Nanking to submit his research to the court. He expected commendation, of course. The accounts vary as to exactly what happened next, but the emperor flew into a rage. Chu Chi-yu's research "slandered the sages and worthies." It "contradicted the explanations of [the Sung Neo-Confucian fathers] Chou Tun-i, Chang Tsai, the Ch'eng brothers, and Chu Hsi." The advisers took the emperor's cue and demanded that harsh penalties be applied. Yang Shih-ch'i urged: "All his writing should be destroyed so that posterity won't be misled by it." The hapless Chu Chi-yu was escorted home under armed guard. Provincial and local officials assembled the literati and students of his home county and conducted a public criticism. Police searched his house for every scrap of his writing and destroyed it. Chu was ordered to be flogged a hundred strokes. He was forbidden thenceforth to call himself a *ju* (Confucian) or to teach anyone ever again. The late Ming historian T'an Ch'ien noted that this sensational crackdown was effective as a deterrent to further intellectual inquiry.[14]

The Yung-lo court went on to embalm approved classical scholarship and orthodox Neo-Confucian commentary in the government-sponsored compendia (*Ta-ch'üan*) of 1415. Clearly, the era of relative intellectual freedom, the national climate in which men like Chu Chi-yu (and earlier, T'ai-ho men like Yen Wei and Hsiao Nan-k'o) had dared to exhibit individual intellectual creativity and prowess was over.[15]

There was, however, a payoff for the men of Kiangsi, T'ai-ho men included. In return for the sacrifice of their moral and intellectual freedom, the gates of opportunity for careers in government were thrown open to them. And collegiality and patronage were the means whereby Yang Shih-ch'i eased the entry of friends and younger men from the reconstituted common-descent groups of T'ai-ho into government service.

Yang Shih-ch'i served as senior grand secretary, the highest post in the Ming realm, from the 1420s until his death in 1444. A master of a fine tactical sense of the right times for outspokenness and reticence, a statesman and diplomat rather than an ethical purist or ideological zealot, Yang left it to the Yung-lo emperor and his successors to dictate national policy. Within those limits, however, Yang and the other grand secretaries (the Three Yangs) worked so effectively with the palace, and with colleagues from all over China, that later generations came to look back upon the first half of the fifteenth century as a golden era, an era when the country enjoyed peace and prosperity; and rulers and officials high and low bent to the tasks of national administration in a spirit of cooperation and harmony.

T'AI-HO COLLEAGUES

The best way to understand T'ai-ho collegiality is to contrast it with An-fu collegiality. An-fu County was northwest of T'ai-ho, in the same Chi-an Prefecture. Liu Ch'iu (1392–1443) was from An-fu and was a Han-lin official. Liu Ch'iu noted that all banquets of An-fu men in Peking (some twenty-two banquets were held, between 1432 and 1434, with ten to twenty guests each time) cleaved to the most stringent norms of frugality, sobriety, and ethically serious purpose. By common agreement, an appointed monitor saw to it that all joking and loud behavior were forbidden.[16] (And Liu Ch'iu died as no T'ai-ho man died in those times: as a martyr, in prison, for his fearless protest of a eunuch-sponsored invasion of Burma.)

When T'ai-ho men gathered for banquets in Nanking or Peking, no such rules applied. Glimpses of their behavior at off-duty social gatherings can be marshaled to underscore the point.

It was important that T'ai-ho men be sociable. Take, for example, Wang Ching-hsien (1365–1420, from Yung-chiang Ward, township

49). He was "generous and mild by nature, and was not contentious when people crossed him." Through recommendation, he was made an assistant instructor in a county school in Hunan. In 1403, he was one of several hundred men recruited as editorial aides for the great encyclopedia project, the *Yung-lo ta-tien*. There were "more than twenty" T'ai-ho men on duty in Nanking at the time; and "late in the day, after work, Wang would join his county compatriots for discussions and jokes and drinking and chess playing, and the clamor would go on until late at night." This went on for several years. (Wang ended his career as instructor in a county school in Szechwan.)[17]

Liang Ch'ien used the occasion of Ou-yang Hsien's departure on home leave to celebrate the same circle of Nanking comrades. Ou-yang Hsien (1368–1422, of Shu-chiang Ward, township 61) was an instructor (8B) in the imperial college. "Ou-yang Hsien is a close friend of Yang Shih-ch'i, expositor-in-waiting in the Han-lin Academy," wrote Liang, "so whenever he has a free day and comes to join the rest of us, he always sends somebody to find Yang and make him come too. Then when everyone has gathered, Ou-yang won't let anyone leave. So the singing and joking, the draining of cup after cup, go on without a break until late at night. Sometimes it goes on to nearly dawn, when we have to call the servants to carry lamps to light our way back. What pleasure! It can happen only because we share interests and bear no resentments against each other."[18]

Liao Lung (1369–1418), of T'ai-ho city, died a lowly assistant instructor in a county school in Hunan. But Yang Shih-ch'i remembered him as impressive looking, well read, and a good talker. "When relaxing with local friends, drinking, or playing chess, he would occasionally come up with some superb quip that would make the whole company collapse in laughter. That is why everyone, young and old, liked having him around. Of course, he would never compromise his basic principles."[19]

Lung Chü (1366–1424, of Kan-chu Ward, township 54) wanted desperately to become an official. Around 1400, Yang Shih-ch'i met him in Wu-chang on the Yangtze. "He invited me onto his boat," Yang recalled,

> and treated me to clear wine, meat, and fish. He wasn't a drinker by nature, but he raised one big cup after another in my behalf. Around midnight he turned abruptly to serious talk. I kidded him: "Talent like yours is rare," I said. "Surely you don't think it'll be hard for you to get to wear the sash of an official, so why are you so worried?" Lung lightened up at once, and he

said: "So this is how far your self-confidence takes you! I'm not as good as you are, so if you're looking up to me, then surely you mean I'm as good as hired!" I can remember that just as though it was all spoken yesterday."[20]

Lung Chü never got an offer.

The convivial T'ai-ho spirit and the long social gatherings edged Ch'en Lien into alcoholism and early death. Ch'en Lien (1366–1410, from Willow Creek) achieved his *chin-shih* degree in 1406 and was appointed a Han-lin bachelor (elite trainee). Gregarious by nature, he was so addicted to drink that after he died, they found a pot and a cup right in his bed. Liang Ch'ien had known him when he was younger, and when he saw him again in Nanking in 1409, he was shocked to see how bad he looked. "His face was withered, his hands trembled as he held his cup, and he was so unsteady he could scarcely stand. Yet he continued his hard drinking. His friends just let him go on like that. I was afraid he might collapse, and I tried to stop him, but to no avail, and he died a year later.[21]

One had to be able to handle oneself to stay in the collegial circle of T'ai-ho men. Lo Chao (1355–1434, of Hsi-yuan Ward, township 46) was a family manager. When he arrived in Nanking accompanying a tax shipment, he was invited to a party at Yang Shih-ch'i's house. Lo was a former *sheng-yuan* (county student) and a former student of Hsiao Ch'i's, so he could hold his own in educated company. "Lo arrived with his friend T'ang Liu," recalled Yang (T'ang Liu was a Han-lin bachelor from Kan-chu Ward, township 54).

> So I got out some rice-beer for us all. We talked about idle matters, but T'ang Liu, who was straitlaced, kept saying things by way of chiding Lo. Lo took it all calmly. He said: "You must like me, or you wouldn't go into this. I appreciate your criticism." After he said that, we went on drinking happily. At first I thought that Lo had been forcefully put down, but the more I observed him, the more I realized that he harbored no ill feelings. Later I too chided Lo about a few things. He looked shocked and said, "It's my fault." He really accepted that. He didn't resent it, and we got along very well afterwards. It is certainly rare for people to listen and yield to correction like that.[22]

K'ang Yen-ying (1372–1435, of P'u-t'ien Ward, township 37) was Yang Shih-ch'i's half-sister's husband. He helped look after Yang's eldest son, then a child living back in T'ai-ho. K'ang was unsociable and easily offended. "Once he came to Nanking to see me," Yang remembered. "At night we were drinking together when I said something too frank, and he took offense. He left at dawn. I apologized and tried to convince him to stay a few days, but he wouldn't. Yet he continued to look after my son Chi, just as he had always done."[23]

It is hard to know just where T'ai-ho men in office in Nanking or Peking held their social gatherings, or where T'ai-ho visitors stayed when in Nanking or Peking. It is clear that Yang Shih-ch'i put up visitors at home, but there were already a few anticipations of the native-place hostels that were to become common in the late Ming and Ch'ing.[24] For example, in the Kiangsi provincial capital of Nan-ch'ang, site of the triennial provincial exams, a former student of Hsiao Ch'i's, now in business, extended hospitality to the T'ai-ho candidates, and his son built a hall or lodging in order to continue and expand that hospitality.[25] In Peking, officials and students and others from T'ai-ho sometimes stayed with P'eng Hsu (1375–1430, of Moon Pond Ward, township 56). P'eng was an archivist (9B) in the national college. Visitors would gather in P'eng's house, "start off by discussing philosophical principles and historical precedents, and then turn to raucous jokes, hardly aware of the late hour."[26]

When it was feasible, T'ai-ho men tried to live in houses near each other in the capital. In 1423, Yang Shih-ch'i prevailed upon Wang Chih to move from the mud and dust and traffic of the east side of the new capital of Peking over to the west side, where Yang and a half-dozen other officials from T'ai-ho and Chi-an Prefecture had homes. Wang Chih had been living with Ou-yang Ho (b. 1387), who was a supervising censor and a relative of Wang's mother. Because Yang "valued local friendships and *shih-hao* [friendly relations extending over generations]," he and the others pooled funds to help buy a just vacated house for Wang Chih. Wang moved in on July 9. Wang listed all his new neighbors by name. All their descendants would want to know all these things. That was what *shih-hao* was all about.[27]

There were, however, a few T'ai-ho men who were not accepted. Despite thick ties of *shih-hao*, despite his good reputation as an official, Investigating Censor P'eng Pai-lien (1386–1433, of Moon Pond Ward, township 56, who was a very distant relative of P'eng Hsu's), did not fit in. In a preface to a eulogy for him, Yang Shih-ch'i openly confessed that he had never liked him. P'eng Pai-lien had been too hard and forthright. He had struck fear in other people and had stirred turmoil in the placid surfaces of social and bureaucratic life. Yang conceded that P'eng usually had had justice on his side. Still, his style of behavior had been unwelcome. "He used to bear himself with a spirited and righteous air," stated Yang. "He hated evil and sympathized with the victims of it. But he would express himself directly and without reservation on any matter at hand, even when he was home on leave, and that is how he provoked resentments."[28]

Did the collegial ethic require that one do everything to help comrades in serious trouble? To a limited extent, it did. It is interesting to note the limitations of the ethic, the reticence of some to honor it.

An ineffectual show of solidarity for a friend in distress might be enough to discharge one's social obligations. Consider the case of Kuo Ting (1356–1434) of the North Gate Kuo descent-group of T'ai-ho city. Kuo was a career government Confucian instructor. Something bad happened with his first marriage; his wife Li took their suckling son and fled back to her own people. In order to get his son back, Kuo needed adequate property in fields and gardens; but his nephews coveted his share, and as long as he was sonless, he could not stop them from asserting their claims. Friends and well-wishers tried to help. Yin Tzu-hou (Kuo Ting's new father-in-law) and P'eng Yen-hui (Kuo's friend) attempted negotiations. Yin To, formerly a student of Kuo's, offered him some of his own fields. Kuo's daughter and son-in-law (of the T'ang surname) offered him fields and a house. All to no avail. No matter. There was no obligation to do more. It was enough for Yang Shih-ch'i to note the deplorable greed shown by Kuo's nephews and the praiseworthy and unselfish help offered him by the others. What was it that caused the flight of wife Li with the baby in the first place? Of that he said nothing at all.[29]

It was the same with colleagues in political trouble. Take the case of Yin Ch'ang-lung. Yin Ch'ang-lung (ca. 1369–1417, of Kuan-t'ang Ward, township 14) was companion to the heir apparent (6A) when he was arrested and executed on the charge of conspiring with the prince of Ku (half-brother and erstwhile ally of the Yung-lo emperor) to carry out a coup d'état. None of his friends thought Yin guilty of this high treason; some thought the evidence against him forged. But neither his T'ai-ho friends nor anyone else tried to protest or intervene in his behalf.

Yin Ch'ang-lung's father was living in Nanking at the time of his son's execution. He received the corpse, and on his departure for T'ai-ho, sympathizers gave him a sheaf of poems done in his honor. Yang Shih-ch'i prefaced these and noted that Yin's father had borne up well under the ordeal, blaming not others but himself for having "disobeyed the ancestors by not giving adequate instructions to his sons and grandsons."[30]

Yin Ch'ang-lung's wife was home in T'ai-ho, but his concubine, his two sons by her, and his son Yin Hao by his regular wife had been living with him in Nanking. Under the law of high treason, they were all scheduled for execution. In an act of self-sacrifice that taxes the imagination, the concubine delivered Yin Hao, as the "last thread" of the descent line, to Yang Shih-ch'i for safekeeping and then surrendered herself and her own two sons to the authorities for execution. Apparently Yang hid Yin Hao for eight years. Documents show that on May 3, 1425, Yang Shih-ch'i notified the new Hung-hsi emperor that Yin Hao was alive and living in the capital with "a local compatriot," that the emperor then ordered Yang to "take care of him," and that Yang then arranged his transportation home.[31]

In 1418, a year after Yin Ch'ang-lung's demise, the Yung-lo government struck down yet another T'ai-ho man. This time the victim was Liang Ch'ien, Han-lin reader-in-waiting (6A) and admonisher to the heir apparent. The Yung-lo emperor was spending much of his time in his new capital, Peking. He had his heir apparent (Chu Kao-chih, later the Hung-hsi emperor, r. 1424–25) remain in Nanking as a kind of subemperor, with some carefully limited administrative responsibilities; but there were tensions between Peking and Nanking and several plots among the Ming princes to depose the heir apparent, with the result that officials in the heir apparent's group of advisers often found themselves under suspicion and vulnerable to the attacks of personal or political enemies. (That was what had happened to Yin Ch'ang-lung.)

Chief among the advisers to Chu Kao-chih was Yang Shih-ch'i. As the arch priest of collegiality, Yang was eager to bring the studious, idealistic, and conscientious heir apparent into a collegial relationship with himself and the other advisers, of whom at least four or five were (even after Yin's execution) T'ai-ho men. Wang Chih, Han-lin senior compiler (6B), was home on mourning leave at the time of Liang's death, but junior compiler (7A) Ch'en Hsun was there serving as an amanuensis to Yang Shih-ch'i.

Tokens of their personal relations with heir apparent Chu Kao-chih were much valued by these T'ai-ho men. Wang Chih treasured a short note scribbled for him on a fan; a prescription for eye medicine the heir apparent had given him; a pass in the future ruler's hand authorizing travel home for his father's funeral. Wang had these keepsakes mounted into a hanging scroll.[32] Yang Shih-ch'i prized a note handwritten by the heir apparent (in which he agreed to Yang's request to release his half-brother from penal servitude).[33] In 1417, the heir apparent presided at a banquet, on which occasion he gave autograph poems to his favorite "literary *shih*," Yang Shih-ch'i and Liang Ch'ien among them.

Then disaster struck. On August 27, 1418, Liang Ch'ien was placed under arrest, charged with having failed to warn the heir apparent not to pardon a military officer—whom the heir apparent had just convicted and sentenced to exile. On October 16, Liang Ch'ien was executed in prison—for "disrespectful" behavior. Yang Shih-ch'i later wrote Liang's tomb inscription, and in it he openly called the execution "unjust" (*fei ming*).

Liang Ch'ien's home in Nanking was thrown into chaos. Ch'en Hsun lived next door, and he tried to keep an eye on things; but in the panic, and with the death a few days later of Liang's wife, much of Liang's writing got lost and scattered, and the autograph poems disappeared, probably stolen by someone. Years later, Liang's eldest son, who had memorized the poems, hired a calligrapher to create facsimiles, which were then affixed to scrolls and treasured as a family heirloom, almost as genuine as the lost originals and good, if second-hand, testimony to the high regard in which the heir apparent Chu Kao-chih had long ago held Liang Ch'ien.[34]

From all this, one gathers that Yang Shih-ch'i intended collegiality among the T'ai-ho group in Ming bureaucracy to serve as a kind of high-level social-support network, an extension to the bureaucratic level of the intrafamily solidarities of T'ai-ho's common-descent groups. As officials, the T'ai-ho men were not expected to defend their friends by acting as a vengeance-seeking mafia, nor were there pressures to organize the morally aroused into a protest group to seek justice. No one sought to get to the bottom of the "unjust" execution of Liang Ch'ien. When unfortunate or terrible things happened to a man, his colleagues rallied and did what they could to help his family, to safeguard his personal effects, and preserve his memory. A desire to preserve their positions and to sustain at all costs their personal bonds to the Ming ruling family seems to explain moral reticence of the T'ai-ho group.

PATRONIZING THE YOUNGER GENERATIONS

The foundation of Yang Shih-ch'i's collegial vision was the belief that native-place ties, strong kinship identities (forged in the ongoing reconstruction of T'ai-ho's common-descent groups), school associations, marriage relations of long standing, and *shih-hao* in some way built a solid footing for effective public service. But how could effective public service be shown to grow out of social ties such as those? For that question, Yang Shih-ch'i had an answer in the form of a local historical model. The meaning of the model was directed at T'ai-ho's younger generations.

The model was a trio of local men: Yang Cho (1322–80, a senior kinsman of Yang Shih-ch'i's); Lo Tzu-li (ca. 1326–ca. 1395, Yang's step-father); and Teng Ch'ung-chih (who was not related to Yang). Yang Shih-ch'i repeatedly used the acronym "Yang-Lo-Teng" to refer to them. Talented students and firm friends, Yang-Lo-Teng were among the first assistant instructors appointed to the T'ai-ho County Confucian school by the new Ming government in 1370. As assistant instructors, the three were remembered many years later as having been "so strict and resolute that people didn't dare offend them."

Lo and Yang passed the Kiangsi provincial exams of 1370 and 1371. As the two were about to depart T'ai-ho, all three took an oath among themselves to the effect that if in official life they ever violated in even the slightest way the Confucian principles they had learned and taught, "each would be too ashamed of himself ever to meet the others again."

And they stayed true to that oath, and they all died impoverished. But the larger point is this: although they were effective as officials, they had troubled careers and never rose very far in Ming government. Recruited by recommendation, Teng was made (and ended up as) a lowly registrar (7B) in a salt bureau in Szechwan. Lo Tzu-li was appointed a vice prefect (5A) in northern Kiangsi; around 1375 he was (unjustly) impeached for "misappropriating jujube wood intended for dyeing uniforms" and was exiled to Shensi Province for the rest of his life. Yang Cho achieved his *chin-shih* degree in 1371, spent some time in punitive exile at a military farm in central China, and ended up as assistant prefect (6A) in Hangchow, where he remained until his dismissal for reasons that are unclear.[35]

How could Yang-Lo-Teng have inspired others as models? For one thing, their story reflected some of the harsher realities of bureaucratic life in the early Ming. They were outstanding local talents who placed ethical self-restraint and conscientious service foremost in their scheme of values. The frustrations and injustices they suffered were a true test of their spiritual strength. The message of the Yang-Lo-Teng example for the aspiring youth of T'ai-ho was that they should form ethically based fellowships, that they should aspire to government office, that they should serve the Ming state unstintingly, and that they should accept low positions, poverty, failure, and even unjust punishment without complaint.

The effect of this model on patronage can be seen in each of the several contexts in which the senior T'ai-ho men in office were in a position to lead and influence their juniors.

The metropolitan and palace examinations were pivotal. Yang Shih-ch'i, Wang Chih, or some other high-ranking official from T'ai-ho served as a chief examiner for the metropolitan *chin-shih* exams in 1412, 1415, 1421, 1427, 1433, 1436, 1439, and 1454. At least one high-ranking T'ai-ho official was a palace examination reader in 1445, 1448, and 1451. All of the fifty T'ai-ho men who passed those exams had something more than the usual patronage bond to their chief examiner: they had someone who knew not only about their individual abilities as potential scholar-officials but also a great deal about their family and social place back in T'ai-ho.

The seniors also knew something of the friendship bonds among the juniors. Ch'en Hsun (when he was Han-lin academician expositor-in-waiting, 5B) kept a running count of the new men as they came through the exam system. "Triennially," he wrote,

> there are several tens of *shih* from T'ai-ho who take the provincial exams, and every time, more than ten of them pass. From 1414 to 1423, four provincial exams were held, and altogether some sixty-odd [actually seventy] passed. This was grand indeed! Thirty-one of them did not come directly for the metropolitan exams, because they wanted to study more and develop themselves first. In 1425, those men gathered at Nan-p'ing [location uncertain] for discussions, questions, and analyses. They hoped to get the clearest possible understanding of things. Their meeting was in line with the words of the *Analects*—that "The superior man on grounds of culture meets with his friends." They weren't simply looking for some way to advance their own prospects; yet they did believe that to learn and not to hold office was not to pursue a useful learning.

A poetry-writing session followed the youths' discussions. Another was held on board a boat en route to Peking for the exams.[36]

From Ch'en Hsun's glosses on these meetings, one notes how the native-place tie, the collegial ethic, and ambition for office were all supposed to mesh together in a frictionless way. A gathering of T'ai-ho men back in the fourteenth century would have been an opportunity for domineering individuals to make their mark. But the collegial mode of the fifteenth century gave no one license to stand out. Rather, it invited everyone to try to fit in as one of a friendly and mutually supportive company in which everyone was equal in the seriousness of his determination to achieve his dream of becoming an official.

Of course, the spectacle of high officials promoting a collegial ethic and, at the same time, extending patronage and protection to younger men from their native county could not escape the attention of others. So the seniors tried to avoid giving an impression of undue local favoritism. Liang Ch'ien, though only a *chü-jen* (he had failed the metropolitan exam of 1397), was nevertheless made a chief examiner for the metropolitan exams in 1415. The consensus of the examiners was that the best exam was that submitted by T'ai-ho man Ch'en Hsun. Liang Ch'ien decided to rank Ch'en number two, not number one. Otherwise, he feared, people would suspect him of partiality. So Ch'en Hsun was ranked number two. Fortunately for Ch'en, the palace examiners (who were not T'ai-ho natives) ranked him first after all.[37] The very same thing happened again in 1421, when Yang Shih-ch'i was a chief examiner and Tseng Hao-ling (1383–1441, from T'ai-ho city) was the candidate.[38]

It is not clear whether some personal difficulty, or a desire to avoid the appearance of collusion based on their common T'ai-ho origin, came into play when Grand Secretary Yang Shih-ch'i blocked Wang Chih's promotion to the grand secretariat in 1443 (and evidently also on a much earlier occasion).[39] Wang reportedly took Yang's rejection of him very hard, though he said nothing of it in his autobiography.[40] As consolation prize, on February 13, 1443, the position of minister of personnel (2A), the most prestigious of all the regular bureaucratic offices, was given to Wang.[41]

With Yang as chief grand secretary and Wang as minister of personnel, aspiring candidates and lower-ranking officials from T'ai-ho had every reason to expect that their merits would not be overlooked in hiring and promotion. As they aged, Yang and the others participated less and less in social activities, but they were regularly asked for interviews and written messages whenever younger T'ai-ho men gathered for a banquet to say good-bye to a comrade about to return home or depart for some official or teaching post in the provinces. The written works of Wang, Yang, and the others contain hundreds of such messages. Typically, the recipient's common-descent group is identified; his immediate ancestors are recalled; his career to date is outlined; and something is said about the place the appointee is about to go to and about how the demands of the task he is about to undertake should be met.

It was often that older men praised their T'ai-ho protégés for accepting low and undesirable posts without murmur. That was the idea behind the Yang-Lo-Teng example. In 1421, Yang Shih-ch'i went so far as to console and counsel the four T'ai-ho men who had completely failed the metropolitan exams. He met with the unfortunates and wrote them a memoir about their meeting. "You four met with me," he wrote.

> I am a close friend of your fathers. You were respectful in demeanor and cheerful in expression and showed no sign of dissatisfaction. I was feeling ashamed for having failed you, but you all joined in saying: "Our studies weren't complete, so we could hardly escape the impartial judgment of the enlightened authorities. It's fortunate for us that we can return home now and study some more." You visited with me several times and took my advice. How different you are from those who suffer some small misfortune, and repress their resentment, or give vent to it! Gain and loss are a matter of fate, and those who know the Confucian Way rest content in fate. This year our T'ai-ho men had exceptional luck on the exams, but you four, who had no luck, are even more exceptional for your ability to seek within yourselves and not put the blame on others.[42]

THE DECLINE AND DESTRUCTION OF T'AI-HO COLLEGIALITY

Besides the help they might extend as examiners, Yang Shih-ch'i and the other senior men were also in a position to boost promising colocals through the in-service promotion system known as *pao-chü* (guaranteed recommendation). This system was used for promoting men to mainly middle-level posts.

Instead of concentrating appointment authority in the Ministry of Personnel, *pao-chü* required all high-level officials in the capital, the minister of personnel included, to propose nominees and then jointly to endorse or reject them. Not surprisingly, the system came under attack as a mask for favoritism and corruption. In 1447, Minister Wang Chih was pressed to defend the system. "Of course those who make the recommendations choose colocals, subordinates, and protégés!" he cried. "How do you know about men, unless you've had some sustained contact with them? There is no classical injunction against recommending even sons and nephews. As Confucius said, 'raise to office those whom you know.' " Excesses and errors, Wang argued, should be remedied after the fact, by way of censorial impeachment. Despite his objections, the system was suspended, and all appointment-making authority was placed in the Ministry of Personnel.[43]

As minister, Wang Chih earned a reputation for conscientious honesty in the discharge of his duties, but he fell twice into grave difficulties in which he was accused of unfair preferment on behalf of T'ai-ho men. In 1446, censors impeached Minister Wang and several others (after each had accused the others of wrongdoing). All were imprisoned. After ten days' investigation, Wang was pronounced guilty of having favored a colocal, Lung Wen (1409–59, of Kan-chu Ward, township 54), when he jumped him from a 7B post to vice director (5B) in the Bureau of Honors in Wang's own Ministry of Personnel. The emperor decided to fine Wang for that, but he restored both him and Lung to their ministry positions.[44]

In fact, Wang Chih had already placed into the ministry at least two other T'ai-ho men: Hsiao I (of Grass Garden Lane, in T'ai-ho's western suburb) was secretary (6A) in the ministry's Bureau of Evaluations; and Hsiao Huan (1397–1461, of Li-yuan Ward, township 48) was on duty in Nanking as director (5A) of the southern personnel ministry's Bureau of Records.

In 1453, Wang Chih and two other top-ranking ministry officials again came under censorial attack for favoritism in promotions. One of the censors' targets was Tseng Meng-chien, son of the deceased Han-lin academician Tseng Hao-ling of T'ai-ho. (To indicate how cross-meshed local, ancestral, familial, and collegial ties could become, it bears noting that Tseng Meng-chien's examiner—he was the fourth-ranking *chin-shih* of 1445–was Ch'en Hsun and that Tseng's older sister was Secretary Hsiao I's mother.)

The problem was that, late in 1452, Tseng Meng-chien had been leapfrogged from a 5B to a 3B position in provincial service. Wang Chih had authorized that unusual promotion, and, when challenged, he offered to resign. The emperor refused his offer and took no action on the promotion. But January 1455 found Wang Chih in trouble yet again. Censors impeached Lin Ts'ung (of Ning-te County, Fukien), chief supervising secretary of the Office of Scrutiny for Personnel, for having colluded with Minister Wang in order to effect the improper protection and promotion of a number of his Fukien compatriots. The emperor demoted Lin over this but pardoned Wang and everyone else accused in the impeachment.[45]

By these times, chief Grand Secretary Yang Shih-ch'i had been dead some ten years, and signs were that the collegial system—openly based on local identities that he had labored all his life to build—was unraveling.

Indeed, a terrible thing happened in the final year of the grand secretary's life. The myth of T'ai-ho social solidarity and moral goodness exploded in his face. His oldest and favorite son, Yang Chi, was the fuse. Bland and suave, Yang Chi was a local entrepreneur who had long known how to manipulate the affection of his father and exploit his power and fame. But late in 1442, one Li Yen (of Nan-kang Ward, township 53) filed suit, charging Yang Chi with a long list of crimes, including perpetrating commercial tax fraud and land and tomb extortion; leading a gang of bondsmen as enforcers; and committing murder. Investigating censors looked into the charges and arrested Yang Chi plus several hundred others implicated with him in the case, among them nineteen scions of pedigreed T'ai-ho families. All confessed to the charges. Yang Shih-ch'i was himself impeached for allowing his son to commit evil. Yang was at this time nearly eighty. He conceded his son's guilt but asked that his son's elite accomplices be absolved of all charges. Old, sick, and deeply distraught, the grand secretary passed away April 2, 1444. Yang Chi was abused by his guards, and in the fall of the same year, he died in prison in Peking. What happened to the others named in the suit is not known.[46]

A month after Yang Shih-ch'i died, the young Cheng-t'ung emperor appointed Yang's former aide and protégé Ch'en Hsun to the grand secretariat in his place. Thus one T'ai-ho man succeeded another in the highest organ of Ming government. (As if that were not enough, in January 1452, Hsiao Tzu, of Nan-ch'i Ward, township 59, was also appointed a grand secretary.)[47]

There was no way that Grand Secretary Ch'en Hsun could fill the shoes of his illustrious T'ai-ho predecessor. He had no vision to offer the realm, and he could do little but try to sustain Yang's legacy of patronage; but for all his combativeness and venom, he was not up to the task of defending that legacy against increasingly heavy assault, both in Peking and in T'ai-ho County itself.

In 1451, while Ch'en was on duty in Peking, in T'ai-ho a bondservant of his charged a local man, one P'eng Te-ch'ing, of plotting to murder the tomb watcher and seize the tomb in which Ch'en's wife (probably his second wife, Kuo Miao-chih, d. 1449) was buried. Somehow, Ch'en was absolutely sure that the charge was true. The emperor sent Investigating Censor Chou Chien to look into the matter. He found the servant's allegations false and malicious.

Ch'en Hsun was outraged, and he took his grievance directly to the young Ching-t'ai emperor. He told the emperor that Chou Chien hated

T'ai-ho and favored An-fu (another county in Chi-an Prefecture). That was so because Chou had once studied the *Spring and Autumn Annals* in An-fu and because he had passed no fewer than twenty An-fu men when earlier he had presided over the Kiangsi provincial exams! Moreover, alleged Ch'en, Chou was a friend of P'eng Te-ch'ing; and to top it all off, the T'ai-ho County magistrate tilted the investigation because Ch'en Hsun's relatives had not bribed him enough![48]

These were ad hominem, petty, and vindictive remarks. The emperor did not think that a grand secretary would knowingly make false statements, but he did not know quite what to believe. The censorate suggested that Investigating Censor Wang Hao conduct a review. That sounded like a good idea, and the emperor endorsed it. In his review, Censor Wang Hao found all of Ch'en Hsun's allegations groundless, and he further demanded that the grand secretary be arrested and prosecuted for behavior unbefitting a man of so high a rank. The emperor thought it might be best just to drop the whole matter, but Ch'en Hsun wanted vindication. He now charged that there was a conspiracy against him. Censor Wang Hao lived on the same Peking lane as officials from powerful An-fu families! Furthermore, Censor Chou Chien had bribed him!

The emperor turned to Lin Ts'ung (who was chief supervising secretary of the Office of Scrutiny for Justice at this time) and asked him to check the grand secretary's latest allegations. Lin returned with a stinging rebuke of Ch'en Hsun and urged his immediate dismissal as a man unfit to hold the post of grand secretary.

According to Lin's report, the burial site in question was actually not Ch'en Hsun's at all. He had used his high position to override the rightful T'ai-ho claimants and seize the site for himself. The original complainant was not really a family servant but Ch'en's ambitious son-in-law Li Yü (of Nan-kang Ward, township 53, and a one-time office manager, 9B, in the Ministry of Justice). The mastermind of the plot was Li's older brother Li Wu, a one-time county assistant instructor. Li Wu was arrested and brought to Peking, but Ch'en managed to get him released.

The emperor agreed with Lin's report, and its terrible indictment of Ch'en Hsun, but he pardoned Ch'en on the basis of his long service. Still, the controversy dragged on for another several months before it disappeared from the record.[49]

Indeed, it appears that the ingredients of Yang Shih-ch'i's good Confucian society—descent-group consciousness, marriage and kinship ties, *shih-hao*—were being turned to criminal purposes on some scale at the local level. By trading on his father's political influence, Yang Chi seems to have set an infectious example for others. Ch'en Hsun had arranged the appointment of Han Yung as Kiangsi governor; and although Han Yung did excellent work in creating rice reserves, as noted in an earlier chapter, he faced insurmountable resistance when in 1453 he tried to crack down on the crime rings in which the "sons and younger brothers and servants" of high officials like Ch'en Hsun, Hsiao Tzu, and Wang Chih were involved. The problem extended beyond T'ai-ho into Chi-an Prefecture generally. In Peking, palace eunuch Hsing An acted as a protector of these rings.[50]

Ch'en Hsun's combative paranoia surfaced again in 1456, when his son Ch'en Ying (b. 1431) failed his provincial examinations (which, as was often the case with officials' sons, he took in the metropolitan prefecture of Shun-t'ien, rather than back home in Kiangsi). Ch'en Hsun was outraged. He provided a detailed list of irregularities in the questions asked and in the grading procedures used. He further alleged that his son had failed because the examiners had not read all of his exam.

The emperor ordered the Ministry of Rites and Grand Secretary Kao Ku to reread all 135 passing exams and to compare them with Ch'en Ying's (and with that of Wang Lun, a son of Grand Secretary Wang Wen, who had also failed). The reviewers found that the failed sons' exams were at least as good as, and in some cases better than, those that had been passed. They also found that one exam had been tampered with. The emperor then ordered the imprisonment and interrogation of the original examiners. But rather than insist that the whole examination be given over again, he simply authorized Ch'en Ying and Wang Lun to take the next year's metropolitan *chin-shih* exam.

The supervising secretaries of the various offices of scrutiny exploded in protest of the unfairness of that decision. Some 1,800 candidates had taken those exams, they pointed out. Only 135 of them could have passed under the quota, so surely the sons of the grand secretaries were not the only ones whose merits had been slighted. Furthermore, because such special pleading on behalf of their own sons showed that neither Ch'en Hsun nor Wang Wen was conducting himself with the dignity and gravity expected of the highest officials of the land, both should be dismissed and punished. The Ching-t'ai emperor acknowledged that the protesters had a valid point, but he declined to take any action.[51]

· · ·

The great palace coup of 1457 terminated, with a dramatic flourish, the remarkable half-century-long dominance of T'ai-ho men at the very top of Ming government. The story of that coup is the subject of a fine study by Philip de Heer.[52] Suffice it here to say that all the events that surrounded that great crisis of imperial authority found the high-level T'ai-ho men—Grand Secretaries Ch'en Hsun and Hsiao Tzu and Minister of Personnel Wang Chih—wanting in compelling vision or effective strategy and clearly out of their depth as national leaders and statesmen, even though they were in the thick of things throughout the crisis years.

The seeds of the crisis were sown in 1449 when the Cheng-t'ung emperor, leading an ill-advised military expedition, was captured and held hostage by the Mongols. Peking was thrown into panic, but Minister of War Yü Ch'ien saved the day, and the dynasty. He deposed the captured emperor and enthroned the emperor's younger brother—the "caretaker" Ching-t'ai emperor. In 1450 the Mongols returned their hostage, and from 1450 until the coup seven years later, the ex-emperor lived in enforced seclusion in the Forbidden City while controversy raged among the high officials about the succession. Did it lie with the Ching-t'ai emperor and his heir? Or with his older brother, the former Cheng-t'ung emperor, and his heir? Late in 1453, the Ching-t'ai emperor's little son and only heir died. Finally, in 1457, a well-planned coup d'état restored the older brother to the throne, and he reigned as the T'ien-shun emperor from then until his death in 1464.

The reputations of Ch'en Hsun, Hsiao Tzu, and Wang Chih were badly damaged in the course of these events. There was no doubt they were guilty of an unclear moral vision. When the Ching-t'ai emperor had insisted on changing the line of succession in favor of his own son, they had objected at first. Then they had changed their minds.[53] The coup of 1457 took them by surprise, and it is small wonder that the coup makers and the restored emperor then forced the ouster of all of them.

Ch'en Hsun (age seventy-one) was flogged and exiled to a garrison in Manchuria. Five years later, he petitioned the throne for his release, which was granted. He died in Peking later the same year, 1462.[54] Hsiao Tzu (age unknown) was removed from civil service and sent home to T'ai-ho, where he died in 1464. Wang Chih (age seventy-eight) was sent home, but with full official honors. He too died in 1464.

Collegial and social harmony in the Yang Shih-ch'i style was dead as well. Recruitment rates of new T'ai-ho men into Ming government fell by half after the coup of 1457. It was time for a different outlook and a new dispensation. There took place after 1457 an important change in the politics of patronage at the Ming court. Instead of an asset, native-place ties became more and more a political liability. New forms of factional alignment emerged, which called for the use of different kinds of political skills. The career of T'ai-ho man Yin Chih, the subject of the next chapter, yields some insights into the new order of things at the center of Ming government.

CHAPTER 7

Cutting Loose

The Provocative Style of
Yin Chih (1427–1511)

The last grand act of patronage that the T'ai-ho ascendancy in central government in Peking undertook was in connection with the metropolitan examinations of 1454. Grand Secretaries Ch'en Hsun and Hsiao Tzu and Minister of Personnel Wang Chih were chief examiners on that occasion.

They passed six men from T'ai-ho. One of them was Yin Chih, whom they ranked second overall in a rank-order list of 349. In the palace exam immediately following, a different set of examiners dropped him to ninety-ninth. Nevertheless, when twenty-one of the new *chin-shih* were selected to be Han-lin bachelors, i.e., elite trainees, Yin Chih was included. In 1456, his traineeship completed, he was appointed a Han-lin junior compiler (7A) and was thus launched on Ming China's most promising career track. He was twenty-nine years old. But he would soon have to make his way through Ming bureaucracy's uncertain and dangerous world without a support group of T'ai-ho sponsors and colleagues.

•   •   •

Yin Chih was completely different from Yang Shih-ch'i, who, as a personality, was complex and elusive. Yang could pontificate; he could dictate ethical principles, but only those that pertained to individual and social behavior. Among friends and peers, he was companionable. Harmony and cooperation were his key values. In 1402, in the interest of achieving national political harmony, he blunted his own moral vision, bowed to the usurper of the Ming throne, and forever after laid himself under a cloud of personal opportunism. He never questioned the moral bases of national power and national policy, or sought to control them, but served his imperial masters with all the finesse he could muster.

Yin Chih (1427–1511) came from T'ai-ho's Hung-fu Ward (township 24).[1] Tales were told of the brilliance he had shown as a child. You measured the intelligence of children by engaging them in verbal challenge-and-response games. You made up a five- or seven-word poetical line, and it was the child's job to think up a matching line that responded to yours in some clever or insightful way. Yin Chih's childhood responses were legendary as put-downs; people long remembered them. It is related that one day he wore a round collar to school. "So even a herd boy has learned to wear a round collar," prompted the schoolmaster. "Surely a blind fellow has never seen an overcoat!" retorted Yin Chih, and everyone roared with laughter.[2] Once Yin Chih fell off a horse and broke his arm. "Breaking the arm was caused by falling off the horse," said Hsiao Huan (1397–1461), a kinsman of Yin's mother and a *chin-shih* degree holder. "When I get back on my feet, I'll mount a dragon!" retorted Yin.[3] Amazing! The lines matched perfectly, and the boy divulged his great ambition in a strikingly direct way.

Born and raised in T'ai-ho as he was, young Yin Chih was fully aware of the advantages of *shih-hao* (generational friendships) and patronage. One day, after having achieved his degree, he paid a call on his metropolitan examiner, Minister of Personnel Wang Chih. He brought with him a portrait of his grandfather, Yin Tzu-yuan. He showed it to Wang Chih and asked him to write an "appreciation" (*tsan*) for it. The elderly minister of personnel was very glad to do that because Yin Tzu-yuan had been an old personal friend. Wang Chih recalled how in 1413 he and Yin Tzu-yuan had shared a house in the capital when Yin was there on temporary assignment as a copyist for the *Yung-lo ta-tien* encyclopedia project; how Yin Tzu-yuan had amused everyone with his jocular recitations of bad poems; and how he had coaxed Wang Chih into drinking far into the night, more than he really wanted. Yin Tzu-yuan left the capital to assume the very low (unranked) post of commissioner of a fishing tax office. When he left, he wondered how Wang Chih would ever manage to have any fun without him. Some years afterwards, home on mourning leave, Wang Chih gave lessons to Yin Tzu-yuan's son (Yin Chih's father)—a private citizen who spent much of his adult life in legal trouble of some sort.[4]

Yin Chih's visit to Wang Chih and Wang's written remarks were quintessential examples of how *shih-hao* was expressed in the T'ai-ho style. They were also among the last such examples. The coup of 1457 not only put an end to the careers of Wang Chih and the other senior men but also lowered the value of county-based friendship and patron-protégé ties, the value of knowing all the intimate details of family and descent-group history. Yin Chih is not known ever to have extended to other T'ai-ho men the net of collegial fellowship that Wang Chih extended to him. After 1457, it no longer mattered to Yin Chih's political identity or career prospects that he was a T'ai-ho native at all. So he sought patronage ties elsewhere. Furthermore, he came to the realization that native-place ties were a political liability and should be avoided.

After the coup of 1457, Junior Compiler Yin Chih placed himself under the patronage of certain other senior officials, including especially Grand Secretary Li Hsien (1408–67), a northerner from Honan Province. There was an old link between Li Hsien and Wang Chih. Early on, Wang Chih had spotted Li Hsien as a young man of character and talent. Li Hsien had served under Wang Chih as his vice minister of personnel (3A). Li Hsien had asked Wang Chih to write his mother's epitaph. Later, Li Hsien wrote Wang Chih's career biography. He also wrote Yin Chih's mother's epitaph. (A story has it that on one early occasion, Yang Shih-ch'i expressed a desire to meet the young Li Hsien. A mutual friend offered to bring Li to Yang's house. Li refused to go. "To go to his house without ever having met him would simply be recognition seeking," he explained; and for that act of self-restraint, Li won much praise for himself.)[5]

Yin Chih served in Peking until 1479 (when he was transferred, in effect politically exiled, to Nanking). From Han-lin junior compiler he was successively promoted to reader-in-waiting (6A), academician expositor-in-waiting (5B), and in 1475 vice minister of rites (3A). In 1486 he returned to Peking, and for several months, during the last year of the Ch'eng-hua emperor's life, he served as a grand secretary. Then the new emperor dismissed him.

Yin's collected works have disappeared,[6] but his personal memoir, the controversial *Chien-chai so-chui lu* (Bits from the studio of candor) survives; and much of it sets down in vivid detail the opinions the author held and the sharp political conflicts he engaged in. Taken together with other sources, it is a useful guide to the exploration of several issues current in the late fifteenth century, among them (1) the pitfalls of patronage based on native-place ties; (2) high-level political infighting, in which Yin Chih was a major player; (3) statecraft; and (4) the rise of philosophical Neo-Confucianism, to which Yin Chih was heatedly opposed.

YIN CHIH'S NEGATIVE ASSESSMENT OF YANG SHIH-CH'I

The *Bits from the Studio of Candor* is notable for its assault on the old T'ai-ho ethic of collegiality, of which the author himself had been a beneficiary in his youth. Yin Chih aimed his shafts directly at Yang Shih-ch'i.

Why assault Yang? After all, it was the common understanding that Grand Secretaries Yang Shih-ch'i, Yang Jung, and Yang P'u (the Three Yangs) had together created an early Ming golden age of peace, prosperity, and political harmony. Later people could not only read about that era but also visualize it. A famous group portrait, done in 1437 in Yang Jung's Apricot Garden in Peking, featured the Three Yangs, plus Wang Chih and Ch'en Hsun and several others, seated or standing in attitudes of lofty elegance and calm repose, crystallizing the mood and sense of the time. The mood was infectious. Several young Han-lin men had a look at it in 1477 and wanted portraits of themselves done just like it.[7]

Yin Chih agreed that the early fifteenth century had been a golden age, but he argued that the Three Yangs had had nothing to do with it. What had happened was a fortuitous conjuncture of larger historical forces—an absence of civil strife, an adequacy of tax revenues, a favorable man-to-land ratio, an effective system of laws, and long official tenures. Far from having created those conditions, the Three Yangs had merely been their passive beneficiaries.

Yin Chih further argued that the practice of friendship, patronage, and protection in imperial bureaucracy could not be based in native-place identities. That practice, he pointed out, had in fact led to a split among the grand secretaries and had opened the way to the rise, in the Cheng-t'ung reign period, of the palace eunuchs who complicated Ming power relations in his own day. He thought Yang Shih-ch'i personally to blame for that development.

What had happened was this. In 1438, T'ai-ho man Liao Mo (1392–1448) was assistant surveillance commissioner (5A) for Fukien Province. He was strict and feared as a supervisor of local officials there. One day, when he was held up by rain en route to the capital with an official document, he was angered by what he took to be acts of disrespect toward him, and he ordered the flogging of the responsible parties, a county magistrate and a local stationmaster. The stationmaster died of his wounds.

This incident occurred in Chien-an County, Fukien, home of Grand Secretary Yang Jung. Friends of the injured parties appealed to Yang Jung for his help. Yang Shih-ch'i was bound to do what he could to defend his local compatriot, Liao Mo. Grand Secretaries Yang Jung and Yang Shih-ch'i agreed that some penalty should be dealt to Liao Mo, but they could not agree on its severity. So they appealed the issue to the throne, specifically the dowager empress, acting as regent for the eleven-year-old Cheng-t'ung emperor. She in turn consulted the palace eunuch Wang Chen. Wang Chen's view was that both grand secretaries were prejudiced in behalf of local protégés and that a compromise penalty, transfer to a post at the same rank but lower in responsibility, should apply to Liao Mo. The empress agreed and, on the child-emperor's behalf, so ordered. That incident, argued Yin Chih, had been key to the rise of Wang Chen and the whole problem of eunuch power in the Ming (Yin lived long enough to witness three successive "eunuch dictatorships").

Yin Chih also castigated Yang Shih-ch'i for his reticence in all the major issues of his long tenure as chief grand secretary. He not only had never spoken out about eunuch power but also had actively, if unthinkingly, abetted it because of "personal interest" (ssu) on behalf of "local friends" (hsiang-ku). Furthermore, he had shied away from the great controversies of his time—the Vietnam intervention, the Burma campaign, and the Cheng Ho expeditions to Southeast Asia and the Persian Gulf.[8]

As for himself, Yin Chih did not favor local friends, and he was not silent in issues of controversy. He was in every way Yang Shih-ch'i's opposite. Yin Chih's biography in the Ming dynastic history excoriates him at length as a wire-pulling practitioner of dirty politics and concludes that "he was intelligent and learned, and versed in bureaucratic procedure, but he was too eager to advance himself, and was by nature conceited and abrasive."[9] Even Yin's panegyrist conceded as much. Fei Hung (1468–1535, from northeastern Kiangsi), later a grand secretary himself, described his old mentor as "tall and so impressive-looking that you could tell at a glance he was a high-ranking official . . . He was knowledgeable, intelligent, and talented," Fei went on to say, and his constant urge was to take personal charge of the affairs of the realm, without affecting an attitude of petty scruple. There were people who disliked his independence and his strong opinions, [which is one reason why] he came to assume authority [as grand secretary] only very late, and was never able to achieve all he wanted. Some people say that because people feared what he wrote, and because he was frank, uninhibited, hard, and resolute, it is no wonder that others shied away from him, and it was just his good fortune that he was able to retire from office with his body still in one piece.[10]

HIGH-LEVEL POWER GAMES

A big battle over control of official appointments broke out in January, 1469. The target was Minister of Personnel Li Ping, a northerner. His principal attackers were Han-lin Reader-in-Waiting P'eng Hua (a younger cousin of Grand Secretary P'eng Shih) and Wang Kai, chief minister of the Court of Judicial Review (3A). Both were southerners, from Chi-an Prefecture. Rumor had it that Wang Kai wanted Li Ping's position for himself.

P'eng and Wang had an important helper in T'ai-ho man Hsiao Yen-chuang, who was supervising secretary of the Office of Scrutiny for Justice (7B) and son of the former Grand Secretary Hsiao Tzu. P'eng and Wang approached Hsiao Yen-chuang with a request that he draw up a detailed impeachment of Li Ping listing examples of irregularities in Li's handling of official selections and appointments.

Hsiao Yen-chuang complied. He wrote and submitted the bill of impeachment. The Ch'eng-hua emperor then gathered a large court conference to consider the charges. Li Ping "admitted his guilt," and the emperor ordered his immediate retirement.

But among the charges against Li was a vague one, "secretly allying with long-time censors, who supported him in his autocracy [*chuan-ch'üan*]." The emperor was prompted to ask Hsiao Yen-chuang exactly whom he was referring to, and he was visibly angered when Hsiao could or would not give an immediate answer to that question. Hsiao's credibility was further damaged when an official whom he had cited in his long bill of impeachment gave a vigorous and credible defense of himself and his record.

Inevitably, then, someone lodged a counterimpeachment against Hsiao Yen-chuang for having made groundless accusations. Although the original indictment against Li Ping was allowed to stand, the em-

peror agreed that Hsiao had been recklessly malicious, and ordered him
removed and demoted to a post station in Szechwan. It is said that Hsiao
was widely disliked for his "intrigue in behalf of powerful people."
No one was sorry to see him go. (Five years later, he was murdered in
Szechwan.)[11]

Yin Chih was Han-lin reader-in-waiting (6A) at the time, and he detailed this whole affair in his personal memoir. He held no brief for his
county compatriot, Hsiao Yen-chuang. He did side with P'eng Hua and
Wang Kai, and he shared their dislike of Li Ping. He identified one of
the "long-time censors," unnamed in Hsiao's indictment, as one Liu Pi,
who supported Li Ping's effort once again to shift appointment powers
from the grand secretaries to the Ministry of Personnel. He also asserted that those censors, after having been alluded to in Hsiao's bill of
impeachment, concocted in retaliation the falsehood that Wang Kai,
P'eng Shih, P'eng Hua, and Hsiao Yen-chuang were all linked in a conspiracy.

By his own testimony, Yin Chih's power brokering saved the day. "I
feared," wrote Yin,

> that everyone from our prefecture was headed for deep trouble, and so I
> asked Grand Secretary Shang [Lu] to hurry and appoint Ts'ui [Kung, a north-
> erner] as minister of personnel, as a sop to the censors and supervising sec-
> retaries, and to put people's minds at ease. Shang Lu understood that Wang
> [Kai] and P'eng [Hua] had been slandered, and indeed Ts'ui was soon given
> the promotion. Ts'ui furthermore relied on my contacts with the grand sec-
> retaries to secure the appointments of Yin [Min, a northerner] and Yeh
> [Sheng, a southerner] as his two vice ministers. Hsiao Yen-chuang was de-
> moted to a post station, and Liu Pi [and several others] were demoted to
> various local positions, and those fellows have no one but themselves to
> blame for the disaster that befell them.[12]

·   ·   ·

Yin Chih went on to relate at length aspects of a long struggle carried
on by his faction of Peking bureaucracy against another, which was al-
lied to the powerful palace eunuch Wàng Chih (fl. 1476–81).

The bureaucratic infighting that plagued the Ch'eng-hua emperor's
reign (1465–87) has sometimes been characterized as having been based
on regional cliques: northerners versus southerners, or to some extent
Shantung men versus Kiangsi men. There is some substance to these
characterizations. After all, regional distinctions among men from the
north, south, and center were built into the quota system for metropolitan examination degrees, and, similarly, provincial citizenship was fun-

damental to the awarding of *chü-jen* degrees. In bureaucracy, there was the rule of avoidance whereby officials were forbidden to hold office in their native provinces. There were also special observances, like the quasi-official "old rule" that placed Ministry of Revenue posts off-limits to men from Chekiang or Kiangsi.[13]

But to call a bureaucratic clique regional or provincial was only valid as a kind of shorthand. The cliques of the Ch'eng-hua era were fuzzily bounded, not sharply defined in regional membership, and they were not useful as rallying symbols in any positive sense. One did not assert one's own membership of a regional clique; one castigated one's enemies as members of a regional clique. One also acted under the fear of being so stigmatized by others. Regional cliques were nothing to boast of, but they did serve as constructs of the paranoid imagination, as in 1469, when Yin Chih feared that certain others were out to "ruin everyone from our region."[14]

The struggle between factions in the Ch'eng-hua era was mainly about spoils. The parties did not raise ideological or philosophical issues. Factional alignments in those years were built on personal connections drawn across powerful institutions—the palace, the grand secretariat, and the Peking ministries, especially the Ministry of Personnel.

The so-called northern faction was headed by a cooperative link-up among key men at each of these three levels. Eunuch Wàng Chih and his secret police bureau, known as the Western Depot constituted the palace component. The key player in the grand secretariat was Liu Hsu. The key player in bureaucracy was Yin Min, who was promoted to minister of personnel in 1473.

The central players in the southern faction (with which Yin Chih aligned himself) were, in the palace, Li Tzu-hsing, an adventurer and charlatan from Kiangsi, whose skills at divination won the confidence of the emperor, and who served as a secret channel for making direct imperial appointments, by-passing the Ministry of Personnel; and in the grand secretariat, Wan An, from Szechwan Province.[15]

There were northerners such as Li Ho and Chang P'u in the southern faction. There were at least three T'ai-ho officials who belonged to the northern faction. One was the courtly and affable Chang Ta (1432–1505) from Hsiu-ch'i in T'ai-ho's western suburb, who held a series of midlevel posts in the Ministry of Works—and who, years later, with his white hair and dark complexion and furrowed face, was featured in a famous group portrait of high officials who were classmates of 1464.[16] Another was Tseng Yen (1425–1497+) of Nan-ch'i in township 4. He was famous because, after many years of failure, he had finally achieved his *chin-shih* degree in 1478 at the advanced age of fifty-three, and with the final palace rank of number one. People said that Tseng's belated triumph inspired aging examination hopefuls all over China.[17] He was appointed Han-lin junior compiler. And yet another was the frank, friendly, and easygoing Lo Ching (1432–1503), Yang Shih-ch'i's step-grandson and librarian to the heir apparent (5B).

In 1475, Yin Chih was promoted to the position of vice minister of rites (3A), five grades above his previous post (5B). This unusual upward leap did not have the endorsement of Minister of Personnel Yin Min. It came directly from the palace, almost certainly through Li Tzu-hsing's special channel to the emperor.[18] It was said that Yin Chih flaunted his new promotion right in Yin Min's face.[19] In any event, in 1479, when Yin Chih returned to Peking after having observed the mourning period for his father, Yin Min managed to engineer his exile to the bureaucratic backwater of Nanking, as vice minister of personnel in the secondary capital. And there Yin Chih languished until 1486.

In 1486, circumstances changed. Yin Min's ally in the grand secretariat had retired the year before. His replacement was P'eng Hua. P'eng Hua and Grand Secretary Wan An were supporters of Yin Chih. Together they arranged with their palace channel, Li Tzu-hsing, to have the emperor recall Yin Chih to assume a post as vice minister of war. The Ministry of Personnel objected to this irregular summons, to no avail.

The recall was joyous news to Yin Chih. His friends in Nanking arranged a send-off banquet in his honor. An older colleague, northerner Wang Shu, wrote the customary covering remarks (*hsu*). Wang conceded that there was no opportunity in Nanking for anyone who aspired to be a statesman. Peking was the hub for information and news, foreign affairs, and important decision making. Peking was where the true statesman had to be. Wang Shu joined everyone in congratulating Yin Chih for having gotten the opportunity at last to put his great talents to use.[20]

Within a few months of his recall to Peking, Yin Chih's friends and factional allies brought about the dismissal of Minister of Personnel Yin Min. They undermined him by pressing corruption charges against his son. A further dozen or so Peking officials were purged for having been allies of Yin Min. (One of those purged was T'ai-ho man Lo Ching. Both Lo Ching and Yin Min's son were married to women of the same K'ung family. Someone else from Chi-an Prefecture was vying with Lo for a position with the heir apparent. Reportedly, Yin Chih helped to smear Lo Ching and arrange his exile to a post in Nanking. Tseng Yen was also sent there.)[21]

YIN CHIH AS STATESMAN

Long and often unscrupulous political infighting finally paid off for Yin Chih. On October 22, 1486, he was appointed a grand secretary and was at last in a position to influence the high policy matters that had long exercised his mind. Yin Chih was, among other things, a statecraft intellectual and scholar, a man who knew and admired Ch'iu Chün (1420–95) and was himself author of a number of statecraft works, now lost or unavailable, which he had began work on as early as 1470.[22]

Over the objections of the other grand secretaries, his ally Wan An in particular, Yin Chih made efforts to involve the often otiose Ch'eng-hua emperor more regularly and personally in the work of government. The emperor was painfully awkward and shy, and Wan An urged that he continue to be approached through his eunuchs, rather than be dealt with face-to-face.[23] Yin Chih disagreed. He wrote as follows:

> As soon as I was appointed [a grand secretary], I wanted to show my grati-
> tude. I was too naive to have inhibitions, and so I spoke up in full [to the
> emperor], hiding nothing. [Grand Secretaries] Wan An and Liu Chi cau-
> tioned me about that, because they were afraid of upsetting the ruler, who
> might then stop communicating. I said: "If he doesn't consult us, then we're
> not responsible for bad policy. If he consults us, and we don't respond fully,
> then we're deceiving him and betraying our traditions and the office we
> hold."
>
> The emperor's assumption was that when officials presented him with
> long memorials full of admonition, they were simply out to make reputations
> for themselves at his expense. So whenever I had matters to discuss with him,
> I just spoke to him without preparing a formal memorial. He'd always agree
> to what I had to say. Sometimes he hesitated at first, and came around later;
> sometimes he listened eagerly and agreed right away. For a year, we had good
> policy results.
>
> Ruler-minister relations have never been easy, but the [Ch'eng-hua] em-
> peror was well meaning and disposed to achieve good rule. If only the grand
> secretaries who served him had done so with sincerity, outstanding results
> might have been achieved. But most of them were only looking out for them-
> selves, and the emperor was never able to achieve his aim of being an active
> ruler who accomplished good things.[24]

Yin Chih's forte lay in formulating reasonable and clear-cut resolutions of difficult and emotion-laden issues. As grand secretary, he had a

hand in the shaping of several high-level decisions that have tradition-
ally been well received. He argued successfully against a planned military suppression of the Miao minority in Kweichow; he helped
negotiate the settlement of a war between Annam and Champa in the
Indo-Chinese peninsula.

Less well received was his work in removing Min Kuei (1430–1511)
from his position as civil governor (hsun-fu) responsible for suppressing
violence in the far south of Kiangsi Province. Many T'ai-ho people were
establishing themselves down there. "Powerful families took in vaga-
bonds to serve as family servants and tenants, who in turn leagued together as robbers, dividing the spoils [with their masters]." Min Kuei's
strategy was to prosecute the powerful families. The families complained of unjust harassment. Yin Chih took up their cause. Through
Li Tzu-hsing, the palace appointments broker, Min Kuei (a southerner
attached to the northern faction) was removed from his position and
transferred elsewhere.[25]

Yin Chih's tenure as grand secretary was cut unexpectedly short by
the death of the thirty-nine-year-old Ch'eng-hua emperor on September
9, 1487. His son and successor, the Hung-chih emperor, age seventeen,
was soon presented with vehement impeachments of the incumbent
grand secretaries. (The most sensational of these impeachments was
that presented by a brilliant Han-lin bachelor, the twenty-one-year-old
Tsou Chih, a native of Szechwan, who castigated all the grand secretaries as self-serving "small men" and Yin Chih in particular as "a shame-
less and dishonest intriguer of villainous intentions".)[26] The southern
faction, which had only just triumphed the year before, was purged by
the new emperor late in 1487. Li Tzu-hsing was put to death in prison.
Yin Chih was dismissed on November 30 on the grounds that he had
achieved his promotions through procedural irregularities. He was allowed to retire with full honors, however.[27]

In 1508 and 1510, when Yin Chih was very old and living in retirement, the regional issue of north versus south came up again, this time
with special virulence. Eunuch dictator Liu Chin and his ally, Grand
Secretary Chiao Fang, made two forceful moves to enhance the place of
northerners in imperial bureaucracy.

First, in 1508, they revised the provincial and metropolitan degree
quotas to bring the north into a position of full equality with the richer
and more heavily populated south.[28] Then, in 1510, they struck a heavy
blow, specifically at Kiangsi. The opportunity to do that came up when
a man from Wan-an County (just south of T'ai-ho) was caught imper-

sonating an ambassador from Southeast Asia. His case came up for adjudication. The dossier crossed Grand Secretary Chiao Fang's desk. There was some blank space at the end of it, in which the grand secretary scribbled a note, unburdening himself of some deeply felt prejudice:

> Kiangsi society has long featured scofflaws like P'eng Hua and Yin Chih and [several others]. Nobody likes them. We should reduce their provincial quota by fifty. Nobody from there should be chosen for positions in the capital. This should be made an order. And the crimes of Wang An-shih, who ruined the Sung dynasty, and Wu Ch'eng, who served the Yuan, [both of them Kiangsi natives], should be posted up in public so that in future we won't hire so many Kiangsi men![29]

The Kiangsi provincial quota was indeed cut for that year. But in that same year, 1510, Liu Chin was executed and his ally Chiao Fang dismissed; and the Kiangsi quota was restored. Clearly, regional struggle in high bureaucracy had gone too far.

Indeed, as the sixteenth century wore on, the fires of regionalism subsided under the impact of a Confucian moral revival—led by such figures as Wu Yü-pi, Ch'en Hsien-chang, and Wang Yang-ming—whose appeal was to the individual and the moral universe, not to the locality or region. It is interesting to note that Yin Chih was a lifelong enemy of the two earlier revivalists, Wu and Ch'en.

YIN CHIH'S ASSAULT ON THE CONFUCIAN REVIVAL

A major new phenomenon that surfaced during Yin Chih's years in government, and provoked his hostility, was the revival of philosophical Confucianism, which had been in limbo since the death of Fang Hsiao-ju in the Nanking slaughter of 1402. In question was not routine knowledge of the approved Confucian curriculum, which every regular official in government studied as a matter of course, but rather the sustained and systematic rethinking of Confucianism's essential meaning, a quest for moral truth and inner certitude. Two great names in this endeavor were Wu Yü-pi (1392–1469) and Ch'en Hsien-chang (1428–1500), both revered icons in their own lifetimes and later. Yet Yin Chih condemned both of them, not so much on purely ideological grounds as for their behavioral shortcomings. Why? What was it about Wu Yü-pi and Ch'en Hsien-chang that angered Yin Chih?

With the Yung-lo emperor's suppression of Confucian freethinking (in the Chu Chi-yu case of 1404) and his sponsorship of the orthodox

Ta ch'üan (Great compendia) on the Five Classics, the Four Books, and Sung Neo-Confucian metaphysics, individual philosophical inquiry was effectively discouraged. One of the first men to resume it, working carefully within the bounds of the official orthodoxy, was Wu Yü-pi.

His father had been a Nanking official. Wu Yü-pi had been with him in Nanking in 1402, and although he was only ten years old at the time, he must have experienced something of what happened in that city. In any case, at the age of seventeen, he gave up his studies for the civil service exams, broke with his father, and returned home to Ch'ung-jen County, Kiangsi (about a hundred miles northwest of T'ai-ho). There he managed his family's small estate, living and dressing as a common peasant while pondering Confucianism's inner meaning. He had no interest in history or institutions, no interest in current politics, no interest in large-scale questions of national sociomoral order or the future of the realm, all issues that had earlier on obsessed Fang Hsiao-ju. Wu's obsession was personal psychic reconstruction, the individual quest for a perfect moral state of mind, an obsession rooted in doctrine that he took from the state-sanctioned orthodoxy itself. This quest he deliberately pursued in conjunction with (rather than as an escape from) the labor, the discomforts, and the random irritations of life at the everyday level of a working commoner.

As word of Wu Yü-pi's endeavor spread, he attracted a following of men who had, for one reason or another, dropped out of the race for socioacademic success. But Wu had to tread carefully for fear that too large a following would attract the suspicions of the authorities, and he drove many would-be truth seekers away. He assured those who became his disciples that there was no easy path to ethical enlightenment. One imagines Wu and his small band of followers (none came from T'ai-ho) looking like so many common peasants grubbing at chores, talking little, each absorbed in using Wu's formula of "seriousness" and "reverence" (*ching*) to advance by slow and halting steps to some final psychic peace.[30]

Wu Yü-pi became a national celebrity, and he was several times invited to come to Peking for consideration for a possible appointment. Finally, in 1457, he accepted, invited by none other than General Shih Heng, one of the leaders of the coup that had just deposed the Ching-t'ai emperor and restored his older brother to the throne of Ming China.

Wu Yü-pi arrived in Peking in June 1458 and stayed there most of the summer. General Shih recommended that he be made an adviser to the heir apparent (5B). The emperor himself arranged a banquet and urged Wu to accept the offer. Wu gave the matter some thought.

The philosopher's behavior in the summer of 1458 struck some observers as seriously flawed. For example, so deep was his gratitude to Shih Heng that he wrote a preface for the general's genealogy. He even went so far as to style himself the general's "protégé" (men-jen).[31] Thirty-year-old Yin Chih, at the time a Han-lin junior compiler, described the celebrated philosopher, a man more than twice his age, in disdainful detail:

> When Wu Yü-pi arrived, the court treated him with courtesy. High officials and eunuchs went to pay calls on him. At first, Wu addressed every official as "excellency." Later on he discriminated, treating powerful people with excessive courtesy, while addressing those without the chin-shih degree dismissively (as hsiu-ts'ai), and not even escorting them to the door [of his lodging]. Whenever he received rich gifts from people in high places, he would go to their homes to express his gratitude. He collected their calling cards and made an album of them, telling people: "This is for my descendants, so they'll see the great honor of this moment." People disparaged Wu for doing that.
>
> I didn't go visit Wu, but one day when Ch'iu Chün and I went to [Grand Secretary] Li Hsien's home to deliver some poems, Wu Yü-pi happened to be there. I noticed that he was wearing a palm-fiber hat with a peaked crown and wide brim. The grand secretary said [to us, in a tone of mock politeness,] that he was too poor a student to grasp Wu's advanced views, so he and Wu were talking on a lower level that he could understand. Li looked at me and grinned: "I just can't follow the old gentleman!" Wu brought out some confused written proposal, and after a while, Li got up in such a way as to suggest that the interview was over. I rose too. Wu bowed to me and said: "May your excellency leave first, because I have a private matter to discuss with the grand secretary."
>
> I bowed and left, and [Wu's] disciple Huang Shun-chung accompanied me partway. I stopped and spoke to him. "Scholars don't wear palm-fiber hats," I said. "Why does Master Wu wear one?" Huang said: "It's just to keep off the sun." "Public affairs can be discussed in public," I continued. "Private affairs shouldn't be discussed at all. By what right does a private person [like Wu] get to discuss private affairs with a grand secretary?" Huang said: "They're just discussing the question whether to accept or decline the offer of an appointment." "He should decide that for himself," I replied. "Why should he ask the grand secretary to decide it?" To that Huang replied: "The court appointed Master Wu adviser to the heir apparent, and it won't accept his refusal; but he feels he can't take the position unless he has the grand secretary's firm support. That's what he's asking about." I said: "How can he tell whether the grand secretary will really support him or not? What he

should think about is his own fitness for the job. I looked at the six-point proposal he prepared. It consists of nothing but the commonplace remarks of a classics student. There's nothing of any use in it. One can gauge his scholarship from the emptiness of his verbiage. You'd best convince him to decline the offer and retire home. Otherwise, he'll be mocked when people find out his substance doesn't match his reputation." "I guess he shouldn't stay," replied Huang.[32]

In the end, Wu Yü-pi did decide to go home. Yin clearly disliked Wu (the Ming dynastic history says the philosopher had earlier slighted him at a banquet).[33] He also related secondhand some derogatory things about Wu Yü-pi that may or may not have been true. But it is clear from the conversation that he thought all the adulation had turned the sixty-seven-year-old philosopher's head, and that intellectually and otherwise he was completely out of his depth in the sophisticated political world of Peking. Wu's continuing pretension to peasant status also irritated him. It was out of place. Wu Yü-pi's renown had stemmed from his life-long commitment to a spartan regimen of farming and studying and a lonely and heroic quest for personal sagehood. His flirtation with power so late in his life appeared to Yin Chih a serious and unforgivable act of misjudgment. Wu Yü-pi was no sage. He was a shallow fraud.

Yin Chih's negative comments on Ch'en Hsien-chang came much later, and from a distance. In 1483, the Ministry of Personnel, acting on the fervent recommendation of provincial officials, summoned Ch'en to Peking. They wanted him to take a special exam, and then to appoint him to some suitable position.

Although he had been a student of Wu Yü-pi's for a time, times had changed, and Ch'en eventually threw off the restraints of the official Confucian orthodoxy that Wu had always accepted. Ch'en held the degree of B-list *chü-jen* and had attended the imperial college. But he was a committed truth seeker; and he returned home to Kwangtung Province, and there, after many years of arduous effort, he finally achieved "consciousness of the oneness of all things, and of his own participation in the dynamic transformation of the universe."[34] As word of Ch'en's unorthodox "philosophy of the natural" spread, his fame grew wider and wider, and his admirers in officialdom implored the court in Peking to place this tall visionary, with the seven moles displayed visibly across his face, in some suitable post high in court circles.[35]

There is no indication that Yin Chih had ever met Ch'en Hsien-chang. At least, when Ch'en gave in to the recommendations made in his behalf and made his celebrated trip to Peking, Yin was posted in

Nanking as vice minister of personnel. In any event, Yin's comments about him were thoroughly derogatory. He reviewed all the basic facts of Ch'en's career and noted that when, long before, Ch'en had finished job training as a *chien-sheng,* and should have taken an appointment, his friends urged him to win fame by refusing outright and going home, which he did. Then, continued Yin, "he devoted himself to strange ideas and high-flown discussion." Upon his arrival in Peking in 1483, Ch'en refused to take any test with the Ministry of Personnel. He then wrote ten poems in praise of his coprovincial, the palace eunuch Liang Fang, and Liang Fang prevailed upon the Ch'eng-hua emperor to let Ch'en go home with the honorary post of examining editor (7B) in the Han-lin Academy; and so philosopher Ch'en departed the capital, in splendor, borne on a palanquin, the road lined with crowds of admirers holding parasols to shade him from the rays of the sun. "How could anyone who knows Confucian morality [*chih tao-i che*] act like that?" Yin demanded to know. "He never achieved his *chin-shih* degree, and so he made use of *tao-hsueh* [dissenting Confucian study] to delude people [about his intelligence]. Had he ever achieved [his degree], he would certainly have turned out to be insatiably ambitious."[36]

YIN CHIH IN RETIREMENT

Yin Chih disbelieved those who laid claim to personal spiritual enlightenment, but he evidenced credulities of his own, particularly with regard to divination and the supernatural. In 1474, while in Peking, he consulted a certain diviner to find out whether his cousin, Yin Chia-yen, had passed his provincial exams in Kiangsi. The signs read positively, and, sure enough, nine days later when the results arrived in Peking, Yin Chia-yen's name was listed. He had passed![37] Yin Chih was reluctant to discuss Li Tzu-hsing, who was imperial appointments broker and a key player in behalf of the southern faction, but there are certainly grounds for supposing that Yin would have seen nothing amiss with either Li's claim to possess divinatory skills or the authority he derived therefrom.

Most of Yin Chih's reports of divination, dreams, and the supernatural have T'ai-ho County, rather than Peking, for their stage. For example, he noted that on May 9, 1493, late in the day, two ghosts lured Madame Hsiao, wife of I Chü-sung of Hou-ku Ward (township 24) into a pond. Family members found her there the next morning, clinging to tree roots so as not to drown. Wife Hsiao stated that the ghosts had

identified themselves as I Chü-sung's dead cousin and his wife and had
stated that they were taking revenge for I Chü-sung's having seized their
tiny home and field and driven out their old mother, who had then died
of cold and hunger. "I describe this in full," concluded Yin, "not just to
record something about ghosts, but also to warn unfilial descendants
who recklessly seize ancestral property and don't take care of their
mothers."[38]

He wrote an uncanny story about Lung Po of Kan-chu Ward (township 63), who was an old county-school classmate. Lung Po achieved his
chin-shih degree in 1466, twelve years after Yin. He was then appointed
magistrate (7A) in Tz'u-ch'i County in Chekiang, where the local gazetteers remember him as having been an unusually fair-minded and effi-
cient judge in legal cases.[39] One day he went to see the prefect, collapsed
while kowtowing, and expired moments after they carried him out of
the yamen. His corpse was returned to his native T'ai-ho, where it was
buried. But twelve years later, geomancers advised his widow and sons
to bury him in some better site. They exhumed him and brought him
home. They opened his coffin. Lung Po looked alive. His skin and hair
were vibrant, and his clothing looked new. They pushed open his eyelids
and observed in amazement how bright the pupils were. Four or five
years they kept his corpse at home, until at last a suitable site for re-
burial was found. "I was a schoolmate of Lung Po," wrote Yin, "and I
knew how fine a man he was; and although I did not see for myself the
extraordinary physical powers [*yun-ch'i,* that he showed in death], my
local in-law Yang Kuang-pi, who is his wife's younger brother, saw it
with his own eyes and told me it was so."[40]

Yin Chih's robust optimism about life shows in his speculations
about portents. He believed that portents that appeared threatening
might in fact be felicitous. Case in point, Tseng Ch'iung of T'ai-ho city
dreamt he was holding a child with no arms and two right ears, a trou-
bling omen perhaps, but one that Tseng's brother correctly interpreted
as an acting out of two written characters (*ch'ü liao*) that meant he
would pass his provincial exams (which indeed he did, in 1477).[41]

Nor was it necessarily an ominous sign when a local landmark self-
destructed. In 1424, an old pagoda collapsed. In 1485, another old pagoda collapsed. Bad signs? Perhaps not, argued Yin, because in 1424
Yang Shih-ch'i had entered the grand secretariat; and, in 1485, Yin
Chih himself had done the same. Other interpretations were possible,
he admitted. The collapse of things depended on fate, while the appointment of men to office depended upon the times; and these kinds

of events did not necessarily link together. But then, was not T'ai-ho county shaped geographically like a tally? The pagodas had sat in separate halves of it, and it was when you *broke* a tally that you placed it in use. So Yin guessed; but he was not absolutely sure of his conclusion. "I simply record this," he noted, "in the hope that in the future someone of intelligence can straighten the matter out."[42]

Yin was less puzzled about the giant fish people had seen swimming in the Yun-t'ing River starting in 1477. The strange part was that the fish swam with its body submerged and its head above the water's surface. The very next year after its first appearance, Tseng Yen became the nation's first-ranking *chin-shih*. In 1486, people saw that fish again, and later that year, Yin Chih became a grand secretary. In 1492 the fish made a third appearance, and, sure enough, the next year, Lo Ch'in-shun (1465–1457, of Hsi-kang Ward, township 28) became the nation's third-ranking *chin-shih*. Yin Chih seems to have felt that the fish portent needed no special explanation.

In the very next entry in his memoir, Yin Chih went on to remark on Lo Ch'in-shun's part in the only true example of "three phoenixes" in all of China's history. Lo Ch'in-shun won his *chin-shih* in 1493. His two brothers passed in 1499. They were coplacental brothers. Happily, their mother and father lived to witness their success. Never before had three brothers, all from the same womb, achieved China's highest socioacademic degree![43]

Lo Ch'in-shun lived to become one of Ming China's leading Confucian scholar-intellectuals. Yin Chih's life thus bridged two distinct ages. In his youth he knew Wang Chih (1379–1462), and in his old age, Lo Ch'in-shun. He must have known young Lo rather well; their homes were only a few miles apart, in Yun-t'ing Canton. When Yin Chih died in 1511, Lo composed a funerary ode in his honor.[44] Lo was certainly familiar with Yin's *Bits from the Studio of Candor* because he later penned his partial agreement with Yin's negative assessments of the philosophers Wu Yü-pi and Ch'en Hsien-chang.[45]

·   ·   ·

So Yin Chih, after his dismissal as grand secretary at the age of sixty, lived out the rest of his long life at home in T'ai-ho. There is talk of his consorting from time to time with retired tutor Li Mu (1426–1508, of Nan-kang Ward, township 53), with whom he and a few others formed a *chen-shuai hui*, or "club of candid directness," where people were free to say anything they desired, and where an older T'ai-ho tradition of poems, drink, and raillery was carried on among the members.[46] There was talk of his forming a "friendship in which age-difference does not matter" (*wang-nien chiao*) with a much younger fellow—the well-traveled and well-connected T'ai-ho artist Kuo Hsu (1456–1532, from T'ai-ho city).[47] Yin was a participant in local learned discussions. He was always eager to receive high-ranking visitors when they came through T'ai-ho; and his physical energies were such that even late in life he walked so fast that younger men complained that they could not keep up.[48]

He yearned, however, to leave T'ai-ho and return once again to high office in Peking. In 1496, in honor of the Hung-chih emperor's birthday, Yin Chih sent up a conventionally ornate expression of felicitations together with a cover statement, which the emperor correctly interpreted as a request for a recall to office. "Yin Chih was impeached, and he has been living in retirement many years, and now he violates regulations by sending up these documents," said the emperor upon receiving them. "Obviously he flatters me in the hope that I will do him a favor. His request is disallowed."[49]

Yin Chih died on December 20, 1511, and his provocative style died with him. Posterity tended to ignore him. The next generation of brilliant young T'ai-ho elites jumped enthusiastically into the new philosophical storms, whose early warning signs Yin Chih had seen and denounced.

CHAPTER 8

Philosophical Furors

Sixteenth-century T'ai-ho was a county undergoing changes. Silver was modifying the old rural economy, creating new opportunities in financing and moneylending, both within the county and beyond. Managerial agents for the emerging corporate lineages were replacing the great landowners who had served as tax captains, and the tax captaincy system itself was withering away. The upper class was reducing its size and encouraging emigration. The population of *sheng-yuan* (county students) had swollen to somewhere around a thousand, even though bureaucratic opportunities for them had declined by nearly half after 1457. No one paid much attention to the local landscape anymore. It was in many ways a different world. There was no longer a consistent T'ai-ho "style" among the elites, no more a proudly self-conscious localism in their sense of identity. Liu Sung or Yang Shih-ch'i would have had a difficult time recognizing the place.

Yet sixteenth-century T'ai-ho was hardly dead. It produced several nationally prominent scholar officials, whose lives and writings provide participant accounts of the new intellectual developments of mid-Ming China, and indications as to how those developments affected life in their native county. If a sense of T'ai-ho "patriotism" no longer commanded the loyalties of these men, what did? If *shih-hao* (generation after generation of friendly relations) had lost value, if Yang Shih-ch'i's ethic of collegiality among county compatriots in and out of office was no longer sustainable, then what kinds of relationships among the local literati took their place? What did it mean for T'ai-ho that two of the great intellectuals of sixteenth-century Ming China—Lo Ch'in-shun and Ou-yang Te—were contemporary native sons? Not what that proud fact would have meant early in the Ming, certainly.

For the scholar-elites of China, those in T'ai-ho County most definitely included, the sixteenth century was profoundly shaped by the new waves of Confucian thought set in motion by Wang Yang-ming (1472–1529). As anyone even slightly familiar with the scene knows, Wang's many followers interpreted him in many different ways (Okada Takehiko identifies an existentialist left wing, a quietist right wing, and an orthodox center).[1] In addition, there were thinkers who disagreed with Wang Yang-ming, among them Chan Jo-shui (1466–1560), Lü Nan (1479–1542), Wei Chiao (1483–1543), and T'ai-ho's own Lo Ch'in-shun (1465–1547). These and other intellectuals, and those in T'ai-ho who followed them, reacted in different ways to the intense controversies regarding power and ethics that consumed men's energies and passions in the sixteenth century. Some cooperated with those in power; others withdrew; and a few braved the lethal dangers of public protest. There was no consistent T'ai-ho response to all this. T'ai-ho's literati made a wide range of personal choices about how best to engage this new world, and their lives and careers were pressured and torn into almost every possible pattern by its polarities and cross-pressures. No Yang Shih-ch'i presided, offering wide-ranging patronage and guidance.

While Lo Ch'in-shun devoted his life to rethinking and refining the state orthodoxy of Ch'eng-Chu Neo-Confucianism, his county compatriot Ou-yang Te (1496–1554) gave himself totally to the task of restating Wang Yang-ming's ideas and propagating them among the intelligentsia, locally and nationally. Wang Ssu (1481–1524) sought to reconcile the ideas of Wang Yang-ming with those of Chan Jo-shui; and, unlike Ou-yang Te, who did not countenance such things, Wang Ssu plunged forthrightly into the "unfathomable abyss" of political-moral protest, not once but several times, ultimately at the price of his life.[2] Liu K'uei (ca. 1489–1552) entered that abyss once, but with a moral attitude altogether different from that of Wang Ssu. Hu Chih (1517–85) tried, but failed, to become another Ou-yang Te. These men all came from the same county of T'ai-ho, but they acted as though in their minds they were inhabitants of completely different planets.

UNDERSTANDING THE WORLD:
LO CH'IN-SHUN VS. OU-YANG TE

The demise of a naive T'ai-ho localism, localism expressed for example in the earlier descriptions of its landscapes or in Yang Shih-ch'i's Yang-Lo-Teng model for local ethical behavior, is perhaps nowhere better demonstrated than in the irreconcilable worldviews espoused by Lo Ch'in-shun, of Hsi-kang Ward (township 28), and Ou-yang Te, of Shu-chiang Ward (township 61). (There is something slightly absurd about providing their local addresses because, even when living at home, they wrote and spoke as national figures. Outsiders, too, scarcely noticed that both were T'ai-ho men.)

Lo Ch'in-shun, the nation's third-ranking *chin-shih* of the class of 1493, had been for a quarter century on the right track for eminent success in Ming bureaucracy. Matters had come to the point that, by the 1520s, he was offered the posts of minister of rites and minister of personnel, and he was put up as a candidate for grand secretary. But in the fall of 1522, Lo was granted leave to go home to tend to his sick father, and he never returned to the official world again, despite many invitations to do so. Why? Lo was extremely reticent about himself, his intellectual development, and his political views, and it is hard to know for sure. T'ai-ho people speculated that his determination permanently to retire was based in part at least upon his publicly stated difference with the new Chia-ching emperor in what was rapidly developing into the so-called Great Rites Controversy (*Ta-li i*, about which more later).[3]

From 1522 until his death (in 1547), Lo Ch'in-shun lived at home in T'ai-ho, and he was a greatly admired and respected figure, though little given to socializing. His personal life was austere and reclusive. He took some part in lineage organization and community compact formation, but he gave his best efforts to a meticulous rethinking and indeed revision of what the orthodox Ch'eng-Chu philosophy had to say on questions of the nature of mind and reality. The results of his researches he published in installments over the years 1528–46 as *K'un-chih chi* (Knowledge painfully acquired). His intended readership was the scholar-elite of all of China. (This is not the place to take up in detail the thought that these texts purvey; Irene Bloom has done that in her *Knowledge Painfully Acquired: The K'un-chih chi by Lo Ch'in-shun*.)[4]

Lo Ch'in-shun sent the first installment of his *Knowledge Painfully Acquired* to his younger brother Lo Ch'in-chung (1476–1529),

who had just resigned as Nanking vice censor-in-chief (3A) and would
die in a matter of months. Lo Ch'in-chung was living in T'ai-ho city. He
read his older brother's work with great care, agreed with much of it,
and complimented him on it in a short letter; but he also ventured to
dispute with his brother's insistence that the "idealist" Sung philosopher Lu Hsiang-shan was, with respect to his view of the mind, in fact
a Buddhist and not a Confucian at all. Lo Ch'in-shun wrote back a detailed and cogent reply which clearly showed his intellectual strategy,
which was to convince the world of his views by means of a painstaking
comparative review of all the pertinent written evidence on a given issue, a searching exploration of the logical implications of that evidence,
and finally the inescapable conclusions.[5]

In 1536, Lo exchanged a series of letters with Ch'en Feng-wu (1475–
1541). Ch'en had been dismissed in 1527 as Nanking censor-in-chief
(2A) and was living at home, on Back Street outside T'ai-ho's west wall.
Ch'en's letters are lost, but Lo's replies show that Ch'en had read Lo's
work with great care. He agreed with Lo's position against subjectivism,
and he conducted with Lo a friendly, serious, and learned debate on
certain topics (such as the meaning of *ching*, or "reverence"). "We who
respect Chu Hsi," wrote Lo in one of his letters to Ch'en,

> are surely obligated to rediscover where he was right, to fix up his slight
> flaws, to rescue him from his minor biases, to synthesize what he left un-
> done, and put the whole [of his thinking] into a pure and finished state so
> that we have no further dissatisfactions with him. That is how in substance
> to respect Chu Hsi. There is no need to labor to make excuses for [his short-
> comings]. If we proceed in this fashion, not only will we be well prepared to
> refute his attackers but our own minds will be enlarged and brightened and
> freed of encumbrances as well.[6]

(The two correspondents addressed each other as national intellectuals;
that they were both T'ai-ho men meant nothing whatever.)

By and large, however, Lo Ch'in-shun found himself disagreeing
with his colocals because more and more of them were coming under
the spell of Wang Yang-ming, the most famous Confucian theorist of
the Ming dynasty. Wang Yang-ming spent many important years in
office in this or that part of Kiangsi. In 1510, he was magistrate of Lu-
ling County. From 1517 to 1519, he was posted in Kan-chou Prefecture
as assistant censor-in-chief (4A) and concurrently as governor (*hsun-fu*)
of southern Kiangsi, where he was charged with pacifying the endemic
disorder in that region. In 1519, he conducted a memorable and suc-

cessful campaign against the revolt of the prince of Ning in northern Kiangsi. From 1520 to 1521, he was governor of all of Kiangsi; and in that capacity, he stopped one day in T'ai-ho County and directed that copies of two tracts of his be sent over to Lo Ch'in-shun. The tracts sought to argue on evidentiary grounds the case for the subjectivist Confucian position.

Lo happened to be home on official leave at that time. He had met Wang Yang-ming earlier, in Nanking. In 1520, Wang's ideas were beginning to attract serious attention. The first installment of his *Ch'uan-hsi lu* (Instructions for practical living) had been published, and Lo had already read it. Lo read Wang's tracts and replied at once by letter. Concrete evidence and logical argument were home turf to Lo, and his refutation of Wang is persuasive even now.[7] Indeed, Wang conceded in his reply to Lo's letter that his scholarship may have been faulty; and he asked for a personal meeting so that he might persuade Lo face-to-face of the validity of his special insights.[8] No meeting came about.

In 1527, Wang was in Kwangsi Province as censor-in-chief and governor, directing military operations against an ethnic disturbance there, and he wrote Lo again, requesting a public meeting with him for an airing of their philosophical differences. Lo declined such a meeting, preferring to outline in a letter what he saw as the major points of dispute between them. But, unexpectedly, Wang died early in 1529, before Lo had actually sent him the letter; so Lo published it, on the grounds that their "exchange was not a private matter only."[9] Lo wrote a funerary tribute to Wang Yang-ming which was generously complimentary, suggesting only that had his life not been cut so suddenly short, he might eventually have come to some clearer understanding of Confucian doctrine.[10]

Lo Ch'in-shun outlived Wang Yang-ming by many years, and he continued to do battle with the legacy of Wang's ideas. But Lo lacked Wang's boundless energy and charismatic personality. He never attracted a following of eager and dedicated young disciples. He was respected and admired, but he was not loved. He avoided personal or group encounters and confined his formidable persuasive powers to carefully crafted written statements. He was, however, actively interested in the publication and dissemination of his *Knowledge Painfully Acquired*, copies of which he sent to scholar-officials all over China. Some recipients saw his work as a welcome salvo in an emerging national ideological battle against elements who in the interest of "discussing mind-study" (*t'an hsin-hsueh*) were "denigrating classical study," "belittling the Ch'eng brothers," and "rejecting Chu Hsi."[11]

．　．　．

As a thinker and as a person, Ou-yang Te was completely different from his older contemporary, Lo Ch'in-shun. Ou-yang passed his provincial examination in 1516, but then he and his father, having heard something of the thought of Wang Yang-ming, leaped to the conclusion that it was orthodox rather than crypto-Buddhist as many others were saying. The Ou-yangs' excitement was such that, with his father's encouragement, Ou-yang Te postponed taking the metropolitan exam, to venture south to Kan-chou to take personal instruction from Wang Yang-ming. Wang had, by this time, worked out a sort of magic key to the release of psychic energy by way of a dramatic breakthrough to self-understanding. "What Wang was then emphasizing," wrote Hsu Chieh many years later in Ou-yang Te's epitaph, "was that the human mind, being conscious, contained all principles within it; and that to the extent that it was unclouded by desire, and was made immeasurably impartial and deeply quiet, it automatically produced a marvelously effective response [to the world]."[12]

Wang Yang-ming conferred regularly with his students even as he directed military operations and civil reconstruction in southern Kiangsi. Young Ou-yang Te stood high in his teacher's regard; Wang fondly called him his "little up-and-coming talent" (*hsiao hsiu-ts'ai*). Ou-yang served as an aide of some sort and as a teaching assistant, whose job was to meet with new students and give them preliminary instruction.[13] In the *Instructions for Practical Living* (Wang's conversations and letters as recorded and edited by disciples), Ou-yang Te appears several times, asking questions. He wondered why the mind seemed to be always "busy," even when nothing was going on. Why was it not quiet and still? Also, it seemed to him that the words "extending the innate knowledge," (*chih liang-chih*) just by themselves, said everything there was to say (Wang corrected him on that). And why did people with the right approach to learning sometimes fail to share it with others? Ou-yang thought it was because self-absorption and personal ambition stood in the way; and Wang seems to have agreed.[14]

Ou-yang Te left after a year or two. He won his *chin-shih* degree in 1523 (he ranked fourteenth in a class of 265 and was one of nine Ou-yang men from Shu-chiang Ward in T'ai-ho who won that degree in the first half of the sixteenth century). He was then posted as magistrate

(5B) in Liu-an Subprefecture, in present-day northern Anhwei Province. His father worried how his son, only in his late twenties, would handle the demands of the job. Indeed, Ou-yang Te wrote Wang Yang-ming that he was having a hard time of it but was beginning to find some leisure moments in which to gather students and "discuss study." Wang wrote back. "I do my discussions of study even when engaged in busy government work," he chided. "Why wait to gather disciples before you do it?"[15] Ou-yang Te also wrote Wang for further clarification on the relationship between "innate knowledge" (liang-chih) and acquired knowledge; on the ability of the innate knowledge to detect and control purposive or manipulative thoughts; about the problem of physical exhaustion limiting one's ability to manage problems of government while simultaneously cultivating one's mind; and about how to avoid "anticipating deceit" in others while at the same time proceeding as though others were not assuming deceit in oneself.[16] These questions were far less naive than those he had posed to Wang a few years earlier in Kanchou.

Ou-yang Te acquitted himself well in Liu-an, and after a few years he was brought up to Peking as a vice director (5B) in the Ministry of Justice. In 1527, the Han-lin Academy was purged and restaffed, and he was made a Han-lin junior compiler (7A), without a salary cut.[17]

In 1532, he was shifted down to Nanking as director of studies (6A) in the imperial college there; and he remained in Nanking, in one post or another, for the next fifteen years. There he worked to develop and spread his own special distillation of Wang Yang-ming's thought: the idea of extending the innate knowledge. But there was a game to be played with the world of power, and Ou-yang Te played it. He and several other T'ai-ho men in Nanking enlisted themselves as protégés of Yen Sung (1480–1565), the controversial Kiangsi man who was made Nanking minister of rites in 1532 and would as chief grand secretary come to exert a dictatorial hand over the realm for some twenty years, 1542–62.[18]

Ou-yang Te actively proselytized while he was in Nanking. One of those he impressed was Hsu Chieh (1503–83), a future chief grand secretary. Hsu Chieh later gave a description of Ou-yang Te's teaching style:

> He used the occasion of having to monitor the students' writing as an opportunity to draw them into the Way. He built a lecture pavilion, and he invited the Nanking students plus learners from all over the realm for lectures and discussions in it. He made his listeners see their errors by considering their doubts and questions in the light of what the classics had to say, verifying

[the answers] in actual situations, relating them to human feeling, and check-
ing them against changing historical conditions. He taught leisurely, so that
the students would end up with their minds at ease. He was certainly a good
debater, and because he was so utterly sincere and even-tempered, students
were attracted to him in ever increasing numbers.[19]

There survives a substantial file of philosophical correspondence dating to the time when Ou-yang Te was in Nanking. In 1534, Lo Ch'in-
shun sent him a copy of his *Knowledge Painfully Acquired.* There followed several long letters between the two men, both natives of T'ai-ho
County, whose epistemologies were each at a completely different end
of the spectrum. They debated such issues as whether received Confucianism really admitted an innate knowledge as something distinct from
acquired knowledge. Their disagreements could not be reconciled. Although Lo Ch'in-shun was thirty years his senior and far superior to
him as a scholar, Ou-yang Te respectfully stuck to his convictions and
refused to concede an inch to his county compatriot.[20]

Ou-yang Te wrote twice to Liu K'uei seeking spiritual advice. Liu
K'uei (ca. 1489–1552), of T'ai-ho city, had won his provincial degree
in 1507. He never passed his *chin-shih.* From 1535 to 1541, he was in
Ch'ao-chou Prefecture, Kwangtung, as vice prefect (5A) in charge of
military personnel administration. Ou-yang and Liu had earlier studied
together under Wang Yang-ming, and they remained fellow-travelers in
the Way that Wang had laid out. However, Ou-yang felt he was not
making progress. He was trying hard, but he was just harvesting
"weeds" for all his efforts. "Selfishness and deviance" were distracting
him. How could he, he asked Liu, "wash his bones and cleanse his mar-
row, and restore his natural wholeness?" How could he recapture the
"child's mind" that Mencius had said should not be lost? Did it have to
be by way of struggle? Should it not return all of a sudden, as Wang
Yang-ming had implied when he said that the "extension of [innate]
knowledge is there in a mental awakening"?[21]

Lo Ch'in-shun wrote some four philosophical letters to the same Liu
K'uei, of which the burden was a debate over central issues raised in
Knowledge Painfully Acquired. Liu disagreed with Lo; but he did dis-
tribute copies of Lo's book to other officials, and he arranged for the
printing of Lo's book in Ch'ao-chou Prefecture in 1537.[22]

Liu was a colocal and an in-law of Lo's. Early in the Ming, such links
would surely have been enough to encourage collegial solidarity and
a common outlook. Later on, Yin Chih might have turned the philo-

sophical differences between the two men into a harsh dispute. But neither of these possibilities materialized. The differences remained, and they remained purely intellectual. Liu's letters are missing, but Lo quotes statements from them in his replies. The letters were not part of a personal feud but open and publishable contributions to what both seem to have understood as a common pursuit of doctrinal truth.

There also took place a three-way exchange of letters among Ou-yang Te, Lo Ch'in-shun, and Hu Yao-shih (1499–1558, of She-pei Ward, township 51, in T'ai-ho). Hu Yao-shih had won his *chin-shih* degree in 1526, 123d in a list of 301. The correspondence between Ou-yang Te and Hu apparently took place in the early 1530s. Hu was then magistrate of T'ai-chou Subprefecture, where Wang Ken (1483–1541), the renowned founder of the so-called left wing of the Wang Yang-ming school, was near the height of his teaching fame. (Hu's young son, at the time a child of ten or so, was strongly attracted to Wang Ken's belief that immediate sagehood could be obtained through an appropriate development of love of self and love of others.)[23]

Ou-yang's letter to Hu Yao-shih was a careful restatement of his own approach. Ou-yang said there were

> certain comrades who just talk about innate knowledge and omit the need actually to extend it. If you just discuss it abstractly and never exert it, then I'm afraid you'll never really grasp what innate knowledge is. Yet you must know what innate knowledge is before you know how to extend it. Innate knowledge is distinct from acquired knowledge. Acquired knowledge is a function of innate knowledge. It is not itself innate knowledge. What you hear and see is a function of intelligence, but hearing and seeing aren't themselves intelligence. The distinction is small, but the implications of it are immense.
>
> I'm afraid, too, that the comrades have recently been discussing only acquired knowledge. Acquired knowledge has to be gotten through study, and you know it by thinking about it. But innate knowledge is the undiluted altruism of the original mind. You don't study it; you know it without thinking about it. What people do, though, is mix in their personal thoughts, and not everything that forms in their minds is an expression of the true altruism of innate knowledge. . . . When Mencius said the child knows [by instinct] to love his parents and respect his elders, he was in fact referring to the natural manifestation of the undiluted altruism of the original mind, and he was trying to get people to extend that original mind to the whole world. When each conscious thought is wholly altruistic, then each conscious thought extends the innate knowledge. I maintain that it is essential that the innate knowledge be involved in every action we undertake. We cannot extend knowledge unless the thoughts we have reflect innate knowledge. This is

what all the sages have taught with respect to the mind. It is Wang Yang-ming's most important idea, as surely you already understand. But I want you to take very seriously the fine distinction [that I raised].[24]

Hu Yao-shih seems to have climbed aboard Ou-yang Te's bandwagon. Hu wrote a letter to Lo Ch'in-shun in which he seems to have wanted to engage the older man in an extended debate. In his reply (which apparently dates to 1537, by which time Hu had been demoted and made a county magistrate in Kwangtung), Lo was not inclined to comply.

> Your very long letter goes into all the details of what is meant by "extending knowledge and rectifying things." You base yourself mainly on [Wang Yang-ming]'s *Instructions for Practical Living,* and you try to make "making the will sincere," "rectifying things," and "extending knowledge" all one and the same thing, erasing their sequence. Admittedly, the original text of the *Great Learning* leaves some loose ends, but the Ch'eng-Chu commentary explains it perfectly well. Their explanation is long, because the matter had lain so long unapprehended, but they wouldn't have said what they said unless their minds were made up about it. The thing is, we engage in "discussion and study" in order to throw light on things we're not clear about, or still have doubts about. Then we have to get together with friends and talk things through, so we can find out what's right, and not lose our direction. But once we've come to a final conclusion, we must then abide by it and not doubt it. What is there to discuss? I've stated my own views in my ["Knowledge Painfully Acquired"], and you say you've read through that, so I can only suppose that the points wherein we differ are as clear as black and white.[25]

Thus here we have a disagreement about whether Confucianism says that the world is to be engaged intellectually as an object, or psychologically as an extension of a primordial altruistic self, a disagreement involving T'ai-ho literati in various far-flung parts of China, in which, once again, the common denominator of their local identity as county compatriots has no meaning.

MORAL AND POLITICAL PROTEST

Political-moral clashes at the highest levels of Ming government throw a great deal of light on some of the major implications of the various philosophical strategies for world understanding that the sixteenth-century Ming intelligentsia were so feverishly engaged in. How should the members of the bureaucratic intelligentsia, as the moral custodians of the realm, react to the presence of perceived evil in the directing levels of government? The matter was often one of life and death. T'ai-ho men took no consistent stand and can be found on almost every side of the issue.

Late in 1529, before the exchanges of letters with Ou-yang Te and Lo Ch'in-shun noted above, Hu Yao-shih was serving in Peking as a supervising secretary (7B) in the Office of Scrutiny for War. As such, he was, along with the censors, one of the corps of *k'o-tao*, or "designated speaking officials," among whose duties were those of critiquing administration and impeaching malfeasance. On December 6, 1529, a censor by the name of Liu An sent up a critique of the ruling style of the young Chia-ching emperor himself. The ruler, he said, was too intent upon achieving immediate results; he was too emotional and too distrustful of his officials; he was relentlessly investigative rather than wise and discerning; and, inevitably, his inappropriate attitudes were infecting the working style of the whole bureaucracy. The Chia-ching emperor read Liu An's criticisms and was not pleased. "Liu An is selling rectitude in order to win a reputation for himself," he retorted. "He affects simple loyalty but his aim is to stir up malice. . . . I might excuse him just to show that I tolerate criticism, but types like him are villainous and deceitful and cannot be let off easily. He is to be remanded to the Embroidered Uniform Guard for interrogation under torture. Report back [what he says]."

How should the rest of the *k'o-tao* respond to the plight of their colleague Liu An? Supervising Secretary Hu Yao-shih took the very dangerous step of submitting a follow-up memorial in Liu An's defense. For that, Hu Yao-shih was imprisoned and interrogated. On December 20, both men were released from prison and demoted to minor posts in the provinces.[26]

Ou-yang Te was a Han-lin junior compiler at that time. He was thirty-three years old, three years older than Hu. Ou-yang Te wrote a message for Hu Yao-shih *chiding* him for what he had tried to do rather than praising him for his righteous valor. In the message, Ou-yang reviewed the preceding eight sour years of contentious relations, including the Great Rites Controversy of 1524, between the Chia-ching emperor and the upper echelons of Ming bureaucracy. He insisted that criticizing the ruler was altogether the wrong strategy for restoring the Way to the realm. Targeting evil and directly attacking it was like raising the dikes to try to stop a river in flood! Unless the officials carried out the Way in their own behavior, unless they themselves had "rectified things and extended innate knowledge," they could not expect enlightenment in other people.[27] (Hu Yao-shih came to agree.

Eventually he got his career back on track, and in 1552 he retired as surveillance commissioner (3A) of Kweichow Province.)[28]

But what of Wang Yang-ming? Early in his career, had Wang himself not done just what Hu Yao-shih had done? In 1506, as a bureau secretary (6A) in the Ministry of War, Wang Yang-ming had memorialized in defense of a colleague who had been imprisoned for denouncing a powerful eunuch. For that he suffered two months' confinement in the infamous Decree Prison, forty lashes, and four years' banishment to a remote post station. (It was while he was in exile in 1508 and 1509 that he experienced an awakening with regard to the meaning of the Confucian injunction to "investigate things and extend knowledge"; it was then that he "began . . . to pronounce the doctrine of the unity of knowledge and action.")[29]

But after his enlightenment, and as he developed his ideas further, Wang avoided the protest style altogether. He preferred to use tactical finesse in dealing with central authority, to carry out his tasks at the regional level, and to spread his ideas among the younger elites of the realm. During the Great Rites protest of 1524, Wang was in temporary retirement at home in Chekiang Province, and although it appears he disagreed with the protesters and sympathized with the position taken by the young Chia-ching emperor, he did not openly commit himself to either side. The Confucian philosopher Chan Jo-shui (1466–1560), who was in Peking at the time as a Han-lin reader-in-waiting (6A), deplored the whole confrontation and, like Wang, declined to place himself on either side of it. Ou-yang Te had just gotten his metropolitan degree in 1523, and it is not clear just where he was in the summer of 1524. There is no record of his having taken any stand on the controversy.

Lo Ch'in-shun, however, did take a stand. Early in 1522, as vice minister of personnel (3A), he drafted and cosigned a memorial protesting the Chia-ching emperor's express intent to change the ritual arrangement he had been pressured to agree to when he was asked to take the throne.[30] The emperor had agreed, in effect, ritually to disown his deceased father and to make himself son of the Hung-chih emperor (r. 1488–1505) by posthumous adoption; the Hung-chih emperor's own son, the Cheng-te emperor (r. 1505–21), had died childless. In that way, it had been argued, the direct imperial line of descent could be kept intact. Otherwise, the Chia-ching emperor would have been causing the ritual extinction of the original line and founding a new branch in its place. But the new emperor rebelled against that arrangement. He decided that, as a filial son, he had every right ritually to honor his father to the maximum extent possible. This was what was at the heart of the so-called Great Rites Controversy.

As noted, Lo Ch'in-shun had left government forever in the fall of 1522 and was not on hand in the summer of 1524 to participate in what amounted to a general strike by Peking bureaucracy against the Chia-ching emperor, which was followed by a mass demonstration by the officials outside one of the palace gates on August 11. The emperor stood firm against the protesters. They were arrested, imprisoned, and tortured. Many were subsequently flogged. Seventeen demonstrators died of the flogging.[31] One of those who demonstrated and died was Han-lin junior compiler Wang Ssu, a T'ai-ho native, a great-grandson of Minister of Personnel Wang Chih, and in himself a intriguing study in the intersection of personality, philosophy, and protest politics.

To a point, Wang Ssu's career reads like an exact rerun of that of Yin Chih, a very different sort of T'ai-ho man of the late fifteenth century. Wang Ssu was the ninety-first *chin-shih* on the list of 1511 (Yin Chih had been ninety-seventh in 1454.) After he won his degree, Wang was then appointed a Han-lin bachelor, as Yin Chih had been. After two years, he was made a Han-lin junior compiler (7A), as Yin Chih had been. As junior compiler, Yin Chih had carried out some major editorial tasks; but Wang Ssu, whatever his designated assignments may have been, at once involved himself in ethical struggles with the throne. (Yin Chih had rejected that approach as valueless from the point of view of effective statecraft and would never have adopted it.)

There was an innate combativeness in Wang Ssu that differentiated him from the consistently shy and reclusive Lo Ch'in-shun and the warm and radiant Ou-yang Te. Wang Ssu underwent a self-induced personality change, by means of which he consciously sought to put an end to his short-fused aggressiveness and to force himself into the mold of the philosophically self-disciplined intelligentsia of his time. At some point, and unfortunately it is not clear just how or why, Wang Ssu decided he could no longer continue to out-argue everyone or scream at people until his neck turned red. He came to believe that substance must replace dazzle, that reticence must replace disputatiousness.[32]

It appears that Wang Ssu was in an early stage of this personality change when, in February 1514, in the wake of a bad portent (a palace fire), the Cheng-te emperor issued a routine call for criticism. Wang sent up a harsh memorial, accusing the emperor of favoritism and inattention to duty. The emperor ignored the memorial.[33] In September of the same year, the emperor ceased holding audiences because, as report had it, he was recuperating from a wound inflicted in a foolish encounter with a tiger. Wang Ssu announced to his colleagues the style of Confucian thinking upon which he was about to base his next memorial of protest. "A minister should serve his ruler as a son serves his father," said Wang, echoing the *Classic of Filial Piety.* "If his father is ill, the son must show concern. If the father errs, the son must remonstrate with him." Wang then wrote and sent up his memorial of protest, which effectively expressed, in a familial way, shock at the emperor's waywardness and misbehavior.[34] This time the emperor took notice. Wang Ssu was exiled to a post station in Kwangtung Province. Luckily, he was spared the usual physical and verbal abuse.

In Kwangtung, the authorities relieved him of his post station duties and invited him to teach in a local academy. Then, somehow, he obtained leave and joined Wang Yang-ming in his headquarters in Kanchou, surely more as a colleague than as a student. He participated in philosophical discussions. He was invited (as were many others) to join Wang Yang-ming in the campaign against the rebellion of the prince of Ning in northern Kiangsi in 1519. Then he went back to Kwangtung and visited with Chan Jo-shui in order to learn of his ideas. Then he returned to the academy and began to teach in earnest. He tried to create a philosophical bridge between Wang Yang-ming's intensely inward focus and the more outward orientation emphasized by Chan. "Wang Yang-ming bases himself upon extending [innate] knowledge," argued Wang Ssu, "while Chan bases himself on the investigation of things. But it's like the debate about how far the sun is from us. Whether you place it near or far, it's still the same sun." It was said that Wang Ssu was popular with the local students, who published an account of his discussions.[35]

In 1522, the new Chia-ching emperor recalled Wang Ssu to Peking and restored him (along with many other exiles) to his original position in the Han-lin Academy. Within barely half a year of his return, Wang was chiding the fifteen-year old emperor for inattention to duty. What, asked Wang, was the point in rehabilitating officials punished in the Cheng-te era if the new ruler declined to consider seriously their views?[36]

By the summer of 1524, the antagonism between the palace and most of Peking bureaucracy over the ritual-constitutional issue of the imperial descent rules, and who had the authority to define them, heated up to the boiling point. The emperor forged ahead with his determination to honor his princely father by posthumously promoting him to emperor. The bureaucracy refused to cooperate. Junior Compiler Wang Ssu was one of many who memorialized in protest; his second memorial on the issue is striking for its extremism and stands as eloquent testimony to the unbearable emotional heat the Great Rites Controversy generated in its final stages. Wang Ssu moved beyond the technical points of ritual that he had raised in his first memorial. Now at stake was the very survival of civilization itself. "It is by way of ritual that we assign correct names, establish the proper distinctions, set aside dubious things, and bring hidden matters to light," argued Wang. "This is what rectifies government and makes the ruler secure. If government is not rectified, then the ruler's position is imperiled and the power of the dynasty can no longer be sustained . . . Ritual error by rulers leads to chaos; by officials, to their punishment. The key to security and order lies in preserving ritual." The emperor's mistake was to put selfish personal feeling ahead of public necessity, to let "partiality toward his parents" (*ssu-ch'in*) override the "orthodox imperial succession" (*cheng-t'ung*). Aside from a handful of sycophants, argued Wang, the entire bureaucracy was of one mind on this issue. Wang insisted that he was expressing not a "private" view but the "unbiased opinion of all the millions of people in the realm."[37]

Wang's passionate memorials show that he saw the world as object, rather than as an extension of the moral self; that he believed that the world as object embodied evil as a hypostatized force and that the outer world featured the private family and the public realm as wholly separate and indeed incommensurable ritual spheres. The error of the emperor and his "sycophants," fraught with dire consequences for the fate of the realm, lay in destroying "public" ritual with a small-minded desire to satisfy a personal sense of filial piety.

Wang Ssu participated in the mass demonstration of officials at the palace. He was among those arrested and lashed thirty times. On August 24, he died of the gruesome effects. His friends thought it tragic that he had no sons to continue his own patriline.[38] Much of his writing was scattered and lost; but a colleague inquired at his home, secured a copy of his philosophical writing (the *Kai-chai hsueh-lu*), and published it "for the benefit of future students."[39]

· · ·

It was different with T'ai-ho man Liu K'uei, mentioned previously as a friend of Ou-yang Te's and a disciple of Wang Yang-ming's. Inasmuch as Liu K'uei was a faithful disciple of Wang Yang-ming, he did not objectify error and confront it, as Wang Ssu had done, in the style of the remonstrating son. His torment was occasioned by a different philosophy.

The situation was this. The year was 1541. On March 1 of that year, Censor Yang Chueh, a northerner, submitted a wide-ranging, scathing indictment of the Chia-ching emperor, accusing him, among other things, of indulging in useless and wasteful construction projects. The emperor retaliated immediately. Yang Chueh was flogged nearly to death and was then placed in the Decree Prison under the cruelest imaginable conditions, detailed at length in Yang's extraordinary prison notes and diaries. Only a few of Yang's *k'o-tao* colleagues dared come to his defense; those who did were immediately arrested and flogged, and several died in excruciating pain.

Liu K'uei's turn came on October 24, 1542. The emperor was of a mind to proceed with the building of a "thunder altar for the protection of the dynasty and the well-being of the people." Liu K'uei had recently been transferred from vice prefect (5A) in Ch'ao-chou to vice director (5B) of the Bureau of Forestry and Crafts in the Ministry of Works. There was a problem about financing the thunder altar, because of the continuing costs of other construction projects. Liu K'uei did not indict the emperor, but he brought the problem to his attention in a low-key memorial which simply described the difficulty and suggested that the construction be postponed until sufficient funds accumulated. Probably he thought writing such a memorial a compulsory instance of extending the innate knowledge.

The only question was whether the emperor would view this memorial as sincere, i.e., as a routine piece of business, or whether he would suspect an ulterior motive. Indeed, the emperor suspected an ulterior motive. He regarded Liu's memorial as obstructive and insincere. Liu had thought he might and had taken care to make arrangements for his funeral. Liu was arrested, flogged heavily, and placed in the Decree Prison alongside Yang Chueh and various others.[40]

Yang Chueh and Liu K'uei were committed Confucians. Yang, a follower of a northern school, sustained through all his horrible sufferings an attitude of angered defiance. Neither man was about to confess his "guilt." Liu K'uei, however, preferred to turn his terrible misfortune inward; rather than blame the ruler for his plight, he resolved to act as though the fault were his, because "his accumulated sincerity had been inadequate to the task of bringing [the emperor] to his senses."[41]

Compared to what Yang Chueh underwent, the penal restrictions placed upon Liu K'uei were light. Liu was allowed visits by his younger brother, and he shared with Yang Chueh and other less fortunate prisoners the food his younger brother supplied him. It was known that Liu K'uei had been a personal disciple of Wang Yang-ming. Because of that, people wanted to interview him. Prisoner though he was, Liu K'uei somehow made himself available. Yu Shih-hsi (1503–80), a northerner and an erudite (8B) in the imperial college, was an ardent follower of Wang Yang-ming's ideas. He heard that Liu had personally studied under the great man. He managed to have a letter delivered to Liu, and to talk to him. Yu Shih-hsi asked: "What is the essential thing in study?" "It lies in establishing sincerity," replied Liu. He went on to relate some personal anecdotes about Wang Yang-ming. Yu asked Liu to describe in detail how Wang had spoken and acted. "Well," replied Liu, "he was after all just an ordinary man."[42]

Communicating with political prisoners was not entirely a safe undertaking. In 1544, however, Lo Ch'in-shun had a poem smuggled in to Yang Chueh. Yang was impressed. "Lo Ch'in-shun has been living at home for years without communicating with the officials," he exclaimed, "and yet now he sends us condemned men a poem. He is a model!"[43]

There is no indication that Ou-yang Te ever tried to communicate with the prisoners or to do anything to help them. He was home in T'ai-ho on mourning leave at the time of his friend Liu K'uei's arrest. When Ou-yang did return to office late in 1546, it was to Nanking that he went, so perhaps he was not in a position to be able to do much.

But Yen Sung, by this time chief grand secretary, was in a position to help. On September 17, 1545, the emperor was advised by the spirits he consulted through his planchette to release Yang Chueh and another prisoner. Yen Sung suggested to the emperor that Liu K'uei's "crime" was similar and that he should therefore be released as well.[44] And he was.

Then, incredibly, less than a month later, they were all rearrested. It is said that the minister of personnel sent up strong memorial of protest against the emperor's use of the planchette in deciding cases. The minister was unaware that it had been through the planchette that the prisoners' release had been decided. Furious at the personal affront, the emperor petulantly had his revenge. Was the release order improperly arrived at? Very well, then, the men will be rearrested! (Not long after, he arrested the minister of personnel and had him sent home in shackles.)[45]

So guards were dispatched to bring back the prisoners. They reached T'ai-ho before Liu K'uei did. Liu K'uei's brother was there, so they arrested him. Liu K'uei heard about all this when he arrived at a post station near T'ai-ho. He decided to buy a boat then and there and return at once to Peking. He would not even visit his family. He sent them a poem. "It is my duty today to exert every effort on behalf of our enlightened ruler," went one of the lines. "How could I bear to consider my own life, even though I've come this far?"[46] Back to Peking he went. Sometime during the night of December 16, 1545, Yang Chueh, who had already been rearrested, heard the clatter of iron fetters and loud yelling as guards placed wooden cangues on two newly arrived prisoners. One of them was Liu K'uei. "What, have they captured and brought in tigers?" joked a guard sitting by Yang. "They haven't forgotten what it's like in fetters," laughed Yang. "But you'll see what they're really like when they start suffering the cold and heat."

One day during this second internment, Yang Chueh and another prisoner decided to eat no more of the terrible prison food. Liu K'uei talked them out of a hunger strike and insisted that they share the food his brother brought him. The emperor's intent, he argued, was to keep them alive, not to kill them. So they shared. Then one day the guards learned that the emperor was upset because his prayers for snow were not answered, and they feared they themselves might be punished for their lack of vigilance (the gods might be withholding snow as a sign of their displeasure with administrative laxity in the prison). For nine days all food to the prisoners was cut off. Finally one guard interceded with his superiors and got it restored.[47]

After two years, in December 1547, the prisoners were freed again, this time for good. By then their long ordeal had made them national celebrities. But what had it all meant? Lo Hung-hsien (1504–64, from Chi-shui County, north of T'ai-ho), a right-wing follower of the Wang Yang-ming philosophy attempted a conclusive answer to that question in a birthday message he wrote for the liberated Liu K'uei. It had all been a test, stated Lo. According to Lo, Liu K'uei's memorial about the thunder altar had been moderate in tone and had dealt with a matter well within the competence of the writer's official duties, as the emperor himself had acknowledged upon "brilliantly investigating its hidden subtleties." There was no great guilt there, but the emperor had not been absolutely sure of Liu's motive,

> so he decided to detain him a while to test his sincerity. He kept him in prison for six years, along with Yang [Chueh] and Chou [I]. The emperor further sent observers to report on the three men's speech and behavior, on their eating and sleeping, and on anything unusual. He was informed that their demeanor was always good, their words never reproachful, and that they ceaselessly engaged in [philosophical] discussion, even when deprived of adequate food and clothing. So he fed them from time to time. The three men's sincerity was all the firmer. Then one day, without waiting for the authorities to request it, the emperor released them. The people of the realm were all moved by the sage emperor's benevolence, and everyone congratulated the three on their good fortune.[48]

It is hard to know what to make of Lo Hung-hsien's extraordinary statement. Could it be that the emperor, by his cruel experiment, had actually performed a meritorious public service? Had the strength of the commitment of the Ming intelligentsia to Confucian moral truth in fact been in serious doubt until Yang Chueh, Chou I, Liu K'uei, and the Chia-ching emperor together cooperated to prove that it was unbreakable?

· · ·

Another issue of protest came up in 1554. It involved Yang Tsai-ming (1514–63), a fifth-generation descendant of Yang Shih-ch'i. As a *sheng-yuan,* Yang Tsai-ming was a brilliant local talent. Ou-yang Te's friend Hsu Chieh noted that firsthand when he was educational intendant in Kiangsi.[49] People said he bore a facial resemblance to his famous ancestor. He carried Yang Shih-ch'i's portrait around with him wherever he went. In 1538, at the age of twenty-four, he achieved his *chin-shih* degree, 162d in a class of 222. After serving as prefectural judge (6B) in the provinces, he was promoted in 1547 to the Ministry of Personnel in Peking. By 1554, he was vice director (5B) in the ministry's Bureau of Evaluations. And there he crossed swords with Grand Secretary Yen Sung.

The all-powerful Yen Sung was a patron and protector of Ou-yang Te (by this time minister of rites in Peking), of other luminaries of the Wang Yang-ming school, of Kiangsi men, and of many others. As Hu Chih tells the story, personnel control had largely fallen into Yen Sung's hands, and because he was in the habit of rewarding and promoting his

supporters and punishing his opponents, he controlled what amounted
to a personal bureaucratic machine. He thought he had a reliable sup-
porter in Yang Tsai-ming. They were coprovincials, after all. Yen Sung
saw to it that Yang's parents were accorded very special honors.

But Yang Tsai-ming was not a party loyalist, as things turned out. As
a personnel evaluator with responsibility for recommending promotions and demotions, he found himself growing increasingly distressed
with the inevitable corruptions of machine politics: "The habits of men
and the affairs of state were becoming ever more skewed and deviant."
So he turned party traitor. "He withdrew into his own mind in order to
spur himself on. He firmly declined all social invitations, and confined
himself to a remote recess of his office. He ordered his servants to lock
his house against importuning visitors and guests. That way, he was
able to effect his will on his own . . . and promote good people, and
demote the bad ones."

Yang Tsai-ming's one-man guerrilla war on machine corruption threatened Yen Sung's people, and clearly it could not be waged for long. On
March 1, 1554, a pretext was found, and the hammer fell. Yang was
demoted to the post of clerk in a county in Fukien.[50]

Yang Tsai-ming must have been taking spiritual advice from Minister
of Rites Ou-yang Te. It is not clear for how long. He sent Ou-yang Te
a personal letter upon or just after his departure from Peking. That letter is lost, but Ou-yang's reply to it survives. In it, Ou-yang endorsed
Yang's belief that the appointments system was corrupt. He also noted
that sudden demotion was a common risk that everyone faced in bureaucratic life. The problem was how to effect the reform of government in such circumstances. "Change and transformation," counseled
Ou-yang Te,

> cannot be brought about by the efforts of one or two men acting over the
> short term. What I wish of you, and people like you, is that you exert a mind
> to illustrate illustrious virtue to the realm, and that you truly make the effort
> to rectify things and extend innate knowledge, because [external] change oc-
> curs only when transformation in our own selves affects affairs. As the Bud-
> dhists say, first oneself is pure, then a hundred selves are pure, then a single
> generation is pure, and finally a hundred generations are pure, and in that
> way a world of pain and suffering turns [by slow degrees] into a land of
> total joy.[51]

So that was it! That was how Ou-yang Te justified his own membership of a machine that he conceded was corrupt. That was how he believed the pure world of philosophy must intersect with the soiled world

of politics. The slogan extend the innate knowledge—which for Ou-yang Te was key to all the rest of Confucian philosophy—was not useful or meaningful in any real-world sense unless a powerful personality bordering on the saintly vested the words with consistent force and, through them, radiated an irresistible charm and glow.

There seems little doubt but that Ou-yang Te radiated such a glow. His official career climaxed in the years 1552–54. In April 1552, he was ordered to return from mourning leave to take appointment as minister of rites (2A) in Peking, and in October, he was made concurrent chancellor of the Han-lin Academy. It happened that there was a dangerously contentious ritual matter on the imperial agenda, a matter potentially as explosive as the Great Rites Controversy of 1524. The issue involved the status of the Chia-ching emperor's oldest surviving son (the future Lung-ch'ing emperor, b. 1537) and the burial ceremony due the son's mother, consort K'ang (d. 1554). The emperor insisted upon degrading his son's status; but the issue lay within the proper scope of the Ministry of Rites, and Ou-yang Te could not let the matter slide. His son Ou-yang Shao-ch'ing helped draft the memorials, so worded as to sustain the son's rights and those of his mother without provoking the emperor into another of his brutal outbursts. Indeed, the emperor backed off slightly. This remarkable feat was later attributed to Ou-yang Te's personal charisma, his "profound and wordless effect upon people."[52] Asked about his success in this matter, Ou-yang reportedly replied: "I seek a thing in my mind, and if my mind knows it to be right, then I resolutely do it, regardless of danger. If I know it to be wrong, then I won't do it, even if it is advantageous to do it. This is what I learned from my teacher [Wang Yang-ming], and it is my way of extending my innate knowledge."[53]

Ou-yang Te died of natural causes in Peking on April 24, 1554. He was fifty-eight years old.

FERMENT AMONG THE COUNTY STUDENTS

In the 1530s and 1540s, the new intellectual currents were clearly having profound effects among the *sheng-yuan* population of T'ai-ho. What were the effects? Did the new waves of Confucian thinking rekindle among them a sense of local or regional solidarity and pride? One reason for posing the second question is that Kiangsi Province, Chi-an Prefecture especially, had become a nationally important center of intellectual activity, so much so that there was a tendency throughout China to see all the many different thinkers of the Wang Yang-ming school there, despite their significant individual differences, as members of a single regional group, the "Chiang-yu Wang-men."[54] There were even built at Ch'ing-yuan Mountain in Lu-ling County, just north of T'ai-ho, residential quarters and a meeting hall for philosophical gatherings and discussions among the "comrades of the nine counties [of Chi-an Prefecture]."[55] Did this regional philosophical venture effectively substitute for the landscape aesthetic that had given the young elites of T'ai-ho such a strong sense of identity in the fifteenth century? The answer is no.

The young elites of sixteenth-century T'ai-ho were passionately in quest of spiritual-intellectual certainty. The right mentor with the right approach might not necessarily be found within local or prefectural boundaries. One might have to venture further.

Take Hu Chih's father, Hu T'ien-feng (1495–1533), an ambitious but destitute young man from a family of smallholders and primary teachers in I-ho Ward (township 51). He was appointed a *sheng-yuan* without stipend in 1523. But he was soon forced to quit and find work tutoring because "the family income was shrinking at the same time that the dependents were increasing in number." He found a job in Yü-tu County in southern Kiangsi, where many other T'ai-ho people were living as sojourners and migrants.

Wang Yang-ming had left southern Kiangsi a few years earlier, but two followers of his were living right there in Yü-tu. Tutor Hu began visiting them to "discuss study." They told him that "the study of the sages emphasizes turning matters inward into the mind, not exhaustive [outward] inquiry." At first, Hu T'ien-feng disagreed with that idea. Then he "half doubted it, and half believed it." Then he described (in an essay called "How I Came to Believe") how his confidence in external inquiry crumbled when one night he got so simple a thing as the correct time completely wrong. "That was," he concluded, "how I came to believe that the study of Master Wang Yang-ming alone had a real basis to it." He made it clear that he had undergone a fundamental intellectual conversion. "At first I did not believe in [Wang Yang-ming's] study because I thought he was at odds with the Sung Confucians. But in fact the Sung Confucians not only said 'that which inheres in things is principle,' they also said 'human nature is principle.' That which inheres in things may well be external, but we cannot say that human nature is external. If it is not external, then principle too is not external. So it is clear from which point we must begin our inquiries."[56]

But Hu T'ien-feng's was not necessarily a widely shared experience. Five students from T'ai-ho were in Nanking in the years 1527–35, as disciples of Lü Nan, a northerner who was teaching there. Lü Nan held Wang Yang-ming in respect, but he insisted that his formulas were too generalized and procrustean. Confucius had varied his message depending upon who was questioning him. "How he brought people along depended upon their character and learning," argued Lü. "He never tried to measure everyone by the same yardstick. But our teachers nowadays have the mistaken idea that they can fashion a few words and make everyone follow them, no matter what their character or state of knowledge might be."[57]

> [A disciple] said that learners had been deeply benefited by Wang Yang-ming's teaching them about innate knowledge.
> To that, [Lü Nan] replied: "That's too impenetrable a phrase. The Sage [Confucius] never taught like that. You can't use that with everybody. People's characters, their stage of progress, and their learning all vary too much. [Confucius] spoke individually to a man's faults, his shortcomings, his prejudices. He never insisted on a single slogan. When he did establish fixed methods for future generations, he spoke of investigating things and extending knowledge, broad learning in culture, and ritual restraint. Impenetrable phrases may be all right for establishing general methods, but they cannot be retailed individually to people."[58]

When Ou-yang Te was teaching in Nanking, Wei Chiao (another Confucian thinker opposed to Wang Yang-ming) wrote him several times, respectfully urging him to discontinue his teaching-through-discussion (*chiang-hsueh*), because it was both empty and heretical, as well as too popular. One should "seek truth from actual affairs," he insisted. Seeking truth from actual affairs was not Ou-yang Te's way at all, and he proved wholly immune to Wei Chiao's friendly counsel. But Wei Chiao found at least one T'ai-ho disciple, whose spiritual-intellectual progress he solicitously monitored.[59]

T'ai-ho's *sheng-yuan* were a mixed lot. Probably most of them were preoccupied with studying for exams. But not all. Tseng Yü-ch'ien (1520–62, of Moon Hill Ward, township 32) was a student leader, actively involved in local issues in the 1530s and 1540s. He led a petition to reform the regional salt distribution laws, as well as a successful protest against stern disciplinary measures that the T'ai-ho magistrate and school officials were about to impose on the student body.[60] Others formed themselves into small cliques and study groups. Some groups took part in ongoing national debates about how to evaluate China's literary and cultural heritage.[61] Other study groups were philosophical, with Wang Yang-ming's ideas their principal focus.

Hu Chih, a brilliant and much sought after local student, drifted in and out of both sorts of groups. In 1542, Ou-yang Te returned home on mourning leave and arranged a series of seminar-style study meetings for the local students in the P'u-chueh monastery in T'ai-ho city. "All the comrades in the city went to those meetings," wrote Hu Chih, "except me." Then, recalled Hu, Ou-yang Ch'ang (1516–67), a stipend student and a distant relative of Ou-yang Te's, "urged me at least to go and pay my respects, and so I accompanied him to the monastery. Ou-yang Te called me by my old name. 'I-chü,' he said, 'why have you taken so long to come?' He asked me my age, and I told him, and he said: 'You sit below so-and-so, who is older than you.' I noted how courteous and direct he was, with no air of self-importance, and that won me over." Ou-yang Te then led a discussion about how to avoid objectifying good and evil. "It was a fault of mine," Hu Chih confessed, "that I was given to fits of anger, and [Ou-yang Te's] words touched me, just as though they had been said especially for me."[62]

The discussions then moved from T'ai-ho city to another Buddhist temple, probably in Hao-ch'i Ward (township 61), home of Ou-yang Te's in-laws, the K'ang.[63] Hu Chih went along, at the urging of Ou-yang Te's son and aide, Ou-yang Shao-ch'ing (1517–74). "Ou-yang Te treated me not as an ordinary fellow but as a son," wrote Hu Chih, "and so Ou-yang Shao-ch'ing befriended me and treated me like a brother."[64] It thus appears that Ou-yang Te did not welcome a mass followership, but instead selected a chosen few to bring into an inner circle of family-like devotees.

At the new discussion site, Hu Chih took further lessons from Ou-yang Te about extending the innate knowledge and "establishing one's will." He was also tutored by *chü-jen* Yang Hai, who was a descendant of Yang Shih-chi and was serving Ou-yang Te as a personal aide. Hu Chih and the other disciples put questions to Yang Hai. Were knowledge and action really the same thing? "We aren't forcing them to be one, they really are one," replied Yang. "Take Chu Hsi. He taught that in order to exhaust principles, one must first abide in seriousness. Is this two things, or one? Confucius at fifteen put his will on learning, and at thirty, he was established. In neither case did he put knowledge first. Not that he deliberately refused to; it's just that if there's action, there is knowledge, and if there is knowledge, there is action. That's why we regard them fundamentally as one."[65]

In spite of the lessons at the new discussion site, Ou-yang Te's philosophy failed to take, and a few years later Hu found himself in a deep quandary about what path he should take. A fellow *sheng-yuan,* Wang T'o (a descendant of Minister of Personnel Wang Chih), urged him to work harder on "study" and suggested that he go north to Chi-shui County and get advice from Lo Hung-hsien, a nationally known Wang Yang-ming follower. Hu Chih did that.

Hu Chih was aware that Lo Hung-hsien differed with Ou-yang Te on the question whether innate knowledge should be identified and stressed as the fulcrum of Wang Yang-ming's thought. For Lo, the key point of departure was not innate knowledge. There was such a thing as innate knowledge, but it was impossible to dredge it up from its bed deep in the mind and project it directly into the world of action. One had first to soak it in meditation, a procedure he called "returning to tranquillity."[66] "What [Lo Hung-hsien] taught us," Hu Chih recalled, "was to maintain tranquillity and reduce desires. While I didn't fully agree with him, I understood very well the part about reducing desires; that it is obvious from the very way we exercise the spirit in everyday affairs that we have to make exacting judgments about the propriety of giving and taking."[67]

Lo Hung-hsien's relationships with his students appear to have been more caring and personal than those of Ou-yang Te with his. Lo regularly corresponded by letter with absent or former disciples (among them at least seven younger T'ai-ho men); and his letters show him worried about their personal well-being, their career difficulties, and often their states of mental depression. He chided them, cajoled them, counseled them, and gave them pep talks.[68] Ou-yang Te's letters to younger men tended to be explicative or didactic; he may well have been personally interested in them, but it is hard to find evidence for that in his letters. Thus for spiritual as well as philosophical reasons, striving young men from T'ai-ho thought nothing of looking beyond the county borders for mentors, guides, and patrons.

In 1549, when Hu Chih joined several other junior T'ai-ho men and organized a formal philosophical study group they called the "Club of Five" (*Wu-jen hui*). Why it was called a Club of Five when its membership was at least six is not clear. At any rate, they drew up a membership register (*hui-chieh*). The register was brought to the attention of Ou-yang Te, who was then in Peking as vice minister of personnel (3A); but someone also took it to Tsou Shou-i, a leading Wang Yang-ming disciple in An-fu County, and Tsou wrote a preface for it (now lost).[69]

All this extracurricular learning the T'ai-ho *sheng-yuan* were pursu-
ing in the mid–sixteenth century was given some support by local men
of means, among them Chang Feng (1501–1573+, of Hou-tung Ward,
township 5) and Kuo Ying-k'uei (c.s. 1529, of Kao-p'ing Ward, township 61). Chang achieved his provincial degree in 1528, failed four
times at the metropolitan level, and in 1556 retired after eighteen years
of good work as a local official. In the 1530s, Chang was a personal
disciple of Ou-yang Te's. But then he went to T'ai-chou in northern
Kiangsu to take instruction from the noted "existentialist" Wang Ken.
Chang made his home a venue for philosophical discussions, the demanding logistics of which his wife, née Liao, helped manage. He later
revised and had printed the philosophical discussions of Wang Ken. And
in 1556 he built at his home in T'ai-ho an academy for local students,
and he also interested himself in the "quietist" doctrines of Tsou Shou-i
and Lo Hung-hsien. A rich man, Chang was principally an enthusiast
and booster, not a thinker in his own right.[70]

Kuo Ying-k'uei was also plugged into nearly all the ongoing philosophical currents. From 1526 to 1529, he attended the imperial college
in Nanking, and there he absorbed the teaching of Chan Jo-shui, whom
he took for his teacher and mentor ever after. In 1529, he and Lo Hung-
hsien became *chin-shih* year-mates, and he got to know Lo very well. In
1533, he was demoted to a post in Huo-ch'iu County in what is now
northern Anhwei Province, where he lectured students in a local academy about the ideas of Ou-yang Te. He spent much of the rest of his life
in T'ai-ho, reportedly living the simple lifestyle of a Confucian student
(*ju-sheng*) and spending all his time attending philosophical discussions.
He was the leader in the funding and building of T'ai-ho's Ts'ui-ho
Academy in 1560. Like Chang Feng, Kuo was an enthusiast, a sociable
man, and a benefactor, not a thinker.[71]

The most striking things about these boosters, as well as about the
sheng-yuan, are their eclecticism and their evident belief that it made no
sense to support T'ai-ho men and T'ai-ho thinkers exclusively. By the
same token, it is clear that despite diminished opportunities in government, the educated elite of T'ai-ho County were full and active participants in the exciting and absorbing intellectual life of sixteenth-century
Ming China. T'ai-ho was neither dull nor dead. In several respects it
was a much more interesting place than it had been in the fourteenth or
fifteenth century. Still, one wonders whether the county had not lost
its sense of specialness and wholeness. Its leading lights were national
figures with national followings; yet so many of its younger men kept

looking elsewhere—to Wang Yang-ming or Wang Ken or Chan Jo-shui, to Lü Nan or Wei Chiao or Lo Hung-hsien or Tsou Shou-i—for philosophical and spiritual guidance.

HU CHIH: A DISCIPLE OF OU-YANG TE?

In the latter part of the sixteenth century, there was certainly a golden opportunity to found a nationally recognized T'ai-ho "school" of Confucian philosophical interpretation in the Wang Yang-ming tradition. It could have focused upon perpetuating Ou-yang Te's doctrine of extending the innate knowledge. There were several former disciples of Ou-yang Te's in T'ai-ho who could have had a hand in founding such a "school," and Hu Chih was poised to assume the leading role in it. In fact, some years after Ou-yang Te's death in 1554, Hu Chih gave indications that some such attempt might be in the offing.

From 1567 to 1569, by then surveillance vice commissioner (4A) in charge of education in Szechwan, Hu Chih took an extended home leave to look after his mother, but he also made a ceremonial visit to Ou-yang Te's tomb and offered a "report" to his shade. Ostensibly an expression of utter devotion, Hu's tomb report actually conveyed a personal interpretation of his teacher's doctrine that the teacher himself might not have recognized as his own. Hu Chih linked the thought of Ou-yang Te historically to the orthodoxy of Confucius and Mencius by way of what he now said was Ou-yang's central phrase—not "extending innate knowledge," as Ou-yang himself would have had it, but the "substance of benevolence."[72]

At about this same time, Hu Chih accepted an invitation to preface a selected edition of Ou-yang Te's writings, compiled by Grand Secretary Li Ch'un-fang, which the Chi-an prefectural government was about to publish. In his preface, Hu Chih seems again to have rethought Ou-yang Te's place in history. In the preface, he adjusted the location of his teacher in the national intellectual genealogy (which he now said began with Confucius and threaded its way to Ou-yang Te by way of Ch'eng Hao and Wang Yang-ming). He also took Ou-yang's central concept of extending the innate knowledge and applied such torque to it as to deflate its importance. The "true substance" of innate knowledge, he argued, lay in an elusive spot where it and heavenly principle coalesced—where the universe became a whole, *without* clean distinctions between inner self and outer reality, tranquillity and engagement. (Ou-yang Te's whole point had been to keep the distinctions; to project the original, altruistic inner self into external engagements.) However, Ou-yang Te was not a good writer, and the phrase "extending innate knowledge" gave readers only a hazy clue to his ideas; and Hu Chih was surely right to emphasize in his preface that to understand Ou-yang Te, one really had to have had personal experience of him.[73]

In 1570, those who had known Ou-yang Te built a sacrificial temple to his memory in T'ai-ho, and the imperial government ordered its officials to conduct seasonal sacrifices in his behalf there.[74] Yet if his chief disciple was giving his doctrine a radical misreading, then any hope for founding of an Ou-yang Te "school" that kept faith with his ideas was surely dimmed.

In fact Hu Chih had tried for years, but in the end failed, to make Ou-yang Te's precepts take hold in his own psyche. Hu Chih's extraordinary "spiritual autobiography" shows that he suffered one personal crisis after another until Ou-yang died in 1554, whereupon his unhappy disciple at last felt himself freed of an impossible burden, got his mind in order, and, at the age of thirty-seven, as Rodney Taylor writes, properly established his "resolve."[75]

Hu Chih's difficult experience demonstrated to his contemporaries that "extending the innate knowledge" could not be simply lifted off the page and put to personal use in the real world by just anyone. Ou-yang Te seems seldom to have been assailed by doubts (at least, he was not at all given to making personal revelations), and the formula obviously worked smoothly and effectively—for him. So if a T'ai-ho "school" based on the ideas of Ou-yang Te failed to establish itself, much of the reason for that failure must be laid to Ou-yang Te himself, attractive a personality though he was, and to the fundamental unteachability of his approach to life.

Hu Chih's departure from Ou-yang Te was not simply philosophical. It extended to politics. It has been noted that Ou-yang Te had no qualms about cooperating with Grand Secretary Yen Sung and his corrupt machine. In contrast, Hu Chih could scarcely conceal his revulsion.

In 1556, on his fourth try, Hu Chih achieved his *chin-shih* degree (forty-first overall in the final palace ranking) and was appointed a bureau secretary (6A) in the Ministry of Justice. His wife, Hsiao Jun-chuang, joined him in Peking, and she urged him, for his career's sake, to ingratiate himself with Yen Sung. Hu Chih adamantly refused, and she backed off. "Yen Sung's residence was a hub of activity day and night," he explained, "and crowded with people seeking favors, but my wife never demanded that I do things I disapproved of, because she was familiar enough with my simple stubbornness to know that I could not be forced."[76]

In Peking, Hu Chih participated in philosophical discussion meetings at the Ling-chi temple and established close ties with the then current generation of intellectual celebrities.[77] They all opposed Yen Sung, in a low-key way.

Hu's student and biographer explained that Yen Sung wanted Hu Chih to be a personal protégé. Both were Kiangsi men. Hu Chih turned down several invitations from Yen Sung. Hu Chih kept saying he was ill and could not come. Yen Sung was incredulous. "How can Hu be so sick all the time?" he asked. In 1560 other Kiangsi men finally prevailed upon Hu to pay a visit. The meeting did not go well. There were policy arguments. Yen Sung was angered, and others at the meeting were upset. Yen Sung soon ordered the transfer of Hu Chih together with his circle of junior oppositionists out of Peking to various posts in the provinces.[78]

Some years later, Hu Chih locked horns with Chang Chü-cheng, who in 1567 had been made a grand secretary and would in a few years become the most powerful man in China. Around 1570, Hu Chih was education intendant in Hukuang Province, and in a letter he tried to persuade Chang of his philosophy. The real key to Confucian doctrine, he wrote, lay in the word "benevolence" (jen). To grasp it, one had to identify mind with universe. Too many of the intelligentsia were ignoring the outer world in favor of a one-sided emphasis on interior "vacuity and tranquillity."[79] Grand Secretary Chang disagreed, and he sent a sharp reply to Hu Chih. According to Chang, the trouble with the intelligentsia of the realm was that they were seeking truth from "language and words" and were not at all interested in achieving concrete results. It was not just a matter of chasing "vacuity and tranquillity." Even when one talked of "exertion" and "seeking benevolence," Chang warned, one fell into the same kind of language trap.[80]

Meanwhile, Chang Chü-cheng proceeded with the spectacularly successful but controversial fiscal reforms that, along with other reforms, have made him one of the most famous figures in China's long history.

There was no room in Chang's world for intellectuals like Hu Chih, and in 1573, Hu Chih resigned and returned home to T'ai-ho.[81]

When he was living in T'ai-ho from 1567 to 1569, Hu Chih busied himself giving advice about the organization of a community compact (hsiang-yueh), a matter discussed in an earlier chapter. Instead of living at home, he stayed with his mother's people, the Chou of Ch'i-t'ien

(Lacquer Field Ward, township 51), and the Chou advanced funds to build facilities to feed and house the students who came to take instructions from him. Reportedly, "several tens" attended the "small meetings" Hu conducted, and "several tens to a hundred" attended the big ones.[82]

Upon his return to T'ai-ho in 1573, construction went ahead on a long planned academy-like building designed especially to house Hu Chih and his many young followers. It was decided to name the new building the Ch'iu-jen (from *ch'iu-jen*, or "seeking benevolence," the Confucian slogan that Hu Chih favored). The principal contributors were two wealthy men, one-time *sheng-yuan*, who had in their youth been attracted to Wang Yang-ming's ideas. The site they chose was scenic, near a Buddhist temple in township 52, and close to the headquarters of the Ch'iu-jen Community Compact that Hu had earlier helped organize. In 1581, Hu Chih moved in; there was a party, everyone wrote poems, and as a memento, a picture was painted of Hu Chih and his principal backers, with the local scenery for background.[83]

And there amid the scenery, in the last major act of his life, Hu Chih completed what he considered to be his major philosophical statement, the *Hu-tzu heng-ch'i* (The balancing and blending of Master Hu). His former student Kuo Tzu-chang helped him to get it published. In a letter to Kuo, Hu Chih explained why he wrote it:

> My intent is this. While earlier thinkers surely advanced this study of ours, they were in some respects inhibited, and didn't dare come out straightforwardly and say everything. They didn't see that by not being straightforward, they couldn't make the Way visible. That is the reason for all the doubts and criticisms raised in discussion circles. Our comrades like to set up separate schools [*men-hu*], and advance curious arguments and extravagant ideas, and they end up contradicting themselves. How can we clarify this study of ours that way? How can we fix men's minds? Was this how the ancients did it, when in a common spirit they discovered a unified Way?
>
> Here I devise no infallible short formula wherewith to set the truth right. Instead, I go at this study of ours exhaustively. I pay no attention to schools or individuals as such, nor do I try to win the world's favor by flattering my predecessors. The substance of my view is that these principles of ours are not forged somewhere outside ourselves; that they proceed from root to branch; and that while it is essential to know the root first, we must not neglect the branches. . . .
>
> Confucius once said that if a thing is not expressed in an appropriately embellished way, it will not travel far. So I have had no choice but to express [my ideas] in a literary style. It is not my desire, in so doing, to advertise

myself. But I've worked very hard on this. Perhaps some future sage will find something of value in it. I care not if people appreciate me through it, or if they condemn me for it.[84]

Hu Chih wrote the *Hu-tzu heng-ch'i* in dialogue form; but the style is not conversational, and so it lacks immediacy. The work also lacks the scrupulous scholarship and logical force of Lo Ch'in-shun's philosophical writing. It makes for difficult reading. While it has been characterized as a statement of subjective moral idealism in the Wang Yangming mode,[85] it does avoid identifying itself with any particular school or thinker or slogan and, as such, is very much a product of an era in which, all across China, Confucian thinkers began to cast off the bonds of personal discipleship and sectarian school affiliation.[86] If no T'ai-ho "school" carried on the work of Ou-yang Te, none would form to carry on the work of Hu Chih either.

· · ·

In spite of all the stellar performances on the national stage of native sons like Lo Ch'in-shun, Wang Ssu, Liu K'uei, Ou-yang Te, and Hu Chih, their efforts did not lay groundwork for the seventeenth century and beyond. The great figures of early Ming T'ai-ho had established a social and moral seedbed for the men of the sixteenth century to take advantage of, but, somehow, the great figures of the sixteenth century left a diminished legacy for the county's future generations. This chapter has suggested that while T'ai-ho's sixteenth century elites rose successfully to the challenges of the new, heavily intellectualized world they lived in, they did so mainly as individuals rather than as county compatriots; and, as individuals, none issued a philosophy of personal endeavor, or of social and political action, that was broad-based or practicable enough to assist large numbers of their local compatriots.

The aesthetic of local landscape, the reconstruction of genealogical identity, and the Yang-Lo-Teng model of moral behavior were all broad-based and practical, and they appealed widely to everyone in T'ai-ho in the late fourteenth and fifteenth centuries. (They were not of immediate relevance to anyone who did *not* live in T'ai-ho.) Yang Shih-ch'i, Wang Chih, and Ch'en Hsun were all consistent among themselves in their statements on these topics.

But the sixteenth-century search for self-discovery, epistemological certainty, and ultimate values was another matter altogether. Different authorities said very different things. Some followed Lo Ch'in-shun.

Many others listened to Ou-yang Te. Some considered the views of Hu Chih. Others listened to Matteo Ricci and became Christian converts. Many more followed the late Ming Buddhist revival. Whatever the choice, large chunks of the fifteenth-century universe tended to drift out of sight: the landscape, the peasants, the crops, the weeds, the family reconstructions, social camaraderie, striving for worldly success—all the tangible things that go to make up a complete life in an ordered civilization, all the particularized and concrete things that the name "T'ai-ho" invoked.

"T'ai-ho" had no special meaning for Buddhists, or Christians, or followers of Ou-yang Te hoping to negotiate the world through extending innate knowledge, or followers of Lo Ch'in-shun trying to understand the world as *ch'i,* or "matter-energy," in the abstract. In the hearts of its leading native sons, T'ai-ho was nothing special anymore.

Conclusion and Epilogue

It should have been clear throughout this work that the focal point of the whole story was not T'ai-ho County in and of itself but the linkages between that county and the larger theater of Ming China. Indeed, there would have been no T'ai-ho County except for the national matrix in which it was so firmly and inextricably embedded. Without the national matrix, with its literary standards and its summons to government service, it is inconceivable that T'ai-ho literati such as Liu Sung or Wang Chih or Hu Chih would ever have emerged in the first place. Without those literati, no evocative descriptions of the settlements and crops and scenery of the county would have been written, no epitaphs in standardized and storylike format would have been composed, and no accounts of the formation of common-descent groups and lineages would ever have been penned. Except for the national context of Ming government, there would have been no T'ai-ho production and tax system to discuss, no avenue of progress from *sheng-yuan* to degree holder to imperial official to take note of. To a some extent, this pattern held all over China. It just happens that a great deal of information is available about Ming T'ai-ho.

Of course, there must have been a T'ai-ho that was purely local or regional, where people spoke only the Kan dialect and worshiped local deities and knew little of the larger world, but that was a T'ai-ho of the lower social class, of peasants and bondservants and laborers. Unfortunately, they are largely invisible because the literati seldom chose

to write about them. It would also be wrong to suppose that just because upper-class T'ai-ho was firmly fixed in a national matrix, one
could go to any other county in Ming China and expect to find exactly the same features. To be sure, there would be basic uniformities:
all counties had a county government, a Confucian school, and something approximating the standard Chinese family system. But the national storehouse of culture was rich and complex, and the particular
strands that the T'ai-ho literati drew from it were never exactly dupli-
cated elsewhere. The *timing* of T'ai-ho's emergence into the national
limelight was also a peculiarity; it would be difficult to find a similar
example for China in the early Ming centuries.

Telling the T'ai-ho story, therefore, is an attempt to answer the question, What do surviving records allow us to say about life in a thriving
part of rural south China from the fourteenth to the sixteenth century?
It is possible to recover a very tactile sense of some aspects of life there,
in particular, a sense of the settlement, use, and appreciation of the local
landscape, a landscape unrepeatable elsewhere in its special detail. And
it was noted that landscape description, so rich in the late fourteenth
and early fifteenth centuries, faded away after about 1460, even though
there were literati aplenty to continue the tradition had they so chosen.
Why did it fade?

The aggregate evidence suggests that the answer lies in the reasons
for the rise of landscape description in the first place. The literati's
eagerness to notice—and to express in a written idiom that any literate person in China could easily grasp—the arrangements and shapes
and colors and textures and smells of the benign world of nature of the
county they lived in was a way of expressing hope and optimism about
life in general, a way of underscoring the sense the younger elites of the
times had that despite the civil war destruction and other hardships,
their moment as comrades had arrived, their sense that the greater
world (the world of government) was calling for them to enter and
rise high in its service. Liu Sung, Wang Chih, and others were not professional naturalists. Nor were they localists, keeping the rest of China
at bay.

The shining sense of optimism for which landscape was metaphor
carried over into descriptions of farming operations, of great and noble
estate proprietors, of a county population dutiful in meeting its obligations, of a people eager to research its ancestors and reorder its common-descent groups and to encourage its daughters to become capable
wives and its sons to study the classics and strive to become officials or

government instructors. Ch'en Hsun and Yang Shih-ch'i understood Confucianism as a worldly social ethic that supported and guided this whole countywide effort at mutual, collective uplift. Even the scenic landscape reflected this kind of Confucianism.

Then things changed. In the writing of the literati of sixteenth-century T'ai-ho, landscape description was scarce, a positive and worldly sense of optimism was missing, and there was no more talk of mutual social uplift across the board in T'ai-ho County. There was a sense that local behavior had begun to go awry, and there was talk of remedying mechanisms, like community compacts and lineage discipline. Chances for government positions were greatly diminished for the growing local student population. More and more families were emigrating. It was not a hopeless world wracked by misery, but it did not inspire celebration.

Even early in the Ming, the great talents of T'ai-ho County had not the slightest intention of staying home, no matter how compelling they said the scenic and other attractions were. How could they stay home and still validate their assumption that ultimately the worth of local people and things could only be established and made known when the best and most capable native sons gained a place at the highest levels of the nation? Had Yang Shih-ch'i never left T'ai-ho to become a grand secretary, or Wang Chih to become a minister of personnel, then all the hundreds of humbler local men and women whose lives they described would have died without trace, and all the common-descent groups whose formation they encouraged, all the scenery they remembered, would never have been preserved. No Ming China, no T'ai-ho.

Yang Shih-ch'i and the other high bureaucratic elites of early Ming looked on their home county from a distance with fondness and pride. It gave them a strong sense of social rootedness, comradeship, and personal identity. And in return they used their stature as high government officials as a platform from which to guide local social reconstruction and to patronize the younger generation of strivers.

But Lo Ch'in-shun and the other high elites of sixteenth-century T'ai-ho no longer related themselves to their home county in that fashion. Their lack of interest in landscape is telling. They also made no effort to visit and get to know everyone in the county. Forms of wealth were more diffuse. Great landowners had given way to a range of lesser figures who helped manage corporate lineage estates. People were moving away. No one appears to have believed that he had enough local knowledge or personal leverage to influence social change across the board throughout the county. No one in government extended any more than a limited patronage to his younger county compatriots, and even when someone like Lo Ch'in-shun or Ou-yang Te did extend such limited patronage, the relationship was wholly personal or philosophical, without the fond rehearsal of ancestry and *shih-hao* and county identity that had been central to such relationships in Yang Shih-ch'i's time. Ming China lived on, but "T'ai-ho" no longer meant anything.

So in sum this study demonstrated that, perhaps inevitably in the case of late imperial China, there is no such thing as pristine local history. T'ai-ho County would be unknowable had not so many of its men become national figures. As national figures, they were not impartial witnesses of local developments; they sought to influence those developments, if not on the county scale, then at least on the personal, familial, or cantonal (community compact) level. As time went on, it was *national* developments (political and intellectual change) that encouraged new and different sets of personal agendas in T'ai-ho's national elites, such that the sixteenth century writers did not select exactly the same topics or write in precisely the same way as their predecessors had done; and so one is never entirely sure to what degree it was T'ai-ho that had changed over the Ming centuries (though it certainly had), or to what degree apparent change was simply due to new predilections and new ways of framing reality on the part of the literati. The question What was life in T'ai-ho like? thus resolves itself into the question What did the writers think life was like? Which is not a trivial rephrasing, because how they thought about it affected it.

EPILOGUE: IN THE SHADOW
OF THE MING DECLINE

By the turn of the seventeenth century, T'ai-ho County's days as a great producer of government officials and national literati were over and done with. The sixteenth-century enthusiasm for Confucian philosophy as such faded. New currents were spreading through China, among which was the lay Buddhist revival.[1] Whether in hot form as religion, or in cool form as philosophy, or as cultural symbolism for new social activities and group occasions, Buddhism seems to have become for many in T'ai-ho the framework of choice for comprehending the world and adapting to it.[2]

Leaders of some of the eminent T'ai-ho lineages began supporting Buddhist institutions and activities of various kinds. Lung Tsung-wu

(1542–1609) sponsored yearly Buddhist festivals.[3] Kuo Tzu-chang, after his retirement in 1612, engaged in religious philanthropy in and around his home ward of Kuan-ch'ao (township 31). He restored temples, established a fund for a tea stall, helped sponsor the maintenance of animal-releasing pools, and chaired a silver-collection drive to buy fields to support perpetual lamps for the temples of Kuan-ch'ao.[4]

But the height of all this Buddhist activity seems to have been reached in the next generation, that of Hsiao Shih-wei (1585–1651), builder of the Spring Floating Garden (described in chapter 1), and his nephew, Hsiao Po-sheng (1619–ca. 1678).

Hsiao Shih-wei (a seventh-generation descendant of the early Ming Confucian teacher, Hsiao Ch'i) was not truly a major figure of his time. He stood in the shadow of the Ming decline; but he made it his business to know the greater luminaries of his time, and he shared with them, besides an intellectual Buddhism, several other enthusiasms characteristic of the era.

Garden building was one of them, and for Hsiao Shih-wei, it was the centerpiece of his social existence. A "garden mania" was infecting wealthy elites all over China; and its accompanying ideology of spectacular self-indulgence, coupled with hospitality toward peers and charity to the poor, certainly captured Hsiao Shih-wei.[5] A friend jested in 1644 that Hsiao had studied to pass the civil service exams simply because he wanted the money and status necessary to build a socially acceptable pleasure garden.[6]

Hsiao achieved his *chin-shih* in 1622, was appointed a messenger (8A), and served in that capacity in Peking until his demotion in 1628 and transfer to Nanking in 1632. He knew some of the leading martyrs of the sensational Tung-lin repression of 1624–26. There are letters to and from Li Ying-sheng (1593–1626) and a poem for Miao Ch'ang-ch'i (1562–1626); but their content is sentimental and aesthetic, and nothing is said of the ethical-political issues around which the Tung-lin heroes had staged their protest.[7] Intermittently Hsiao visited his garden in T'ai-ho; he was there in 1630 when he commented on an alluring actress he had just seen in a performance of T'ang Hsien-tsu's romantically passionate drama, *The Peony Pavilion*.[8]

In Peking and Nanking, Hsiao was close to the nationally famous scholar-aesthete Ch'ien Ch'ien-i (1582–1664), with whom he could discuss concubines and poetry and Buddhist philosophy. In 1639, he invited Ch'ien to visit the Spring Floating Garden.[9] Hsiao was friendly with (perhaps he helped sponsor) the local T'ai-ho branch of the national Restoration Society (*Fu she*), although he seems not to have been a member of it himself.

The Restoration Society, founded in east China in 1629, dedicated itself to ethical renewal and official preferment for its members. It was made up of locally recruited literary clubs (*she*), mainly in east China and the lower Yangtze region. Hsiao's friend Ch'en Chi-t'ai (from northern Kiangsi) was active in developing a constituency of clubs in Kiangsi Province. All that is known is that some ten to twenty T'ai-ho literati formed a K'uai-ko (Happy Tower) club, named after the famous local landmark, thanks at least in part to Ch'en Chi-t'ai's efforts. T'ai-ho County's participation in the Restoration Society was the heaviest in Chi-an Prefecture, but the greatest participation came from northern Kiangsi, where by the seventeenth century most of the civil service degrees were being won as well.[10]

After Hsiao Shih-wei's death in 1651, his nephew and heir Hsiao Po-sheng proved himself a capable continuator of his uncle's enterprise in T'ai-ho. As noted in chapter 1, he rebuilt upon the war-battered ruins of his uncle's famed garden-estate a new resort; the list of his visitors there constitutes a veritable catalog of the great scholar-loyalists of the era. Hsiao Po-sheng was as good as his uncle had been at social contact making.[11]

Hsiao Po-sheng was even more involved in Buddhist-inspired local charity than his uncle had been. In the 1660s, he spent "several thousand" piculs of rice to help pay people's tax arrears and redeem the children they had been forced to sell, and to feed prisoners in the T'ai-ho County prison.[12] In 1672, he went further and assigned in perpetuity the proceeds of certain fields to prisoner relief. The abbots of the Hsiao family Buddhist temple were asked to manage this endowment.[13]

In 1673, the Manchu conquest of China threatened to come completely undone when General Wu San-kuei declared his independence in the southwest and made hurried plans to force the Manchus back to Manchuria. Kiangsi Province was caught in the middle of this crisis. From 1674 to 1677, Chi-an Prefecture and T'ai-ho County came under Wu San-kuei's banner, at least in part voluntarily. Hsiao Po-sheng had earlier welcomed the Ch'ing occupation. Then he turned against it. He was accused of providing grain supplies for sections of Wu San-kuei's army. The Ch'ing authorities arrested him, and he died in custody, in or about the year 1678.[14]

And the T'ai-ho story, as traced through the lives of its leading elites, already dim early in the seventeenth century, disappears after 1678 and cannot be traced any further. Life went on, but the county produced only a handful of *chin-shih* in the Ch'ing period (1644–1912), and scarcely anything is known of any of them.

Despite the wars and destruction of the fourteenth century, the T'ai-ho literati of the period had emerged well positioned to enter Ming service in great numbers and to become major participants in national life. But somehow the wars and destruction of the seventeenth century left the literati of that time enervated. Hsiao Shih-wei and Hsiao Po-sheng worked hard to make social connections with leading scholar-elites from many parts of China, but they were dead-end connections, as things turned out. None of them opened doors to the new cultural and bureaucratic worlds of Manchu China. After a long and successful record of adapting to the shifting tides of Ming China, the men of T'ai-ho seem, at last, to have run out of luck, or of energy, in the Ch'ing.

Notes

CHAPTER 1

Much of this chapter and portions of the next one appeared in article form in John W. Dardess, "A Ming Landscape: Settlement, Land Use, Labor, and Estheticism," *Harvard Journal of Asiatic Studies* 49, no. 2 (December 1989): 295–364.

1. *Chiang-hsi nung-yeh ti-li* (Nanchang, 1982), 159.

2. I follow the nomenclature of Timothy Brook, "The Spatial Structure of Ming Local Administration," *Late Imperial China* 6, no. 1 (1985): 1–55. The T'ai-ho data are from *T'ai-ho hsien-chih* (1826; reprint, Taipei, 1989), 1:24 ff.

3. An understanding reflected, for example, in Kuo Tzu-chang's statement of 1607 that T'ai-ho's "population [*hu-k'ou*] numbered over 250 *li*." Cf. Kuo Tzu-chang, *Ch'ing-lo kung i-shu* (T'ai-ho, printed ed., 1882), 18.15b–16b.

4. John Nieuhoff, *The Embassy of Peter de Goyer and Jacob de Keyser from the Dutch East India Company to the Emperor of China in 1655*, in *Voyages and Travels*, ed. John Pinkerton (London, 1811), 7:243.

5. Yang Wan-li, *Ch'eng-chai chi* (Ssu-pu ts'ung-k'an ed.), 74.7b–8b (inscription for the Yuan-ming building).

6. Wang Chih, *I-an chi* (SKCSCP ed., 8th ser.), A6.13a–14a (preface to poems for the Ching-hsiu studio); *Chi-an fu-chih* (Kiangsi, 1875), 52.2ab (Chin Yu-tzu, poem on the studio). The quotation is from Wang Chih.

7. Hsiao Ch'i, *Cheng-ku hsien-sheng chi* (ms. ed.), C34a–36b (lament for Liu O).

8. Lo Ta-hung, *Tzu-yuan wen-chi* (Ming woodblock ed.), 3.28a–29b (preface to poems for Magistrate Chang).

9. There are several examples of this movement. Around 1400, Tseng Shih-min, "tired of the disorder, filth, and noise" of the inner city, moved out to

rural Yueh-kang (Moon Hill Ward, township 32). Mme Kuo (1353–1432), also a hater of city life, spent her declining years with her sons on their detached rural estates somewhere to the west. Hu Chih wrote that he lived for four years somewhere in the western suburb, but, disliking the "marketplace clamor" there, he moved in 1546 to an "out-of-the-way lane," where he had a garden: "I wield the hoe, leaving the books behind. . . . Here the reddening oranges, frost-touched, are ready to drop, and the fragrant red hollyhocks embrace the sun." The references are Wang Chih, B5.37b–39a (description of farming joys in Yueh-kang) and A8.13b–15b (epitaph for one of Mme. Kuo's sons); Hu Chih, *Heng-lu ching-she ts'ang-kao* (SKCSCP ed., 4th ser.), A5.3b–4b (poems on moving house). Also in the early 1400s, Wang Chih described in detail how Yang Ssu-ch'ing escaped the din and crowding of the inner city by buying a hundred *mou* of what had been garden just outside the city and building a large family compound there. Wang Chih, A1.39b–41b (inscription for the Chi-ch'ing hall).

10. Wang Chih, A2.33b–35a (inscription for the Keng-tu hall); Hsiao Tzu, *Shang-yueh chü-shih chi* (woodblock ed., 1494), 14.12b–14a (epitaph for Hsiao Mu, 1368–1432); Wang Chih, A6.44b–46a (departing message for Tseng Yung-li, i.e., Tseng Chin, 1380–1458) and B33.9a–10b (epitaph for Tseng Chin).

11. See the detailed soil map accompanying Wu Pen-chung et al., "T'ai-ho ch'ü t'u-jang," *Chiang-hsi sheng ti-chih tiao-ch'a-so ti-chih hui-k'an,* no. 6 (July 1941): 157–88.

12. Described in Dardess, "A Ming Landscape," 308–11.

13. Ch'en Hsun, *Fang-chou wen-chi* (printed ed., 1593), A5.17a–18a (preface to the Shuang-ch'i Cheng genealogy).

14. Dirk Bodde, "Marshes in Mencius and Elsewhere," in *Ancient China: Studies in Early Civilisation,* ed. David T. Roy and T. H. Tsien (Hong Kong, 1978), 157–66.

15. J. G. Hawkes, *The Diversity of Crop Plants* (Harvard, 1983), 83–87.

16. Liu Sung, *Ch'a-weng shih-chi* (SKCSCP ed., 5th ser.), 8.41b (poem for Lo Hui-ch'ing).

17. Liang Ch'ien, *Po-an chi* (SKCSCP ed., 6th ser.), 6.13b–14b (preface to poems for Elder Yao).

18. Liu Sung, *Ch'a-weng wen-chi* (Ming woodblock ed.), 6.18b–20b (inscription on the repair of the T'ien-i yuan, T'ai-ho county).

19. Liu Sung, *shih-chi,* 1.36b–37a (poem, on T'ao-yuan [a ward in township 12]).

20. Ibid., 5.53ab (poem, late on the tenth day of the twelfth month . . . we viewed vegetable plots by a house).

21. Lo Ch'in-shun, *Cheng-an ts'un-kao* (SKCSCP ed., 4th ser.), 19.17b–18a (poem, felicitations for Hsiao Yu-jung).

22. Liu Sung, *shih-chi,* 7.45b (poem, looking into a garden).

23. Ibid., 2.23b–24a (poem, looking at West Garden).

24. Hu Chih, *Heng-lu ching-she ts'ang-kao,* A7.1ab (poem, on returning home from the Hai-chih ssu on an autumn day).

25. Liu Sung, *shih-chi,* 8.50a (poem, on the road at Ho-ch'i).

26. Ibid., 4.36ab (poem, stripping ramie).

27. Wang Chih, B37.35a–36a (appreciation of a painting of radish in the Wei-ts'ai studio). The radish name here is *lu-fu*.

28. Liu Sung, *shih-chi*, 2.7ab (poems on living in poverty); 2.7b–9b (poems on garden life); 7.34a–35a (poems on looking after the melons and vegetables in the east garden).

29. Ibid., 6.35a (poem, again on the peasant house in the old ward).

30. Ibid., 2.5b–6a (poem, crossing South Drain to visit a friend).

31. Ibid., 2.7ab; 6.30b–31a (poem, field family at Shui-k'ou); 6.35b (poem, on my delight at the arrival of the family slave [*chia-t'ung*]); 8.16b (poem, mountain family at Shih-t'ang).

32. Chou Shih-hsiu, *Ch'u-jao chi* (SKCSCP ed., 4th ser), 3.4ab (poems on field families).

33. Liu Sung, *shih-chi*, 1.36b–37a (poem, on T'ao-yuan).

34. Ibid., 8.16b.

35. Ibid., 8.31b (poem, observing the wild fire).

36. Ibid., 8.26a (poem, clearing after rain).

37. As a retired imperial official, an aged Wang Chih toured his rice fields by sedan chair. His sons marshaled "several hundred tenants and bondsmen [*tien-p'u*]" to transplant the shoots, and all these laborers sang to the beat of a gong while they worked. It was a gala occasion that lasted the whole day. Cf. Yin Chih, *Chien-chai so-chui lu* (1507; reprint, Taipei, 1969), 156.

38. Wang Chen, *Nung shu* (SKCSCP ed., *pieh-chi*), 11.13b ff.

39. *Chiang-hsi fu-i ch'üan-shu* (1611; reprint, Taipei, 1970), 4:1385 ff.

40. John Brinckerhoff Jackson, *Discovering the Vernacular Landscape* (New Haven, 1984), 45–47.

41. John L. Buck, *Chinese Farm Economy* (Nanking, 1930), 17–18; Jacob A. Hoefer and Patricia Jones Tsuchitani, *Animal Agriculture in China: A Report of the Visit of the CSCPRC Animal Sciences Delegation* (Washington, 1980), 10, 77–92.

42. Lo Ch'in-shun, *Cheng-an ts'un-kao*, 16.17ab (poem, song of the Hsueh-ku lou).

43. Liu Sung, *shih-chi*, 4.35ab (poem, lament for the cow).

44. Chou Shih-hsiu, 3.4ab (poems on field families).

45. Ibid., 2.6b–7a (herder's song).

46. Liu Sung, *Ch'a-weng wen-chi*, 10.22b–25b (preface to the Hsiao genealogy).

47. Roger B. Swain, *Field Days: Journal of an Itinerant Biologist* (New York, 1983), 1–8.

48. Liu Sung, *shih-chi*, 1.36b–37a (poem, on T'ao-yuan).

49. Chou Shih-hsiu, 3.4ab; Liu Sung, *shih-chi*, 2.19b (poems).

50. Lo Ch'in-shun, *Cheng-an ts'un-kao*, 19a.13a–14a (poem and commentary); Ch'en Hsun, poems section, 3.16a–18a (eight scenes from the library at Pei-ch'i); Chou Shih-hsiu, 2.7ab (wood collector's song). Quotations are from Chou.

51. Yang Shih-ch'i, *Tung-li ch'üan-chi* (SKCSCP ed., 7th ser.), A2.12b–14a (inscription for the Ch'iao-hsueh chai).

52. Chou Shih-hsiu, 4.36a–39a (biography of the southern wood collector who found the true Way).

53. Liu Sung, *shih-chi*, 8.14b (poem, visit to the mountain home of a secluded gentleman of the Hu surname).

54. Hua Shu, ed., *Ming shih hsuan-tsui* (reprint, Taipei, 1974), 4.24a (Hsiao Tzu [d. 1464], poem about his home in Nan-kao).

55. Liu Sung, *shih-chi*, 7.15a (poem, accompanying Shu Po-yuan over the bridge from Shuang-chiang-k'ou).

56. Liang Ch'ien, 6.55a–56b (message for Yen Hsuan-yen).

57. Liu Sung, *shih-chi*, 6.51a (poem, on the road at Ho-ch'i on the ninth day).

58. Ibid., 6.51b (poem, on the old fisherman's secluded home at Ho-ch'i).

59. Ibid., 5.91b (poem, the gardens and ponds of the Hsiao of Yun-t'ing Canton).

60. Ibid., 5.91b (poem); *Chi-an fu-chih*, 50.24b–25a and 53.32b.

61. Liang Ch'ien, 16.14b–16a (colophon to an epitaph).

62. Liu Sung, *shih-chi*, 2.14b (poem on hunting dogs).

63. Chou Shih-hsiu, 4.32b–33a (accounts of three righteous acts).

64. Liu Sung, *shih-chi*, 8.20b (poem, night alarm).

65. Ibid., 4.44ab (poem, cow and tiger).

66. Ou-yang To, *Ou-yang Kung-chien kung i-chi* (Ming woodblock ed.), 18.6a–8a (epitaph for Hsiao Hsien, 1472–1539).

67. *T'ai-ho hsien-chih* (Kiangsi, 1879), 19.48a–50a (Yang Chia-chen, letter to Vice Magistrate Chu about canton troops).

68. Ch'en Mo, *Hai-sang chi* (SKCSCP ed., 4th ser), 2.29a (poem, on a painting of fishing joys).

69. Yang Shih-ch'i, B62.43a–44b (poem, fishing in autumn).

70. Chou Shih-hsiu, 2.6a (fisherman's song).

71. Yang Shih-ch'i, B43.14a–15a (biography of the fisherman of the rapids). The word "rapids" refers to the infamous shoals of the Shih-pa-t'an on the Kan River south of T'ai-ho. Yen Tsung-tan's boat was probably a freighter.

72. Wang Chih, A5.5b–7a (preface to funeral poems for Liu Chung-kao [Liu Ang]); Yang Shih-ch'i, B32.11b–13a (epitaph).

73. Liu Sung, *shih-chi*, 6.29ab (poem, Lang-ch'uan).

74. *Tsao-chih shih-hua* (Shanghai, 1983), 173; *T'ai-ho hsien-chih* (1879), 2.22b ff.

75. Liu Sung, *shih-chi*, 4.58b–59a (poem, on gypsum).

76. *Ming shih-lu* (reprint, Taiwan, 1965), 113:7052, 7134–37, 7155.

77. Liu Sung, *Ch'a-weng wen-chi*, 6.4a–6a (description of Wa-ch'üan).

78. *Chi-an fu-chih*, 50.57b (T'an Sheng, poem on popular customs).

79. Yang Shih-ch'i, B50.1a–8a (record of tomb visits) and B53.4b–5b, 14b–15b (letters to family members).

80. *Chi-an fu-chih*, 53.81a.

81. Wang Chih, B5.10a–12a (description of Shang-yuan-t'ang); *T'ai-ho hsien-chih* (1879), 2.22b ff.

82. Liu Sung, *Ch'a-weng wen-chi*, 14.12a–13b.

83. Ou-yang Te, *Ou-yang Nan-yeh hsien-sheng* (Woodblock ed., 1558), 17.19b–21a (preface to poems on Sung-kang [Pine Hill], dated 1533).

84. Edward Schafer, "T'ang," in *Food in Chinese Culture: Anthropological and Historical Perspectives*, ed. K. C. Chang (New Haven, 1977), 130; Li Hui-lin, "The Domestication of Plants in China: Ecogeographical Considerations," in *The Origins of Chinese Civilization*, ed. David N. Keightley (Berkeley, 1983), 43.

85. Liu Sung, *shih-chi*, 6.51ab (poem, on Liu Ken's mountain estate).

86. Ibid., 3.34b–35b.

87. Ibid., 4.31b–32a (poem, picking wild vegetables).

88. Ibid., 2.5b–6a.

89. Ibid., 2.1b–2a (poem about a reclusive garden waterer) and 2.10b–11a (poem, distress over the drought).

90. Ibid., 4.71a (poem, in the east garden, wild amaranth spreads of itself in the autumn rain).

91. Ibid., 6.15b (poem, staying with the Wen of Wu-ch'i on an overcast night).

92. Ibid., 7.16b (poem, seeing people take *Echinochloa crus-galli* as I passed below a mountain); 7.46a (poem, crossing the Kan from Shui-nan on the eighth month, eleventh day). See also Spencer C. H. Barrett, "Crop Mimicry in Weeds," *Economic Botany* 37 (1983): 255–82.

93. Wang Chih, A2.16a–23b (description of a trip to Mount Wu).

94. *Chi-an fu-chih*, 50.54ab (Wang Chih, poem on a painting of Han-lin Senior Compiler Hsiao [Tzu]'s thatched hall at Nan-ch'i).

95. Wang Chih, B8.44a–45a (preface to poems on eight scenes at Lu-kang).

96. Ibid., B3.26a–27b (description of the detached estate at Nan-yuan).

97. Liang Ch'ien, 4.42b–44a (inscription on the repair of the Lung-ch'eng ssu).

98. Ibid., 4.41a–42b (inscription for a physician's retreat).

99. Wang Chih, A2.38b–40a (inscription for a group of paintings).

100. Ch'en Ch'ang-chi, *Lung-chin-yuan chi* (Ming woodblock ed.), 1.16b–20a (biography of Kuo Ch'ing-k'uang [Kuo Hsu]).

101. Lo Ta-hung, 10.26a–36a (epitaph); Chiao Hung, ed., *Kuo-ch'ao hsien-cheng lu* (1594; reprint, Taipei, 1965), 8:5057–58 (Tsou Yuan-piao, epitaph). The quotation is from Lo.

102. Shih Jun-chang, *Hsueh-yü t'ang wen-chi* (SKCSCP ed., 3d ser.), 14. 16a–17b (description of a trip to Mount Yü-hua).

103. Wang Chih, A1.6b–8a (inscription for the altar and brick building on Mount Wang).

104. *T'ai-ho hsien-chih* (1826), 5:2128–35 (Wang Yü-k'uo, description of Tzu-yao shan [i.e., Mount Wang]).

105. Hsiao Shih-wei, *Hsiao-chai jih-chi*, in *Li-tai ming-jen jih-chi hsuan*, ed. Teng Chin-shen (Canton, 1984), 145.

106. Shih Jun-chang, 14.10a–11a (description of a tour of the Ch'un-fou Garden).

107. *Chi-an fu-chih*, 5.19a–20a (Hsiao Shih-wei, excerpted account).

108. Frederic Wakeman Jr., "Romantics, Stoics, and Martyrs in Seventeenth-Century China," *Journal of Asian Studies* 43 (August 1984): 633.

109. Ch'ien Ch'ien-i, *Mu-chai ch'u-hsueh chi* (Ssu-pu ts'ung-k'an ed.), 28.28b–29b (preface to Hsiao Po-yü's [Hsiao Shih-wei's] commentary on the *Awakening of Faith*). For the main text, see Yoshito S. Hakeda, trans., *The Awakening of Faith Attributed to Asvaghosha* (New York, 1967).

110. Hsiao Shih-wei, *Hsiao-chai jih-chi*, 146–47.

111. H. L. Li, *The Garden Flowers of China* (New York, 1959), 123.

112. Shih Jun-chang, poems section, 4.6a (passing T'ai-ho County) and 6.15b–16a (on the road from Chi-chou to T'ai-ho).

113. *Chi-an fu-chih*, 20.35b–39b; 47.73a–74b.

114. Shih Jun-chang, 14.10a–11a.

115. *T'ai-ho hsien-chih* (1826), 5:2147 (Wang Yü-k'uo, description of a tour of Lake T'ao). Fang I-chih's visits in T'ai-ho have been detailed in Yü Ying-shih, *Fang I-chih wan-chieh k'ao* (Hong Kong, 1972), and Jen Tao-pin, *Fang I-chih nien-p'u* (Hofei, 1983).

116. Shih Jun-chang, poems section, 26.25b–26a (poems on the Ch'un-fou Garden), 7.9b (the lotus pond in the Tun-p'u), and 18.21ab (song about the T'ai-ho vodka); *Chi-an fu-chih*, 51.1ab (Wei Hsi, poem); *Chi-an fu-chih*, 53.92b–93a (Wang Shih-chen [1634–1711], remark about the Hsiao wealth). The quotation is from Shih, 26.25b–26a.

117. *T'ai-ho hsien-chih* (1826), 5:2147–49 (Wang Yü-k'uo, description of a tour of Lake T'ao).

118. *Chi-an fu-chih*, 3.11b–12a (Wei Hsi, account).

CHAPTER 2

1. The relevant literature here is enormous. For a summary statement, see Philip C. C. Huang, *The Peasant Family and Rural Development in the Yangzi Delta, 1350–1988* (Stanford, 1990), 329–31.

2. See especially Joseph P. McDermott, "Charting Blank Spaces and Disputed Regions: The Problem of Sung Land Tenure," *Journal of Asian Studies* 44 (November 1984): 13–41. Brief descriptions of local conditions can be found in Robert P. Hymes, *Statesmen and Gentlemen: The Elite of Fu-Chou, Chiang-Hsi, in Northern and Southern Sung* (Cambridge, 1986), 22–23, for Fu-chou Prefecture, Kiangsi, in the Sung; and Jerry Dennerline, *The Chia-ting Loyalists: Confucian Leadership and Social Change in Seventeenth-Century China* (Yale, 1981), 88–89, 264–41, 272–73, for Chia-ting County in the Yangtze delta in the Ming. Dennerline (p. xv) has also had to maneuver around "the lack of any detailed data on local agriculture, land ownership, family economies, and the like," and he, understandably, prefers analyzing personal networks to deploying class terms such as "landlord" and "peasant." Hui-chou Prefecture, in present-day Anhwei Province, is exceptionally rich in such local documentation; some of the literature is noted in Evelyn S. Rawski, "Research Themes in Ming-Qing Socioeconomic History—The State of the Field," *Journal of Asian Studies* 50 (February, 1991): 84–111. Tenurial landlordism from an econometric perspec-

tive is treated in Chao, *Man and Land in Chinese History* (Stanford, 1986), chap. 8.

3. This is the thrust of Joseph W. Esherick and Mary B. Rankin, eds., *Chinese Local Elites and Patterns of Dominance* (Berkeley, 1990). See especially the editors' concluding remarks, pp. 305–45.

4. Robert M. Hartwell, "Demographic, Political, and Social Transformations of China, 750–1550," *Harvard Journal of Asiatic Studies* 42, no. 2 (December 1982): 395.

5. For the earlier irrigation work and its periodic repair, see *Chiang-hsi t'ung-chih* (Kiangsi, 1881), 63.7a; Liu Yueh-shen, *Shen-chai Liu hsien-sheng wen-chi* (reprint, Taipei, 1970), 469–71 (epitaph for Li I-fei, 1259–1336); Wang Chih, *I-an chi* (SKCSCP ed., 8th ser.), B6.30b–32a (preface to poems for the Yuan-ming lou); Hu Chih, *Heng-lu ching-she ts'ang-kao* (SKCSCP ed., 4th ser), B3.6a–8a (inscription for the Tun-tien t'ang) and B10.1a–3a (epitaph for Hu Hsi, 1498–1580). Three inscriptions, dating to 1052, 1534, and the eighteenth century, have recently been found. The 1052 inscription includes an engraved map. See *Chung-kuo li-shih-hsueh nien-chien* (Beijing, 1989), 438. For the fourteenth-century irrigation work, see Wu Ssu-tao, *Ch'un-ts'ao-chai chi* (Ssu-ming ts'ung shu ed.), 10.5b–7a (epitaph for the builder's son, Liu Jen-shou, 1304–65); Wang Chih, B17.36a–38a (preface to the genealogy of the K'an-ch'i Liu). The agricultural writers were literati from the Tseng common-descent group of T'ai-ho city in the Sung, who were still prominent in Ming times, although their interest in the subject had lapsed. For a discussion of them and their books, see Sudō Yoshiyuki, *Sōdai keizaishi kenkyū* (Tokyo, 1962), 24, 51–53. The text of Tseng An-chih's *Ho p'u* (Guide to the grains) of 1094, which was long lost, has been rediscovered in a local genealogy; see *Chung-kuo li-shih-hsueh nien-chien* (Beijing, 1987), 326.

6. Population figures are from *Chi-an fu-chih* (Kiangsi, 1875), 15.7b–8a; *Chiang-hsi t'ung-chih* (1881), 47.15ab; and *Chung-kuo 1982 nien jen-k'ou p'u-ch'a tzu-liao* (Beijing, 1985), 178.

7. Recent conditions in T'ai-ho County have been so bad that they bear little relation to past history. The county has suffered serious soil erosion: between 1957 and 1979, there was a 15 percent loss of cropland; and despite the likelihood that only the worst land has been removed from cultivation, T'ai-ho's per-*mou* yield of foodstuffs is among the lowest in the province. Irrigation systems, so prominent in the Sung and Ming, have all but disappeared. Sugarcane and sweet potatoes have supplanted rice and other traditional crops. T'ai-ho's 1982 population, which looks large enough by historical standards, is said to be insufficient to meet labor demands. Far from exporting population, either permanently or seasonally, as it did in the middle and late Ming, the county (and, indeed, much of the province) now has to import labor on a seasonal basis. See Judith Banister, *China's Changing Population* (Stanford, 1987), and especially *Chiang-hsi nung-yeh ti-li* (Nanchang, 1982).

Some rural people were too poor to consume rice every day. Hu Chih's grandfather, Hu Hsing-kung (1469–1527), an impoverished primary teacher, was for a while reduced to a diet of "taro and mixed cabbage and beans," but he studied so intently that he didn't mind the hunger. See Hu Chih, *Heng-lu ching-she ts'ang-kao*, A8.21b (generational account of the Hu family).

8. Liu Sung, *Ch'a-weng wen-chi* (Ming woodblock ed.), 10.5a–6b (message for Wu Ming-li, continuing on his journey).

9. Wang Chih, A2.23b–25b (inscription for the Tun-pen t'ang).

10. Ibid., B6.34b–36b (message to T'ai-ho magistrate Cheng, on his departure). Cheng Lin was appointed magistrate in 1416.

11. Ibid., B18.14a–15b (preface to poems for Magistrate Shen, about to take office [in T'ai-ho]). Shen Yü was appointed in 1427.

12. Ch'en Hsun, *Fang-chou wen-chi* (printed ed., 1593), A4.22b–23b (message for Vice Magistrate Ch'iu Chung-yeh, returning to T'ai-ho). Ch'iu's tenure in T'ai-ho was 1440–46.

13. Liu Sung, *Ch'a-weng wen-chi*, 14.12a–13b (postscript to an inscription for the Kuo family retreat).

14. In Shih-kang (Stone Hill Ward, township 10) lived Liu Sung's mother's people, the Shih-kang Hsiao, whose lands produced peaches, pears, mandarin oranges, persimmons, cabbage, leek, melon, edible bamboo, taro, and rice, together with pond-bred fish and livestock (zebu cattle and goats). Liu Sung described in detail the formalities and orderly routines observed by these people, and remarked that "inwardly I used to envy all this, since my own home was poor by comparison." He went on to say that "once I heard the elders talk about Hsiao Pao-sun, who was an accounts keeper and the son of Hsiao Ssu-lien, a facilitated degree holder of the late Sung [thirteenth century]. He was one of the richest men in the county. For several tens of *li* around his home, all of the gardens, fields, mountains, and forests were his, none of it sold to an outside surname." He ended by noting that this gigantic estate was later twice damaged in civil wars, and rebuilt, though on a reduced scale. See Liu Sung, *Ch'a-weng wen-chi*, 10.22b–25b (preface to the Hsiao genealogy).

15. Wang Chih, A1.31b–33b (description of the joys of farming).

16. Ibid., B5.20a–21b (inscription for the detached estate at Ch'ang-ch'i).

17. For example, Chao Kang and Ch'en Chung-i, "Chung-kuo li-shih-shang-ti tzu-ying ti-chu," *Shih-huo yueh-k'an*, n.s., 9, nos. 5–6 (October 1979): 178 (full article, 169–193).

18. Ch'en Hsun, A3.37b–39a (preface to poems on the detached estate at Lung-men).

19. Liang Lan, *Ch'i-le shih-chi* (SKCSCP ed., 8th ser.), 8b (poem, on enjoying myself in the western garden plots) and 32b–33a (poem, on coming home from farming). Liang Lan's son, Liang Ch'ien (1366–1418), expanded his father's garden and diversified its produce. Out a second-story studio window, itself shaded dark by pine and bamboo, one could now view water caltrop planted in a willow-ringed pond. Nearby, a stone path transected an herb garden. From the doorway of the house one could hear fish splash and orioles twitter. "My home," wrote Liang Ch'ien, "is in T'ai-ho's Willow Creek, where there are several tens of *mou* of garden plots. There are several thousand bamboo, hundreds of peach and plum trees, and tens of beds growing rape-turnip, cabbage, ginger, sugar cane, cress [*Nasturtium montanum*], black mustard [*Brassica juncea*], barberry [*Lycium chinense*], and chrysanthemum. . . . And not

even the costliest delicacies can surpass the lettuce gathered in the spring snow, or the leek harvested after the frost." Cf. Ch'en T'ien, ed., *Ming-shih chi-shih* (reprint, Taipei, 1971), 2:716 (Liang Ch'ien, poem on the Ai-ts'ui studio) and 2:270 (Liang Ch'ien, poem on garden life); Liang Ch'ien, *Po-an chi* (SKCSCP ed., 6th ser.), 7.18b–19a (preface to the Le-p'u poems). The quotation is from this last source.

20. Liu Sung, *Ch'a-weng shih-chi* (SKCSCP ed., 5th ser.), 3.34b–35b (poem, on a painting of fall colors in a plain); Hsu Hung, ed., *Ming ming-ch'en wan-yen lu* (SKCSCP ed., 6th ser.), 12.1a–4b (Yin Chih, biography of Liu Sung).

21. Liu Sung, *shih-chi*, 2.11b (poem, expressing my mind).

22. Ibid., 2.12a (poem, visiting a field-father).

23. Ibid., 8.25b (poem, rising early at a peasant house) and 2.60b–61a (poem, returning from observing the harvest below the mountain, in the sixth month, late in the day).

24. Ibid., 2.67ab (poem, in gratitude for the field-father's invitation to have some rice-beer).

25. Ibid., 8.25b (poem, observing the transplanting of rice shoots).

26. Ch'en Hsun, A8.3a–4b (epitaph).

27. Chou Shih-hsiu, *Ch'u-jao chi* (SKCSCP ed., 4th ser.), 6.19a–21b (description of eight inspiring scenes at Chü-kang). The contrast of the Chou home base is with the densely clustered, citylike living arrangements of other rural families, such as the Hsiao of Jen-ch'eng Ward (township 25), the Liu of Chuan-chiang Ward (township 52), the Cheng of Shuang-ch'i in Ta-jui Ward (township 35), or the Chou of Ch'i-t'ien Ward (township 51). See Wang Chih, B3.49a–50b (inscription for the Chi-shan t'ang); Yin Ch'ang-lung, *Yin Na-an hsien-sheng i-kao* (ms. ed.), ch. 4, no p. (preface to the Hsiao genealogy); Chou Shih-hsiu, 5.43a–44b (departing message for Assistant Instructor Liu Chung-heng, en route to Shih-ch'eng); Ch'en Hsun, A5.17a–18a (preface to the Shuang-ch'i Cheng genealogy); Lo Ch'in-shun, *Cheng-an ts'un-kao* (SKCSCP ed., 4th ser.), 2.1a–2b (inscription for the Ying-hsi building) and 2.16b–18a (inscription for the Shih-te hall); *T'ai-ho hsien-chih* (Kiangsi, 1879), 24.44a–45a (Hu Kuang, inscription for the Kao-ming building); Wang Chih, B6.29a–30b (postscript to Chou Chih-kang's Kao-ming lou poems) and B6.30b–32a (preface to the Yuan-ming lou poems).

28. Liu Sung, *shih-chi*, 2.19b (poem, on a field family).

29. Chou Shih-hsiu, 1.17b (poem, on a field family).

30. Ibid., 3.4ab (poems on field families).

31. Yang Shih-ch'i, *Tung-li ch'üan-chi* (SKCSCP ed., 7th ser.), A16.11b–13a (epitaph).

32. Ibid., A16.11b–13a and A17.5b–8a (epitaph for Hsiao Lien).

33. Ibid., B30.11a–12b (epitaph for Hsiao Tzu); Ch'en Hsun, A5.8a–11a (preface to the T'ao-yuan Hsiao genealogy). Liang Ch'ien, 16.4ab (colophon to the genealogy) and 4.1a–2b (inscription for their academy); Wang Chih, A5.12a–13b (preface to the genealogy) and A3.2b–4a (inscription for the I-shout'ang); Yang Shih-ch'i, B23.22a–23a (postscript to the Hsiao genealogy), B1.16b–18b (inscription for the Ching-i t'ang), B3.1a–2b (inscription for the Wan-i chai), B4.13b–14b (inscription for the Ching-yueh t'ang), A4.8ab (pref-

ace to the Shih-t'ai poems), and A9.15b-18a (colophon to the Lucky Fungus poems and essays in honor of the Hsiao); Lo Ch'in-shun, 8.2a-4a (preface to poems for the Yung-ch'ing t'ang).

34. Hsiao Tzu, *Shang-yueh chü-shih chi* (woodblock ed., 1494), 18.16b-18b (epitaph).

35. Wang Chih, B33.38b-40b (epitaph).

36. Ibid., B28.34b-36b (epitaph). In the Yung-lo era, some of T'ai-ho's tax captains were required to do more than collect taxes. The emperor's building and expansion programs required some to build residences in the new capital (Peking) and others to superintend logging teams in the wild mountains of southern Hunan. See Wang Chih, B27.37a-39b (epitaph for Tuan Feng, 1365–1441, of Fishpond Lane in the western suburb), B28.26a-28b (epitaph for Kuo Tung-wei, 1393–1459, of Ch'ien-ch'i [or Ao-t'ou], township 62), and B28.24a-26a (epitaph for Yang Meng-pien's son, township 43); Ch'en Hsun, A7.45b-47b (epitaph for Yueh Hsu, 1390–1447, of Ho-ch'i Ward, township 62). None of these rich T'ai-ho men forced to live in Peking are mentioned in Satō Manabu's detailed study of the whole policy in *Tōyō gakuhō* 64, nos. 1–2 (1983): 69–98. The heat, pestilence, and corruption of the Hunan logging camps are discussed in Hsiao Tzu, 19.6b-7b (biography of Hsiao Pang-yen, of Huang-kang, perhaps in township 67); Wang Chih, B26.54b-57a (epitaph for Tseng Ku, 1380–1437, of Shang-mo Ward, township 28); Yang Shih-ch'i, B46.1a-4b (preface to a lament for P'eng Pai-lien, 1386–1433).

37. Ou-yang Te, *Ou-yang Nan-yeh hsien-sheng wen-chi* (woodblock ed., 1558), 20.11b-12b (preface to a revision of the Sha-li Chang genealogy).

38. Ch'en Hsun, A5.32a-33b (preface to the Chang-ch'i Hsiao genealogy).

39. Wang Chih, A8.7b-9b and B28.8b-10b (two epitaphs for Wang T'ien-ti).

40. Hsiao Tzu, 18.15a-16b (epitaph for Hsiao Chi).

41. Yang Shih-ch'i, B1.16b-18b (inscription for the Ching-i t'ang). Yü Yao was from Fukien Province; see *P'u-t'ien hsien-chih* (1879; reprint, Taipei, 1968), 547.

42. *Ming shih-lu* (Taiwan, 1965), 25:1323-28; *Wan-li T'ai-ho chih* (1579; reprint, Taipei, 1989), 331 ff.; Wang Chih, B33.56a-59a (epitaph for Yang Tzu-p'ei, 1391–1455, of township 62). Yang Tzu-p'ei, very distantly related to Yang Shih-ch'i, could donate only fifteen hundred piculs. For that, his name was engraved on a stela. His family was already exempted from services because his son was a government Confucian instructor.

43. *Ming shih-lu,* 30:3386.

44. Ch'en Hsun, A9.35a-36b (epitaph for Chi-an prefect Li Chi).

45. *Ming shih-lu,* 33:4767-68.

46. Ibid., 34:5096.

47. Ibid., 35:5532; *Wan-li T'ai-ho chih,* 334-36.

48. Liu Ch'iu, *Liang-ch'i wen-chi* (SKCSCP ed., 11th ser.), 4.25b (inscription for the Chung-shun t'ang).

49. Yang Shih-ch'i, B53.18a-23a (family letters).

50. Wang Chih, B33.48a-50a (epitaph). In the seventeenth century, Yen Shu-ching did the same thing; cf. Kuo T'ing-hsun, ed., *Pen-ch'ao fen-sheng jen-wu k'ao* (1622; reprint, Taipei, 1971), 19:6279-81.

51. Yang Shih-ch'i, B40.26b–28b (epitaph for Wang's wife, née Hsiao, 1333–1412).

52. Hsiao Tzu, 16.31a–32a (account of conduct).

53. Wang Chih, B32.14a–16a (epitaph). One great-grandson, Lo Chün, won his *chin-shih* degree in 1448 and ended his career as a prefect (4A); unfortunately, nothing is known of any other descendants or of the disposition of the original estate.

54. Wang Chih, B17.7b–9a (preface to funerary poems); Yang Shih-ch'i, A18.23b–25a (epitaph).

55. Wang Chih, A8.24b–27a; Ch'en Hsun, A7.43a–45a (epitaphs for Lung Ts'an, 1384–1447); Wang Chih, B31.39b–41b (epitaph for Lung Shu-chao); Ch'en Hsun, B4.27a–28b (epitaph for Lung Kuei, i.e., Shu-hsuan). The quotation is from this last source.

56. Wang Chih, B24.38a–41b (epitaph for Lung Wen); Hsu Yu-chen, *Wu-kung chi* (SKCSCP ed., 4th ser.), 4.60a–61b (departing message for Lung Shih-hsi, i.e., Lung Kuang); Yueh Cheng, *Lei-po kao* (SKCSCP ed., 3d ser.), 5.5a–6b (departing message for Lung Shu-tan). The Lung marriage connections with T'ai-ho's high elites were many: Lung Wen's son Chün was married to one of Wang Chih's granddaughters, and Lung Kuang's younger sister was married to Yang Shih-ch'i's second son; and further generational marriage interconnections could easily be discovered. Lung Wen bribed his way into a promotion and transfer to Nanking at the time of the palace coup of 1457; see *Ming shih-lu*, 37:6419.

57. Liu Sung, *Ch'a-weng wen-chi*, 13.4b–5b (postscript to the Lü family record of equal inheritance).

58. Ou-yang Te, 25.19a–22a (epitaph).

59. Wang Chih, A6.5b–7b (epitaph for Liang Hun).

60. Yang Shih-ch'i, B39.17b–22a (epitaph for Ch'en Yung).

61. Wang Chih, B27.16a–18a (epitaph for Wang Yen-jui).

62. Wu K'uan, *P'ao-weng chia-ts'ang chi* (Ssu-ming ts'ung shu ed.), 77.3a–5b; and Li Tung-yang, *Li Tung-yang chi* (new ed., Changsha, 1984), 3:358 (epitaphs for Hsiao Chen).

63. Yang Shih-ch'i, A4.19b–20b (message for Ou-yang Yun-hsuan, on his departure); Ou-yang To, *Ou-yang Kung-chien kung i-chi* (Ming woodblock ed.), 17.1a–2b (epitaph for Ou-yang Yung); Ho Liang-chün, *Ho Han-lin chi* (1565; reprint, Taipei, 1971), 2:753–63 (epitaph for Ou-yang Mien and his wife); Kandice J. Hauf, "The Jiangyou Group: Culture and Society in Sixteenth-Century China" (Ph.D diss., Yale University, 1987), 147. The quotation is from Ou-yang To.

64. Ou-yang Te, 6.1a–14b (family letters); Hu Chih, *Heng-lu ching-she ts'ang-kao*, A10.23b–25a.

65. Ch'en Ch'ang-chi, *Lung-chin-yuan chi* (Ming woodblock ed.), 2.48b–50b. The governor was Weng P'u, for whose career see Chiao Hung, *Kuo-ch'ao hsien-cheng lu* (1594; reprint, Taipei, 1965), 3:2043–44. The prefect was T'ao Ta-nien; Ch'en Ch'ang-chi, 3.44a–46b (an inscription). Apparently only by slow degrees were T'ai-ho's dikes and reservoirs all counted and assessed for tax, however. The definitive count was not made earlier than 1581–82, perhaps not

until as late as 1598. The county budget of 1610 lists reservoirs only, some seventeen thousand *mou* in extent, and these reservoirs appear to have been taxed at a very favorable rate, the same as the rate for the lowest grade of paddy. See *Chiang-hsi fu-i ch'üan-shu* (1611; reprint, Taipei, 1970), 4:1385–1430.

66. Ch'en Ch'ang-chi, 5.63a–68b (letter to Inspector Wei Ch'ien-chi [1509–60] discussing famine relief methods). A major famine in 1637 was handled very differently; the magistrate prevailed upon wealthier people to contribute funds toward the purchase of gruel, and feeding stations were opened in Buddhist and Taoist temples where needy people lined up a thousand at a time to receive doles. Cf. *T'ai-ho hsien-chih* (1826; reprint, Taipei, 1989), 7:2922–27 (Yang Chia-chen, "What I heard and saw about famine relief in 1637").

67. The major study of the inflow of foreign silver into China is William S. Atwell, "International Bullion Flows and the Chinese Economy, *Circa* 1530–1650," *Past and Present*, no. 95 (1982): 68–90.

68. Liu Sung, *Ch'a-weng wen-chi*, 11.23a–24b (preface to the genealogy of the Heng-kang Yuan).

69. Wang Li, *Lin-yuan wen-chi* (SKCSCP ed., 1st ser.), 12.1a–2a (lament for Wang Kung-min).

70. Liu Sung, *Ch'a-weng wen-chi*, 17.27a–28a (epitaph).

71. Hu Chih, *Heng-lu ching-she ts'ang-kao*, A26.14a–16b (epitaph).

72. Ibid., B10.11a–12b (epitaph).

73. Louis J. Gallagher, S.J., trans., *China in the Sixteenth Century: The Journals of Matthew Ricci, 1583–1610* (New York, 1953), 244–47; Matthieu Ricci, S.J., and Nicolas Trigault, S.J., *Histoire de l'éxpedition chrétienne au royaume de la Chine, 1582–1610* (Bellarmin, 1978), 700 (index).

74. Lo Ta-hung, *Tzu-yuan wen-chi* (Ming woodblock ed.), 5.42a–44a (preface to the seventieth birthday [celebration] for my in-law, Wu Hsiang-shan). Lo Ta-hung was a famous scholar-official from Chi-shui County, north of T'ai-ho. Wu's granddaughter was married to one of Lo Ta-hung's nephews.

75. It was related that the Wu had run a local ferry since the Sung era. They funded the construction and repair of the ferryboats from an endowment in rice paddies. A family of the Liu surname held a hereditary contract, sealed with the county seal, to serve the Wu as boatmen; but at some point in the Ming era, the Wu sold the field endowment to someone surnamed Lo. One day, boatman Liu Chang came weeping to one of Wu Hsiang-shan's sons and begged him to resume the family obligation of managing the ferry. So "a thousand men of the six [subbranches] of the Wu lineage contributed funds to extend the field endowment, build boats, renovate the boathouse, and restore the Liu to their hereditary ferry service." Lo Ta-hung, 7.23a–24a (inscription for a stela at the ferry crossing).

76. That did not rule out elite tax cheating, as evidenced by the perennial problem of "empty grain" (*hsu-liang*), i.e., rice tax the registers showed as due but unpaid or uncollectible, owing to one or another form of ownership concealment (*kuei-chi, fei-chi*). A few citations of rice-tax shortfalls survive in the literature: 15,000 piculs in 1512; 4,942 in 1533; 1,659 in 1539; 1,950 in 1587. The total rice tax (according to the county budget of 1610) was 34,760.6996

piculs. Except in 1512, therefore, cheating resulted in marginal losses of 5 percent to 14 percent. In each of the cases cited, the magistrates took remedial action.

77. Ou-yang To, 5.10a–11b (preface to the revised comprehensive tax registers of T'ai-ho); Chang Mou, epitaph for Magistrate Lu Chen (1464–1519), in Chiao Hung, ed., *Kuo-ch'ao hsien-cheng lu,* 3:1705–8.

78. Ou-yang To, 17.10a–12b.

79. Ch'en Ch'ang-chi, 5.75b–76b (epitaph).

80. Ou-yang To, 1.4a–5b (account of an investigation into empty grain in T'ai-ho). In 1539, Kuo Yuan-ch'ang and four other upright locals discovered another tax shortfall, and the magistrate forced the ward scribes to gather all the household heads together so as to eliminate fraud case by case. The ward scribes' work was then audited by the "hundred and ten township scribes." The end product was a new master register in which "the households' [quota of taxes] matched the tithings, the tithings matched the wards, the wards matched the townships, and the townships the county." These registers were then printed and posted where everyone could see them. See Ou-yang To, 5.10a–11b (preface to the collected registers).

81. Ou-yang Te, 25.25b–29a (epitaph).

82. Ou-yang To, 17.16a–17a (epitaph).

83. Hu Chih, *Heng-lu ching-she ts'ang-kao,* A26.6a–7b (epitaph).

84. Ibid., A26.20a–31a (biography).

85. Ibid., B10.11a–12b (epitaph).

86. Kuo Tzu-chang, *Pin-i sheng Yueh-ts'ao* (printed ed., 1590), 6.23b–26a (biography).

87. Wang Shih-hsing, *Kuang-chih i* (reprint, Beijing, 1981), 81.

88. Timothy Brook, "The Spatial Structure of Ming Local Administration," *Late Imperial China* 6, no. 1 (1985): 38.

89. Just how lineage segments mapped onto fiscal households is better known in other localities in China. T'ai-ho lacked a statistically minded native son like Yeh Ch'un-chi, who made detailed studies of this matter in his native Hui-an County, Fukien, in the sixteenth century. See Yeh Ch'un-chi, *Shih-tung chi* (SKCSCP ed., 5th ser.).

90. *T'ai-ho hsien-chih* (1879), 24.40b–42b (Tsou Yuan-piao, inscription for the Ch'en ancestral temple).

91. Ou-yang Te, 20.14b–16b (preface to seventieth birthday honors for the virtuous widow Hsiao).

92. Quoted in *T'ai-ho hsien-chih* (1826), 2:569–70. The extant gazetteer of 1579 is lacking the first five *chüan,* in which the quoted text would have appeared.

93. *T'ai-ho hsien-chih* (1826), 2:558.

94. See Ray Huang, *Taxation and Governmental Finance in Sixteenth-Century Ming China* (Cambridge, 1974), 109–112.

95. Chang Huang, *T'u-shu pien* (1613; reprint, Taipei, 1971), 24:10188–202. The same effect was noted in Hunan around 1600, where Hung Mao-te wrote that "without *ting* all the tax is laid on the land. The people see the land

as poison and abandon it as quickly as possible." Cf. Peter C. Perdue, *Exhausting the Earth: State and Peasant in Hunan, 1500–1850* (Harvard, 1987), 62.

96. Kuo Tzu-chang, *Ch'ing-lo kung i-shu* (T'ai-ho, printed ed., 1882), 31.15a–18a (family instructions).

97. *Chi-an fu-chih* (Kiangsi, 1875), 15.43a–44a (Tseng T'ung-heng, record of field investigation). The boast was not wholly empty; the results of the survey ended up in the county budget of 1610, whose areal totals for rice fields coincide rather well with the rice fields shown on a detailed U.S. Army map of 1954. From 1607 to 1613, when P'u Chung-yü was T'ai-ho magistrate, the tax complaints he heard had little to do with unequal assessments. To be sure, P'u warned the people against false registry and tax engrossment (*kuei-chi* and *pao-lan*), but local complaints at the time targeted the duties and powers of the receivers and checkers and shippers, who, though compensated for their work by payments in silver, were squeezing excessive charges from the people. Cf. Kuo Tzu-chang, *Ch'ing-lo kung i-shu,* 26.1a–2b (stela in honor of Magistrate P'u, on his departure).

CHAPTER 3

1. For example, when Lo Meng-chao died in 1434, his son Lo Ch'ung-pen, at the time a secretary (6A) in the Ministry of Justice, came crying to Grand Secretary Yang Shih-ch'i asking that he write a *mu-piao*. Yang agreed to do so. He stated that he had known the dead man personally and had already written an epitaph for his wife and another for Ch'ung-pen's brother (Yang Shih-ch'i, *Tung-li ch'üan-chi* [SKCSCP ed., 7th ser.], B30.12b–15b). Wang Chih wrote Lo Meng-chao's *mu-chih ming* (Wang Chih, *I-an chi* [SKCSCP ed., 8th ser.], B30.29a–31a), and Ch'en Hsun wrote a *chuan* for him as well (Ch'en Hsun, *Fang-chou wen-chi* [printed ed., 1593], A10.1a–2b).

2. A baby is one *sui* the day it is born and turns two *sui* on the first day of the following lunar new year. Lunar new year's day falls in January or February of a Western-style year (in the decade 1390–1400, it fell in the period from January 17 to February 12). A *sui*-age varies from one to two years higher than a Western-style age, with an average of one and a half years. See Stevan Harrell, ed., *Chinese Historical Microdemography* (Berkeley, 1995), 19, n. 7. Whenever exact birth and death dates aren't known, I have added one year to given *sui* ages.

3. Liang Ch'ien, *Po-an chi* (SKCSCP ed., 6th ser.), 13.9b–11a, 11ab; Yang Shih-ch'i, A17.8a–12b. The problem of excluding dead children is also characteristic of Chinese lineage registers; see Ted A. Telford, "Survey of Social Demographic Data in Chinese Genealogies," *Late Imperial China* 7, no. 2 (December 1986): 118–48, esp. 125. The T'ai-ho epitaphs do not substantiate Telford's assertion that "die young" (if it is equivalent to "died early," *tsao tsu*) means death before the age of fifteen to twenty *sui;* it can simply mean that a person died before his father or mother did, or was that a person was dead as of the time his father or mother's epitaph was written up. See Telford, "Patching the Holes in Chinese Genealogies: Mortality in the Lineage Populations of Tong-

cheng county, 1300–1880," *Late Imperial China* 11, no. 2 (December 1990): 116–36, esp. 121.

4. The result is a list larger than the one I reported in John W. Dardess, "Ming Historical Demography: Notes from T'ai-ho County, Kiangsi," *Ming Studies*, no. 17 (fall 1983): 60–77.

5. Note, however, that where all live births are routinely counted, as among the Chinese population in the United States, Chinese births have a notably higher sex ratio than white births (107.1:100, as compared to 105.6:100, for the years 1960–82). See W. H. James, "The Sex Ratio of Oriental Births," *Annals of Human Biology* 12, no. 5 (September–October 1985): 485–87.

6. *Ming shih-lu* (reprint, Taiwan, 1965), 73:1459–60.

7. Chu Kuo-chen, *Yung-ch'uang hsiao-p'in* (Pi-chi hsiao-shuo ta-kuan ed., reprint, Taipei, 1962), 2:2129.

8. Ou-yang Te, *Ou-yang Nan-yeh hsien-sheng wen-chi* (woodblock ed., 1558), 26.25b–28a.

9. *Chi-an fu-chih* (Kiangsi, 1875), 47.11b–14a.

10. For the references, see Dardess, "Ming Historical Demography: Notes from T'ai-ho County, Kiangsi," 66. There are two different versions of the 1982 T'ai-ho County sex ratio: one comes out to 101:100, the other to 102.7:100. See *Chung-kuo 1982 nien jen-k'ou p'u-ch'a 10% ch'ou-yang tzu-liao* (Beijing, 1983), 100; and *Chung-kuo 1982 nien jen-k'ou p'u-ch'a tzu-liao* (Beijing, 1985), 178–79. However, the 1982 sex ratio for the whole province is 106.5; 100 (see pp. 22–23 of the latter source). Infanticide claimed the lives of 10 percent of the girl babies of the Ch'ing imperial clan and as much as 20–25 percent of the girl babies of the Liaoning peasantry in north China; see James Lee et al., "The Last Emperors: An Introduction to the Demography of the Qing (1644–1911) Imperial Lineage," in *Old and New Methods in Historical Demography,* ed. David S. Reher and Roger Schofield (Oxford, 1993), 361–82.

11. Listed in T'an Ch'ien, *Kuo ch'ueh* (reprint, Beijing, 1958), 1:9–19.

12. Yang Shih-ch'i, B40.1a–2b. She married Hsiao Fen, of the Peach Spring Hsiao in township 12. She was herself a Willow Creek Ch'en, a granddaughter of Ch'en Mo, Yang Shih-ch'i's tutor and uncle. For a general view of this matter, see Bao-Hua Hsieh, "The Acquisition of Concubines in China, Fourteenth–Seventeenth Centuries," in *Chin-tai Chung-kuo fu-nü yen-chou,* no. 1 (1993): 125–200.

13. Ch'en Ch'ang-chi, *Lung-chin-yuan chi* (Ming woodblock ed.), 5.72a–75b (*mu-chih ming* for Hsiao Ai and his wife née Ch'en).

14. Wang Chih, A6.21b–23a (preface to the *Nü-chiao hsu-pien*). Li Shih-mien (1374–1450) added a comment to this book; see Li Shih-mien, *Ku-lien wen-chi* (SKCSCP ed., 3d. ser.), 8.28a–29a.

15. Wang Chih, B33.56a–59a.

16. Ibid., B25.46a–48a. Madame Tseng was from the Tseng common-descent group of Sandalwood Lane in T'ai-ho City West and was the principal wife of Yin Ch'un of Mountain Field Ward (township 31). Wang Chih thought her a model wife.

17. Chiao Hung, ed., *Kuo-ch'ao hsien-cheng lu* (1594; reprint, Taipei, 1965), 4:2469–71 (Kuo Tzu-chang, *mu-chih ming*).

TABLE 5

FEMALE FERTILITY FOR THE
FAN LINEAGE, 1475–1574

	Average N children per consort	Completed family size
1 consort	2.18	2.18
2 consorts	1.48	2.97
3 consorts	1.60	4.79
4 consorts ·	—	—

SOURCE: Data from Harriet Zurndorfer, *Change and Continuity in Chinese Local History: The Development of Hui-chou prefecture, 800–1800* (Leiden, 1989), 193.

18. Lu Jung, *Shu-yuan tsa-chi che-ch'ao* (Chi-lu hui-pien ed.), 182.13b–14a; also Liang Wei-shu, *Yü-chien tsun-wen* (reprint, Shanghai, 1986), 2:582.

19. Ch'en Hsun (Wang Hsiang, *nien-p'u* for Ch'en Hsun); A9.27a–28b (epitaph for Tseng Ching); and A9.28b–31b (epitaph for Kuo Miao-chih).

20. Lu Jung, *Shu-yuan tsa-chi che-ch'ao*, 181.28a.

21. Gary S. Becker, *A Treatise on the Family* (Cambridge, Mass., 1981), 44, 48.

22. Liu Ts'ui-jung has found comparable effects in north China lineages; see her *Ming Ch'ing shih-ch'i chia-tsu jen-k'ou yü she-hui ching-chi pien-ch'ien* (Taipei, 1992), 91. However, Harriet Zurndorfer's data for the Fan lineage of Hui-chou Prefecture, Anhwei Province, 1475–1574, show lower female fertility and a similar general trend, but nothing so neat as in T'ai-ho (see table 5). See her *Change and Continuity in Chinese Local History: The Development of Hui-chou Prefecture, 800–1800* (Leiden, 1989), 193.

23. The procedure is discussed in Nathan Keyfitz, *Applied Mathematical Demography*, 2d ed. (New York, 1985), 330.

24. For the upper-class population to reproduce itself, sets of children had the statistical task of replacing only slightly more than their two parents. This is because of the small contribution extra consorts made to the size of the completed family of children.

25. In certain lineages of Hunan Province up to 1650, Liu Ts'ui-jung has found short-term male growth rates of some 2 percent per annum. There were also periods of negative growth, which she correlates with the effects of local natural disasters. See her "Formation and Function of Three Lineages in Hunan," in *Chin-shih chia-tsu yü cheng-chih pi-chiao*, ed. Chung-yang yen-chiu-yuan chin-tai-shih yen-chiu so (Taipei, 1992), 1:346–47.

26. The inability of "a significant fraction" of lineage males (broadly defined here as "upper class" males) to marry has also been noted in T'ung-ch'eng County, Anhwei, for the period 1520–1661. See Ted A. Telford, "Covariates of Men's Age at First Marriage: The Historical Demography of Chinese Lineages," *Population Studies* 46, no. 1 (March 1992): 19–35.

27. See, for example, Fu I-ling, "Ming-tai Chiang-hsi ti kung-shang-yeh jen-k'ou chi ch'i i-tung," in *Ming Ch'ing she-hui ching-chi-shih lun-wen-chi*, ed. Fu I-ling (Beijing, 1982), 187–97.

28. Sung Lien, *Sung Wen-hsien kung ch'üan-chi* (Ssu-pu pei-yao ed.), 10.18a–19a (eulogy for Liu O).

29. Yang Shih-ch'i, A22.20b–22b (biography).

30. Wang Chih, A1.4b–6b (inscription for the Tz'u-hsun t'ang, Hall of Maternal Instruction); Yang Shih-ch'i, B2.21a–23a (inscription for the same) and A16.1a–3a (epitaph for P'eng Hsu); Wang Chih, B34.10b–12a (biography of Liu Ling).

31. Ch'en Hsun (Wang Hsiang, *nien-p'u* for Ch'en Hsun), s.a. 1400.

32. Yang Shih-ch'i, B33.33a–34a (epitaph for Madame Liu).

33. See his biography in L. Carrington Goodrich and Fang Chaoying, eds., *Dictionary of Ming Biography* (New York, 1976), 2:1535–8.

34. Wang Chih, B36.57b–60b (a memoir about [step]-grandmother Li).

35. Ibid., A8.30a–32b (epitaph for Ou-yang Huai) and B33.59a–62a (epitaph for Madame Ch'en).

36. Ibid., B34.34a–36a (letter of instructions to son Wang Chü).

37. Ibid., A8.5b–7b (epitaph for Liang Hun); Yang Shih-ch'i, A20.8b–11a (epitaph for same); Ch'en Hsun, A10.2b–4b (biography of same); Wang Chih, A10.34a–36a (epitaph for Madame Liu) and B25.4a–6a (epitaph for Ch'en Shun-chih); Yang Shih-ch'i, A21.15b–17a (epitaph for same); Liang Ch'ien, 8.5a–8a (account of conduct for Ch'en Chung-shu); Hsieh Chin, *Wen-i chi* (SKCSCP ed., 4th ser.), 13.8a–10a (epitaph for same); Yang Shih-ch'i, B39.4a–6b (epitaph for Ch'en Chung-heng) and B42.7b–10b (epitaph for Ch'en Shang); Wang Chih, A9.23a–25b (epitaph for Liang Chiung).

38. Lo Ch'in-shun, *Cheng-an ts'un-kao* (SKCSCP ed., 4th ser.), 13.11a–14a (epitaph for Wang Ch'iu); Ou-yang To, *Ou-yang Kung-chien kung i-chi* (Ming woodblock ed.), 19.1a–3a (epitaph for Jen Lien-chen).

39. Lo Ch'i, *Kuei-feng chi* (SKCSCP ed., 4th ser.), 16.14a–17a (epitaph for Lo Fu).

40. Wolfram Eberhard, *Social Mobility in Traditional China* (Leiden, 1962), 106–7, 110.

41. Lo Hsiang-lin, ed., *K'o-chia shih-liao hui-pien* (Hong Kong, 1965), 76, 150, 191, 239, 293–94.

42. Wang Chih, B17.36a–38a (preface to the genealogy of the K'an-ch'i Liu).

43. Ibid., A8.27a–3a (epitaph for Wang Tsai) and A8.30a–32b (epitaph for Ou-yang Huai).

44. *Ch'ang-yuan hsien-chih* (1541; reprint, Shanghai, 1981), 5.35b.

45. Wang Hsien-ch'ien, *Hsu-shou-t'ang wen-chi* (reprint, Taipei, 1966), 2:675, 767; Wang K'ai-yun, *Hsiang-ch'i-lou wen-chi* (reprint, Taipei, 1966), 583.

46. T'an Ch'i-hsiang, "Chung-kuo nei-ti i-min shih—Hu-nan p'ien," *Shih-hsueh nien-pao* 1, no. 4 (1932): 47–104.

47. *Ming-tai Liao-tung tang-an hui-pien* (Shenyang, 1985), 1:16–18.

48. *Feng-t'ien t'ung-chih* (1927; reprint, Shenyang, 1983), 4:4131.

49. *Chiang-hsi t'ung-chih* (Kiangsi, 1881), 12.37a (Chou Yung, memorial requesting the establishment of a heavier official presence [in Nan-Kan]).

50. Ch'en Ch'ang-chi, 3.3b–5b (message for Military Defense Vice Commissioner Kao Pai-p'ing [Kao Shih-yen]).

51. Hai Jui, *Hai Jui chi* (reprint, Beijing, 1962), 1:202–8.

52. *Kan-chou fu-chih* (Kiangsi, 1873), 69.39b–40b (Huang Ta-chieh, letter to prefect Yang, demanding an end to illegal registry).

53. Kuo Tzu-chang, *Pin-i-sheng Yueh-ts'ao* (printed ed., 1590), 4.22a–24a (inscription for the sacrificial fields in honor of the Kuo ancestor).

54. See Frederick W. Mote and Denis Twitchett, eds., *The Cambridge History of China* (Cambridge, 1988), vol. 7, pt. 1, pp. 384–89.

55. See Wu Chin-ch'eng, "Ming-tai Hu-pei nung-ts'un ti she-hui pien-ch'ien yü shen-shih," *Shih-huo* 17, nos. 1–2 (June 1988): 65–87.

56. *Yun-hsi hsien-chih* (1936; reprint, Taipei, 1975), 3:793.

57. *Yun-yang hsien-chih* (1870; reprint, Taipei, 1970), 275; Ou-yang Te, 6.14b–16b (letter to junior kinsmen in Chu-shan).

58. Niida Noboru, *Chūgoku hōseishi kenkyū* (Tokyo, 1959), 3:261–62; Wei Ch'ing-yuan et al., *Ch'ing-tai nu-pei chih-tu* (Beijing, 1982), 96, 128 n. 1; M. Abramson et al., "Tsziansi," *Problemy Kitaia*, no. 14 (1935): 108–110. There is a large literature on bondage in Ming China, the terms of which differed from region to region. For a general overview, see Nishimura Kazuyo, "Mindai no doboku," *Tōyōshi kenkyū* 38, no. 1 (1980): 24–50; and especially Wu Chen-han, "Ming-tai ti chu-p'u kuan-hsi," *Shih huo pan-yueh-k'an* 12, nos. 4–5 (August 1982): 147–63.

59. Hu Chih, *Heng-lu ching-she ts'ang-kao* (SKCSCP ed., 4th ser.), A22.2b–5a (biography). Hsiao Ch'uan was the husband of Hu Chih's aunt.

60. Yang Yin-ch'iu, *Lin-kao wen-chi* (SKCSCP ed., 2d ser.), 2.47a–55a (account of conduct for Madame Liang, his wife).

61. Ou-yang To, 17.3b–5b (epitaph).

62. Hu Chih, *Heng-lu ching-she ts'ang-kao*, A24.13a–18b (account of conduct for his mother, Madame Chou, 1497–1577).

63. Quoted in *T'ai-ho hsien-chih* (Kiangsi, 1879), 2.19b–20b.

64. Hu Chih, *Heng-lu ching-she ts'ang-kao*, B8.16a–20a (epitaph). Kuo Ch'i-shih was Kuo Tzu-chang's grandfather.

65. Yang Yin-ch'iu, 2.1a–4a (biography of Chang T'ing).

66. Ibid., 2.4a–7a (biography).

67. Ibid., 2.33a–38b (epitaph).

68. *Chi-an fu-chih*, 20.35ab.

69. Ibid., 20.36ab; *Yung-hsin hsien-chih* (1874; reprint, Taipei, 1975), 4:1214–15; Fu I-ling, "Ming-mo nan-fang ti 'tien-pien,' 'nu-pien,' " *Lishi yan-jiu*, no. 5 (1975): 61–67. The last quotation is from *Yung-hsin hsien-chih*.

70. *T'ai-ho hsien-chih* (1826; reprint, Taipei, 1989), 2:677–79; *Ch'ing-tai nung-min chan-cheng-shih tzu-liao hsuan-pien* (Beijing, 1984), 1:284–86.

71. See in particular Stevan Harrell, "Introduction: Microdemography and the Modeling of Population Process in Late Imperial China," in *Chinese Historical Microdemography,* ed. Stevan Harrell (Berkeley, 1995), 1–20.

72. Michel Cartier, "Nouvelles données sur la démographie chinoise à l'époque des Ming," *Annales: Économies, sociétés, civilisations* 28 (1973): 1341–59.

CHAPTER 4

1. The terms "descent group" and "lineage" and the distinction between them are taken from Patricia B. Ebrey and James L. Watson, eds., *Kinship Organization in Late Imperial China, 1000–1940* (Berkeley, 1986), 5.

2. Information about the common-descent groups of T'ai-ho is not as complete or systematic as it is for some other parts of south China. Some south China gazetteers of the nineteenth and early twentieth centuries carry a section called "registry of lineages" (*shih-tsu piao*). For example, Lu-ling, a large county bordering T'ai-ho to the north, lists in its gazetteer of 1911 some thirty-five hundred lineages large and small for a population of some 1.7 million (as of 1871). For Hui-chou Prefecture in Anhwei Province, there was a special register, first published in 1316 and later updated, listing seventy-four "large lineages" (*ta tsu*). These texts still survive. But nothing like a a countywide survey of common-descent groups or lineages was ever conducted in T'ai-ho; and although some twelve hundred extant lineage books are listed in Akigorō Taga's catalog, some forty of them from Kiangsi, none of them is from T'ai-ho. See Harriet Zurndorfer, "The *Hsin-an ta-tsu chih* and the Development of Chinese Gentry Society, 800–1600," *T'oung Pao* 67, nos. 3–5 (1981): 154–215; and Taga Akigorō, *Sōfu no kenkyū: Shiryō hen* (Tokyo, 1960).

3. Hsiao Ch'i, *Cheng-ku hsien-sheng wen-chi* (Hsiao-shih shih-chi ed.), 9a–10b (preface to poems and other pieces relating to the Lung family library).

4. Ibid., 40b–42a (colophon).

5. Liu Sung, *Ch'a-weng wen-chi* (Ming woodblock ed.), 13.2b–3a (introduction to Lo Tzu-li's genealogy).

6. Ch'en Mo, *Hai-sang chi* (SKCSCP ed., 4th ser.), 8.13a–15a (epitaph for Lo Ta-k'o, 1286–1359); Wang Chih, *I-an chi* (SKCSCP ed., 8th ser.), A6.10b–12b (preface to the Nan-ch'i Tseng genealogy).

7. Chou Shih-hsiu, *Ch'u-jao chi* (SKCSCP ed., 4th ser.), 5.69b–70a (preface to the Chou genealogy).

8. Ch'en Hsun, *Fang-chou wen-chi* (printed ed., 1593), A5.32a–33b (preface to the genealogy of the Hsiao of Chang-ch'i in T'ai-ho). The source does not explain why it was felt that the genealogy was in danger; perhaps in cases of confiscation, government agents seized anything that appeared to have value.

9. Lo Ta-hung, *Tzu-yuan wen-chi* (Ming woodblock ed.), 3.56b–58a (preface to the genealogy of the Lo of T'ao-chin-i). T'ao-chin Ward was in township 42, T'ai-ho.

10. Yang Shih-ch'i, *Tung-li ch'üan-chi* (SKCSCP ed., 7th ser.), A4.10a–11b (preface to the Ts'ai genealogy).

11. Wang Li, *Lin-yuan wen-chi* (SKCSCP, 1st ser.), B3.10a–11a (preface to the Ho-ch'i Hu genealogy).

12. Ch'en Mo, 9.6a–7a (postscript to Liu Ching-an's genealogy).

13. Wang Chih, B16.7b–9a (preface to the Sha-ch'i Liu genealogy).

14. Yang Shih-ch'i, B12.10a–11b.

15. Ibid., B12.6b–7a (preface to the T'ai-yuan Hsu genealogy). T'ai-yuan (also known as Ta-yuan) was a ward in township 33.

16. Ch'en Hsun, A5.25a–26b (preface to the Chou-hsia Lo genealogy). There were two Chou-hsia Wards in T'ai-ho, one in township 49, the other in township 53.

17. Yang Shih-ch'i, A4.10a–11b (preface to the Ts'ai genealogy).

18. Ibid., B23.13ab (postface to the Shang-mo Tseng genealogy). Shang-mo Ward was in township 28.

19. Wang Chih, B23.27a–28b (preface to poems composed on the occasion of Yang Meng-pien's return south). Yang Meng-pien (from Shang-yuan-t'ang Ward, township 43) was a very wealthy man who claimed a relationship to Yang Shih-ch'i. Yang Shih-ch'i spurned him. This matter is discussed later in the chapter.

20. Yang Shih-ch'i, B5.14b–15b (inscription for the Le-chih t'ang).

21. Ibid., B51.7b–8b (family letter).

22. Wang Chih, A5.19b–21b (preface to the Ch'ing-ch'i Ch'en genealogy). Ch'ing-ch'i (Clear Creek) was on the east side of T'ai-ho city. It was not a ward.

23. Yang Shih-ch'i, B13.29a–30b (postface to the genealogy of the Hung-kang Yuan). Hung-kang (or Heng-kang) Ward was in township 33.

24. Ibid., B12.20ab (postface to the Ho-shan Liu genealogy). Ho-shan was said to lie ten *li* southeast of T'ai-ho city. It is not known to have been the name of a ward. Later descendants lived in Ta-yuan Ward (township 33).

25. Ch'en Hsun, A5.28a–29b (preface to the Feng-kang Kuo genealogy). The Feng-kang Kuo are better known as the Ta-kang Kuo. Ta-kang (Big Hill Ward) was in township 29.

26. Yang Shih-ch'i, B12.22ab (preface to the Nan-ching Hu genealogy). Nan-ching (South Path Ward) was in township 55.

27. Ibid., A2.14a–15b.

28. Yeh Sheng, *Shui-tung jih-chi* (reprint, Taipei, 1968), 2:697–98.

29. Ch'en Mo, 9.30a–31a (postface to Hsiao T'ien-yü's genealogy). Yang Shih-ch'i, B23.27b–28a, is word-for-word the same. Since Yang was Ch'en's student, he may have written the piece under Ch'en's direction, or in his behalf. The Hsiao in question were Sha-hu Hsiao, also known as Hsi-t'ang Hsiao, and were most likely from township 7 (another Hsi-t'ang Ward was located in township 59).

30. Yang Shih-ch'i, B23.8b–9b (postface to the P'eng genealogy).

31. Ibid., B23.24b–25a (a note on interloping). Wang Chih seems to have rescinded his endorsement, because it does not appear in his collected works.

32. Wang Chih, A5.19b–21b (preface to the Ch'ing-ch'i Ch'en genealogy); Ch'en Hsun, A5.11a–12b (preface to the same).

33. Yang Shih-ch'i, B13.25ab (preface to the Liu genealogy). Liu I lived at Hsia-ts'un in township 41. The Chu-lin Liu were based in township 38.

34. Ch'en Hsun, A5.5b–8a (preface to the Kuan-ch'ao Kuo genealogy). Ch'en's second wife was a Kuan-ch'ao Kuo.

35. Chou Shih-hsiu, 5.69b–70a (preface to the Chou genealogy).

36. Liu Sung, *Ch'a-weng wen-chi*, 14.18a–19a (colophon to a biography of Chou Tun-i, kept by Chou So-an).

37. Yang Shih-ch'i, B12.8a–9b (preface to the Shu-yuan Lo genealogy).

38. Chiao Hung, ed., *Kuo-ch'ao hsien-cheng lu* (1594; reprint, Taipei, 1965), 1:402–4 (Ch'en Shang [1378–1413], biography of Yang Shih-ch'i).

39. As he relates in his account of conduct for his father, Liang Lan (1343–1410). See Liang Ch'ien, *Po-an chi* (SKCSCP ed., 6th ser.), 8.11b–18a.

40. Chou Shih-hsiu, 6.39b–40a (colophon to documents regarding Kuo Ts'ung-lung's surname restoration).

41. *T'ai-ho hsien-chih* (1826; reprint, Taipei, 1989), 7:2914–16 (Liu Yeh, argument in favor of Liu Shih-te [Ssu-te]'s restoring his surname).

42. See Ann Waltner, *Getting an Heir: Adoption and the Construction of Kinship in Late Imperial China* (Honolulu, 1990). Patricia Ebrey has made a thorough analysis of the diverging interests of family (*chia*) and descent-group (*tsung*) in her "Conceptions of Family in the Sung Dynasty," *Journal of Asian Studies* 43 (February 1984): 219–45, esp. 232.

43. Yin Ch'ang-lung, *Yin Na-an hsien-sheng i-kao* (ms. ed.), ch. 4 (preface to the Liang genealogy).

44. Ou-yang To, *Ou-yang Kung-chien kung i-chi* (Ming woodblock ed.), 117.12b–14a (epitaph for Wang Chih, 1460–1528).

45. Hu Chih, *Heng-lu ching-she ts'ang-kao* (SKCSCP ed., 4th ser.), A10.25b–28a (preface to a revision of the Chueh-yü K'ang genealogy).

46. Lo Ch'in-shun, *Cheng-an ts'un-kao* (SKCSCP ed., 4th ser.), 9.20a–21a (preface to the Lei-kang K'ang genealogy).

47. Yin T'ai, *Tung-lu-t'ang chi* (SKCSCP ed., 5th ser.), 1.76b–79b (preface to the T'ai-ho K'ang genealogy).

48. Lo Hung-hsien, *Nien-an wen-chi* (SKCSCP ed., 5th ser.), 12.42a–44b (preface to the T'ai-ho Teng genealogy).

49. Ch'en Hsun, A3.22a–23b (preface to poems written in honor of Ch'en Kung-i [Ch'en I, d. 1472], on his departure to take up the post of assistant governor [4A] of Ying-t'ien [Nanking]).

50. Ch'en Ch'ang-chi, *Lung-chin-yuan chi* (Ming woodblock ed.), 5.97a–99b.

51. Liu Sung, *Ch'a-weng wen-chi*, 14.20a–21a (a note on the family record of the Kuan-ch'ao Kuo).

52. Liang Ch'ien, 16.12a–13b (colophon to the family record of the Kuan-ch'ao Kuo).

53. Ch'en Hsun, A5.5b–8a (preface to the Kuan-ch'ao Kuo genealogy).

54. Kuo Tzu-chang, *Ch'ing-lo kung i-shu* (T'ai-ho, printed ed., 1882), 18.23b–25b (preface to the genealogy of the Chien-ch'i Kuo). Chien-ch'i appears to be another name for Ao-t'ou, in T'ai-ho township 62.

55. Ibid., 31.12a–15a (message to the heads of the five lineages about revising the genealogy).

56. Ch'en Hsun, A5.28a–29b (preface to the Feng-kang [Ta-kang] Kuo genealogy); Ch'en Ch'ang-chi, 2.82a–84a (preface to the revised genealogy of the Ta-kang Kuo). Ch'en Ch'ang-chi's mother was a Ta-kang Kuo.

57. Wang Chih, B7.30a–32a (preface to the Kao-p'ing Kuo genealogy); Lo Hung-hsien, *Nien-an wen-chi*, 12.36b–39b (preface to the same).

58. The Ch'ing dynasty considered Kiangsi lineage conglomerates a threat and sought to break them up. See Alexander Woodside, "Emperors and the Chinese Political System," in *Perspectives on Modern China*, ed. Kenneth Lieberthal et al. (Armonk, 1991), 11–12.

59. Liu Sung, *Ch'a-weng wen-chi*, 6.7b–9a (inscription on the rebuilding of the Yueh family's Chui-yuan t'ang).

60. Liu Chiang-sun, *Yang-wu-chai chi* (SKCSCP ed., 1st ser.), 17.15a–17b (inscription for a bronze image of the Jade Emperor in the Lin-yen Taoist temple).

61. Yang Shih-ch'i, B22.21b–22b (end note to the Yang genealogy) and B23.15b–16a (end note on the Yang genealogical chart).

62. *T'ai-ho hsien-chih* (1826), 5:2176–80 (Tsou Yuan-piao [1551–1624], inscription for the Ch'en ancestral temple).

63. Ou-yang Te, *Ou-yang Nan-yeh hsien-sheng wen-chi* (woodblock ed., 1558), 26.1a–3b (epitaph for Ch'en Te-ming, 1478–1545).

64. *T'ai-ho hsien-chih* (1826), 5:2180–83 (Tsou Yuan-piao, inscription for the Lung ancestral temple); T'ang Hsien-tsu, *T'ang Hsien-tsu shih-wen chi* (new ed., Shanghai, 1982), 2:1177–86.

65. *T'ai-ho hsien-chih* (1826), 5:2176–80 (Tsou Yuan-piao [1551–1624], inscription for the Ch'en ancestral temple).

66. Tsou Yuan-piao, *Yuan-hsueh chi* (SKCSCP ed., 5th ser.), 5B.33b–36a (inscription commemorating the lineage temple for all the Nan-ch'i Hsiao).

67. Ou-yang To, 3.1a–2a (inscription for the sacrificial fields of the Kuan-ch'ao Kuo lineage).

68. Ibid., 16.3a–6a (epitaph for Tseng Hsien, 1451–1535); Lo Ch'in-shun, *Cheng-an ts'un-kao*, 1.29b–31b (inscription for the ancestral temple in honor of prefect Tseng Su-an [Tseng Yü, Hsien's father]).

69. Lo Ch'in-shun, *Cheng-an ts'un-kao*, 1.28a–29b (inscription in honor of the additional sacrificial fields acquired by the Shang-mo Tseng).

70. Ou-yang To, 3.2a–4a (account of the yearly sacrifices of the middle branch [*chung fang*] of the Wang).

71. Ou-yang To, 17.10a–12b (epitaph for Chang Ssu).

72. Li Pang-hua, *Ming tsung-hsien Li Chung-su kung chi* (printed ed., 1842), 9.8a–10a (preface to regulations for the general temple [for the Li] of the nine counties [of Chi-an Prefecture]).

73. Hu Chih, *Heng-lu ching-she ts'ang-kao*, B3.6a–8a (inscription for the Tun-tien t'ang).

74. Ibid., B10.1a–3b (epitaph for Hu Hsi, 1498–1580).

75. Lo Ch'in-shun, *Cheng-an ts'un-kao*, 14.16b–19a (epitaph).

76. Kuo Tzu-chang, *Ch'ing-lo kung i-shu*, 31.15a–18a (family instructions).

77. Lo Ch'in-shun, *Cheng-an ts'un-kao*, 7.27a–28a (preface to the Yun-t'ing community compact) and 16.3a–6a (epitaph for Tseng Hsien).

78. Chiao Hung, ed., *Kuo-ch'ao hsien-cheng lu*, 4:2469–71 (Kuo Tzu-chang, epitaph for Tseng Yü-hung).

79. Hu Chih, *Heng-lu ching-she ts'ang-kao*, A10.22a–23a (postscript to the T'ai-ho community compact); A10.25b–28a (preface to the Chueh-yü K'ang ge-

nealogy); A26.9b–14a (epitaph for Hu Shun-chü, 1522–76); B3.6a–8a (inscription for the Tun-tien t'ang); B5.5b–7b (preface to an appreciation of the painting of three retired elders at the Ch'iu-jen school); and B10.11a–12b (epitaph for Hu Hou, fl. sixteenth century).

80. See Shen Yen-ch'ing, *Huai-ch'ing i-kao* (1862; reprint Taipei, n.d., as ser. 38, no. 378, of Chin-tai Chung-kuo shih-liao ts'ung-k'an), A3.9b–16a (letter to the Chi-an prefect about conditions in T'ai-ho); ch. B1–B4 consist of detailed lawsuits and public notices. Shen was appointed magistrate of T'ai-ho in 1843.

81. See Hilary J. Beattie, *Land and Lineage in China: A Study of T'ung-ch'eng, Anhwei, in the Ming and Ch'ing Dynasties* (Cambridge, England, 1979); Jerry Dennerline, "Marriage, Adoption, and Charity in the Development of Lineages in Wu-hsi from Sung to Ch'ing," in *Kinship Organization in Late Imperial China 1000–1940,* ed. Patricia B. Ebrey and James L. Watson (Berkeley, 1986), 170–209; Timothy Brook, "Family Continuity and Cultural Hegemony: The Gentry of Ningbo, 1368–1911," in *Chinese Local Elites and Patterns of Dominance,* ed. Joseph W. Esherick and Mary B. Rankin (Berkeley, 1990), 27–50; and William T. Rowe, "Success Stories: Lineage and Elite Status in Hanyang County, Hubei, c. 1368–1949," in *Chinese Local Elites and Patterns of Dominance,* ed. Joseph W. Esherick and Mary B. Rankin (Berkeley, 1990), 51–81.

82. Robert P. Hymes, *Statesmen and Gentlemen: The Elite of Fu-Chou, Chiang-Hsi, in Northern and Southern Sung* (Cambridge, 1986).

83. Rowe, "Success Stories," 80.

CHAPTER 5

1. Wang Ao, *Chen-tse ch'ang yü* (Ming-Ch'ing shih-liao hui-pien ed., 1st ser.), A.30a; Chu Kuo-chen, *Yung-chuang hsiao-p'in* (Pi-chi hsiao-shuo ta-kuan ed., reprint, Taipei, 1962), 2:1939.

2. *Fen-sheng fu-an chin-shen pien-lan* (reprint, Shanghai, [1990?]).

3. Kuo Tzu-chang, *Ch'ing-lo kung i-shu* (T'ai-ho, printed ed., 1882), 19.19a–21a (preface to the genealogy of the Huang-kang Hsiao).

4. Yang Shih-ch'i, *Tung-li ch'üan-chi* (SKCSCP ed., 7th ser.), A4.23b–24b (message for Tseng Ts'un-shan); Ch'en Hsun, *Fang-chou wen-chi* (printed ed., 1593), B3.18a–19b (inscription for the Chi-shan t'ang).

5. Ph. de Heer, *The Care-Taker Emperor: Aspects of the Imperial Institution in Fifteenth-Century China as Reflected in the Political History of the Reign of Chu Ch'i-yü* (Leiden, 1986).

6. *Ming shih-lu* (reprint, Taiwan, 1965), 32:4513.

7. Wang Chih, *I-an chi* (SKCSCP ed., 8th ser.), B13.4b–6a (message for Assistant Instructor Ch'en); Ch'en Hsun, A9.23a–27a (epitaph for Ch'en Yung); *Ming Shih-lu,* 33:4942, 4950. Lin Ts'ung (1417–82), from Fukien Province, went on to have an outstanding career; he had locked horns with Ch'en Hsun earlier on a wholly different matter. See *Ming shih-lu,* 32:4415, 4492–93, 4496–98; 33:4664–5; also 34:5381–2.

8. *Ming shih-lu,* 35:5690–92.

9. Ibid., 34:5433–34.

10. Ibid., 37:6342.

11. The total is reported in Cheng Hsiao, *Chin yen* (1566; reprint, Taipei, 1969), 189.

12. *Ming shih-lu*, 12:1421–2.

13. Ibid., 18:959–61, 998.

14. Ibid., 55:1994–5.

15. Ibid., 95:1451.

16. Ibid., 98:1001–2.

17. Ibid., 42:1283–4.

18. Chiao Hung, ed., *Kuo-ch'ao hsien-cheng lu* (reprint, Taipei, 1965), 1:402–4 (Ch'en Shang, biography of Yang Shih-ch'i).

19. Yang Shih-ch'i, B40.26b–28b (epitaph for Mme Hsiao, 1333–1412).

20. Wang Chih, B16.13b–15a (message for Hsiao Li-ching, returning to T'ai-ho) and B12.7a–8b (message for Vice Magistrate Hsiao Ssu-ching, on departing for Tz'u-li County).

21. Lo Hung-hsien, *Nien-an wen-chi* (SKCSCP ed., 5th ser.), 8.16a–18a (a statement for Hsiao T'ien-ch'ung, i.e., Hsiao Lung-yu); Ch'en Ch'ang-chi, *Lung-chin-yuan chi* (Ming woodblock ed.), 5.76b–79a (epitaph for Hsiao's father) and 3.79b–81a (message for Hsiao T'ien-ch'ung, on his departure north); Hu Chih, *K'un-hsueh chi,* in *Ming-ju hsueh-an,* ed. Huang Tsung-hsi (reprint, Taipei, 1965), 221–24. The quotation is from Lo's statement to Hsiao.

22. Yang Shih-ch'i, B31.12a–14a (epitaph for Yuan Chün, 1354–1424). Wang Chih recalled that when he was a *sheng-yuan* in the years preceding 1403, his class had numbered twenty in all. Wang Chih, B16.25a–26b.

23. Ch'en Hsun, A3.19a–20b and A4.4a–5b.

24. *T'ai-ho hsien-chih* (1826; reprint, Taipei, 1989), 5:1860–64 (Tseng Meng-chien, inscription for the rebuilding of the Temple of Literature).

25. Yang Shih-ch'i, A8.12b–14a.

26. Ch'en Hsun, A7.43a–45a (epitaph for Lung Ts'an).

27. See Ch'en Hsun (Wang Hsiang, *nien-p'u* for Ch'en Hsun), s.a. 1401.

28. Ibid., s.a. 1403, 1414.

29. *Ming shih-lu,* 35:5641–2.

30. Ibid., 41:1091–2.

31. Yang Shih-ch'i, A3.4a–5a (message for Tseng Shih-jung).

32. Ibid., A22.20b–22b (biography of Ch'en Meng-hsing).

33. *Ming shih-lu,* 41:1091–2.

34. Hu Chih, *Heng-lu ching-she ts'ang-kao* (SKCSCP ed., 4th ser.), A8.20a–32a (generational account of the Hu family). The letters are quoted on pp. 22b–25b.

35. *Ming shih-lu,* 64:1410; Chu Ta-shao, ed., *Huang Ming ming-ch'en mu-ming* (reprint, Taipei, 1969), 3:899–911 (Han Pang-ch'i, epitaph for Ch'en Feng-wu).

36. L. Carrington Goodrich and Fang Chaoying, eds., *Dictionary of Ming Biography* (New York, 1976), 1:843; *Ming shih-lu,* 66:2280 ff.; Tilemann Grimm, "Ming Educational Intendants," in *Chinese Government in Ming Times,* ed. Charles O. Hucker (New York, 1969), 142. So popular was Kiangsi Educational Intendant Shao Pao (1460–1527) that eight years after he left his

post, former students commissioned T'ai-ho artist Kuo Hsu to do a portrait of him from memory; the result bore no resemblance to its subject, but Shao Pao appreciated it nonetheless. See Shao Pao, *Jung-ch'un t'ang hsu-chi* (SKCSCP ed., 5th ser.), 8.23ab (appreciation of a small portrait by Kuo Hsu).

37. Hu Chih, *Heng-lu ching-she ts'ang-kao*, B9.20a–22b (epitaph for Ch'en Ts'an).

38. Ibid., A23.32b–41a (account of conduct for Yang Tsai-ming).

39. Lo Ch'in-shun, *K'un-chih chi* (reprint, Beijing, 1990), 201–2.

40. Kuo Tzu-chang, *Ch'ing-lo kung i-shu*, 3a (Kuo K'ung-yen, *nien-p'u* for Kuo Tzu-chang).

41. Hu Chih, *Heng-lu ching-she ts'ang-kao*, 22.12a–14a (epitaph for Tseng Ch'iu-t'an).

42. *T'ai-ho hsien-chih* (1826), 6:2222–4 (Hsiao Tzu-shang, message for Yin Ch'ang-lung, on his departure as *sui-kung*).

43. Wang Chih, B2.24b–26b (inscription for the North Hall).

44. Ch'en Hsun (Wang Hsiang, *nien-p'u* for Ch'en Hsun, passim).

45. Hu Chih, *K'un-hsueh chi*, 221; Hu Chih, *Heng-lu ching-she ts'ang-kao*, A25.10a–13b (epitaph for Ou-yang Ch'ang), A24.1ab (account of conduct for Ou-yang Shao-ch'ing), and B11.23a–25a (biography of Yang Hai). Hu Chih's spiritual autobiography, the *K'un-hsueh chi*, has been the focus of some interesting literary and psychological research, notably by Wu Pei-yi and Rodney Taylor. Wu, *The Confucian's Progress: Autobiographical Writings in Traditional China* (Princeton, 1990), deals extensively with that text and its later influence on Kao P'an-lung (pp. 100–128). Wu also translates the *K'un-hsueh chi* in an appendix (pp. 243–51). Rodney Taylor's studies include "Journey into Self: The Autobiographical Reflections of Hu Chih," *History of Religions* 21 (May 1982): 321–38; and "Acquiring a Point of View: Confucian Dimensions of Self-Perception," *Monumenta Serica* 34 (1979–80): 145–70, in which he compares the spiritual testaments of Hu Chih and Kao P'an-lung (1562–1626). Neither writer tries to place Hu Chih in local, social, or national political context.

46. For the numbers of candidates taking the Kiangsi exams in the years indicated, see Han Yung, *Han Hsiang-i kung chia-ts'ang wen-chi* (reprint, Taipei, 1970), 2:557–61 (for 1456); Li Shun-ch'en, *Yü-ku chi* (SKCSCP ed., 5th ser.), 5.20b–22a (for 1534); *Ming-tai teng-k'o-lu hui-pien* (reprint, Taipei, 1969), 13:6901 and 23:12085 (for 1558 and 1627).

47. *Ming shih-lu*, 95:1304.

48. Ibid., 25:1440–41. When provincial *chü-jen* quotas were raised in 1440 (Kiangsi's to sixty-five), the idea was to generate more B-list *chü-jen* to fill teaching vacancies. It was the opinion of the authorities that the "tribute students" (*sui-kung*) in the imperial colleges, having failed all exams themselves, made very poor government teachers.

49. The quotas and the numbers of degree candidates, can be found out for many of the exams given in the Ming. See Wada Masahiro, "Mindai kyojinsō no keisei katei ni kansuru ichi kōsatsu," *Shigaku zasshi* 87, no. 3 (March 1978): 43; *Ming-tai teng-k'o-lu hui-pien*, 14:7339, 15:7943, 18:9123; Yang Shih-ch'i, B6.9b–11a, 13b–15a, B9.9b–10b; and Ch'en Hsun, B2.15a–16a and A3.43b–45a (see table 6).

TABLE 6

PASS RATES FOR MING
CHIN-SHIH CANDIDATES

	Quota	N (Candidates)	% Pass
1421	200	3,000	7
1427	100	2,000	5
1430	100	2,000	5
1442	150	1,000	15
1445	150	1,200	13
1457	300	3,000	10
1469	250	3,300	8
1478	350	4,000	9
1496	300	3,500	9
1550	320	4,500	7
1559	300	4,600	6
1562	300	4,500	7
1568	400	4,500	9
1574	300	4,500	7

SOURCES: Data from Wada Masahiro, "Mindai Kyojinso no Keisei Katei ni Kansuru ichi Kosatsu," *Shigaku zasshi* 87, no. 3 March 1978): 43; *Ming-tai teng-k'o-lu hui-pien* (reprint, Taipei, 1969), 14: 7339, 15: 7943, 18: 9123; Yang Shih-ch'i, *Tung-li chüan-chi* (SKCSCP ed., 7th ser.), B6.9b–11a, 13b–5a, B9.9b–10b; and Ch'en Hsun, *Fang-chou wen-chi* (printed ed., 1593), B2.15a–16a and A3.43b–45a.

50. Ch'en Hsun, A3.43b–45a; *Ming shih-lu,* 63:868.

51. Ch'en Hsun, A3.43b–45a (message for Instructor Hsiao, on his departure for Ch'ang-chou).

52. See Ho Ping-ti, *The Ladder of Success in Imperial China* (New York, 1964), 246 ff.

53. Yang Shih-ch'i, B6.9b–11a, B6.13b–15a, and B9.9b–10b.

54. Ch'en Hsun, B2.15a–16a (message on the departure [from Peking] of Assistant Instructor Lo Ching-hsun).

55. See Tani Mitsutaka, "Mindai kansei no kenkyū," *Shigaku zasshi* 73, no. 4 (April 1964): 56–81; 73, no. 6 (June 1964): 69–82.

56. This count is taken from the *Ming shih-lu,* entries for the Chia-ching reign period (1522–66) and later, passim.

57. Ibid., 23:779–80.

58. See Ma Tai-loi, "The Local Education Officials of Ming China, 1368–1644," *Oriens Extremus* 22 (1975): 11–27. Despite the handicaps, some famous men in Ming China spent at least a part of their careers as government teachers; see Wu Chih-ho, *Ming-tai ti ju-hsueh chiao-kuan* (Taipei, 1991).

59. Yang Shih-ch'i, A6.3a–4b (message for Wang Ching-hsien).

60. The ages of four T'ai-ho men at the time they entered one of the imperial colleges as *sui-kung chien-sheng* are known. The ages are 34, 34, 50, and 69. Four men (not necessarily the same four) are known to have spent 1, 3, 5, and

16 years, respectively, as college students. The data include five ages at the time of first official posting: 35, 39, 40, 50, and 57.

61. Ou-yang Te, *Ou-yang Nan-yeh hsien-sheng wen-chi* (woodblock ed., 1558.), 24.37b–40b (epitaph).

62. Lo Ch'in-shun, *Cheng-an ts'un-kao* (SKCSCP ed., 4th ser.), 1.29b–31b (inscription for the temple). The county was Ch'ing-yuan, but the gazetteer of Kuang-chou Prefecture fails to list Tseng among the assistant instructors appointed to Ch'ing-yuan County in Ming times.

63. *Ming shih-lu*, 68:3003–4.

64. Ibid., 80:4211, 86:6569–70.

65. Ch'en Ch'ang-chi, 5.80a–82a (epitaph).

66. Hu Chih, *Heng-lu ching-she ts'ang-kao*, B9.3a–5a (epitaph).

67. *Ming shih-lu*, 56:2128; *T'ai-p'ing hsien-chih* (1540; reprint, Shanghai, 1981), 4.7a. The quotation is from the latter source.

68. For the mathematics of such "economic hierarchies," see Nathan Keyfitz, *Applied Mathematical Demography*, 2d. ed. (New York, 1985), 199–200.

69. Ho Ping-ti, *The Ladder of Success in Imperial China*, 231, 246–8. In the Ch'ing dynasty, T'ai-ho County produced a total of eighteen *chin-shih*, about a 90 percent drop from its level of achievement in the Ming. See Hans Bielenstein, "The Regional Provenance of *Chin-shih* during Ch'ing," *Bulletin of the Museum of Far Eastern Antiquities*, no. 64 (1992): 5–178, 46.

70. Lo Ch'i, *Kuei-feng chi* (SKCSCP ed., 4th ser.), 5.26a–27b (message for Kiangsi Education Intendant Su, on his departure).

71. James B. Parsons once considered from a national perspective the prominent success of certain "clans" (common-descent groups and lineages) in placing their members in Ming bureaucracy. His study focused on central bureaucracy, plus a small sample of the rest of the bureaucracy. He identified as a clan everyone with the same surname living in the same county. Nine T'ai-ho clans appear in his tables (pp. 211–2). The Hsiao, for example, appear as a single clan; however, in fact, there were at least twenty wholly distinct common-descent groups of the Hsiao surname in T'ai-ho. Similarly, there were several completely distinct groups of the other surnames—Ch'en, Wang, Liu, Tseng, Kuo, Li, Yang—that he listed. Of those that he listed, only the Ou-yang was a recognized single common-descent line. See Parsons, "The Ming Dynasty Bureaucracy: Aspects of Background Forces," in *Chinese Government in Ming Times: Seven Studies*, ed. Charles O. Hucker (New York, 1969), 175–232.

72. Some well-to-do landowners and family managers of sixteenth-century T'ai-ho opposed the idea of encouraging sons to take up Confucian studies. They argued that it was a waste of resources to support their education, and the belt-tightening penury of a Confucian lifestyle was unacceptable to them. See Yang Yin-ch'iu, *Lin-kao wen-chi* (SKCSCP ed., 2d ser.), 2.20b–24a (epitaph for T'ung Ni, 1531–95).

CHAPTER 6

1. There is substantial evidence to support this assertion. The great Neo-Confucian theorist Wu Ch'eng (1249–1331), a native of Fu-chou Prefecture,

Kiangsi, complained about the behavior of men from Chi-an Prefecture in several places in his collected works. One occasion was his epitaph for K'ang Jui-sun of T'ai-ho's Shen-ch'i Ward (township 4). The rich landowners of K'ang's area were hot-tempered and grasping, he noted. The merchants were much too aggressive. Quiet and shy people were laughed at by the predatory majority. K'ang Jui-sun himself had been hard-drinking and violent in his youth. See Wu Ch'eng, *Wu Wen-cheng chi* (SKCSCP ed., 2d ser.), 63.1a–4a. The works of T'ai-ho natives Hsiao Ch'i, Ch'en Mo, and Liu Sung sustain this theme.

2. The example of Lo Fu-jen, "honest Lo," from Chi-shui County, is discussed in L. Carrington Goodrich and Fang Chaoying eds., *Dictionary of Ming Biography* (New York, 1976), 1:974–75.

3. The civil war and usurpation have been well handled in Edward L. Dreyer, *Early Ming China: A Political History, 1355–1435* (Stanford, 1982), chap. 5.

4. T'an Ch'ien, *Kuo ch'ueh* (reprint, Beijing, 1958), 1:844.

5. Ku Ying-t'ai, *Ming-shih chi-shih pen-mo* (1658; reprint, Taipei, 1956), 1:209.

6. T'an Ch'ien, *Kuo ch'ueh*, 1:849; *T'ai-ho hsien-chih* (1826; reprint, Taipei, 1989), 6:2580–84 (Liang Ch'ien, account of conduct for Chou Shih-hsiu); Chiao Hung, ed., *Kuo-ch'ao hsien-cheng lu* (1594; reprint, Taipei, 1965), 8:4740 (Yang Shih-ch'i, biography of Chou) and 8:4740–42 (Kuo Tzu-chang, biographical notes on Chou).

7. Ku Ying-t'ai, *Ming-shih chi-shih pen-mo*, 1:211. The belief was strongly held that there had been such a pact, and many later writers condemned Yang Shih-ch'i for moral cowardice in backing out of it. See, for example, Wu T'ing-han, *Wu T'ing-han chi* (reprint, Beijing, 1984), 106.

8. *T'ai-ho hsien-chih* (1826), 6:2409–12 (Chou Shih-hsiu, letter to general editor Fang Hsi-chih [Fang Hsiao-ju]).

9. Yang Shih-ch'i recited parts of his life story to Ch'en Shang, a young T'ai-ho protégé. See Chiao Hung, ed., *Kuo-ch'ao hsien-cheng lu*, 1:402–4 (Ch'en Shang [1378–1413], biography of Yang Shih-ch'i).

10. Ibid.

11. T'an Ch'ien, *Kuo ch'ueh*, 1:815.

12. Ibid., 1:845.

13. The point is elaborated in John W. Dardess, *Confucianism and Autocracy: Professional Elites in the Founding of the Ming Dynasty* (Berkeley, 1983), chap. 5.

14. T'an Ch'ien, *Kuo ch'ueh*, 1:937; *Ming shih-lu* (reprint, Taiwan, 1965), 10:581; Chiao Hung, ed., *Kuo-ch'ao hsien-cheng lu*, 1:398 (Wang Chih, biography of Yang Shih-ch'i).

15. Yen Wei (1280–1355, from T'ai-ho city), arrogant and ambitious as a youth, ended up a private tutor in the households of several high ranking Mongol elites in the Yuan capital of Ta-tu; there he authored a text called the *Wu-ching ta-i* (General idea of the Five Classics). Several people had a look at the manuscript; some thought it better than Chen Te-hsiu's *Ta-hsueh yen-i*, a widely read Neo-Confucian text of the Sung. Someone showed Yen's work to

emperor Tugh Temür (Wen-tsung, r. 1328–32). People said the emperor liked it, but nothing came of it. Hsiao Nan-k'o was an uncle of Liu Sung's, who lived most of his life as a private tutor in the Kiangsi provincial capital of Nan-ch'ang. Liu Sung met him in an inn in Hsing-kuo County, southeast of T'ai-ho, probably in the 1340s. "He took out his annotations to the Four Books and Five Classics and he let me look at them and he said: 'I'm old now, and soon I'll give all these to you.' Then he pounded on the table and called for rice-beer. He drank several tens of cups and devoured a plateful of meat. He was loud and spirited and arrogant. I never saw him again after that." Cf. Liu Sung, *Ch'a-weng wen-chi* (Ming woodblock ed.), 17.18b–22b (epitaph for Yen Wei) and 10.22b–25b (preface to the Hsiao genealogy).

16. Liu Ch'iu, *Liu Liang-ch'i wen-chi* (Ch'ien-k'un cheng-ch'i chi ed.), 228(7).6ab, 11b–12a (prefaces to banquet poems).

17. Wang Chih, *I-an chi* (SKCSCP ed., 8th ser.), B29.44a–46a (epitaph).

18. Liang Ch'ien, *Po-an chi* (SKCSCP ed., 6th ser.), 6.47a–48b (preface to poems in honor of Ou-yang Hsien's departure); Wang Chih, B30.1a–3b (epitaph for Ou-yang Hsien).

19. Yang Shih-ch'i, *Tung-li ch'üan-chi* (SKCSCP ed., 7th ser.), B38.16b–18a (epitaph).

20. Ibid., A18.23b–25a (epitaph).

21. Liang Ch'ien, 13.7b–9a (preface to an appreciation of Ch'en Lien); Yang Shih-ch'i, A18.16b–18a (epitaph).

22. Yang Shih-ch'i, B30.12b–15b (epitaph); also Wang Chih, B30.29a–31a (epitaph), and Ch'en Hsun, *Fang-chou wen-chi* (printed ed., 1593), A10.1a–2b (biography).

23. Yang Shih-ch'i, B39.3b–4a (a partially damaged epitaph).

24. Native-place hostels are discussed in Ho Ping-ti, *Chung-kuo hui-kuan shih-lun* (Taipei, 1966).

25. Wang Chih, B3.40b–41b (inscription for the I-ching t'ang).

26. Yang Shih-ch'i, A16.1a–3a (epitaph for P'eng Hsu); Wang Chih, B23.25b–27a (postface to poems written in honor of Hsiao Yu-lung's departure). P'eng Hsu's experiences as a fatherless child in danger of becoming a slave were discussed in an earlier chapter.

27. Wang Chih, A4.9b–11a (preface to poems celebrating his moving house).

28. Yang Shih-ch'i, B46.1a–4b; Wang Chih, A9.21a–23a (epitaph).

29. Yang Shih-ch'i, B31.19a–21b (epitaph for Kuo Ting).

30. Ibid., A4.4a–5a (preface to poems in honor of Yin Neng-ching's departure).

31. The Yin Ch'ang-lung case is not covered by the *Veritable Records*. In connection with a petition to rehabilitate Yin Ch'ang-lung and place his tablet in the T'ai-ho hall of honor (Hsiang-hsien tz'u) in 1516, a number of documents, biographies, testimonials, and other materials were collected, and these are gathered in ch. 9 of Yin Ch'ang-lung, *Yin Na-an hsien-sheng i-kao* (ms. ed). See also Shen Te-fu, *Wan-li yeh-huo pien* (1619; new ed., Beijing, 1980), 2:709, 807.

32. Ch'en Hsun, A10.8b–9a (colophon on handwriting by Jen-tsung).

33. Ibid., A10.10b–11a (colophon to a scroll).

34. *Ming shih-lu,* 14:2094–95; Yang Shih-ch'i, A17.8a–12b (epitaph) and A9.13b–14b (colophon to autograph poems by Jen-tsung); Ch'en Hsun, B5.4b–5b (same subject); see also Ch'en Hsun (Wang Hsiang, *nien-p'u* for Ch'en Hsun), s.a. *wu-hsu* (1418).

35. Yang Shih-ch'i, A22.12b–15b (biography of Lo Tzu-li), A22.6a–8a (biography of Yang Cho), A9.15b–18a (colophon to the lucky fungus poems of the Peach Spring Hsiao), B7.1a–2a (message for District Medical School Principal Teng Ch'ien), and B9.15a–16b (message for Teng Chia-mou); Ch'en Mo, 5.4b–5b (message for Yang Cho); Ch'en Hsun, A3.33b–35a (message for Wang Tzu, appointed T'ai-ho assistant instructor); *Wan-li T'ai-ho chih* (1579; reprint, Taipei, 1989), 465–67 (biographies of Yang, Lo, and Teng).

36. Ch'en Hsun, A3.23b–24b (preface to poems done at a "literary meeting") and A10.13ab (colophon to poems done aboard ship, and kept by Wang Tzu).

37. Ch'en Hsun (Wang Hsiang, *nien-p'u* for Ch'en Hsun), s.a. *i-wei* (1415).

38. *Ming shih-lu,* 25:1526; Yang Shih-ch'i, B27.21a–24a; Wang Chih, A9.30a–32b (epitaphs for Tseng Hao-ling); Liu Ch'iu, *Liang-ch'i wen-chi* (SKCSCP ed., 11th ser.), 22.19a–22a (account of conduct for Tseng); Liang Wei-shu, *Yü-chien tsun-wen* (reprint, Shanghai, 1986), 2:665–66. Tseng was a surprise choice for such high grades on either exam. He impressed outsiders as reticent and dull, and when he died in office as Han-lin academician expositor-in-waiting, his official obituary merely commended his affability, sincerity, and good writing style. There wasn't much more to say.

39. *Ming shih* (Kuo-fang yen-chiu-yuan ed.), 3:2002–4 (biography of Wang Chih); Shen Te-fu, *Wan-li yeh-huo pien,* 1:181. One theory has it that Yang resented Wang Chih's repeated warnings about the evil doings of his beloved oldest son, Yang Chi. Cf. Ho Liang-chün, *Ssu-yu-chai ts'ung-shuo* (reprint, Beijing, 1983), 60.

40. Wang Chih, B33.65b–68b (autobiographical epitaph). In this piece, Wang states that he was indeed made a grand secretary sometime early in the Yung-lo era. He doesn't say how he lost that status.

41. *Ming shih-lu,* 26:2017.

42. Yang Shih-ch'i, B6.9b–11a (message for Liu Ting). Much the same sentiment is expressed in B9.9b–10b (message for Lo Ching).

43. *Ming shih-lu,* 29:2952–55; *Ming shih,* ch. 71.

44. *Ming shih-lu,* 28:2850–52.

45. Ibid., 33:4866–69, 4872–73; 34:5381–82.

46. Ibid., 26:1973; 27:2082–83, 2439; Yang Shih-ch'i, C3.28a–29b (regarding the suit filed by the T'ai-ho plaintiffs).

47. *Ming shih-lu,* 32:4551.

48. Ibid., 32:4415; *Chiang-hsi t'ung-chih* (Kiangsi, 1881), 127.10b; Ch'en Hsun, A9.28b–31b (epitaph for Kuo Miao-chih).

49. *Ming shih-lu,* 32:4492–93, 4496–97, 4498, 4664–65, 4759.

50. Shih Chien, *Hsi-ts'un chi* (SKCSCP ed., 3d ser.), 7.29b–33b (epitaph for Chu Sheng, 1396–1457). Chu Sheng was the principal investigator of these

crime rings. See also Goodrich and Fang, eds., *Dictionary of Ming Biography,* 1:498–503, 561–62 (biographies of Han Yung and Hsing An).

51. *Ming shih-lu,* 35:5710–15, 5718–20. This exam controversy is also discussed in Goodrich and Fang, eds., *Dictionary of Ming Biography,* 1:970–71 (biography of Liu Yen).

52. Ph. de Heer, *The Care-Taker Emperor: Aspects of the Imperial Institution in Fifteenth-Century China as Reflected in the Political History of the Reign of Chu Ch'i-yü* (Leiden, 1986).

53. Besides de Heer, cf. *T'ai-ho hsien-chih* (1826), 7:2868–72 (Kuo Tzu-chang, preface to Ch'en Hsun's collected works) and 5:1769–71 (Hsiao Tzu, memorial against changing the succession); Goodrich and Fang, eds., *Dictionary of Ming Biography,* 2:1358–61 (biography of Wang Chih).

54. *Ming shih-lu,* 38:6853–57; Ch'en Hsun (Wang Hsiang, *nien-p'u* for Ch'en Hsun), s.a. *jen-wu* (1462). The *nien-p'u* of Ch'en Hsun was written by Assistant Instructor Wang Hsiang, who was not a T'ai-ho native, but he was evidently a protégé eager to present his subject in his best light. The *shih-lu,* or *Veritable Records,* for the Cheng-t'ung, Ching-t'ai, and T'ien-shun reigns (1435–64) were compiled in 1467, and these spare no effort to show Ch'en Hsun in his worst moments. For the compilation of the *shih-lu,* see Wolfgang Franke, *An Introduction to the Sources of Ming History* (Kuala Lumpur, 1968).

CHAPTER 7

1. There was a distant blood relationship between the Hung-fu Yin and Yin Ch'ang-lung's people, who lived some miles away in Kuan-t'ang Ward (township 14). This relationship had no known bearing upon Yin Chih's career.

2. Chu Kuo-chen, *Yung-ch'uang hsiao-p'in* (Pi-chi hsiao-shuo ta-kuan ed., reprint, Taipei, 1962), 2:2069.

3. Chiao Hung, ed., *Kuo-ch'ao hsien-cheng lu* (1594; reprint, Taipei, 1965), 1:455–59 (Ch'eng K'ai, biography of Yin Chih). Yin was still alive when Ch'eng K'ai wrote this.

4. Wang Chih, *I-an chi* (SKCSCP ed., 8th ser.), B37.26b–27a (portrait appreciation) and B9.17b–19a (preface to poems in honor of Yin Tzu-yuan's departure).

5. Ch'eng Min-cheng, *Huang-tun wen-chi* (SKCSCP ed., 3d ser.), 40.4a (account of conduct for Li Hsien).

6. Yin's *Ch'eng-chiang pieh-chi* survives, but it consists mainly of official papers, which he edited and published in order, as he states in the preface, to show his descendants how high he had risen in his career.

7. L. Carrington Goodrich and Fang Chaoying, eds., *Dictionary of Ming Biography* (New York, 1976), 2:1521; Ni Yueh, *Ch'ing-ch'i man-kao* (Wu-lin wang-che i-chu ed.), 16.16a–17b (account of a group portrait of Han-lin yearmates).

8. Yin Chih, *Chien-chai so-chui lu* (Li-tai hsiao-shih ed.), 8b–9b; Wang Chih, A7.35b–37b (epitaph for Liao Mo); T'an Ch'ien, *Kuo ch'ueh* (reprint, Beijing, 1958), 2:1563–64. There was a common belief in the realm that Yang

Shih-ch'i had abetted the rise of eunuch power; different stories, some of them probably apocryphal, circulated to show that he had done so. See, for example, Cheng Hsiao, *Chin yen* (1566; reprint, Taipei, 1969), 164–65.

9. *Ming shih* (Kuo-fang yen-chiu-yuan ed.), 3:1998–99.

10. Fei Hung, *T'ai-pao Fei Wen-hsien kung chai-kao* (1555; reprint, Taipei, 1970), 3:1509–17 (epitaph for Yin Chih).

11. *Ming shih-lu* (reprint, Taiwan, 1965), 40:371; 42:1219, 1269–73; 45:2536–37; *Ming shih*, 3:1996, 2080–82 (biographies of P'eng Hua and Li Ping); Sun Hsu, *Sha-ch'i chi* (SKCSCP ed., 8th ser.), 14.39ab (comment on Hsiao Yen-chuang).

12. Yin Chih, *Chien-chai so-chui lu* (Li-tai hsiao-shih ed.), 28a–30a.

13. See *Ming shih-lu*, 12:1238, for the rule barring Chekiang and Kiangsi men from holding positions in the Ministry of Revenue. The rule certainly worked in the case of T'ai-ho men; none was ever assigned a regular post in the Ministry of Revenue.

14. Yin Chih, *Chien-chai so-chui lu* (Li-tai hsiao-shih ed.), 30a.

15. Detailed inside information on these connections may be found in Han Pang-ch'i, *Yuan-lo chi* (SKCSCP ed., 4th ser.), 19.7ab.

16. Li Tung-yang, *Li Tung-yang chi* (new ed., Changsha, 1984), 3:39–40 (preface to poems on the group portrait); Goodrich and Fang, eds., *Ming Biographical Dictionary*, 1:881; *Ming shih-lu*, 61:62–3 (obituary note for Chang Ta).

17. Ni Yueh, *Ch'ing-ch'i man-kao*, 19.11b–13a (message for Tseng Yen on his retirement).

18. *Ming shih-lu*, 45:2705.

19. *Ming shih*, 3:1998–99 (biography of Yin Chih).

20. Wang Shu, *Wang Tuan-i kung wen-chi* (reprint, Taipei, 1970), 61–64 (departing message for Vice Minister of War Yin Chih).

21. *Ming shih-lu*, 59:3741–43 (obituary for Lo Ching). See also *Ming shih-lu*, 50:4757–58 and 51:178–80; Li Tung-yang, *Huai-lu t'ang kao* (reprint, Taipei, 1975), 7:3401–6 (epitaph for Lo Ching).

22. See Hung-lam Chu, "Intellectual Trends in the Fifteenth Century," *Ming Studies*, no. 27 (spring 1989): 1–33. In 1470, Yin Chih's proposal to compile a Ming history and a *Ta Ming t'ung-tien* (Comprehensive encyclopedia of Ming institutions) was accepted by the throne. See *Ming shih-lu*, 42:1453–54. Fei Hung's epitaph for Yin Chih lists all his statecraft publications.

23. *Ming shih*, 3:1995–96 (biography of Wan An).

24. Yin Chih, *Chien-chai so-chui lu* (Li-tai hsiao-shih ed.), 46ab.

25. *Ming shih-lu*, 50:4733–34; *Ming shih*, 3:1998–99 (biography of Yin Chih) and 3:2149 (biography of Min Kuei); Wang Ao, *Chen-tse chi* (SKCSCP ed., 5th ser.), 29.14a–17b (epitaph for Min Kuei). The quotation is from the *Ming shih-lu*.

26. Tsou Chih, *Li-chai i-wen* (SKCSCP ed., 9th ser.), 1.1a–7b (memorial of impeachment). Tsou Chih was soon arrested on a charge unrelated to this memorial, and he died of disease in exile in Kwangtung.

27. *Ming shih-lu*, 51:116–117.

28. Ibid., 63.868; Goodrich and Fang, eds., *Dictionary of Ming Biography*, 1:233–34 (biography of Chiao Fang).

29. *Ming shih,* 5:3447 (biography of Chiao Fang); *Ming shih-lu,* 64:1313–14. The quotation is from the *Ming shih.*

30. Yang Hsi-min, *Shih-wu-chia nien-p'u* (reprint, Taipei, 1966), 4:1526. There is a large literature about Wu Yü-pi and his disciples. There is a biography of Wu in Goodrich and Fang, eds., *Dictionary of Ming Biography,* 2:1497–1501. See also Wing-tsit Chan, "The Ch'eng-Chu School of Early Ming," in *Self and Society in Ming Thought,* ed. Wm. Theodore de Bary (New York, 1970), 29–51; and Helmut Wilhelm, "On Ming Orthodoxy," *Monumenta Serica* 29 (1970–71): 1–26.

31. T'an Ch'ien, *Kuo ch'ueh,* 2:2072–73.

32. Yin Chih, *Chien-chai so-chui lu* (Li-tai hsiao-shih ed.), 23ab. For the events of Wu Yü-pi's disastrous visit, see *Ming shih-lu,* 36:6217–19, 6224–26, 6251–52; and T'an Ch'ien, *Kuo ch'ueh,* 2:2057, 2069, 2072–73.

33. Cf. Goodrich and Fang, eds., *Dictionary of Ming Biography,* 2:1500.

34. Ibid., 1:154 (biography of Ch'en Hsien-chang). See also Jen Yu-wen, "Ch'en Hsien-chang's Philosophy of the Natural," in *Self and Society in Ming Thought,* ed. Wm. Theodore de Bary (New York, 1970), 53–92.

35. For a memorial that recommends fervently that Ch'en be invited to Peking, see P'eng Shao, *P'eng Hui-an chi* (SKCSCP ed., 3d ser.), 1.8b–ff. Ch'en's appearance is described in Lin Chün, *Chien-su chi* (SKCSCP ed., 5th ser.), A10.14a–16a (inscription for a memorial temple in honor of Ch'en Hsien-chang).

36. Yin Chih, *Chien-chai so-chui lu* (Li-tai hsiao-shih ed.), 45ab. Cf. Goodrich and Fang, eds., *Dictionary of Ming Biography,* 1:896–98 (biography of Liang Fang). Yin Chih neglected to state that the request to the palace to confer the Han-lin appointment upon Ch'en Hsien-chang was prepared by his archenemy Yin Min, the minister of personnel. See Lin Chün, *Chien-su chi,* D1a–2b (chronological biography of Lin Chün). The official *Veritable Records* are hostile to Ch'en Hsien-chang, remarking unfavorably upon his philosophical unorthodoxy and upon his eagerness for fame and recognition. *Ming shih-lu,* 48:4128–30.

37. Yin Chih, *Chien-chai so-chui lu* (Li-tai hsiao-shih ed.), 44b.

38. Ibid., 54b–55a.

39. *Ning-po fu-chih* (1741; reprint, Taipei, 1957), 3:1380.

40. Yin Chih, *Chien-chai so-chui lu* (Li-tai hsiao-shih ed.), 36a.

41. Ibid., 53b.

42. Ibid., 54a.

43. Ibid., 53b–54a.

44. Lo Ch'in-shun, *Cheng-an ts'un-kao* (SKCSCP ed., 4th ser.), 15.1ab.

45. Cf. Irene Bloom, trans., *Knowledge Painfully Acquired: The K'un-chih chi by Lo Ch'in-shun* (New York, 1987), 146–47.

46. Lo Ch'in-shun, *Cheng-an ts'un-kao,* 13.16b–19b (epitaph for Li Mu). Cf. Goodrich and Fang, eds., *Dictionary of Ming Biography,* 1:1269, for the "club of candid directness" as a sometime elite social institution in Ming China.

47. *Ming Wen-hai* (SKCSCP ed., 7th ser.), 466.21a–23a (Liu Chieh, epitaph for Kuo Hsu); Ch'en Ch'ang-chi, *Lung-chin-yuan chi* (Ming woodblock ed.), 1.16b–20a (biography of Kuo Hsu).

48. Fei Hung, *T'ai-pao Fei Wen-hsien kung chai-kao,* 17.25b–30b (epitaph for Yin Chih).

49. *Ming shih-lu,* 55:2073–74.

CHAPTER 8

1. Okada Takehiko, *Ōyōmei to Minmatsu no jogaku* (Tokyo, 1971).

2. Wang's exceptional moral courage was remarked upon admiringly by the late Ming historian Shen Te-fu. Cf. Shen Te-fu, *Wan-li yeh-huo pien* (1619; new ed., Beijing, 1980), 2:508.

3. *Wan-li T'ai-ho chih* (1579; reprint, Taipei, 1989), 535; Also cf. Irene Bloom, trans., *Knowledge Painfully Acquired: The K'un-chih chi by Lo Ch'in-shun* (New York, 1987), 4.

4. See also Bloom, "On the 'Abstraction' of Ming Thought: Some Concrete Evidence from the Philosophy of Lo Ch'in-shun," in *Principle and Practicality: Essays in Neo-Confucianism and Practical Learning,* ed. Wm. Theodore de Bary and Irene Bloom (New York, 1979), 65–125.

5. Lo Ch'in-shun, *K'un-chih chi* (reprint, Beijing, 1990), 113–115, 170. Bloom has not dealt with Lo Ch'in-shun's relationships with contemporaries, relationships about which there remain quite a few letters written by him and to him.

6. Lo Ch'in-shun, *K'un-chih chi,* 133.

7. Translated in Bloom, *Knowledge Painfully Acquired,* 175–85. See also Wing-tsit Chan, trans., *Instructions for Practical Living and Other Neo-Confucian Writings by Wang Yang-ming* (New York, 1963), 263–64.

8. Chan, *Instructions,* 157–65.

9. Ibid., 188.

10. Lo Ch'in-shun, *Cheng-an ts'un-kao* (SKCSCP ed., 4th ser), 15.4b–5a.

11. Ts'ui Hsien, *Huan tz'u* (SKCSCP ed., 6th ser.), 10.13a–14b (on Lo's seventieth birthday); 10.14b–15b (letter to Lo); and 6.15a–16a (reply to Lo).

12. Hsu Chieh, *Shih-ching-t'ang chi* (Ming printed ed.), 19.32a–38a.

13. Wang Yang-ming, *Wang Yang-ming ch'üan-chi* (reprint, Taipei, 1964), 425; *T'ai-ho chih,* 554.

14. Chan, *Instructions,* 66–67, 194–95, 235.

15. Wang Yang-ming, *Wang Yang-ming ch'üan-chi,* 425.

16. Chan, *Instructions,* 150–57.

17. *Ming shih-lu* (reprint, Taiwan, 1965), 74:1815, 76:2474, 76:2486.

18. Yen Sung, *Ch'ien-shan-t'ang chi* (ms. ed.), *fu-lu,* portrait appreciations, composed and signed in 1532 by T'ai-ho men Ou-yang Te and Ch'en Ch'ang-chi, and in some later year by Ch'en Te-wen, a vice director in the Ministry of Works. Ou-yang Te's written works also contain a number of flattering messages for Yen Sung.

19. Hsu Chieh, *Shih-ching-t'ang chi,* 19.32a–38a; also reprinted in Chiao Hung, ed., *Kuo-ch'ao hsien-cheng lu* (1594; reprint, Taipei, 1965), 2:1390–92.

20. Ou-yang Te, *Ou-yang Nan-yeh hsien-sheng wen-chi* (woodblock ed., 1558), 1.14a–18b, 18b–24a, 24ab; Lo Ch'in-shun, *K'un-chih chi,* 117–21, 121–23.

21. Ou-yang Te, 2.29ab and 3.21ab.

22. Lo Ch'in-shun, *K'un-chih chi*, 124–27, 132–33, 176–77, 182–83.

23. Hu Chih, *Heng-lu ching-she ts'ang-kao* (SKCSCP ed., 4th ser), A26.9b–14a (epitaph for Hu Shun-chü); L. Carrington Goodrich and Fang Chaoying, eds., *Dictionary of Ming Biography* (New York, 1976), 2:1382–85 (Julia Ching, biography of Wang Ken).

24. Ou-yang Te, 1.33b–34b (response to Hu Yang-chai, i.e., Hu Yao-shih). Ou-yang's philosophical letters are not individually dated; his editor places this one along with a number of others in a section that he dates to the years 1529–34.

25. Lo Ch'in-shun, *K'un-chih chi*, 160–61.

26. *Ming shih-lu*, 76:2524–26. Hu Yao-shih's memorial is given in *T'ai-ho hsien-chih* (1826; reprint, Taipei, 1989), 5:1818–22.

27. Ou-yang Te, 17.4a–6a (message to Hu [Yao-shih], on his departure for the south).

28. Ch'en Po-ch'üan, ed., *Chiang-hsi ch'u-t'u mu-chih hsuan-pien* (Nan-chang, 1991), 368–70 (Hu Shun-chü, epitaph for Hu Yao-shih).

29. Chan, *Instructions*, xxv.

30. Lo Ch'in-shun, *K'un-chih chi*, 208; *Ming shih-lu*, 71:352–53.

31. The Great Rites dispute has been thoroughly studied in Carney T. Fisher, *The Chosen One: Succession and Adoption in the Court of Ming Shizong* (Sydney, 1990). On this and other protests in Ming history, cf. John W. Dardess, "Ming Officials and Modern Intellectuals: Some Enduring Configurations of Moral-Political Protest in China" (paper presented at the research conference entitled The Continuing Relevance of Traditional Chinese Institutions and Values in the Context of Modern China, East-West Center, University of Hawaii, May 1993).

32. Tsou Shou-i, *Tung-kuo hsien-sheng wen-chi* (Ming printed ed.), 3.1a–3a (preface to the *Kai-chai wen-chi*). The *Kai-chai wen-chi*, the collection of Wang Ssu's written works, is apparently now lost.

33. *Ming shih-lu*, 66:2215–17; *Ming shih* (Kuo-fang yen-chiu-yuan ed.), 3:2242 (biography of Wang Ssu).

34. *Ming shih*, 3:2242; See *T'ai-ho hsien-chih* (1826), 5:1788–90, for the full memorial.

35. *Ming shih-lu*, 66:2348; *Wan-li T'ai-ho chih*, 548–49. The account of his lectures (a *yü-lu* or *ch'uan-lu*) appears no longer to be extant. The academy he lectured at was the Ching-han Academy in Ch'eng-hai County; I have not been able to find much information about it. The quotation is from the *Wan-li T'ai-ho chih*.

36. *Ming shih-lu*, 71:599.

37. *T'ai-ho hsien-chih* (1826), 5:1790–92, 1792–96.

38. Hsia Liang-sheng, *Tung-chou ch'u-kao* (SKCSCP ed., 4th ser), 14.48a (poem of lament for Wang Ssu). Wang Ssu had a wife, a concubine, and two daughters.

39. Chu Che, *T'ien-ma shan-fang i-kao* (SKCSCP ed., 4th ser.), 2.18b–19b (postface to the *Kai-chai hsueh-lu*). The work is now apparently lost. Chu Che noted a particular argument in it—that "the vacuity in the Way of Heaven con-

sists solely of mind, and that the vacuity in the human mind consists solely of desire. The learner's job is done when he is no longer burdened by private desires, such that the substance of the mind engages the world with clear immediacy and in each instance according to principle."

40. *Ming shih-lu,* 82:5269–70; Chiao Hung, ed., *Kuo-ch'ao hsien-cheng lu,* 4:2180–81 (T'ang Po-yuan, biography of Liu K'uei). *T'ai-ho hsien-chih* (1826), 5:1804–7, contains the text of Liu K'uei's memorial.

41. Chiao Hung, ed., *Kuo-ch'ao hsien-cheng lu,* 4:2180 (T'ang Po-yuan, biography of Liu K'uei).

42. *Ming shih,* 5:3190 (biography of Yu Shih-hsi); Huang Tsung-hsi, *Ming-ju hsueh-an* (reprint, Taipei, 1965), 187. The quotation is from Huang Tsung-hsi.

43. Yang Chueh, *Yang Chung-chieh chi* (SKCSCP ed., 5th ser.), 6.12b–13a.

44. *Ming shih-lu,* 84:5736; T'an Ch'ien, *Kuo ch'ueh* (reprint, Beijing, 1958), 4:3676.

45. The minister of personnel here was Hsiung Chia (1478–1554). *Ming shih,* 3:2297–98 (biography of Hsiung Chia); Chiao Hung, ed., *Kuo-ch'ao hsien-cheng lu,* 2:1033–34 (Chang Ao, epitaph for Hsiung Chia). The other prisoner was Chou I (1506–69). Chiao Hung, ed., *Kuo-ch'ao hsien-cheng lu,* 5:3042 (Chiang Pao, epitaph for Chou I).

46. Chiao Hung, ed., *Kuo-ch'ao hsien-cheng lu,* 4:2180.

47. Yang Chueh, 2.10b–16a (prison diary); *Wan-li T'ai-ho chih,* 539–42 (biography of Liu K'uei).

48. Lo Hung-hsien, *Nien-an wen-chi* (SKCSCP ed., 5th ser.), 11.48a–51a (message to Liu Ch'ing-ch'uan [Liu K'uei] on his sixtieth birthday). In 1541, Lo Hung-hsien had himself offended the emperor in a memorial that touched on the sensitive question of the imperial succession. He was admonisher to the heir apparent (6B), and was dismissed from civil service for his remarks. He spent the rest of his life at home, engaging in tax and service reform, conducting cartographical and other research, and developing and teaching his own version of the Wang Yang-ming doctrines. See Goodrich and Fang, eds., *Dictionary of Ming Biography,* 1.980–84.

49. Hsu Chieh, *Shih-ching-t'ang chi,* 12.6a–7a (message for Yang Tzu-hsu [Yang Tsai-ming]).

50. A prefectural judge by the name of Kuo Lai-ch'ao was placed on the Ministry of Personnel's promotions list. Yang Tsai-ming thought Kuo quite acceptable. Why not? Yang had read and admired Kuo's writing, and Kuo also had an "outstanding" rating attached to his personnel file. Censors, however, discovered disrespect in Kuo's preparation of a routine memorial to the emperor, and they furthermore reported that Kuo had been "unreasonably greedy and oppressive" in his work as judge. The high officials of the ministry acknowledged their error and issued an apology. The emperor ordered them fined, but he considered Yang Tsai-ming the main culprit, guilty of evilly and deliberately misrepresenting Kuo's record. See *Ming shih-lu,* 87:7100–01; Hu Chih, *Heng-lu ching-she ts'ang-kao,* A23.36b (epitaph for Yang Tsai-ming).

51. Ou-yang Te, 5.43b–44b (letter in reply to Yang Wu-tung [Yang Tsai-ming]).

52. Chiao Hung, ed., *Kuo-ch'ao hsien-cheng lu*, 2:1392–93 (Li Ch'un-fang, stela for the imperially authorized temple in honor of Ou-yang Te).

53. Hsu Chieh, *Shih-ching-t'ang chi*, 19.32a–38a (spirit-way stela for Ou-yang Te); also in Chiao Hung, ed., *Kuo-ch'ao hsien-cheng lu*, 2:1390–92.

54. Huang Tsung-hsi makes this and other regional groupings of the Wang Yang-ming school in his *Ming-ju hsueh-an*. Ch. 16–24 of that work provide excerpts of the thought of no fewer than twenty-nine Kiangsi men, only three of which were from T'ai-ho (Ou-yang Te, Liu K'uei, and Hu Chih). Kandice J. Hauf, "The Jiangyou Group: Culture and Society in Sixteenth-Century China" (Ph.D. diss., Yale University, 1987) is a pioneering attempt to study the lives and ideas of four leading figures: Nieh Pao, Tsou Shou-i, Ou-yang Te, and Lo Hung-hsien.

55. Described in John Meskill, *Academies in Ming China: A Historical Essay* (Tucson, 1982). Around 1542, Ou-yang Te attended one of the "meetings of the comrades of the nine counties" held at Ch'ing-yuan Mountain, and there discussed differing interpretations of Wang Yang-ming's thought with Nieh Pao, Tsou Shou-i, and Lo Hung-hsien. Ou-yang Te's son Ou-yang Shao-ch'ing accompanied him and "got to hear things he had never heard before, which he faithfully recorded, eventually amassing a container full of notes." The notes are lost. See Hu Chih, *Heng-lu ching-she ts'ang-kao*, A24.4a (account of conduct for Ou-yang Shao-ch'ing, 1517–74). The account also relates that as a boy in Nanking in the company of his father in the 1530s, Ou-yang Shao-ch'ing was attracted to the philosophy of Chan Jo-shui, who was living nearby, until one night Ou-yang had a mystical experience. He dreamt that he rode a horse past Chan's house and soon came upon a strange new place, where Wang Yang-ming sat at the the gate. Wang called him over, smiled, and impressed a seal upon the palms of the young man's hands; Wang then pulled open his jacket and impressed the seal over his heart.

56. Hu Chih, *Heng-lu ching-she ts'ang-kao*, A8.27a–30a (a generational account of the Hu); Lo Hung-hsien, *Nien-an wen-chi*, 15.40a–42b (epitaph for Hu T'ien-feng).

57. Lü Nan, *Ching-yeh-tzu nei-p'ien* (reprint, Beijing, 1992), 87–88, also cf. 52. The five T'ai-ho men were K'ang Shu (1495–1569) of T'ai-ho city; Ou-yang Ch'ien-yuan, a distant relative of Ou-yang Te's; and three Ch'en men from Willow Creek, including Ch'en Ch'ang-chi, who prefaced the *Ching-yeh-tzu nei-p'ien*. All five were provincial degree holders at the time of the discussions; only Ch'en Ch'ang-chi later achieved his *chin-shih*.

58. Lü Nan, *Ching-yeh-tzu nei-p'ien*, 87–88, 121–22. The five T'ai-ho men were K'ang Shu (1495–1569) of T'ai-ho city; Ou-yang Ch'ien-yuan, a distant relation of Ou-yang Te's, and three Ch'en men from Willow Creek, including Ch'en Ch'ang-chi, who prefaced Lü's work. Ho Liang-chün tended to agree with Lü about Wang Yang-ming; he asserted that Wang Yang-ming was a true genius, whom "middling talents" simply could not follow, struggle as they might. Cf. Ho Liang-chün, *Ssu-yu-chai ts'ung-shuo* (reprint, Beijing, 1983), 32.

59. Wei Chiao, *Chuang-ch'ü i-shu* (SKCSCP ed., 5th ser.), 3.73ab, 4.6b–7a, 4.25ab, 4.55b–56a, 14.5b–6b. There is only one letter to Wei Chiao in Ou-yang

Te's works, and it does not seem to bear directly on Wei's objections. Ou-yang Te, 3.9ab. Ou-yang also wrote Lü Nan. Ou-yang Te, 2.25ab. Wei Chiao's T'ai-ho disciple was Wang Tsung-yin of Nan-fu Ward (township 61), a *chü-jen* of 1528 and later a magistrate. Wei Chiao, *Chuang-ch'ü i-shu*, 4.53b–54b, 69b–70b.

60. Hu Chih, *Heng-lu ching-she ts'ang-kao*, B8.20a–25a (epitaph).

61. Ibid., B11.29b–37a (biographies of Ch'en Liang-ching [1518–61], Lo Meng-fu, and Lo P'eng).

62. Hu Chih, *K'un-hsueh chi*, in *Ming-ju hsueh-an*, ed. Huang Tsung-hsi (reprint, Taipei, 1965), 221.

63. The Buddhist temple in question, the Hai-chih ssu, is not given in the gazetteers, at least not under that name. But it seems to have been located close to Hu Chih's home in township 51, as one of his poems suggests. Hu Chih, *Heng-lu ching-she ts'ang-kao*, A7.1ab.

64. Hu Chih, *Heng-lu ching-she ts'ang-kao*, A24.1ab (account of conduct for Ou-yang Shao-ch'ing). Hu Chih was three months older than Ou-yang Shao-ch'ing.

65. Hu Chih, *Heng-lu ching-she ts'ang-kao*, B11.23a–25a (biography of Yang Hai).

66. Goodrich and Fang, eds., *Dictionary of Ming Biography*, 1:983.

67. Hu Chih, *K'un-hsueh chi*, 221.

68. Such letters are among those included in Lo Hung-hsien, *Nien-an wen-chi*, ch. 2–4. His T'ai-ho correspondents included Hu Chih, Wang T'o, Ou-yang Ch'ang, Tseng Yü-ch'ien, Tseng Yü-chien, Tseng Yü-hung, and Tseng Yü-yeh (the Tsengs were kinsmen from Moon Hill Ward, township 32).

69. Hu Chih, *K'un-hsueh chi*, 222; *Heng-lu ching-she ts'ang-kao*, B8.20a–25a (epitaph for Tseng Yü-ch'ien, 1520–62). The other members were Lo Ch'ao, Hsiao Lung-yu, Wang T'o, and Ou-yang Ch'ang. Except for Hu Chih, all failed in their careers: Tseng became a primary tutor, Hsiao eventually purchased a post as a county vice magistrate, and Ou-yang Ch'ang was still a *sheng-yuan* when he died. So too, it appears, were Lo and Wang.

An older friend of Hu Chih's was successful in Fukien, however. Wang Chu (1500–54, of Hollow Street, in T'ai-ho's western suburb) won his *chü-jen* degree in 1525, but he spent the next quarter century as a private teacher in T'ai-ho and an active member of the local study groups that gathered to develop and spread the ideas of Wang Yang-ming. In 1549, he was appointed instructor in P'u-t'ien County in Fukien. The provincial education intendant was Chu Heng, from Wan-an County, just south of T'ai-ho. Chu Heng set up a series of venues for intensive discussion of Wang Yang-ming's thought, and he had Instructor Wang run these sessions in P'u-t'ien. Hundreds of *sheng-yuan* attended, and "their old habits of clinging to classical text and commentary [in the Ch'eng-Chu tradition] were completely changed." Local scholar-officials were highly impressed. Wang died suddenly in 1554; a public mourning ceremony was held at the P'u-t'ien school. It turned out he was so poor that all he owned was a ragged blanket and a tattered mat, and the costs of his funeral and burial had to be met by contribution. Wang Shen-chung, *Tsun-yen chi* (SKCSCP ed., 8th ser.), 24.20b–21a (letter to Wang Wu-yang, i.e., Wang Chu) and 19.5ab (eulogy); Ch'en Ch'ang-chi, *Lung-chin-yuan chi* (Ming woodblock ed.), 3.74a–75b (message for Wang on his departure for P'u-t'ien); *P'u-t'ien hsien-chih* (1879; reprint, Taipei, 1968), 268. The quotation is from the *P'u-t'ien hsien-chih*.

What Wang Chu tried to do at the county level was mirrored by what, at the same time, Ou-yang Te and others tried to do at the national level, in Peking. Information about the mass meetings held in Peking from 1553 to 1554 seems inexplicably scarce, but Ou-yang Te (minister of rites) and several other high officials conducted a series of lecture-discussions over a period of two months at the Ling-chi kung, a Taoist temple inside the Imperial City, for the purpose of introducing a younger generation of officials to Wang Yang-ming's thought. "Thousands" attended these affairs. See Hsu Hsueh-mo, *Shih-miao shih-yü lu* (reprint, Shanghai, 1991), 21.14a–15a; Lo Ju-fang, *Hsu-t'an chih-ch'üan* (reprint, Taipei, 1960), 297–98. The Ling-chi kung sessions are mentioned only briefly by Meskill, *Academies in Ming China,* 131, and Joanna F. Handlin, *Action in Late Ming Thought: The Reorientation of Lü K'un and Other Scholar-Officials* (Berkeley, 1983), 43.

70. Hu Chih, *Heng-lu ching-she ts'ang-kao,* A26.20a–31a (biographical account, written while Chang was still alive); A25.20b–22b (epitaph for Madame Liao, 1524–69); A10.15a–17b (preface to the reprinting of the *Wang Hsin-chai i-lu*); Ou-yang To, *Ou-yang Kung-chien kung i-chi* (Ming woodblock ed.), 11.2a–3b (message for Chang Feng).

71. *Wan-li T'ai-ho chih* (1579; reprint, Taipei, 1989), 557–58; *Wan-li Chi-an fu-chih* (1585; reprint, Beijing, 1991), 375–76 (biographies of Kuo Ying-k'uei); *Shou-chou chih* (1550; reprint, Shanghai, 1981), 5.78a.

72. There was, stated Hu, an "original mind." It was Mencius's "mind of not being able to bear others' [misfortunes]." Certain lofty-minded men (surely he meant Lo Hung-hsien and Tsou Shou-i here) erred by drowning themselves in "vacuity and tranquillity." Men of low mind (Grand Secretaries Yen Sung? Hsu Chieh?) engaged in the power-based manipulation of others. Only Ou-yang Te's "original mind," when made manifest, steered the student away from either of those errors. See Hu Chih, *Heng-lu ching-she ts'ang-kao,* A21.16b–17b (tomb report).

73. Ibid., A10.22a–26b (preface to the *Ou-yang Nan-yeh hsien-sheng wen-hsuan*).

74. *Ming shih-lu,* 94:1233.

75. Rodney L. Taylor, "Acquiring a Point of View: Confucian Dimensions of Self-Perception," *Monumenta Serica* 34 (1979–80): 145–70.

76. Hu Chih, *Heng-lu ching-she ts'ang-kao,* B9.18a (epitaph for Hsiao Jun-chuang, 1517–81).

77. These were Lo Ju-fang (1515–88), Tsou Shan (Tsou Shou-i's son), Keng Ting-hsiang (1524–96), and Chiang Pao (1514–93). Lo Ju-fang served alongside Hu Chih in the Ministry of Justice (his career as lecturer and teacher has been dealt with by Joanna F. Handlin in *Action in Late Ming Thought,* 41–54). Keng Ting-hsiang, another major intellectual figure, would later write Hu Chih's epitaph, as well as an earlier piece celebrating key phases in Hu Chih's intellectual development. See Keng Ting-hsiang, *Keng T'ien-t'ai hsien-sheng*

wen-chi (reprint, Taipei, 1956), 3:1205–8, 1225–43. Chiang Pao was a Han-lin junior compiler. They were all among Ming bureaucracy's brightest and best.

78. Kuo Tzu-chang, *Pin-i sheng Yueh-ts'ao* (printed ed., 1590), 6.1a–20a (account of conduct for Hu Chih).

79. Hu Chih, *Heng-lu ching-she ts'ang-kao,* A20.17a–19a (letter to Chang).

80. Chang Chü-cheng, *Chang T'ai-yueh wen-chi* (reprint, Shanghai, 1984), 262 (22.2ab, letter to Hu Chih).

81. Hu Chih was on his way to Peking when he was informed that his mother was ill, and he then decided to retire. He sent an *i-nan* (foster son, i.e., personal bondservant) by the name of Hu An ahead to Peking with a written retirement request. He also sent Grand Secretary Chang a long letter, in which he raised issues he said he had originally planned to raise with him in person. He urged that more be done to acclimate the young Wan-li emperor to his moral role. He argued that officials should not be promoted solely on the basis of their concrete accomplishments. He asked that Chang intervene to heal a growing partisan split between followers of Chu Hsi and followers of Wang Yang-ming. He demanded that Chang rescind his tax reforms because they were causing hardship all over China. Chang seems to have ignored the letter. Hu's request to retire was approved. His mother soon recovered from her illness. Cf. Hu Chih, *Heng-lu ching-she ts'ang-kao,* A20.40b–42a (memorial requesting retirement) and A20.21b–25b (official letter to Chang).

82. One gifted student who came for a short while in 1568 to take instruction was Kuo Tzu-chang (1543–1618, of Kuan-ch'ao Ward, township 31). Hu's lesson for him dwelt on "seeking benevolence," which Hu explained as a quest without intentionality or emotion, where "the learning of the Sages begins." Another gifted student, and future national luminary, who studied with Hu Chih around this time was Tsou Yuan-piao (1551–1624) of Chi-shui County. Cf. Kuo Tzu-chang, *Ch'ing-lo kung i-shu* (T'ai-ho, printed ed., 1882), 5a (*nien-p'u*); Goodrich and Fang, eds., *Dictionary of Ming Biography,* 2:1312–14; *Ming shih,* 4:2763–65 (biography of Tsou Yuan-piao).

83. Hu Chih, *Heng-lu ching-she ts'ang-kao,* B5.5b–7b (preface and appreciation for the portrait). The two contributors were K'ang Tsung-wang, probably of Chueh-yü Ward (township 52) and Yueh I-ning, of Ho-ch'i Ward (township 65).

84. Hu Chih, *Heng-lu ching-she ts'ang-kao,* B4.5a–7a (letters to Kuo Hsiang-k'uei [Tzu-chang]). Kuo was serving in Fukien at this time and may have published the *Hu-tzu heng-ch'i* there. It was also published in Ch'ang-chou, with a preface by the famed litterateur Wang Shih-chen (1526–90). See Wang Shih-chen, *Yen-chou shan-jen hsu-kao* (reprint, Taipei, 1970), 6:2581–85. The Ssu-k'u ch'üan-shu chen-pen edition of Hu Chih's works contains the entirety of the *Hu-tzu heng-ch'i,* under the label *tsa-chu,* or "miscellaneous writings." Hu Chih, *Heng-lu ching-she ts'ang-kao,* A28.1a–A30.117b.

85. Goodrich and Fang, eds., *Dictionary of Ming Biography,* 1:624–25 (biography of Hu Chih).

86. A phenomenon noted by Handlin, *Action in Late Ming Thought,* 14, and, indeed, throughout the book.

CONCLUSION AND EPILOGUE

1. For the late Ming Buddhist revival, see Pei-yi Wu, "The Spiritual Auto-biography of Te-ch'ing," in *The Unfolding of Neo-Confucianism,* ed. Wm. Theodore de Bary (New York, 1975), 67–92; Kristin Yü Greenblatt, "Chu-hung and Lay Buddhism in the Late Ming," in ibid., 93–140; Chün-fang Yü, *The Renewal of Buddhism in China: Chu-hung and the Late Ming Synthesis* (New York, 1981); Hsu Sung-p'eng, *A Buddhist Leader in Ming China: The Life and Thought of Han-shan Te-ch'ing* (University Park, Pa., 1979). Late Ming Buddhism preached a kind of social gospel of good works and positive engagement with the world.

2. The Buddhist revival was a China-wide phenomenon. Timothy Brook has argued that it constituted a social challenge, the construction of a new world of local social action that was disengaged from the long-dominant embrace of the imperial state. See his *Praying for Power: Buddhism and the Formation of Gentry Society in Late-Ming China* (Harvard, 1993).

3. T'ang Hsien-tsu, *T'ang Hsien-tsu shih-wen chi* (new ed., Shanghai, 1982), 2:1177–86 (epitaph).

4. Kuo Tzu-chang, *Ch'ing-lo kung i-shu* (T'ai-ho, printed ed., 1882), 12.10b–11a, 11b–12a; 26.19b–20a, 25a–26a, 26a–27a; 28.14b–15b (inscriptions and other pieces).

5. Cf. Joanna F. Handlin Smith, "Gardens in Ch'i Piao-chia's Social World: Wealth and Values in Late-Ming Kiangnan," *Journal of Asian Studies* 51 (February 1992): 55–81.

6. Hsiung Ming-yü, *Wen-chih hsing-shu* (printed ed., 1660), 2.52a–55a (inscription for the Hsiao-yuan).

7. Li Ying-sheng, *Lo-lo chai i-chi* (Ch'ang-chou hsien-che i-shu ed.), ch. 3 (letter to Li) and 7.24ab, 8.18b–19a (letters to Hsiao); Miao Ch'ang-ch'i, *Ts'ung-yeh-t'ang ts'un-kao* (Ch'ang-chou hsien-che i-shu ed.), appendix, 14ab (poem from Hsiao).

8. Hsiao Shih-wei, "Random notes from the Spring Floating Garden," quoted in Mao Hsiao-t'ung, ed., *T'ang Hsien-tsu yen-chiu tzu-liao hui-pien* (Shanghai, 1986), 2:1162–63. As young men, Hsiao Shih-wei and Ch'en Chi-t'ai (1567–1641) attended a banquet at T'ang's home; the host praised Hsiao's literary talent, and Hsiao remained for the rest of his life an aficionado of T'ang's dramas. See T'ang Hsien-tsu, *T'ang Hsien-tsu shih-wen chi,* 2:1100–01.

9. Ch'ien Ch'ien-i, *Mu-chai yu-hsueh chi* (Ssu-pu ts'ung-k'an ed.), 18.7a–8b (preface to Hsiao's *Ch'un-fou-yuan chi*) and 15.6b–8b (poem); Chou Liang-kung, ed., *Lai-ku-t'ang ch'ih-tu hsin-ch'ao* (reprint, Taipei, 1972), 3:498–500 (short letters by Hsiao to Ch'ien Ch'ien-i and others).

10. See William F. Atwell, "From Education to Politics: The Fu She," in *The Unfolding of Neo-Confucianism,* ed. Wm. Theodore de Bary (New York, 1975), 333–67; Jerry Dennerline, *The Chia-ting Loyalists: Confucian Leadership and Social Change in Seventeenth-Century China* (New Haven, 1981), which has much to say about the Restoration Society; Hsieh Kuo-chen, *Ming Ch'ing pi-chi t'an-ts'ung* (Beijing, 1962), 48–53, on Hsiao Shih-wei; and Hsieh Kuo-chen,

Ming Ch'ing chih chi tang-she yun-tung k'ao (Taipei, 1967), 155 ff., on the Restoration Society in Kiangsi. See also Ch'en Chi-t'ai, *I-wu chi* (reprint, Taipei, 1977), 1:17–18, 177–78, 2:459–60 (notes for T'ai-ho club members); *Chi-an fu-chih* (Kiangsi, 1875), 37.40b. The *Fu-she hsing-shih chuan-lueh* (printed ed., 1831) lists nineteen T'ai-ho members (Chi-an Prefecture had forty-five total, and Nan-ch'ang ninety-five). Information about the K'uai-ko club and its members is very scarce, owing to the heavy Ch'ing purge and destruction of late Ming writing. T'ai-ho writing was hit hard. Cf. *Ssu-k'u ch'üan-shu tsung-mu* (reprint, Taipei, 1964), 8:12, 36, 158, and passim.

11. The famous names include Wei Hsi (1624–81), P'eng Shih-wang (1610–83), Fang I-chih (1611–71), Mao Ch'i-ling (1623–1716), Shih Jun-chang (1619–83), and Wu Wei-yeh (1609–72).

12. Wu Wei-yeh, *Mei-ts'un chia-ts'ang kao* (reprint, Taipei, 1970), 2:623–25 (message for Hsiao Meng-fang [Po-sheng] on his fiftieth birthday).

13. *Chiang-hsi t'ung-chih* (Kiangsi, 1881), 153.13a–14a (inscriptions by P'eng Shih-wang and Chang Chen-sheng).

14. Liu Hsien-t'ing, *Kuang-yang tsa-chi* (reprint, Beijing, 1985), 83.

Bibliography

I. SOURCES OF MING AND CH'ING DATA

Ssu-k'u ch'üan-shu chen-pen 四庫全書珍本 is abbreviated SKCSCP. *Chüan,* a section in a book, is abbreviated ch.

Chang Chü-cheng (1525–82). 張居正 *Chang T'ai-yueh wen-chi* 張太岳集 47 ch. Reprint, Shanghai, 1984.

Chang Huang (1527–1608), ed. 章潢 *T'u-shu pien* 圖書編 127 ch. 1613. Reprint, 30 vols., Taipei, 1971.

Ch'ang-yuan hsien-chih 長垣縣志 9 ch. 1541. Reprint, Shanghai, 1981.

Ch'en Ch'ang-chi (ca. 1501–ca. 1570). 陳昌積 *Lung-chin-yuan chi* 龍津原集 6 ch. Ming woodblock ed.

Ch'en Chi-t'ai (1567–1641). 陳際泰 *I-wu chi* 己吾集 14 ch. Reprint, 2 vols., Taipei, 1977.

Ch'en Hsun (1385–1462). 陳循 *Fang-chou wen-chi* 芳洲文集 10+6 ch. Printed ed., 1593.

Ch'en Mo (1305–ca. 1389). 陳謨 *Hai-sang chi* 海桑集 10 ch. SKCSCP ed., 4th ser.

Ch'en T'ien (1849–1921), ed. 陳田 *Ming-shih chi-shih* 明詩紀事 Reprint, 6 vols., Taipei, 1971.

Cheng Hsiao (1499–1566). 鄭曉 *Chin yen* 今言 1566. Reprint, Taipei, 1969.

Ch'eng Min-cheng (b. 1445). 程敏政 *Huang-tun wen-chi* 篁墩文集 93 ch. SKCSCP ed., 3d ser.

Chi-an fu-chih 吉安府志 53 ch. Kiangsi, 1875.

Chiang-hsi fu-i ch'üan-shu 江西賦役全書 8 Vols. 1611. Reprint, Taipei, 1970.

Chiang-hsi t'ung-chih 江西通志 180 ch. Kiangsi, 1881.

Chiao Hung (1541–1620), ed. 焦竑 *Kuo-ch'ao hsien-cheng lu* 國朝獻正錄 1594. 119 ch. Reprint, 8 vols., Taipei, 1965.

Ch'ien Ch'ien-i (1582–1664). 錢謙益 *Mu-chai ch'u-hsueh chi* 牧齋初學集 110 ch. Ssu-pu ts'ung-k'an ed.

———. *Mu-chai yu-hsueh chi* 牧齋有學集 50 ch. Ssu-pu ts'ung-k'an ed.

Chou Liang-kung (1612–72), ed. *Lai ku-t'ang ch'ih-tu hsin-ch'ao* 賴古堂尺牘新抄 Reprint, 3 vols., Taipei, 1972.

Chou Shih-hsiu (1354–1402). 周是修 *Ch'u-jao chi* 芻蕘集 6 ch. SKCSCP ed., 4th ser.

Chu Che (1486–1552). 朱淛 *T'ien-ma shan-fang i-kao* 天馬山房遺稿 8 ch. SKCSCP ed., 4th ser.

Chu Kuo-chen (1557–1632). 朱國禎 *Yung-ch'uang hsiao-p'in* 湧幢小品 32 ch. Pi-chi hsiao-shuo ta-kuan ed. 筆記小説大觀 Reprint, Taipei, 1962.

Chu Ta-shao (c.s. 1547), ed. 朱大韶 *Huang Ming ming-ch'en mu-ming* 皇明名臣墓銘 8 ch. Reprint, 4 vols., Taipei, 1969.

Fei Hung (1468–1535). 費宏 *T'ai-pao Fei Wen-hsien kung chai-kao* 太保費文憲公摘稿 20 ch. 1555. Reprint, 3 vols., Taipei, 1970.

Feng-t'ien t'ung-chih 奉天通志 5 vols. 1927. Reprint, Shenyang, 1983.

Fen-sheng fu-an chin-shen pien-lan 分省撫按縉紳便覽 2 ts'e. Reprint, Shanghai, [1990?].

Fu-she hsing-shih chuan-lueh 復社姓氏傳略 Printed ed., 1831.

Hai Jui (1513–87). 海瑞 *Hai Jui chi* 海瑞集 2 Vols. Reprint, Beijing, 1962.

Han Pang-ch'i (1479–1555). 韓邦奇 *Yuan-lo chi* 苑洛集 22 ch. SKCSCP ed., 4th ser.

Han Yung (1422–78). 韓雍 *Han Hsiang-i kung chia-ts'ang wen-chi* 韓襄毅公家藏文集 15 ch. Reprint, 2 vols., Taipei, 1970.

Ho Liang-chün (1506–73). *Ho Han-lin chi* 何翰林集. 1565. Reprint, Taipei, 1971.

———. 何良俊 *Ssu-yu-chai ts'ung-shuo* 四友齋從説 Reprint, Beijing, 1983.

Hsia Liang-sheng (1480–1538). 夏良勝 *Tung-chou ch'u-kao* 東洲初稿 14 ch. SKCSCP ed., 3d ser.

Hsiao Ch'i (1325–96). 蕭岐 *Cheng-ku hsien-sheng chi* 正固先生集 3 ch. Ms. ed.

———. *Cheng-ku hsien-sheng wen-chi* 正固先生文集 1 ch. Hsiao-shih shih-chi ed. 蕭氏世集 In Hsiao Po-sheng (1619–ca. 1678), ed. 蕭伯升 *Hsiao-shih shih chi* 蕭氏世集 Printed ed., 1678.

Hsiao Tzu (d. 1464). 蕭鎡 *Shang-yueh chü-shih chi* 尚約居士集 Woodblock ed., 1494.

Hsieh Chin (1369–1415). 解縉 *Wen-i chi* 文毅集 16 ch. SKCSCP ed., 4th ser.

Hsiung Ming-yü (1579–1649). 熊明遇 *Wen-chih hsing-shu* 文直行書 30 ch. Printed ed., 1660.

Hsu Chieh (1503–83). 徐階 *Shih-ching-t'ang chi* 世經堂集 26 ch. Ming printed ed.

Hsu Hsueh-mo (1522–93). 徐學謨 *Shih-miao shih-yü lu* 世廟識餘錄 26 ch. Reprint, Shanghai, 1991.

Hsu Hung (c.s. 1480), ed. 徐紘 *Ming ming-ch'en wan-yen lu* 明名臣琬琰錄. 24 ch. SKCSCP ed., 6th ser.

Hsu Yu-chen (1407–72). 徐有貞 *Wu-kung chi* 武功集 5 ch. SKCSCP ed., 4th ser.

Hu Chih (1517–85). 胡直 *Heng-lu ching-she ts'ang-kao* 衡廬精舍藏稿 30+11 ch. SKCSCP ed., 4th ser.

———. *K'un-hsueh chi.* In *Ming-ju hsueh-an,* edited by Huang Tsung-hsi, 221–224. 62 ch. Reprint, Taipei, 1965.

Hua Shu (1589–1643), ed. 華淑 *Ming-shih hsuan-tsui* 明詩選最 8 ch. Reprint, Taipei, 1974.

Huang Tsung-hsi (1610–95), ed. 黃宗義 *Ming-ju hsueh-an* 明儒學案 62 ch. Reprint, Taipei, 1965.

Kan-chou fu-chih 贛州府志 78 ch. Kiangsi, 1873.

Keng Ting-hsiang (1524–96). 耿定向 *Keng T'ien-t'ai hsien-sheng wen-chi* 耿天基先生文集 20 ch. Reprint, 4 vols., Taipei, 1970.

Ku Ying-t'ai (d. 1689+). 谷應泰 *Ming-shih chi-shih pen-mo* 明史紀事本末 1658. 80 ch. Reprint, 4 vols., Taipei, 1956.

Kuo T'ing-hsun (fl. 1570–1625), ed. 過庭訓 *Pen-ch'ao fen-sheng jen-wu k'ao* 本朝分省人物考 1622. Reprint, 30 vols., Taipei, 1971.

Kuo Tzu-chang (1543–1618). 郭子章 *Ch'ing-lo kung i-shu* 青螺公遺書 35 ch. T'ai-ho, printed ed., 1882.

———. *Pin-i sheng Yueh-ts'ao* 蠙衣生粵草 10 ch. Printed ed., 1590.

Li Pang-hua (1574–1644). 李邦華 *Ming tsung-hsien Li Chung-su kung chi* 明總憲李忠肅公集 16 ch. Printed ed., 1842.

Li Shih-mien (1374–1450). 李時勉 *Ku-lien wen-chi* 古廉文集 SKCSCP ed., 3d ser.

Li Shun-ch'en (1499–1559). 李舜臣 *Yü-ku chi* 愚谷集 SKCSCP ed., 5th ser.

Li Tung-yang (1447–1516). 李東陽 *Huai-lu-t'ang kao* 懷麓堂稿 20+30+10+30 ch. Reprint, 8 vols., Taipei, 1975.

———. *Li Tung-yang chi* 李東陽集 New ed., 3 vols., Changsha, 1984.

Li Ying-sheng (1593–1626). 李應昇 *Lo-lo-chai i-chi* 落落齋遺集 10 ch. Ch'ang-chou hsien-che i-shu ed. 常州先哲遺書.

Liang Ch'ien (1366–1418). 梁潛 *Po-an chi* 泊菴集 16 ch. SKCSCP ed., 6th ser.

Liang Lan (1343–1410). 梁蘭 *Ch'i-le shih-chi* 畦樂詩集 1 ch. SKCSCP ed., 8th ser.

Liang Wei-shu (1587–1662). 梁維樞 *Yü-chien tsun-wen* 玉劍尊聞 Reprint, 2 vols., Shanghai, 1986.

Lin Chün (1452–1527). 林俊 *Chien-su chi* 見素集 28+7+12+2 ch. SKCSCP ed., 5th ser.

Liu Chiang-sun (ca. 1258–1317). 劉將孫 *Yang-wu-chai chi* 養吾齋集 32 ch. SKCSCP ed., 1st ser.

Liu Ch'iu (1392–1443). 劉球 *Liang-ch'i wen-chi* 兩溪文集 24 ch. SKCSCP ed., 11th ser.

———. *Liu Liang-ch'i wen-chi.* 劉兩溪文集 20 ch. Ch'ien-k'un cheng-ch'i chi ed. 乾坤正氣集.

Liu Hsien-t'ing (1648–95). 劉獻廷 *Kuang-yang tsa-chi* 廣陽雜記 Reprint, Beijing, 1985.

Liu Sung (1321–81). 劉崧 *Ch'a-weng wen-chi* 槎翁文集 18 ch. Ming woodblock ed.

———. *Ch'a-weng shih-chi* 槎翁詩集 8 ch. SKCSCP ed., 5th ser.

Liu Yueh-shen (b. 1260). 劉岳申 *Shen-chai Liu hsien-sheng wen-chi* 申齋劉先生文集 15 ch. Reprint, Taipei, 1970.

Lo Ch'i (1447–1519). 羅玘 *Kuei-feng chi* 圭峰集 30 ch. SKCSCP ed., 4th ser.

Lo Ch'in-shun (1465–1547). 羅欽順 *Cheng-an ts'un-kao* 整菴存稿 20 ch. SKCSCP ed., 4th ser.

———. *K'un-chih chi* 困知記 (Knowledge painfully acquired). Reprint, Beijing, 1990.

Lo Hung-hsien (1504–64). 羅洪先 *Nien-an wen-chi* 念菴文集 22 ch. SKCSCP ed., 5th ser.

Lo Ju-fang (1515–88). 羅汝芳 *Hsu-t'an chih-ch'üan* 盱壇直詮 2 ch. Reprint, Taipei, 1960.

Lo Ta-hung (c.s. 1586). 羅大紘 *Tzu-yuan wen-chi* 紫原文集 12 ch. Ming woodblock ed.

Lu Jung (1436–97). 陸容 *Shu-yuan tsa-chi che-ch'ao* 菽園雜記摘抄 7 ch. Chi-lu hui-pien ed.

Lü Nan (1479–1542). 呂楠 *Ching-yeh-tzu nei-p'ien* 涇野子內篇 Reprint, Beijing, 1992.

Miao Ch'ang-ch'i (1562–1626). 繆昌期 *Ts'ung-yeh-t'ang ts'un-kao* 從野堂存稿 8 ch. Ch'ang-chou hsien-che i-shu ed.

Ming shih 明史 332 ch. 1736. Kuo-fang yen-chiu-yuan ed. New ed., 6 vols. Taipei, 1962.

Ming shih-lu 明實錄 133 Vols. Reprint, Taiwan, 1965.

Ming-tai Liao-tung tang-an hui-pien 明代遼東檔案滙編 2 Vols. Reprint, Shenyang, 1985.

Ming-tai teng-k'o-lu hui-pien 明代登科錄彙編 22 Vols. Reprint, Taipei, 1969.

Ming wen-hai 明文海 480 ch. SKCSCP ed., 7th ser.

Ni Yueh (1444–1501). 倪岳 *Ch'ing-ch'i man-kao* 清溪漫稿 24 ch. Wu-lin wang-che i-chu ed.

Ning-po fu-chih 寧波府志 36 ch. 1741. Reprint, 4 vols., Taipei, 1957.

Ou-yang Te (1496–1554). 歐陽德 *Ou-yang Nan-yeh hsien-sheng wen-chi* 歐陽南野先生文集 30 ch. Woodblock ed., 1558.

Ou-yang To (1487–1544). 歐陽鐸 *Ou-yang Kung-chien kung i-chi* 歐陽恭簡公遺集 22 ch. Ming woodblock ed.

P'eng Shao (1430–95). 彭韶 *P'eng Hui-an chi* 彭惠菴集 10+1 ch. SKCSCP ed., 3d ser.

P'u-t'ien hsien-chih 莆田縣志 36 ch. 1879. Reprint, Taipei, 1968.

Shao Pao (1460–1527). 邵寶 *Jung-ch'un-t'ang chi* 容春堂集 20+14+8+9 ch. SKCSCP ed., 5th ser.

Shen Te-fu (1578–1642). 沈德符 *Wan-li yeh-huo pien* 萬曆野獲編 1619. New ed., 3 vols., Beijing, 1980.

Shen Yen-ch'ing (1813–53). 沈衍慶 *Huai-ch'ing i-kao* 槐卿遺稿 6+6 ch. 1862. Reprint, Taipei, n.d., as ser. 38, no. 378, of Chin-tai Chung-kuo shih-liao ts'ung-k'an. 近代中國史料叢刊

Shih Chien (1434–96). 史鑑 *Hsi-ts'un chi* 西村集 8+1 ch. SKCSCP ed., 3d ser.

Shih Jun-chang (1619–83). 施閏章 *Hsueh-yü t'ang wen-chi* 學餘堂文集 28+50 ch. SKCSCP ed., 3d ser.

Shou-chou chih 壽州志 8 ch. 1550. Reprint, Shanghai, 1981.

Ssu-k'u ch'üan-shu tsung-mu 四庫全書總目 9 Vols. Reprint, Taipei, 1964.

Sun Hsu (1474–1547). 孫緒 *Sha-ch'i chi* 沙溪集 23 ch. SKCSCP ed., 8th ser.

Sung Lien (1310–81). 宋濂 *Sung Wen-hsien kung ch'üan-chi* 宋文憲公全集 53 ch. Ssu-pu pei-yao ed. 四部備要.

T'ai-ho hsien-chih 泰和縣志 48 ch. Kiangsi, 1826. Reprint, 7 vols., Taipei, 1989.

———— 30 ch. Kiangsi, 1879.

T'ai-p'ing hsien-chih 太平縣志 8 ch. 1540. Reprint, Shanghai, 1981.

T'an Ch'ien (1594–1658). 談遷 *Kuo ch'ueh* 國榷 104 ch. Reprint, 6 vols., Beijing, 1958.

T'ang Hsien-tsu (1550–1616). 唐顯祖 *T'ang Hsien-tsu shih-wen chi* 唐顯祖詩文集 50+1 ch. New ed., 2 vols., Shanghai, 1982.

Tsou Chih (1466–91). 鄒智 *Li-chai i-wen* 文齋遺文 5 ch. SKCSCP ed., 9th ser.

Tsou Shou-i (1491–1562). 鄒守益 *Tung-kuo hsien-sheng wen-chi* 東郭先生文集 9 ch. Ming printed ed.

Tsou Yuan-piao (1551–1624). 鄒元標 *Yuan-hsueh chi* 願學集 8 ch. SKCSCP ed., 5th ser.

Ts'ui Hsien (1478–1541). 崔銑 *Huan tz'u* 洹詞 12 ch. SKCSCP ed., 6th ser.

Wang Ao (1450–1524). 王鏊 *Chen-tse ch'ang-yü* 震澤長語 2 ch. Ming-Ch'ing shih-liao hui-pien ed., 1st ser. 明清史料彙編

————. *Chen-tse chi* 震澤集 36 ch. SKCSCP ed., 5th ser.

Wang Chen (fl. 1313). 王禎 *Nung shu* 農書 22 ch. SKCSCP ed., *pieh-chi*. 別輯

Wang Chih (1379–1462). 王直 *I-an chi* 抑菴集 13+37 ch. SKCSCP ed., 8th ser.

Wang Hsien-ch'ien (1842–1918). 王先謙 *Hsu-shou-t'ang wen-chi* 虛受堂文集 15 ch. Reprint, 2 vols., Taipei, 1966.

Wang K'ai-yun (1833–1916). 王闓運 *Hsiang-ch'i-lou wen-chi* 湘綺樓文集 8 ch. Reprint, Taipei, 1966.

Wang Li (1314–86). 王禮 *Lin-yuan wen-chi* 麟原文集 12+12 ch. SKCSCP ed., 1st ser.

Wang Shen-chung (1509–59). 王慎中 *Tsun-yen chi* 遵巖集 25 ch. SKCSCP ed., 8th ser.

Wang Shih-chen (1526–90). 王世貞 *Yen-chou shan-jen hsu-kao* 弇州山人續稿 211 ch. Reprint, 18 vols., Taipei, 1970.

Wang Shih-hsing (1547–98). 王士性 *Kuang-chih i* 廣志繹 5 ch. Reprint, Beijing, 1981.

Wang Shu (1416–1508). 王恕 *Wang Tuan-i kung wen-chi* 王端毅公文集 9+2 ch. Reprint, Taipei, 1970.

Wang Yang-ming (1472–1529) 王陽明（守仁）. *Wang Yang-ming ch'üan-chi* 王陽明全集. 38 ch. Reprint, Taipei, 1964.

Wan-li Chi-an fu-chih 萬曆吉安府志 36 ch. 1585. Reprint, Beijing, 1991.

Wan-li T'ai-ho chih 萬曆泰和志 10 ch. (ch. 1–5 missing). 1579. Reprint, Taipei, 1989.

Wei Chiao (1483–1543). 魏校 *Chuang-ch'ü i-shu* 莊渠遺書 12 ch. SKCSCP ed., 5th ser.

Wu Ch'eng (1249–1331). 吳誠 *Wu Wen-cheng chi* 吳文正集 100 ch. SKCSCP ed., 2nd ser.

Wu K'uan (1436–1504). 吳寬 *P'ao-weng chia-ts'ang chi* 匏翁家藏集 77 ch. Ssu-pu ts'ung-k'an ed.

Wu Ssu-tao (ca. 1314–90). 烏斯道 *Ch'un-ts'ao-chai chi* 春草齋集 12 ch. Ssu-ming ts'ung shu ed. 四明叢書.

Wu T'ing-han (ca. 1490–1559). 吳廷翰 *Wu T'ing-han chi* 吳廷翰集 Reprint, Beijing, 1984.

Wu Wei-yeh (1609–72). 吳偉業 *Mei-ts'un chia-ts'ang kao* 梅村家藏稿 58 ch. Reprint, 3 vols., Taipei, 1970.

Yang Chueh (1493–1549). 楊爵 *Yang Chung-chieh chi* 楊忠介集 13+3 ch. SKCSCP ed., 5th ser.

Yang Hsi-min, ed. 楊希閔 *Shih-wu-chia nien-p'u* 十五家年譜 Reprint, 4 vols., Taipei, 1966.

Yang Shih-ch'i (1365–1444). 楊士奇 *Tung-li ch'üan-chi* 東里全集 25+3+62+3 ch. SKCSCP ed., 7th ser.

Yang Wan-li (1127–1206). 楊萬里 *Ch'eng-chai chi* 誠齋集 133 ch. Ssu-pu ts'ung-k'an ed.

Yang Yin-ch'iu (1547–1601). 楊寅秋 *Lin-kao wen-chi* 臨皋文集 4 ch. SKCSCP ed., 2d ser.

Yeh Ch'un-chi (fl. mid–16th cent.). 業春及 *Shih-tung chi* 石洞集 18 ch. SKCSCP ed., 5th ser.

Yeh Sheng (1420–74). 業盛 *Shui-tung jih-chi* 水東日記 40 ch. Reprint, 2 vols., Taipei, 1968.

Yen Sung (1480–1565). 嚴嵩 *Ch'ien-shan-t'ang chi* 鈐山堂集 40 ch. Ms. ed.

Yin Ch'ang-lung (ca. 1369–ca. 1417). 尹昌隆 *Yin Na-an hsien-sheng i-kao* 尹訥菴先生遺稿 10 ch. Ms. ed.

Yin Chih (1427–1511). 尹直 *Ch'eng-chiang pieh-chi* 澄江別集 3 ch. Printed ed., 1504.

———. *Chien-chai so-chui lu* 謇齋瑣綴錄 Ms. ed. 1507. Reprint, Taipei, 1969.

———. *Chien-chai so-chui lu.* 1 ch. Li-tai hsiao-shih ed.

Yin T'ai (1506–79). 尹臺 *Tung-lu-t'ang chi* 洞麓堂集 10 ch. SKCSCP ed., 5th ser.

Yueh Cheng (1418–72). 岳正 *Lei-po kao* 類博稿 10+2 ch. SKCSCP ed., 3d ser.

Yun-hsi hsien-chih 鄖西縣志 14 ch. 1936. Reprint, 4 vols., Taipei, 1975.

Yun-yang hsien-chih 鄖陽縣志 8 ch. Hupei, 1870. Reprint, Taipei, 1970.

Yung-hsin hsien-chih 永新縣志 7 vols. 1874. Reprint, Taipei, 1975.

II. OTHER REFERENCES

Abramson, M., et al. "Tsziansi." *Problemy Kitaia*, no. 14 (1935): 89–157.

Atwell, William S. "From Education to Politics: The Fu She." In *The Unfolding of Neo-Confucianism,* edited by Wm. Theodore de Bary, 333–67. New York, 1975.

————. "International Bullion Flows and the Chinese Economy, *circa* 1530–1650." *Past and Present,* no. 95 (1982): 68–90.

Banister, Judith. *China's changing population.* Stanford, 1987.

Barrett, Spencer. C. H. "Crop Mimicry in Weeds." *Economic Botany* 37 (1983): 255–82.

Beattie, Hilary J. *Land and Lineage in China: A Study of T'ung-ch'eng, Anwei, in the Ming and Ch'ing Dynasties.* Cambridge, England, 1979.

Becker, Gary S. *A Treatise on the Family.* Cambridge, Mass. 1981.

Bielenstein, Hans. "The Regional Provenance of *Chin-shih* during Ch'ing." *Bulletin of the Museum of Far Eastern Antiquities,* no. 64 (1992): 5–178.

Bloom, Irene. "On the 'Abstraction' of Ming Thought: Some Concrete Evidence from the Philosophy of Lo Ch'in-shun." In *Principle and Practicality: Essays in Neo-Confucianism and Practical Learning*, edited by Wm. Theodore de Bary and Irene Bloom, 65–125. New York, 1979.

————, trans. *Knowledge Painfully Acquired: The K'un-chih chi by Lo Ch'in-shun.* New York, 1987.

Bodde, Dirk. "Marshes in Mencius and Elsewhere." In *Ancient China: Studies in Early Civilisation,* edited by David T. Roy and T. H. Tsien, 157–66. Hong Kong, 1978.

Brook, Timothy. "The Spatial Structure of Ming Local Administration." *Late Imperial China* 6, no. 1 (1985): 1–55.

————. "Family Continuity and Cultural Hegemony: The Gentry of Ningbo, 1368–1911." In *Chinese Local Elites and Patterns of Dominance*, edited by Joseph W. Esherick and Mary B. Rankin, 27–50. Berkeley, 1990.

————. *Praying for Power: Buddhism and the Formation of Gentry Society in Late-Ming China.* Harvard, 1993.

Buck, John L. *Chinese Farm Economy.* Nanking, 1930.

Cartier, Michel. "Nouvelles données sur la démographic chinoise à l'époque des Ming." *Annales: Économies, sociétés, civilisations* 28 (1973): 1341–59.

Chan, Wing-tsit, "The Ch'eng-Chu School of Early Ming." In *Self and Society in Ming Thought,* edited by Wm. Theodore de Bary, 29–51. New York, 1970.

————, trans. *Instructions for Practical Living and Other Neo-Confucian Writings by Wang Yang-ming.* New York, 1963.

Chao, Kang. *Man and Land in Chinese History.* Stanford, 1986.

Chao Kang and Ch'en Chung-i 趙岡, 陳鍾毅 "Chung-Kuo li-shih-shang-ti tzu-ying ti-chu" 中國歷史上的自營地主 [Managerial landlords in Chinese history]. *Shih-huo yueh-k'an,* n.s., 9, nos. 5–6 (October 1979): 169–93.

Ch'en Po-ch'üan, ed. 陳柏泉 *Chiang-hsi ch'u-t'u mu-chih hsuan-pien* 江西出土墓志選編 [Selected texts from tombstones unearthed in Kiangsi]. Nanchang, 1991.

Chiang-hsi nien-chien 江西年鑑 [Kiangsi yearbook]. Nanchang, 1936.

Chiang-hsi nung-yeh ti-li 江西農業地理 {Kiangsi agricultural geography]. Nanchang, 1982.

Ch'ing-tai nung-min chan-cheng-shih tzu-liao hsuan-pien 清代農民戰爭史資料選編 [Selected sources on the history of peasant rebellion in the Ch'ing], vol. 1, pt. 2. Beijing, 1984.

Chu, Hung-lam. "The Debate over Recognition of Wang Yang-ming." *Harvard Journal of Asiatic Studies* 48 (June 1988): 47–70.

―――. "Intellectual Trends in the fifteenth Century." *Ming Studies*, no. 27 (spring 1989): 1–33.

Chung-kuo 1982 nien jen-k'ou p'u-ch'a 10% ch'ou-yang tzu-liao 中國1982年人口普查10%抽樣資料 [Ten percent sampling materials from the 1982 census of China]. Beijing, 1983.

Chung-kuo 1982 nien jen-k'ou p'u-ch'a tzu-liao 中國1982年人口普查資料 [Material from the 1982 census of China]. Beijing, 1985.

Chung-kuo li-shih-hsueh nien-chien 史國歷史學年鑑 [China history yearbook]. Beijing, 1987.

―――. Beijing, 1989.

Dardess, John W. *Confucianism and Autocracy: Professional Elites in the Founding of the Ming Dynasty.* Berkeley, 1983.

―――. "Ming Historical Demography: Notes from T'ai-ho County, Kiangsi." *Ming Studies*, no. 17 (fall 1983): 60–77.

―――. "A Ming Landscape: Settlement, Land Use, Labor, and Estheticism in T'ai-ho County, Kiangsi." *Harvard Journal of Asiatic Studies* 49, no. 2 (December 1989): 295–364.

―――. "Ming Officials and Modern Intellectuals: Some Enduring Configurations of Moral-Political Protest in China." Paper presented at the Conference entitled The Continuing Relevance of Traditional Chinese Institutions and Values in the Context of Modern China, East-West Center, University of Hawaii, May 1993.

de Heer, Ph. *The Care-Taker Emperor: Aspects of the Imperial Institution in Fifteenth-Century China as Reflected in the Political History of the Reign of Chu Ch'i-yü.* Leiden, 1986.

Dennerline, Jerry. *The Chia-ting Loyalists: Confucian Leadership and Social Change in Seventeenth-Century China.* New Haven, 1981.

―――. "Marriage, Adoption, and Charity in the Development of Lineages in Wu-hsi from Sung to Ch'ing." In *Kinship Organization in Late Imperial China, 1000–1940,* edited by Patricia B. Ebrey and James L. Watson, 170–209. Berkeley, 1986.

Dreyer, Edward L. *Early Ming China: A Political History, 1355–1435.* Stanford, 1982.

Eberhard, Wolfram. *Social Mobility in Traditional China.* Leiden, 1962.

Ebrey, Patricia B. "Conceptions of the Family in the Sung Dynasty." *Journal of Asian Studies* 43 (February 1984): 219–45.

Ebrey, Patricia B., and James L. Watson, eds., *Kinship Organization in Late Imperial China, 1000–1940.* Berkeley, 1986.

Esherick, Joseph W., and Mary B. Rankin, eds. *Chinese Local Elites and Patterns of Dominance.* Berkeley, 1990.

Fisher, Carney T. *The Chosen One: Succession and Adoption in the Court of Ming Shizong.* Sydney, 1990.

Franke, Wolfgang. *An Introduction to the Sources of Ming History.* Kuala Lumpur, 1968.

Fu I-ling 傅衣凌 "Ming-mo nan-fang ti 'tien-pien,' 'nu-pien'" 明末南方的

'佃變', '奴變' ["Tenant revolts" and "slave revolts" in south China in late Ming]. *Li-shih yen-chiu*, no. 5 (1975): 61–67.

———. "Ming-tai Chiang-hsi ti kung-shang-yeh jen-k'ou chi ch'i i-tung" 明代江西的工商業人口及其移動 [The industrial and commercial population of Ming Kiangsi and its movement]. In *Ming Ch'ing she-hui ching-chi-shih lun-wen chi*, edited by Fu I-ling, 187–97. Beijing, 1982.

Gallagher, Louis J., S. J., trans. *China in the Sixteenth Century: The Journals of Matthew Ricci, 1583–1610*. New York, 1953.

Goodrich, L. Carrington, and Fang Chaoying, eds. *Dictionary of Ming Biography*. 2 Vols. New York, 1976.

Greenblatt, Kristin Yü. "Chu-hung and Lay Buddhism in the Late Ming." In *The Unfolding of Neo-Confucianism* edited by Wm. Theodore de Bary, 93–140. New York, 1975.

Grimm, Tilemann. "Ming Educational Intendants." In *Chinese Government in Ming Times: Seven Studies* edited by Charles O. Hucker, 129–47. New York, 1969.

Hakeda, Yoshito S., trans. *The Awakening of Faith Attributed to Asvaghosha*. New York, 1967.

Handlin, Joanna F. *Action in Late Ming Thought: The Reorientation of Lü K'un and Other Scholar-Officials*. Berkeley, 1983.

Harrell, Stevan, ed. *Chinese Historical Microdemography*. Berkeley, 1995.

Hartwell, Robert M. "Demographic, Political, and Social Transformations of China, 750–1550." *Harvard Journal of Asiatic Studies* 42, no. 2 (December 1982): 365–442.

Hauf, Kandice J. "The Jiangyou Group: Culture and Society in Sixteenth-Century China." Ph.D. diss., Yale University, 1987.

Hawkes, J. G. *The Diversity of Crop Plants*. Harvard, 1983.

Ho Ping-ti. *The Ladder of Success in Imperial China*. New York, 1964.

———. *Chung-kuo hui-kuan shih-lun* 中國會館史論 [An historical survey of *Landsmannschaften* in China]. Taipei, 1966.

Hoefer, Jacob A., and Patricia Jones Tsuchitani. *Animal Agriculture in China: A Report of the Visit of the SSCPRC Animal Sciences Delegation*. Washington, D.C., 1980.

Hsiao Shih-wei (1585–1651). *Hsiao-chai jih-chi*. In *Li-tai ming-jen jih-chi hsuan* 歷代名人日記選 [Select diaries of famous men through the ages], edited by Teng Chin-shen 鄧進深 Canton, 1984.

Hsieh, Bao-Hua. "The Acquisition of Concubines in China, fourteenth–seventeenth Centuries." *Chin-tai Chung-kuo fu-nü yen-chiu*, no. 1 (1993): 125–200.

Hsieh Kuo-chen 謝國禎 *Ming Ch'ing pi-chi t'an-ts'ung*. 明清筆記談叢 [Scholars' notebooks of the Ming and Ch'ing]. Beijing, 1962.

———. *Ming Ch'ing chih chi tang-she yun-tung k'ao* 明清之際黨社運動考 [Studies of clique movements in the Ming and Ch'ing]. Taipei, 1967.

Hsu Sung-peng. *A Buddhist Leader in Ming China: The Life and Thought of Han-shan Te-ch'ing*. University Park, Pa., 1979.

Huang, Philip C.C. *The Peasant Family and Rural Development in the Yangzi Delta, 1350–1988*. Stanford, 1990.

Huang, Ray. *Taxation and Governmental Finance in Sixteenth-Century Ming China*. Cambridge, 1974.

Hymes, Robert P. *Statesmen and Gentlemen: The Elite of Fu-Chou, Chiang-Hsi, in Northern and Southern Sung*. Cambridge, 1986.

Jackson, John Brinckerhoff. *Discovering the Vernacular Landscape*. New Haven, 1984.

James, W.H. "The Sex Ratio of Oriental Births." *Annals of Human Biology* 12, no. 5 (September–October 1985): 485–87.

Jen Tao-pin 任道斌 *Fang I-chih nien-p'u* 方以智年譜 [Chronological biography of Fang I-chih]. Hofei, 1983.

Jen Yu-wen. "Ch'en Hsien-chang's Philosophy of the Natural." In *Self and Society in Ming Thought* edited by Wm. Theodore de Bary, 53–92. New York, 1970.

Keyfitz, Nathan. *Applied Mathematical Demography*. 2d ed. New York, 1985.

Lee, James, Cameron Campbell, and Wang Feng. "The Last Emperors: An Introduction to the Demography of the Qing (1644–1911) Imperial Lineage." In *Old and New Methods in Historical Demography* edited by David S. Reher and Roger Schofield, 361–82. Oxford, 1993.

Li, H.L. [Li Hui-lin]. *The Garden Flowers of China*. New York, 1959.

Li Hui-lin. "The Domestication of Plants in China: Ecogeographical Considerations." In *The Origins of Chinese Civilization*, edited by David N. Keightley, 21–63. Berkeley, 1983.

Liu Ts'ui-jung. "Formation and Function of Three Lineages in Hunan." In *Chin-shih chia-tsu yü cheng-chih pi-chiao lun-wen chi*, edited by Chung-yang yen-chiu-yuan chin-tai-shih yen-chiu so, vol. 1. Taipei, 1992.

———. 劉翠溶 *Ming Ch'ing shih-ch'i chia-tsu jen-k'ou yü she-hui ching-chi pien-ch'ien* 明清時期家族人口與社會經濟變遷 [Family population and socioeconomic change in Ming and Ch'ing]. Taipei, 1992.

Lo Hsiang-lin, ed. 羅香林 *K'o-chia shih-liao hui-pien* 客家史料彙編 [Sources on Hakka history]. Hong Kong, 1965.

Ma Tai-loi. "The Local Education Officials of Ming China, 1368–1644." *Oriens Extremus* 22 (1975): 11–27.

McDermott, Joseph P. "Charting Blank Spaces and Disputed Regions: The Problem of Sung Land Tenure." *Journal of Asian Studies* 44 (November 1984): 13–41.

Mao Hsiao-t'ung, ed. 毛校同 *T'ang Hsien-tsu yen-chiu tzu-liao hui-pien* 唐顯祖研究資料彙編 [Sources for the study of T'ang Hsien-tsu]. 2 Vols. Shanghai, 1986.

Meskill, John. *Academies in Ming China: A Historical Survey*. Tucson, 1982.

Mote, Frederick W., and Denis Twitchett, eds. *The Cambridge History of China*. Vol. 7, pt. 1. (The Ming Dynasty, 1368–1644). Cambridge, 1988.

Nieuhoff, John. *The Embassy of Peter de Goyer and Jacob de Keyser from the Dutch East India Company to the Emperor of China in 1655*. Vol. 7 of *Voyages and Travels*, ed. John Pinkerton. London, 1811.

Niida Noboru 仁井田陞 *Chūgoku hōseishi kenkyū* 中國法制史研究 [Studies in Chinese legal history]. 4 Vols. Tokyo, 1959–64.

Nishimura Kazuyo 西村かずよ "Mindai no doboku" 明代の奴僕 [Ming slaves]. *Tōyōshi kenkyū* 38, no. 1 (1980): 24–50.

Okada Takehiko 岡田武彦 *Ōyōmei to Minmatsu no jogaku* 王陽明と明末の儒學 [Wang Yang-ming and late Ming Confucianism]. Tokyo, 1971.

Parsons, James B. "The Ming Dynasty Bureaucracy: Aspects of Background Forces." In *Chinese Government in Ming Times: Seven Studies* edited by Charles O. Hucker, 175–232. New York, 1969.

Perdue, Peter C. *Exhausting the Earth: State and Peasant in Hunan, 1500–1850.* Harvard, 1987.

Rawski, Evelyn S. "Research Themes in Ming-Qing Socioeconomic History—The State of the Field." *Journal of Asian Studies* 50 (February 1991): 84–111.

Ricci, Mattieu, S.J., and Nicolas Trigault, S.J. *Histoire de l'éxpedition chrétienne au royaume de la Chine, 1582–1610.* Bellarmin, 1978.

Rowe, William T. "Success Stories: Lineage and Elite Status in Hanyang County, Hubei, c. 1368–1949." In *Chinese Local Elites and Patterns of Dominance* edited by Joseph W. Esherick and Mary B. Rankin, 51–81. Berkeley, 1990.

Satō Manabu 佐藤學 "Minsho Pekin e no fuminsō kyōsei ijū ni tsuite—iwayuru 'fuko' no kiseki o chūshin ni" 明初北京への富民層強制移居住について—所謂「富民」の軌跡を中心に [Forced residence of the rich in Peking in early Ming, with special reference to the so-called rich households]. *Tōyō gakuhō* 64, nos. 1–2 (1983): 69–98.

Schafer, Edward. "T'ang." In *Food in Chinese Culture: Anthropological and Historical Perspectives* edited by K.C. Chang, 85–140. New Haven, 1977.

Smith, Joanna F. Handlin. "Gardens in Ch'i Piao-chia's Social World: Wealth and Values in Late-Ming Kiangnan." *Journal of Asian Studies* 51 (February 1992): 55–81.

Spence, Jonathan. *The Death of Woman Wang.* Penguin, 1979.

Sudō Yoshiyuki 周藤吉之 *Sōdai keizaishi kenkyū* 宋代經濟史研究 [Studies in Sung economic history]. Tokyo, 1962.

Swain, Roger B. *Field Days: Journal of an Itinerant Botanist.* New York, 1983.

Taga Akigorō 多賀秋五郎 *Sōfu no kenkyū: Shiryō hen* 宗譜の研究・史料編 [Genealogy studies: Sources]. Tokyo, 1960.

T'an Ch'i-hsiang 譚其驤 "Chung-kuo nei-ti i-min shih—Hu-nan p'ien" 中國內地移民史—湖南篇 [History of internal migrations in China—Hunan]. *Shih-hsueh nien-pao* 1, no. 4 (1932): 47–104.

Tani Mitsutaka 谷光隆 "Mindai kansei no kenkyū" 明代監生の研究 [Imperial college students in the Ming]. *Shigaku zasshi* 73, no. 4 (April 1964): 56–81; 73, no. 6 (June 1964): 69–82.

Taylor, Rodney. "Acquiring a Point of View: Confucian Dimensions of Self-Perception." *Monumenta Serica* 34 (1979–80): 145–70.

———. "Journey into Self: The Autobiographical Reflections of Hu Chih." *History of Religions* 21 (May 1982): 321–38.

Telford, Ted A. "Survey of Social Demographic Data in Chinese Genealogies." *Late Imperial China* 7, no. 2 (December 1986): 118–48.

———. "Patching the Holes in Chinese Genealogies: Mortality in the Lineage Populations of Tongcheng County, 1300–1880." *Late Imperial China* 11, no. 2 (December 1990): 116–36.

———. "Covariates of Men's Age at First Marriage: The Historical Demography of Chinese Lineages." *Population Studies* 46, no. 1 (March 1992): 19–35.

Tsao-chih shih-hua 造紙史話 [Historical talks about paper making]. Shanghai, 1983.

Wada Masahiro 和田正廣 "Mindai kyojinsō no keisei katei ni kansuru ichi kōsatsu" 明代舉人層の形成過程に關する—考察 [The process of formation of the class of provincial degree holders in the Ming]. *Shigaku zasshi* 87, no. 3 (March 1978): 36–71.

Wakeman, Frederic Jr. "Romantics, Stoics, and Martyrs in Seventeenth-Century China." *Journal of Asian Studies* 43 (August 1984): 631–65.

Waltner, Ann. *Getting an Heir: Adoption and the Construction of Kinship in Late Imperial China*. Honolulu, 1990.

Wei Ch'ing-yuan et al. 衛慶遠 *Ch'ing-tai nu-pei chih-tu* 清代奴婢制度 [The Ch'ing slave system]. Beijing, 1982.

Wilhelm, Helmut. "On Ming Orthodoxy." *Monumenta Serica* 29 (1970–71): 1–26.

Woodside, Alexander. "Emperors and the Chinese Political System." In *Perspectives on Modern China* edited by Kenneth Lieberthal, Joyce Kallgren, Roderick MacFarquhar, and Frederic Wakeman Jr., 1–30. Armonk, N.Y., 1991.

Wu Chen-han 吳振漢 "Ming-tai ti chu-p'u kuan-hsi" 明代的主僕關係 [Master-slave relations in the Ming]. *Shih-huo pan-yueh-k'an* 12, nos. 4–5 (August 1982): 147–63.

Wu Chih-ho 吳智和 *Ming-tai ti ju-hsueh chiao-kuan* 明代的儒學校官 [Confucian teaching officials in the Ming]. Taipei, 1991.

Wu Chin-ch'eng 吳金成 "Ming-tai Hu-pei nung-ts'un ti she-hui pien-ch'ien yü shen-shih" 明代湖北農村的社會變遷與紳士 [Social change and scholar-gentry in the villages of Hupei in the Ming]. *Shih-huo* 17, nos. 1–2 (June 1988): 65–87.

Wu, Pei-yi. "The Spiritual Autobiography of Te-ch'ing." In *The Unfolding of Neo-Confucianism* edited by Theodore de Bary, 67–92. New York, 1975.

———. *The Confucian's Progress: Autobiographical Writings in Traditional China*. Princeton, 1990.

Wu Pen-chung et al. 吳本忠 "T'ai-ho ch'ü t'u-jang" 泰和區土壤 [Soils of T'ai-ho district]. *Chiang-hsi sheng ti-chih tiao-ch'a-so ti-chih hui-k'an,* no. 6 (July 1941): 157–188.

Yü, Chün-fang. *The Renewal of Buddhism in China: Chu-hung and the Late Ming Synthesis*. New York, 1981.

Yü, Ying-shih. 余英時 *Fang I-chih wan-chieh k'ao* 方以智晚節考 [Fang I-chih: His last years and his death]. Hong Kong, 1972.

Zurndorfer, Harriet. "The *Hsin-an ta-tsu chih* and the Development of Chinese Gentry Society, 800–1600." *T'oung Pao* 67, nos. 3–5 (1981): 154–215.

———. *Change and Continuity in Chinese Local History: The Development of Hui-chou Prefecture, 800–1800*. Leiden, 1989.

Index

Compositor: J. Jarrett Engineering, Inc.
Chinese compositor: Asco Trade Typesetting
Text: 10/13 Sabon
Display: Sabon
Printer: Thomson-Shore
Binder: Thomson-Shore